Jesus and Paul in the Context of Judaism and Early Christianity

Jesus and Paul in the Context of Judaism and Early Christianity

COLLECTED ESSAYS

DONALD A. HAGNER

PICKWICK *Publications* · Eugene, Oregon

JESUS AND PAUL IN THE CONTEXT OF JUDAISM AND EARLY CHRISTIANITY
Collected Essays

Copyright © 2025 Donald A. Hagner. All rights reserved. Except for brief quotations in critical publications or reviews, no part of this book may be reproduced in any manner without prior written permission from the publisher. Write: Permissions, Wipf and Stock Publishers, 199 W. 8th Ave., Suite 3, Eugene, OR 97401.

Pickwick Publications
An Imprint of Wipf and Stock Publishers
199 W. 8th Ave., Suite 3
Eugene, OR 97401

www.wipfandstock.com

PAPERBACK ISBN: 979-8-3852-2624-5
HARDCOVER ISBN: 979-8-3852-2625-2
EBOOK ISBN: 979-8-3852-2626-9

Cataloguing-in-Publication data:

Names: Hagner, Donald A., author.

Title: Jesus and Paul in the context of Judaism and early Christianity : collected essays / Donald A. Hagner.

Description: Eugene, OR: Pickwick Publications, 2025.

Identifiers: ISBN 979-8-3852-2624-5 (paperback). | ISBN 979-8-3852-2625-2 (hardcover). | ISBN 979-8-3852-2626-9 (ebook).

Subjects: LCSH: Jesus Christ. | Paul, the Apostle, Saint. | Judaism (Christian theology)—History of doctrines. | Judaism—Relations—Christianity. | Christianity and other religions.

Classification: BS2361.3 H34 2025 (print). | BS2361.3 (ebook).

03/24/25

Contents

Preface vii

Acknowledgments ix

PART ONE | JESUS

1. Reclaiming Jesus for Judaism 3
2. Radical Gospel Criticism and the Modern Jewish Study of Jesus 37
3. The Jesus Quest and Jewish-Christian Relations 48
4. Matthew: Apostate, Reformer, Revolutionary? 71
5. New Things from the Scribe's Treasure Box (Matt 13:52) ... 90

PART TWO | PAUL

6. Paul in Modern Jewish Thought 107
7. Balancing the Old and the New 132
8. Paul as a Jewish Believer—According to His Letters ... 145
9. Paul's Quarrel with Judaism 175
10. Paul and Judaism: Testing the "New Perspective" 203
11. Paul's Christology and Jewish Monotheism 227
12. The Apostle Paul's Christianity as an Expression of His Jewish Faith ... 248
13. The Newness of Paul's Gospel 265

PART THREE | JUDAISM AND CHRISTIANITY

14	Another Look at "The Parting of the Ways"	279
15	A Positive Theology of Judaism from the New Testament	319
16	Jesus: Bringer of Salvation to Jew and Gentile Alike	336

Appendix 1: Passages Pointing to Discontinuity/Supersession/Displacement   353

Appendix 2: Passages Pointing to Continuity/Ongoing Significance/Salvation   361

Preface

IT WAS NEARLY SIXTY years ago, when I was working on a Master of Theology degree at Fuller Seminary that my mentor, Everett Harrison, suggested that the Jewish study of the NT could be an interesting area in which to write my master's thesis. I did find it to be a fascinating subject, and I ended up writing on "The Teaching of Jesus in Modern Jewish Scholarship," which some years later I developed into a book, *The Jewish Reclamation of Jesus: An Analysis and Critique of Modern Jewish Study of Jesus* (Grand Rapids: Zondervan, 1984; reprint Wipf & Stock, 1997), summarized here in the first essay. Over the decades this interest has continued and broadened to include Paul, the separation of the church and the synagogue, Jewish-Christian dialog, and anti-Semitism among other things.

Although some have disagreed with my conclusion that there is a generally recognizable *Jewish* view of Jesus, I continue to maintain that Jewish scholarship exhibits a pattern of common traits resulting in a distinctively Jewish view of Jesus. This goes beyond the obvious uniting conclusion concerning what Jesus was *not*.

The thorough Jewishness of Jesus, Paul, and the NT writings has rightly become established as a fixed point in the universe of NT scholarship. This is a positive legacy of the labors of twentieth century scholars. However, already in the 1990s this good emphasis began to be pushed by some to the extreme conclusion that Christianity is best understood as a sect of Judaism. The Gospel of Matthew was described as reflecting "Christian Judaism" (see, e.g., David Sim, *The Gospel of Matthew and Christian Judaism: The History and Social Setting of the Matthean Community* [Edinburgh: T. & T. Clark, 1998]). In the past decade, a handful of scholars, both Jewish and gentile, have energetically been propagating the notion that even Paul is best understood as being fully *within* Judaism, reflecting what they call "Apostolic Judaism" (see, e.g., *Paul Within*

PREFACE

Judaism: Restoring the First Century Context to the Apostle, Mark D. Nanos and Magnus Zetterholm, eds. [Minneapolis: Fortress, 2015]). I am convinced that these new approaches make a crucial mistake in ignoring the emphasis throughout the NT on the *radical newness* of the experience of the early Christian communities and the gospel they proclaimed (see my book, *How New is the New Testament? First Century Judaism and the Emergence of Christianity* [Grand Rapids: Baker, 2018]).

The essays collected in the present volume reflect my interest in these and related issues. They were written over a considerable period of time and reveal some development in my conclusions. I have left the essays in their original form and resisted the temptation to update them, since they are useful as they are and the later essays often bring discussions down to the present. The main justification for reprinting these essays, however, is that quite a few of them were originally published in unusual places, making them difficult to access.

The essays, as will be seen, are in three groups. The first of these contains five essays on Jesus; the second, and largest, group, eight essays on Paul; and the third group, three general essays on Judaism and Christianity.

I am grateful to editors and original publishers for the permission to reprint these essays. Finally, I want to thank the Rev. Fran Gardner-Smith, for her superb help in launching this project by tracking down the original essays and getting them from print into digital format, and also to thank the kind people at Wipf & Stock for taking the essays the rest of the way to their new home, where I hope they will be of benefit to a cadre of new readers.

DONALD A. HAGNER
Pentecost, 2024

Acknowledgments

THE AUTHOR GRATEFULLY ACKNOWLEDGES the sources of the original publication of these essays:

1. "Reclaiming Jesus for Judaism," *Ung Teologi* (Oslo, Norway) 29 (1996) 15–40.
2. "Radical Gospel Criticism and The Modern Jewish Study of Jesus," *Mishkan* 33 (2000) 4–12.
3. "The Quest and Jewish-Christian Dialogue" in *The Handbook of the Study of the Historical Jesus*, edited by T. Holmén and Stanley E. Porter (Leiden: Brill, 2011) 3:1055–77.
4. "Matthew: Apostate, Reformer, Revolutionary?" *NTS* 49 (2003) 193–209.
5. "New Things from the Scribe's Treasure Box (Mt 13:52)," *ExpT* 109 (1998) 329–34.
6. "Paul in Modern Jewish Thought," in *Pauline Studies: Essays Presented to Professor F. F. Bruce on His 70th Birthday*, edited by D. A. Hagner and M. J. Harris (Exeter/Grand Rapids: Paternoster/Eerdmans, 1980) 143–65.
7. "Balancing the Old and the New: The Law of Moses in Matthew and Paul," *Interpretation* 51 (1997) 20–30.
8. "Paul as a Jewish Believer in Jesus—According to His Letters" in *Jewish Believers in Jesus: The Early Centuries*, edited by O. Skarsaune and R. Hvalvik (Peabody, MA: Hendrickson, 2007) 96–120.
9. "Paul's Quarrel with Judaism," in *Anti-Semitism and Early Christianity*, edited by Craig A. Evans and Donald A. Hagner (Minneapolis: Fortress, 1993) 128–50.

10. "Paul and Judaism: Testing the 'New Perspective'" in *Revisiting the Pauline Doctrine of Justification: A Challenge to the New Perspective*, by Peter Stuhlmacher and Donald A. Hagner (Downers Grove, IL: InterVarsity, 2001) 75–105.

11. "Jewish Monotheism and Paul's Christology," in *Perspectives on Christology. Essays in Honor of Paul King Jewett*, eds. R. Muller and M. Shuster (Grand Rapids: Zondervan, 1991) 19–38.

12. "The Apostle Paul's Christianity as an Expression of his Jewish Faith," in *Da Gesù a Paola: Evangelizzare la gioia del Regno. Scritti in onore di Bernardo Estrada nel suo 70° compleanno*, ed. Giuseppe de Virgilio (Rome: EDUSC, 2020) 199–213.

13. "The Newness of Paul's Gospel," in *God's Glory Revealed in Christ: Essays in Biblical Theology in Honor of Thomas R. Schreiner*, edited by Denny Burn, James Hamilton Jr., and Brian Vickers (Nashville: B & H Academic, 2019) 99–108.

14. "Another Look at 'The Parting of the Ways,'" in *Earliest Christian History: History, Literature, and Theology. Essays from the Tyndale Fellowship in Honor of Martin Hengel*, edited by Michael F. Bird and Jason Maston, WUNT 2/320 (Tübingen: Mohr Siebeck, 2012) 381–427.

15. "A Positive Theology of Judaism from the New Testament," *Svensk Exegetisk Årsbok* 69 (2004) 7–28.

16. "Jesus: Bringer of Salvation to Jew and Gentile Alike," in *Who Was Jesus? A Jewish-Christian Dialogue*, edited by C. A. Evans and P. Copan (Louisville: Westminster John Knox, 2001) 45–58.

PART ONE
Jesus

1

Reclaiming Jesus for Judaism

Jesus in Modern Jewish Scholarship

THE TWENTIETH CENTURY SAW an astonishing turn-about in the perception of Jesus among Jewish scholars.[1] For nineteen centuries the Jewish attitude towards Jesus was expressed only by the occasional deprecation that broke an otherwise resentful silence. The classic example of the negative view of Jesus is found in the *Toledot Yeshu* (the "Story [lit. 'generations'] of Jesus"), a biting parody of the gospel story. This folk-tale, based partly on Talmudic traditions, was first written down around the tenth century and in varying forms continued to dominate the popular Jewish

---

1. The subject is discussed fully in my book *The Jewish Reclamation of Jesus: An Analysis and Critique of the Modern Jewish Study of Jesus* (Grand Rapids: Zondervan, 1984; reprint Wipf & Stock, 1997), upon which the present article is largely based. Among earlier studies of Jewish scholarship on Jesus the following may be particularly recommended: G. Lindeskog, *Die Jesusfrage im neuzeitlichen Judentum* (Uppsala: Almquist & Wiksells, 1938; reprinted with a new postscript, Darmstadt: Wissenschaftliche Buchgesellschaft, 1973); *Judarnas Jesus* (Stockholm: Schalom, 1972); and the two books of J. Jocz, *The Jewish People and Jesus Christ* (1949; 3rd ed.; Grand Rapids: Baker, 1979) and *The Jewish People and Jesus Christ After Auschwitz: A Study of the Controversy Between Church and Synagogue* (Grand Rapids: Baker, 1981). Now to be added is W. Vogler, *Jüdische Jesusinterpretationen in christlicher Sicht* (Weimar: Böhlaus, 1988). From the Jewish perspective the following must be mentioned: S. Ben-Chorin, *Jesus im Judentum* (Wuppertal: Brockhaus, 1970), of which an English distillation is available in "The Image of Jesus in Modern Judaism," *JEcSt* 11 (1974) 401–30; and P. Lapide, *Israelis, Jews and Jesus*, trans. P. Heinegg (Garden City, NY: Doubleday, 1979).

perception of Jesus from the medieval period to the nineteenth century.[2] It is not difficult to understand this derisive view of Jesus, given the long and painful history of the "Christian" persecution of the Jews.[3]

In our century, however, Jews have for the first time begun to write positively about Jesus. This new approach, made possible by the rise of liberal or Reform Judaism, on the one hand (Orthodox Jews have been slow to participate), and radical New Testament criticism on the other, regards Jesus as belonging to Judaism rather than to Christianity. In this so-called Jewish reclamation of Jesus, Jewish scholars in a flood of publications[4] have attempted to extract from the synoptic Gospels (John being less suitable for this purpose) a Jesus who fits entirely within the categories and boundaries of Judaism. They accordingly stress the Jewishness of Jesus and his teaching, constructing him as a prophetic reformer of Judaism, a preacher of righteousness like an Amos or Isaiah, or as an apocalyptic proclaimer of doom like the writers of the apocalyptic literature.

Jewish scholars have naturally welcomed the conclusions of radical critical scholarship concerning the historical Jesus. In the early modern period, beginning with H. S. REIMARUS, through F. C. BAUR and more recently R. BULTMANN, down to the "Jesus Seminar" in our own day, a wedge has been driven between Jesus and the faith of the post-resurrection church. Jesus, it is argued, was a preacher of righteousness who intended to reform Judaism in light of imminent apocalyptic judgment, and hence one who was not essentially different from John the Baptist. It was the early church, and especially Paul, who turned Jesus, the proclaimer of the Kingdom, into the proclaimed One, the Lord of the

---

2. Convenient summaries of different versions of the *Toledot* may be found in J. Klausner, *Jesus of Nazareth* (New York: Macmillan, 1925. See also S. Krauss, *Das Leben Jesu nach jüdischen Quellen* (Berlin: Calvary, 1902).

3. On this exceptionally important subject much has been written. I know of no better place to begin than with the moving books of J. Isaac, *Jesus and Israel*, trans. S. Gran (New York: Holt, Rinehart & Winston, 1971) and *The Teaching of Contempt: Christian Roots of Anti-Semitism*, trans. H. Weaver (New York: Holt, Rinehart & Winston, 1964).

4. Lapide can conclude in the 1970s that more was written about Jesus by Jews in the preceding quarter century than in the preceding eighteen centuries. *Israelis, Jews and Jesus*, 31-32. A recent book on Jesus by a Jewish scholar is an exception to the genre of books treated here. J. Neusncr perceptively writes: "It is disingenuous to offer Jesus a standing, within Judaism. that Christianity rightly finds trivial and beside the point" (*A Rabbi Talks with Jesus. An Intermillennial, Interfaith Exchange* [New York: Doubleday, 1993] 15). Neusner's book by sharp contrast is devoted to showing from the Gospel of Matthew that Jesus was not loyal to the Torah.

church—thus creating Christianity and departing dramatically from the intention of Jesus.

This conception of Jesus rests on *a priori* assumptions rather than on objective evidence. The Gospels as they stand simply do not support the conclusion that Jesus was a preacher of righteousness not very different from other such preachers in Israel's history. According to radical critical scholarship, however, the Gospels are so heavily influenced by the post-resurrection faith of the writers, which is regarded as being read back into the narratives, that they cannot be taken as presenting a true portrait of Jesus as he actually was. Indeed, among the criteria devised by these scholars to test the historical reliability of the sayings of Jesus is that of "dissimilarity," namely that only sayings not paralleled by the theological convictions of the early church[5] may be accepted with any degree of confidence as having been spoken by Jesus. This means, of course, that much of the Gospel tradition is automatically rejected. It is obvious how this approach of radical critical scholarship has facilitated the Jewish reclamation of Jesus. Material objectionable to the Jewish perspective can be dismissed from the start. All the better that the "enlightened" conclusions[6] have come initially from the Christian side itself!

The Jewish scholars who have written about Jesus are naturally from different backgrounds and often come to varying conclusions, as we shall see. It is nevertheless the case that the amount of agreement between them is impressive, and it is often justifiable to generalize about what may be called "the Jewish perspective" on a particular issue. We are concerned here only with Jewish scholars who have written substantial studies of Jesus and his teaching. The earliest of these are the British scholars CLAUDE GOLDSMID MONTEFIORE[7] (1858-1938) and IS-

---

5. See R. H. Stein, "The 'Criteria' for Authenticity," in *Gospel Perspectives*, vol. 1, eds. R. T. France and D. Wenham (Sheffield: JSOT Press, 1980) 225-63 and C. A. Evans, "Authenticity Criteria in Life of Jesus Research," *Christian Scholars' Review* 19 (1989) 6-31. One of the other criteria goes quite against the convictions of Jewish scholars and is usually rejected by them, viz., that sayings of Jesus paralleled in first-century Judaism cannot be safely accepted as authentic.

6. Not all the conclusions of radical critical scholarship. of course, are accepted by Jewish scholars. The latter tend, for example, to respect the historical reliability of much more of the Gospel narrative (though, of course, by no means all of it).

7. *The Synoptic Gospels*, 2 vols., 2nd ed. (London: Macmillan, 1927; reprint, New York: Ktav, 1968). *Some Elements of the Religious Teaching of Jesus According to the Synoptic Gospels* (London: Macmillan, 1910; reprint, New York: Arno, 1973); *Rabbinic Literature and Gospel Teaching* (London: Macmillan, 1930; reprint, New York: Ktav, 1970). In this and the following notes I list only the major, pertinent works of the authors in view.

RAEL ABRAHAMS[8] (1858–1925). Proceeding more or less chronologically, we come next to JOSEPH KLAUSNER (1874–1960), a Lithuanian Jew, who in 1920 settled in Israel, and the author of what is probably the best-known book (and in fact one of the best books) on Jesus by a Jewish author.[9] Among the more recent authors are the distinguished American scholar, SAMUEL SANDMEL[10] (1911–1979); the German-born Israeli journalist, SCHALOM BEN-CHORIN[11] (1913–99); the Austrian-born professor of comparative religion at Hebrew University in Jerusalem, DAVID FLUSSER[12] (1917–2000); journalist-scholar, PINCHAS LAPIDE[13] (1922–1997); and Hungarian-born Oxford scholar, GEZA VERMES[14] (1924–2013).

In the review that follows we proceed topically, covering Jesus and the Law, the ethical teaching of Jesus, the teaching of Jesus concerning relationship to God, and finally the question of Jesus himself.[15]

---

8. *Studies in Pharisaism and the Gospels,* First Series (Cambridge: Cambridge University Press, 1917); Second Series (Cambridge: Cambridge University Press, 1924; reprint of both volumes, New York: Ktav, 1967).

9. *Jesus of Nazareth: His Life, Times, and Teaching,* trans. H. Danby (New York: Macmillan, 1925; reprint, New York: Beacon, 1964); *From Jesus to Paul,* translated from the Hebrew original of 1939 by W. F. Stinespring (London: Macmillan, 1943; reprint, New York: Beacon, 1961).

10. *We Jews and Jesus* (New York: Oxford University Press, 1965; reprint, 1973); *A Jewish Understanding of the New Testament* (Cincinnati: Hebrew Union College Press, 1956; reprint, New York: Ktav/Anti-Defamation League, 1974).

11. *Bruder Jesus: Der Nazarener in jüdische Sicht* (Munich: List, 1967); *Jesus im Judentum* (Wuppertal: Brockhaus, 1970), summarized in "The image of Jesus in Modern Judaism," *Journal of Ecumenical Studies* 11 (1974) 401–30.

12. *Jesus,* trans. R. Walls (New York: Herder & Herder, 1969).

13. *Der Rabbi von Nazareth: Wandlungen des jüdischen Jesusbildes* (Trier: Spee, 1974); *Israelis, Jews and Jesus,* trans. P. Heinegg (Garden City, NY: Doubleday, 1978).

14. *Jesus the Jew: A Hisiorian's Reading of the Gospels* (New York: Macmillan, 1973; reprinted many times); *Jesus and the World of Judaism* (Philadelphia: Fortress, 1984).

15. We deliberately leave aside the issue of the trial and the death of Jesus, subjects upon which Jewish scholars have written much. This special topic receives full treatment in David Catchpole, *The Trial of Jesus: A Study in the Gospels and Jewish Historiography from 1770 to the Present Day* (Leiden: Brill, 1971). See too W. Horbury, "The Trial of Jesus in Jewish Tradition," in *The Trial of Jesus,* ed. E. Bammel (London: SCM, 1970); and Paul Barnett, *The Trials of Jesus: Evidence, Conclusions, and Aftermath* (Grand Rapids: Eerdmans, 2024).

I. JESUS AND THE LAW

Because of the supreme importance of the Torah in Judaism,[16] the question of Jesus' attitude to the law has been the focus of much Jewish study of Jesus. On this question most Jewish scholars go against the conclusions of radical-critical Christian scholars. The latter, for the most part, have concluded that on such matters as the sabbath, prohibition of divorce, and the food laws, Jesus broke with the law in some significant sense. Jewish scholars, by contrast, regard Jesus as being very conservative in his attitude to the law. They find in Jesus' statement, according to Matthew, that he had "come not to abolish but to fulfill" the law, and that not the slightest item "will pass from the law until all is accomplished" (Matt 5:17–18), something that rings true to the Jewishness of Jesus. Much of radical-critical scholarship, on the other hand, denies that Jesus said these words, regarding them instead as the creation of the evangelist.

Only a few Jewish scholars have concluded that Jesus made a break with the law, and even they conclude that the break was a modest one that in no way lessens the Jewishness of Jesus. They certainly do not see that break as having the christological significance that much Christian scholarship finds in it. Montefiore has used very forceful language concerning Jesus' break with the law, referring to it as "a new departure" and "a break from the Judaism of his age."[17] Jesus' attitude to the law "was novel and even revolutionary."[18] Montefiore has in mind primarily Jesus' consistent emphasis upon the moral laws over the ceremonial laws, the stress on the priority of the inward over the outward, and the surpassing importance of the law of love.[19] In Montefiore's opinion Jesus lacks the consistency of the rabbis, and contradicts his own assertion of loyalty to the law.[20]

---

16. This point hardly needs to be supported, but it is worth recalling the opening of the Mishnaic tractate Pirke Abot, the "Sayings of the Fathers," with the statement of Simeon the Just that "By three things is the world sustained: by the Law, by the [Temple-]service, and by deeds of loving kindness" (Abot 1:2; trans. H. Danby). These are commonly regarded as the three pillars of Judaism.

17. "The Religious Teaching of the Synoptic Gospels in Its Relation to Judaism," *Hibbert Journal* 20 (1921–22) 438.

18. *Elements of the Religious Teaching*, 44.

19. Cf. Joseph Jacobs, "Jesus of Nazareth—In History," in *Jewish Encyclopedia*, 7:162.

20. "The Originality of Jesus," *Hibbert Journal* 28 (1929-30) 102-3.

Sandmel admits that Jesus broke with the law if he said the words of Mark 7:15 ("There is nothing outside a person that by going in can defile"), since this contradicts the food prohibitions of Leviticus 11 and Deuteronomy 14. Yet in Sandmel's opinion, because these words stand in tension with other material in the Gospel tradition we cannot be sure of their authenticity.[21]

More Jewish scholars attempt to handle the complexity of the subject by concluding that while Jesus did not break with the law, he did differ from the perspective of rabbinic Judaism (i.e. the Judaism of the Pharisees). Abrahams argues that Jesus was fully faithful to the law, but that his interpretation of it differed from that of the Pharisees. Jesus merely took advantage of an allowable freedom in the exegesis of the law.[22] At the same time, however,—and this is of great importance—Jesus treated "morality as an autonomous principle."[23]

Klausner too concludes that Jesus remained faithful to the law, including even the ceremonial law. Jesus, however, made the latter clearly subordinate to the moral law and his teachings thus contain "a kernel of opposition to Judaism," which Paul first brought to fruition when he abolished the ceremonial laws.[24] In Klausner's opinion, Jesus was guilty of an "exaggerated Judaism" that in the end must be regarded as a "non-Judaism."[25] The point made by scholars belonging to this category is perhaps put best by A. COHEN: "He isolated morality from the halachic framework in which it was embedded."[26] In this perspective, Jesus has another, different way of being faithful to the Torah, than that of the Pharisees.

Almost all the more recent writers on Jesus conclude not only that Jesus was faithful to the law, but also that there was no essential difference between him and rabbinic Judaism. Despite Jesus' special sense of authority ("But I say to you"), Ben-Chorin maintains that Jesus is not to be differentiated from the Pharisees, but that he offers interpretation of the intent of the law in the same way that *Hillel* or *Shammai* do.[27]

---

21. *We Jews and Jesus*, 136–38.
22. *Studies in Pharisaism*, 1:134.
23. *Studies in Pharisaism*, 2:vi.
24. *Jesus of Nazareth*, 369ff.
25. *Jesus of Nazareth*, 374ff.
26. *The Parting of the Ways* (London: Lincolns-Prager, 1954) 80. Cf. K. Kohler, *The Origin of the Synagogue and the Church* (New York: Macmillan. 1929) 218, 222.
27. *Bruder Jesus*. 16–17; 75–76.

Flusser is one of the strongest proponents of this view. He states that "Jesus did not oppose any prescription of the Written or Oral Mosaic Law."[28] The places in the Gospels that may lead a reader to the opposite conclusion are, according to Flusser, the result of distorted wording that reflects not what Jesus said, but the later disagreement between the synagogue and the church. With regard to the law, Jesus is indistinguishable from the Pharisees. A virtually identical view of the matter is held by Lapide, who can write: "Jesus was and remained a Torah-true Jew, who never and nowhere (in Matthew, Mark, and Luke) transgressed against the Mosaic and rabbinic legislation."[29]

Vermes also regards Jesus as loyal to the whole law, arguing that the disagreements between Jesus and the Pharisees amount only to in-house debates that were typical of the Pharisees. The one instance in the synoptic Gospels where Jesus seems to go against the essentials of Judaism, in the opinion of Vermes, is in Mark 7:19 where, however, the Greek redactor misunderstood an Aramaic pun and mistakenly wrote "Thus he declared all foods clean."[30]

There seems to be, then, a clear trend among Jewish scholars to reclaim Jesus for Judaism, even in the area of Jesus and the law. It is clear, however, that this area is not without difficulty for these scholars. Their attempt to understand all of the teaching of Jesus under the spotlight of Matt 5:17–20 is not convincing. Even that passage is capable of being understood in more than one way. While this is not the place to give a full exegesis of the passage, already the fact that it is the law *and the prophets* that are in view should suggest that the passage is not to be adequately understood apart from the reality of fulfillment. If Jesus upholds the law, it is not simply the law as it stands that he upholds, but the law as definitively interpreted by him in the new eschatological situation of the dawning Kingdom.

Totally underestimated by the majority of Jewish scholars is the authority of Jesus and the central importance of his teaching. The "But I say to you" of the antitheses (Matt 5:21–48) points to a unique authority, but so too does the confident exposition of righteousness in the sermon itself, as the astonished crowds indicate: "for he taught them as one having authority, and not as their scribes" (7:29). His demeanor and teaching

28. "Jesus," in *Encyclopedia Judaica*, 10:13.

29. *Der Rabbi von Nazareth*, 52.

30. *Jesus the Jew*, 28–29, 40. Jesus' distinctive lay in his emphasis on interiority and purity of intention.

point to an unparalleled authority in relation to the law, as for example concerning the sabbath (cf. Mark 2:23—3:6; "the Son of Man is lord even of the sabbath," 2:28), divorce (Mark 10:2-9), and the food laws (Mark 7:14-23). As W. D. Davies puts it, "the attitude of Jesus to the Law implies his Messianic awareness or consciousness."[31]

Even the Jewish scholars who do recognize the unusual nature of Jesus' authority often make no attempt to explain it or to pursue possible implications. Either that authority is regarded as somehow being possible within a rabbinic framework, or, if not, it is regarded as the result of later theological tendencies read back into the Gospel narratives. The issue of Jesus and the law is one of very great importance—one that must be faced squarely by those who would reclaim Jesus for Judaism. J. Jeremias writes:

> Thus it was Jesus himself who shook the foundations of the ancient people of God. His criticism of the Torah, coupled with this announcement of the end of the cult; his rejection of the Halakah and his claim to announce the final will of God, were the decisive occasion for the action of the leaders of the people against him, finally brought into action by the cleansing of the Temple. They took Jesus to be a false prophet. This accusation brought him to the cross.[32]

The issue of Jesus and the law will remain problematic for Jewish scholars since a correct understanding of it is not possible apart from coming to terms with the personal claims of Jesus and his identity as the Messiah of Israel.[33]

II. THE ETHICAL TEACHING OF JESUS

Fundamental to the teaching of Jesus is his proclamation of the dawning of the Kingdom (cf. Mark 1:15; Luke 11:20-24; 17:20-21). Jewish

---

31. W. D. Davies, *Christian Origins and Judaism* (Philadelphia: Westminster. 1962) 46.

32. J. Jeremias, *New Testament Theology: The Proclamation of Jesus*, trans. J. Bowden (London: SCM, 1971) 211.

33. R. Banks perceptively concludes, with reference to Matthew, "It therefore becomes apparent that it is not so much *Jesus'* stance towards the Law that he is concerned to depict: It is how 1he *Law* stands with regard to him, as the one who brings it to fulfilment and to whom all attention must now be directed." *Jesus and the Law in the Synoptic Tradition*, SNTSMS 28 (Cambridge: Cambridge University Press. 1975) 226; cf. 25-52.

scholars admit the centrality of the Kingdom in the teaching of Jesus, but they regard Jesus as expecting an imminent coming of the Kingdom, i.e. a future, eschatological Kingdom, rather than proclaiming the presence of the Kingdom in and through his ministry. According to Jewish scholars, Jesus was of course mistaken in his expectation of an imminent coming of the Kingdom. Ben-Chorin expresses a universal Jewish opinion when he writes: "No, there is still no kingdom, no peace, and no redemption ... Jesus of Nazareth was not the promised one because he did not redeem the world."[34]

For Jewish scholars, Jesus resembles John the Baptist in the sense that he was an apocalyptic preacher of repentance and righteousness in light of the imminent coming of the Kingdom, which was to involve the fulfillment of Israel's national-political hopes. Yet some of these scholars admit that there is a paradoxical element in the teaching of Jesus concerning the Kingdom. Montefiore notes, for example, that although Jesus "nearly always" spoke of a future Kingdom, in some sense he also regarded the Kingdom as present in his ministry.[35] On Matt 12:28 Montefiore can write: "The Kingdom of God has already begun with the appearance of Jesus the Messiah. The rule of the devil and his agents is passing away; the rule of God, the new era, has begun."[36] Klausner, too, can admit that for Jesus "in real fact, the kingdom of heaven had already begun: in a certain sense it had come."[37] Similarly, Flusser concludes that Jesus "is the only Jew of ancient times known to us, who preached not only that men were on the threshold of the end of time, but that the new age of salvation had already begun."[38]

That this involves a christological claim is for the most part admitted by Jewish scholars. Klausner writes that for Jesus "the Messiah was, therefore, already in the world, and so the kingdom of heaven, the kingdom of the Messiah, was likewise in existence in the world."[39] Montefiore points in the same direction: "The Kingdom of God which he announces

---

34. *Jesus im Judentum*, 67–68 Further, "we know of no enclave of redemption in the midst of an unredeemed world."

35. *Synoptic Gospels*, 1:61; 2:161; *Rabbinic Literature*, 131.

36. *Synoptic Gospels*, 2:193.

37. *Jesus of Nazareth*, 403; cf. 406, where this fact is admitted to be a real difference between Judaism and Jesus.

38. *Jesus*, 88. For Jesus, the kingdom of heaven is "the eschatological rule of God that has dawned already," *Jesus*, 91.

39. *Jesus of Nazareth*, 403.

is not only God's kingdom; it is also his kingdom."⁴⁰ Yet, of course, just as Jewish scholars deny that the kingdom has come, so they deny that Jesus was who he thought he was. These Gospel assertions, indeed, bring one close to the heart of the Christian faith. In Klausner's words, this "two-fold misapprehension of Jesus—the nearness of the kingdom of heaven and his Messiahship—perpetuated his memory and created Christianity."⁴¹

Although the ethical teaching of Jesus is inseparable from the whole of the Gospel, and in particular from the claim of the dawning kingdom and the identity of Jesus, Jewish scholars find in the ethical teaching what they regard as the most promising ground for the reclamation of Jesus. In his study of the Jewish parallels to the Sermon on the Mount, G. FRIEDLANDER concludes that four-fifths of it "is exclusively Jewish."⁴² Klausner, speaking of the ethical teaching in general, expresses the Jewish conclusion forcefully and in italicized words: "Throughout the Gospels there is not one item of ethical teaching which cannot be paralleled either in the Old Testament, the Apocrypha, or in the Talmudic and Midrashic literature of the period near to the time *of* Jesus."⁴³

In fact, however, there are points at which the ethical teaching of Jesus proves to be problematic for the Jewish perspective. While Jesus' summary of the law by means of the two-fold love commandment (Matt 22:37–40; Mark 12:30–31) may reflect contemporary Jewish ethics, as Jewish scholars stress, the command to love one's enemies is another matter. A quite remarkable admission is made by Flusser who regards the teaching of Jesus on this point as "unique and incomparable," especially in its stress of love towards one's enemies. "Christianity surpasses Judaism, at least theoretically, in its approach of love to all men."⁴⁴ Lapide refers to the command to love one's enemies as "the only new thing in the Sermon on the Mount,"⁴⁵ and Abrahams writes that "We do not find

---

40. "The Significance of Jesus for His Own Age," *Hibbert Journal* 10 (1911–12) 776.

41. *Jesus of Nazareth*, 405.

42. *The Jewish Sources of the Sermon on the Mount* (London: Routledge, 1911; reprint, New York: Ktav, 1969), but Ben-Chorin also regards the Sermon as Jewish in content and finds in it "no originality" (*Bruder Jesus*, 83).

43. *Jesus of Nazareth*, 384.

44. "A New Sensitivity in Judaism and the Christian Message," *Harvard Theological Review* 61 (1968) 126, where Flusser can also say "In Judaism hatred is practically forbidden but love to the enemy is not prescribed."

45. *Okumene aus Christen und Juden* (Neukirchen-Vluyn: Neukirchener, 1972) 138.

in the Rabbinic literature a parallel to the striking paradox *Love your enemies*."⁴⁶

The common complaint of Jewish scholars, with Matthew 23 in mind, is that Jesus himself did not abide by his own teaching concerning the love of one's enemies. But to regard Matthew 23 as an expression of hatred of the Pharisees is to misunderstand the passage. To be sure, Jesus is harsh in his opposition to their errors. It is arguable, however, that this harshness is itself the result of a love for the Pharisees (cf. 23:37b), and not hatred of them. (For Jesus' attitude to his enemies, cf. Luke 23:34, although the verse is lacking in a number of important manuscripts).

Closely related to the exhortation to love one's enemies is the teaching of Jesus, "Do not resist an evildoer. But if anyone strikes you on the right cheek, turn the other also" (Matt 5:39; cf. Luke 6:28-29). A few Jewish scholars such as Montefiore and Sandmel find this teaching to be basically in keeping with the spirit of the Rabbis, although carried to an extreme.⁴⁷ Others stress the radical and unrealistic nature of the teaching and hence its difference from the Jewish perspective. Flusser points to the passive resistance to evil advocated by the Qumran community as affording a Jewish parallel, but nevertheless regards the teaching as "indeed revolutionary, subversive."⁴⁸

In the view of Ben-Chorin, the radical character of the doctrine is to be explained by Jesus' belief in the shortness of time before the end of the present age.⁴⁹

Another teaching of Jesus that is striking from the Jewish perspective is the so-called Golden Rule of Matt 7:12, "In everything do to others as you would have them do to you." The claim of many Jewish scholars that there is no essential difference between this and the negative form of the rule found in Jewish sources, i.e., "What is hateful to thyself do not

---

46. *Studies in Pharisaism*, 1:164. Cf. Montefiore, *Rabbinic Literature*, 103. Friedlander denies this, but the "parallels" he cites are hardly convincing. *Jewish Sources*, 73.

47. Montefiore, *Rabbinic Teaching*, 52-54; Sandmel, *We Jews and Jesus*, 132. Sandmel admits, however, "I know nothing in Judaism which parallels the Christian counsel to turn the other cheek."

48. *Jesus*, 89; cf. 80-84. According to Friedlander, the teaching "revolutionized the spirit of all law" and if followed would mean the destruction of society (*Jewish Sources*, 66).

49. *Bruder Jesus*, 79. Probably D. Daube is closer to the mark when he argues that this teaching has to do with personal rights and honor rather than the laws of society. *The New Testament and Rabbinic Judaism* (London: Athlone, 1956) 254-65.

PART ONE | JESUS

do unto thy neighbor,"[50] is not convincing. This is admitted by Abrahams, who argues that "the negative form is the more fundamental of the two, though the positive form is the fuller expression of practical morality."[51] Ben-Chorin regards the positive form as more radical than the negative, but nevertheless not new.[52]

A further strain within the teaching of Jesus that is alien to the Jewish perspective is that of self-renunciation and asceticism. "Deliberate, voluntary, and complete renunciation is not put forward as an ideal by the Rabbis."[53] The other-worldliness of Jesus as reflected for example in his attitude toward material joys and in his negative view of wealth (e.g. Luke 18:22) is unrabbinic in tone.[54] From the Jewish point of view, the same must be said concerning such things as voluntary celibacy (Matt 19:12),[55] the sacrificial attitude toward family relationships (Luke 14:26), and the absolute prohibition of divorce.[56]

A major problem for the attempt of Jewish scholarship to reclaim Jesus is the radical and absolute character of Jesus' ethical teaching. Klausner repeatedly calls it "extremist" and Ben-Chorin refers to the way of Jesus as "so radical that it surpasses the human dimension."[57] Jewish scholars thus emphasize the impracticability of Jesus' ethical teaching, both at the social and the individual level. The idealism of this teaching is thought to be self-defeating and the cause of its wide neglect by Christians.[58] Montefiore and Vermes, on the other hand, point to the spirit of the teachings and their hyperbolic character.[59]

Jewish scholars are unanimous in the conclusion that the explanation of the radical character and absoluteness of Jesus' ethical teaching is due to Jesus' expectation of an imminent eschatological denouement. In

50. E. g., Tobit 4:15; BT *Shab.* 3la, as set forth by Hillel.
51. *Studies in Pharisaism*, 1:22.
52. *Bruder Jesus*, 17, 80.
53. Montefiore, *Rabbinic Literature*, 355. Cf. Friedlander, *Jewish Sources*, 67.
54. Montefiore, *Rabbinic Literature*, 16, 140, 281. Cf. Friedlander, *Jewish Sources*, 180.
55. Ben-Chorin believes it impossible that Jesus had a negative view of marriage and argues that Jesus was himself married like every rabbi in Israel. *Bruder Jesus*, 128ff.
56. See Friedlander, *Jewish Sources*, 52, 55, 175; Montefiore, *Rabbinic Literature*, 138–39; Abrahams, *Studies in Pharisaism*, 1:121.
57. *Bruder Jesus*, 78.
58. See especially Klausner, "Christian and Jewish Ethics," *Judaism* 2 (1953) 16–30.
59. Montefiore: "Jesus, I am sure, was thinking of something which *is* practicable." "The Old Testament and Its Ethical Teaching," *Hibbert Journal* 16 (1917–18) 242; Vermes, *Jesus and the World of Judaism*, 53.

Montefiore's words, "Much of the moral teaching of the gospel is relative to that one overmastering idea [the End], even when the idea itself is not definitely expressed."[60] The ethic of Jesus is thus seen, to use the language of ALBERT SCHWEITZER, as an "interim" ethic, to be practiced in the short time prior to the coming of the end of the age.[61] In Lapide's view, "The high torah-morality has everything to do with this [the expectation of the end]."[62]

For Jewish scholars, then, while much of the ethical teaching of Jesus rings true to the rabbinic perspective, it can on occasion go far beyond anything found in the rabbis. The resultant tension is well reflected in the conclusion of Klausner, who while asserting that there is "not a single ethical sentence in the whole of the New Testament" that does not find a parallel in Jewish literature of that era, paradoxically adds "nevertheless, there is something distinctive and specific in the moral law of Christianity which is not found in the moral law of Judaism."[63] Flusser forthrightly admits the surprising newness in these words: "Revolution broke through at three points: the radical commandment of love, the call for a new morality, the idea of the kingdom of heaven."[64]

It is the obvious desire of Jewish scholars to salvage as much of the ethical teaching of Jesus as they can. The entire tendency is captured in the oft-quoted words of Klausner, with which his book on Jesus ends: "If ever the day should come and this ethical code be stripped of its wrappings of miracles and mysticism, the Book of the Ethics of Jesus will be one of the choicest treasures in the literature of Israel for all time."[65] Klausner generalizes here, since it is clear from earlier in his book, as we have seen, that not all the teaching of Jesus is acceptable to him. But that aside, a serious question remains: Can the ethical teachings of Jesus be taken out of their eschatological context, stripped of their christological implications, and made into an ethical code book without doing violence to their intent?

60. *Elements of the Religious Teaching*, 77.

61. Cf. Abrahams, *Studies in Pharisaism*, 1:68; Friedlander. *Jewish Sources*, 262-63; Ben-Chorin, *Bruder Jesus*, 79; Klausner, *Jesus of Nazareth*, 405. According to Klausner, this mistaken expectation of Jesus is fundamental to the creation of Christianity

62. *Okumene aus Christen und Juden*, 141.

63. "Christian and Jewish Ethics,"16; cf. *Jesus of Nazareth*, 384. Klausner attributes the difference to an "exaggerated Judaism" of Jesus that ultimately led to a "non-Judaism."

64. *Jesus*, 65. Cf. Montefiore, *The Old Testament and After* (London: Macmillan, 1923) 240-47.

65. *Jesus*, 414. For a similar statement, see Vermes, *Jesus and the World of Judaism*, 57.

Certainly the ethical teaching of Jesus is basically Jewish and can be paralleled in Jewish writings of that era and in the rabbinic literature. Yet, as we have seen, it also repeatedly goes beyond the rabbinic perspective. Jesus calls his disciples to an unconditional love of others, including their enemies; to the positive action of the Golden Rule; to a new concept of service and humility; to nonretaliation in the face of evil; to self-renunciation and to a lifestyle that opposes the materialism of this world. His call to a discipleship of uncompromising commitment involves an absoluteness that is incomprehensible, if taken on its own terms, apart from the good news of the dawning kingdom Jesus brings. Only with this new proclamation of the kingdom—not its imminence, but its presence—can the ethical teaching of Jesus, with all its idealism, be adequately understood. Jesus' ethics are not "interim" ethics, nor are they merely hyperbolical. They are the ethics of the kingdom.

It is the dawning of the kingdom that makes possible a new order of life and a new relation with the Father. The perfection of that new order is exemplified in the absoluteness of Jesus' ethical teachings. These teachings do not constitute a new code of ethics to be substituted for the Law, but are rather a description of kingdom righteousness.[66] They are eschatological ethics, but brought to the present in advance of the final consummation of the age. They are not legislative, but descriptive.

If the ethical teaching of Jesus cannot be understood apart from his proclamation of the kingdom, neither can the latter be understood apart from the person of Jesus. Thus in the last analysis the understanding of Jesus' ethical teaching depends on one's interpretation of the person of Jesus.

III. THE TEACHING OF JESUS CONCERNING RELATIONSHIP TO GOD

Jewish scholars regard the religion of Jesus as thoroughly Jewish. WELL-HAUSEN's words are frequently cited with approval: "Jesus was not a Christian: he was a Jew. He did not proclaim a new faith, but taught men to do the will of God."[67] These words are of course true, yet they do not

---

66. T. W. Manson, *The Teaching of Jesus*, 2nd ed. (Cambridge: Cambridge University Press, 1963) 301.

67. *Einleitung in die drei ersten Evangelien* (Berlin: Reimer, 1905) 113. Quoted, e.g., by Klausner, *Jesus of Nazareth*, 95 Lapide, *Okumene aus Christen und Juden*, 90; Ben-Chorin, *Jesus im Judentum*, 7; Vermes, *Jesus and the World of Judaism*, 18.

tell the whole truth. For all the continuity of Jesus with Judaism, we also confront an unavoidable newness.

The starting point for any comparison must be the admission that Judaism is properly understood a "covenantal nomism," i.e. the pursuit of the righteousness of the law, but within the prior framework of God's grace as experienced in the covenant.[68] It is thus a distortion to regard Judaism as a legalism, where the Jew must earn his or her way with God. Montefiore quotes the daily prayer of the early rabbinic Jew: "Not because of our righteous acts do we lay our supplications before thee, but because of thine abundant mercies. What are we? What is our piety? What our righteousness?"[69]

It is furthermore the case that Judaism and Christianity are parallel at many other points. Thus, as Friedlander reminds us, the teaching of the Beatitudes is found also in Isaiah and the Psalms.[70] The rabbis on the whole would have emphasized the moral above the ceremonial, as did Jesus; they too stressed the importance of thought and intention as well as deed; they too stressed the priority of mercy over sacrifice; and even the revolutionary statement of Mark 7:15 is "only an application of a principle which runs on all fours with theirs."[71]

At the same time there are differences between Judaism and Christianity. The latter is after all not a nomism. Jewish scholars have called attention to the differences. Sandmel points out that "it is in answering the question how can man fulfill the will of God that a strand in Christianity is the antithesis of the Jewish way."[72] Self-effort in doing the deeds of the law and thereby attaining righteousness is vitally important in Judaism. Vermes makes the remarkable admission that "In the inter-testamental period . . . relation with the Father grows to be less of a privilege conferred on Israel as a people, and increasingly on merit."[73] Montefiore writes that "It is not all grace. It is partly man's own effort."[74] Ben-Chorin stresses the neces-

---

68. See especially E. P. Sanders, *Paul and Palestinian Judaism* (Philadelphia: Fortress, 1977).

69. *Rabbinic Literature*, 19.

70. *Jewish Sources*, 23.

71. Montefiore, *Rabbinic Literature*, 316, 42, 242, and for the quote, 25.

72. *We Jews and Jesus*, 132.

73. *Jesus and the World of Judaism*, 39.

74. *Rabbinic Literature*, 201. Thus, although there are some parallels of free grace in the rabbinic literature, Jesus' teaching may be regarded as "comparatively new and original." *Religious Teaching*, 98.

sity of grace and notes at the same time that "The Law was given to Israel, in order that we might fulfill it . . . I myself must do it. Since no one else can take my place—I myself must fulfill it in the probationary test of this life."[75] Abrahams refers to a "synergism" and quotes Akiba, according to Abot 3.20, "The world is judged by grace, yet all is according to the amount of work," adding, "The antinomy is the ultimate doctrine of Pharisaism."[76]

That grace holds a more important place for Jesus than in Judaism is admitted by several Jewish scholars. Klausner notes that in the Jewish view God requires justice and thus will not acquit the guilty (Nah 1:3), while for Jesus, "sinners and non-sinners, evil and good, ungodly and righteous, all alike are of the same worth in God's sight."[77] According to Flusser, Gospel passages such as Matt. 20:1–16 and Luke 13:1–5 undermine the concept of the justice of God so that "All the norms of the usual concepts of the righteousness of God are abrogated."[78] At the same time, however, he maintains that "a relaxation of the compensatory doctrine" and a "new Jewish sensitivity concerning the divine justice" in Judaism prepared the way for the radical message of Jesus.[79] The association of Jesus with sinners is called by Montefiore "something both great and new," "a new and gracious characteristic of Jesus," to which "there are no parallels in the Rabbinic literature."[80]

Repentance is "the corner-stone of Jewish piety," on the other hand, and "Nothing that Jesus says about it beats, or goes beyond, what the Rabbis say about it."[81] Abrahams, however, states that Pharisaism "was inclined to leave the initiative to the sinner, except that it always

---

75. *Jesus im Judentum*, 71.

76. *Studies in Pharisaism*, 1:146–47. Montefiore too notes that the rabbis were satisfied with inconsistency at this point and maintained propositions not capable of harmonization. *Rabbinic Literature*, 163.

77. *Jesus of Nazareth*, 379–80.

78. *Jesus*, 82. Flusser adds that this view is "incommensurable to reason," that "it leads to the preaching of the kingdom in which the last will be first." Flusser considers the view "demonic" because the customarily important virtues are made empty. Although the view "is at once profoundly moral," it is also "beyond good and evil."

79. "A New Sensitivity in Judaism and the Christian Message," *Harvard Theological Review* 61 (1968) 111;
119. Cf. *Jesus*, 65–69.

80. *Rabbinic Literature*, 372, 221.

81. Montefiore, *Rabbinic Literature*, 273, 260. Yet elsewhere Montefiore writes: "What is new and striking in the teaching of Jesus is that this process of repentance takes an *active* turn." *Synoptic Gospels*, 2:249.

maintained God's readiness to take the first step. Jesus in his attitude towards sin and sinners was more inclined to take the initiative."[82]

There is a gravity about the human condition in the perspective of Jesus that is lacking in the rabbinic perspective. According to the rabbis, the evil inclination within us, the *yeṣer ha-ra,* can be overcome by the study and practice of the law. For Jesus, however, the overcoming of evil is a part of the dawning of the kingdom and both are dependent on his death (cf. Mark 10:45). Sandmel describes the difference this way: for Jews sin is "an act or action"; for Christians it is "a state, a condition of man." He continues by noting that in the Jewish view, "man must make his own atonement, not have atonement wrought for him."[83] Prayer and repentance are the only means of atonement needed for forgiveness and restoration. The "Pauline" doctrine — as it is regarded — of humanity trapped by sin and in need of a savior is rejected as un-Jewish.

While the idea of a vicarious suffering of the righteous on behalf of sinful Israel is recognized as authentically Jewish, most Jewish scholars who accept that Jesus foretold his death deny that he understood it as an expiatory sacrifice.[84] It was at a later "Greek" stage of the gospel development, according to Flusser, when the connection was made between the Suffering Servant of Isaiah and Jesus. So too, Montefiore, although admitting the Jewishness of the idea of vicarious sacrifice, believes that the second half of Mark 10:45 ("to give his life a ransom for many") involves Pauline terminology and cannot have been spoken by Jesus.[85] Ben-Chorin, by contrast, does not regard it as impossible that Jesus himself combined the image of the Son of Man (Daniel 7) and that of the Suffering Servant of God (Isaiah 53). He concludes that Jesus may well have seen his death as "a kind of offering."[86]

There is an obvious tendency, then, for Jewish scholarship to deny that Jesus viewed his own death as a vicarious atonement.[87] Verses such

---

82. *Studies in Pharisaism,* 1:58.

83. *We Jews and Jesus,* 45–47.

84. Flusser: "Jesus did not intend to die in order to expiate the sins of others by his own brief passion" (*Jesus,* 98). He writes elsewhere, however, that "if as Christians believe, the martyr was at the same time the Messiah, then his death has a cosmic importance" (*Encyclopedia Judaica,* 10:14).

85. *Synoptic Gospels,* 1:260.

86. *Bruder Jesus,* 158; *Jesus im Judentum,* 42–43.

87. The new revision of Schürer cautiously allows the idea of a suffering Messiah in Judaism, but concludes that the literature analyzed does not contain "the slightest allusion to an expiatory suffering of the Messiah." E. Schürer, *The History of the Jewish*

as Mark 10:45 and Matt 26:28 ("for this is my blood of the covenant, which is poured out for the forgiveness of sins") are either ignored or relegated to post-resurrection theology.

As is true for so much of what is examined in the preceding pages, the doctrine of the fatherhood of God as held by Jesus is both to a degree in continuity with Judaism and also to a degree new. To begin with, Jesus was not the first to affirm the fatherhood of God and, on the whole, the teaching of Jesus is not different from the best of rabbinic teaching.[88] Jewish scholars reject the common notion that for the first-century Jew God was remote and inaccessible. At the same time, however, Montefiore can admit that Jesus brought a new sense of intimacy and a new frequency in his use of Father for God: "This regular conception of God as Father, in proportion to the intensity and vividness of the feeling which suggested it, was something which may fitly be called original."[89]

Both Flusser and Vermes have challenged the view of Jeremias that Jesus is unique in addressing God as "my Father" (rather than "our Father") and in using the intimate term *Abba* (Mark 14:36 and parallels).[90] They both refer to a passage in the Babylonian Talmud (Taanit, 23b) concerning Hanan. grandson of Honi the circle-drawer, who refers to God as "the Abba who gives rain."[91] They do not comment on the fact that the passage involves only an indirect reference to God as Abba, prompted by the lighthearted cry of the children, and that God is actually addressed by Hanan as "Master of the world."[92] The arguments of Flusser and Vermes hardly seem sufficient to overthrow the case made by Jeremias.

Jesus did not depart from Judaism in his reference to God as Father. But in his frequent and consistent use of "Father" in addressing God, his use of the first personal pronoun "my Father" and in his use of Abba, he goes considerably beyond Jewish convention. Klausner rightly concludes

---

People in the Age of Jesus Christ, new rev. ed. by G. Vermes, F. Millar, M. Black, vol. 2 (Edinburgh: T. & T. Clark, 1979) 549 (Appendix on "The Suffering Messiah").

88. Montefiore, *Rabbinic Literature*, 109.

89. "The Originality of Jesus," *Hibbert Journal* 27 (1929-30) 104. Klausner refers to an "excessive emphasis" upon the fatherhood of God by Jesus. *Jesus of Nazareth*, 378. Friedlander denies that "the Fatherhood of God is expounded by Jesus with more depth and intensity than by the great prophets and teachers of Israel who lived before the age of Jesus." *Jewish Sources*, 126-27.

90. *The Central Message of the New Testament* (London: SCM, 1965) 9-30; *The Prayers of Jesus*, SBT 2/6 (London: SCM, 1967) 11-65.

91. Flusser, *Jesus*, 145; Vermes, *Jesus and the World of Judaism*, 42.

92. Jeremias makes these points about the talmudic passage. *Central Message*, 19.

that the data point to Jesus' messianic consciousness: "Jesus looked upon himself as the Messiah, and as the Messiah he was closer to God than any other human being."[93] We are thus again pointed in the direction of the person of Jesus.

It is indeed the centrality of Jesus in the synoptic Gospels that remains problematic for Jewish interpreters of Jesus. A verse such as Matt 11:27, "All things have been handed over to me by my Father; and no one knows the Son except the Father, and no one knows the Father except the Son and anyone to whom the Son chooses to reveal him," presents a particular difficulty.

Montefiore finds it difficult to believe that Jesus could have uttered the words.[94] Flusser does not do justice to the passage when he draws a parallel with the hymns of Qumran and tries to explain it as reflecting "the mentality of the charismatic apocalyptic who has access to the mysteries of God, through which he is able 'to enlighten the minds of many.'"[95] Klausner faces the difficulty more squarely when he writes: Judaism does not associate the Messiah with the God-head, nor attribute to the Messiah a deciding role in the day of redemption: Judaism knows nothing of redemption through an intermediary or intercessor between God and man."[96]

The central position of Jesus is reflected in other places in the synoptic Gospels. His exhortation to take up the cross and to follow him (Mark 8:34 and parallels; cf. Matt 10:38) remains problematic for the Jewish perspective. Montefiore says that "For 'Jesus' must be substituted 'God and his Law,'"[97] and presumably he would require the same substitution for the words immediately preceding and following Matt 10:38: "Whoever loves father or mother more than me is not worthy of me; and whoever loves son or daughter more than me is not worthy of me . . . Those who find their life will lose it, and those who lose their life for my sake will find it." Ben-Chorin regards the words "on my account" in the beatitude of Matt 5:11 as indeed "new," but as due to the post-Easter kerygmatic tradition.[98]

---

93. *Jesus of Nazareth*, 378. This "overemphasis of the divine Fatherhood in relation to himself" led ultimately to his exaltation in the christology of Paul. 392.

94. *Synoptic Gospels*, 2:173.

95. *Jesus*, 96.

96. *Jesus of Nazareth*, 406.

97. *Rabbinic Literature*, 231.

98. *Bruder Jesus*, 74.

Other passages of a similar nature tend to be ignored by Jewish scholars. Thus they have little to say about such statements as Matt 10:32–33 (cf. Luke 12:8–9): "Everyone therefore who acknowledges me before others, I also will acknowledge before my Father in heaven; but whoever denies me before others, I also will deny before my Father in heaven"; or Matt 10:40 (cf. Luke 9:48): "Whoever welcomes you welcomes me, and whoever welcomes me welcomes the one who sent me" (cf. the inverted form of this logion in Luke 10:16). Jewish scholars typically discount such passages as inauthentic creations of the early church, reflecting its post-resurrection perspective. Klausner's view is representative when he concludes that "in spite of himself" Jesus became "in the thought of the next Christian generation," the "Son of God" and a "ransom for many."[99]

In all of this—as in his unparalleled stance of authority in relation to the established religious institutions of Israel—Jesus presents an unprecedented claim of personal significance and a deliberate advance on anything that Judaism had previously known. While the material or the imagery of Jesus' teaching is not original or unparalleled in rabbinic Judaism, the essential content remains by its nature new, original, and of definitive importance.

Jesus' announcement of the arrival of the kingdom of God, his authoritative interpretation and fulfillment of the Law, his heightened ethical imperatives, together with his unique consciousness of the surpassing importance of his person and mission, indicate a pivotal turning point in history that involves a new conception of humanity's relationship with God.

IV. THE IDENTITY OF JESUS

The teaching of Jesus is inseparable from the personal claims of Jesus. The difficulty of Jewish scholars in explaining the teaching of Jesus at crucial points is related to their reluctance to face the claims of Jesus concerning himself in the synoptic Gospels. The Jewish scholar H.-J. SCHOEPS recognizes these claims as "the most decisive point," when he refers to "the unique self understanding of Jesus, the messianic

---

99. *Jesus of Nazareth*, 405. Friedlander notes the difficulty of the central position of Jesus by calling attention to the worship of Jesus: "Several times in Matthew, and once in Mark, we are told that the people 'worshiped' Jesus. In no case did he reject the worship, or rebuke those who offered it to him. This aspect of prayer and worship is indeed, both new and un-Jewish." *Jewish Sources*, 118.

son-of-man consciousness, which contains the key to the understanding of his character."[100]

A true understanding of Jesus is not possible, if the sole concern of the investigation is to demonstrate the Jewishness of Jesus. The Jesus of the Gospels in fact resists being squeezed into a rabbinic mold. Yet, as with the teaching, Jewish scholars have tried to categorize Jesus among other Jewish religious authorities. For this purpose a wide variety of designations is available, some of which overlap and others of which are relatively flexible in meaning. We take up first the categories that are more acceptable, and then those that are less acceptable to Jewish scholars. The varying acceptability of these designations seems directly proportionate to the extent that they enable Jesus to be placed securely within a typical Jewish framework.

Pharisee. In light of the controversies and growing hostility between Jesus and the Pharisees in the Gospels, it may at first seem unlikely that Jesus would be identified as a Pharisee. Yet it is true that the bulk of Jesus' teaching is not innovative but shares the perspective of much of Pharisaic Judaism. As we have seen above, a basic element of the Jewish reclamation of Jesus is the conclusion that he was a faithful upholder of the Torah and that he taught an ideal righteousness in the spirit of true Pharisaism.

Most Jewish scholars stress the similarity of Jesus with the Pharisees, even when they admit that Jesus differed from them on significant points (e.g., Abrahams, Montefiore). S. UMEN notes differences, but concludes that "Jesus' approach to the law was Pharisaic" and that "the spirit of Jesus is Pharisaic."[101] So too, A. FINKEL comes to the conclusion that the approach of the disciples of Hillel's school "was close in spirit to that of the teacher of Nazareth."[102]

Other Jewish scholars do refer to Jesus as a Pharisee. Klausner does so, albeit with considerable qualification.[103] With more boldness P. WINTER writes "in historical reality, Jesus was a Pharisee."[104] Ben-Chorin is of the same opinion. Jesus was called "rabbi," his teaching was

100. Schoeps, "Jesus," in *Gottheit und Menschheit* (Stuttgart: Steingrüben, 1950) 70. We would add that it is also the key to the understanding of his teaching.

101. *Pharisaism and Jesus* (New York: Philosophical Library, 1963) 121; cf. 128–29. Cf. M. Buber, *Two Types of Faith*, trans. N. P. Goldhawk (London: Routledge & Paul, 1951) 137.

102. *The Pharisees and the Teacher of Nazareth* (Leiden: Brill, 1964) 134.

103. *Jesus of Nazareth*, 319.

104. *On the Trial of Jesus*, 2nd ed., revised and edited by T. A. Burkill and G. Vermes (Berlin: de Gruyter, 1974) 186; cf. 171.

both in form and content that of a Pharisee.¹⁰⁵ H. MACCOBY is particularly forceful: "Jesus was not only educated as a Pharisee; he remained a Pharisee all his life . . . As a Rabbi, Jesus was a typical Pharisee teacher. Both in style and content, his religious teachings show an unmistakable affinity to Pharisaism, and especially to the teachings of the great apostle of Pharisaism, Hillel."¹⁰⁶

A few Jewish scholars, however, deny that Jesus should be considered a Pharisee. In Vermes's view, "It would be a gross overstatement to portray him as a Pharisee himself."¹⁰⁷ Sandmel buys fully into the radical-critical skepticism of much modern scholarship concerning the historical Jesus: "I simply do not know enough about him to have an opinion, and I simply do not have enough to set him, as it were, in some one single category."¹⁰⁸

Despite obvious similarities between Jesus and the Pharisees, it is very difficult to believe that this designation does justice to the Jesus of the Gospels. Can that Jesus really be put alongside Hillel and Shammai as offering a third rabbinic route? As we have seen, Jesus not only at several points inclines away from Pharisaic tradition (e.g., in the neglect of ritual handwashing and fasting; and in his association with sinners), but with unparalleled authority departs from the literal teaching of the written Torah, in the relaxing of sabbath injunctions, and (implicitly) the dietary laws and in his prohibition of divorce. Despite legitimate parallels, Jesus cannot be understood when pressed into the Pharisaic mold.

Essene. Many Jewish scholars have seen similarities between Jesus and the Essenes. One of the earliest Jewish writers on Jesus, HEINRICH GRAETZ, called attention to the asceticsm and otherworldly perspective of Jesus and concluded that "although it cannot be proved that Jesus was admitted into the order of the Essenes, much of his life and work can only be explained by the suppostition that he had adopted their fundamental principles."¹⁰⁹ In Abrahams' view "It is undeniable that certain features of his teaching are Essenic," and Kohler describes Jesus as representing

---

105. *Bruder Jesus.* Cf. "Jesus und Paulus in jüdischer Sicht," *Annual of the Swedish Theological Institute* 10 (1976) 20–30.

106. *Revolution in Judaea: Jesus and the Jewish Resistance* (London: Ocean, 1973; reprint, New York: Taplinger, 1981) 106–7.

107. *Jesus the Jew,* 35.

108. *We Jews and Jesus,* 108. Yet he does not see any "profound distance between Jesus and his fellow Jews," 138.

109. *History of the Jews* (London: Nutt, 1891–92) 11:150. Cf. Sandmel, *We Jews and Jesus,* 61ff.

"the acme and the highest type of Essenism."[110] The discovery of the Dead Sea Scrolls encouraged other Jewish scholars to see some influence of the Qumran community upon Jesus and Christianity.[111] Others, however, strongly dissent from associating Jesus with the Essenes.[112] While there are some similarities, Jesus can hardly be explained adequately as an Essene.

Zealot. The category of Zealot has some appeal for Jewish scholars since they are nearly unanimous in their conclusion that Jesus was put to death by the Romans on the charge of sedition. Lapide thus describes Jesus as an *Heilspolitiker* whose goal was to overthrow Roman rule and establish a messianic kingdom of God in its place.[113] Maccoby, though denying that Jesus was actually a Zealot, regards Jesus as holding "a revolutionary vision, involving the overthrow of Roman power."[114] According to Vermes, although Jesus was put to death by the Romans as a revolutionary, this is to be explained from his being from Galilee, a traditional hotbed of rebellion. In Vermes's opinion, "he was not a social reformer or a nationalistic revolutionary, notwithstanding recent claims to the contrary."[115] In fact, few Jewish scholars have actually classified Jesus as a Zealot.

Hasid (Miracle Worker). Several Jewish scholars regard the deeds rather than the words of Jesus as determinative for a correct understanding of him. Kohler was one of the earliest to parallel Jesus with other famous Jewish healers and wonder workers, such as the first-century Galilean *Hanina ben Dosa*.[116] A couple of decades later, SAMUEL S. COHON. also concluded that Jesus was a Galilean Hasid, whose teaching placed him with "the people of the Iand" and "in the teaching company of the Hasidim who stood outside of Pharisaism."[117] Vermes, the author of the most potent Jewish analysis of Jesus to be published in

---

110. Abrahams: *Studies in Pharisaism*, 1:16; Kohler, "Jesus of Nazareth — In Theology," in *Jewish Encyclopedia*, 7:169.

111. Cf. Ben-Chorin, *Bruder Jesus*, Cf. Flusser, *Jesus*, 76-78.

112. E.g., Sandmel, *We Jews and Jesus*, 106; J. Carmichael, *The Death of Jesus* (New York: Macmillan, 1962) 109-10; M. Mansoor, *The Dead Sea Scrolls* (Leiden: Brill, 1964) 160-68.

113. *Der Rabbi von Nazareth*, 25-40. Lapide quotes approvingly S. G. F. Brandon, *Jesus and the Zealots* (Manchester: Manchester University Press, 1966).

114. *Revolution in Judaea*, 120. Jesus was not a Zealot, but an apocalyptist who looked for miraculous deliverance.

115. *Jesus and the World of Judaism*, 50; cf. *Jesus the Jew*, 50.

116. "Jesus of Nazareth — In Theology," in *Jewish Encyclopedia*, 7.167.

117. "The Place of Jesus in the Religious Life of His Day," *JBL* 8 (1927) 108. Reprinted in J. B. Agus, ed., *Judaism and Christianity* (New York: Arno, 1973) 82-108.

recent years, presents a schema similar to Kohler's. He stresses Jesus' role as healer and exorcist and places him fully within charismatic Judaism, as "the paramount example of the early Hasidim or Devout."[118] Galilee was known for producing just that type of charismatic holy men. Flusser holds a similar view, arguing that the gospels present a picture of Jesus which "is not so much of a redeemer of mankind as of a Jewish miracle worker and preacher."[119] He too draws parallels between Hanina ben Dosa and Jesus. This category again contains some truth, but cannot do justice to the Jesus of the synoptic Gospels.

Prophet. With this category we move away from the various Jewish sects and groups of the first century to a higher level of distinctiveness. Since the prevailing sentiment at that time was that prophecy was dead, to describe Jesus as a prophet or even as "prophetic" is to consider him unique among his contemporaries. It may, then, at first glance seem a little surprising that "prophet" is one of the more popular designations for Jesus among Jewish scholars. The advantage of this designation is that it is in keeping with the Jewishness of Jesus and yet allows in him a certain freedom with respect to the religious life of his day. To affirm that Jesus was a prophet is, of course, not to say that he was the eschatological prophet (i.e., of Deut 18:15-19).

Montefiore is above all the champion of Jesus as prophet. The teaching of Jesus resembled that of the prophets in practically every detail. With the prophets he stresses the inward, not the outward; the spirit, not the letter; the motive, not the deed; a true spirituality, not externalism or formalism.[120] Montefiore is indeed unabashed in his praise of Jesus, whom he describes as "one of the greatest and most original of our Jewish prophets," "a sort of eighth-century prophet born out of season."[121] Similarly, L. J. EDGAR writes: "Not only was Jesus a prophet but there is good ground for believing that he was a prophet true to the essentials of Judaism."[122]

---

118. *Jesus the Jew,* 79.

119. *Jesus,* 8. Unlike Vermes, however, Flusser also regards Jesus as "Pharisaic in general outlook," 13.

120. *Some Elements of the Religious Teaching of Jesus,* 102; *Synoptic Gospels,* passim.

121. "What a Jew Thinks about Jesus," *Hibbert Journal* 33 (1934-35) 516. In another place, Montefiore writes: "Jesus occupies the remarkable position of resuming the work and role of the prophets. He is in the genuine succession to Amos and Isaiah. It is most just that the title of prophet is, in Luke, repeatedly ascribed to him." *The Old Testament and After,* 229.

122. *A Jewish View of Jesus* (London: Jewish Religious Union for the Advancement

Although for Vermes Jesus the charismatic Hasid is automatically associated with the prophetic tradition of the Bible, but, as a miracle-worker, he is in the lineage of Elijah and Elisha, rather than the classical prophets.[123] Without committing himself on the question, Flusser concludes that Jesus saw himself as a prophet, though not as the eschatological prophet.[124]

There are Jewish scholars, on the other hand, who regard the designation "prophet" as improper for Jesus. Despite the admitted similarities between the teaching of Jesus and that of the prophets, Klausner, who was a Zionist, rejects the suggestion that Jesus was a prophet because "he lacks the Prophet's political perception and the Prophet's spirit of national consolation in the political-national sense."[125] Ben-Chorin disallows that in any sense Jesus may properly be regarded as a prophet since he does not use the formula "Thus says the Lord."[126] Kohler denies the title of prophet to Jesus because of his egocentric manner.[127]

Jesus is without question similar to the prophets. He repeats and carries forth their teachings. Yet he cannot satisfactorily be subsumed under the title of prophet. In comparison with the prophets, Jesus' sense of personal authority and significance seems obtrusive. "More than a prophet is here."[128]

If the data of the synoptic Gospels are taken seriously, we are forced to consider other categories for classifying Jesus. This brings us to what for Jewish scholars are clearly less acceptable designations for Jesus. If it is granted that Jesus thought of himself or his mission in any of these

---

of Liberal Judaism, 1940) 6. H. G. Enelow is of a similar persuasion: "In his own way Jesus did what the Prophets had done: He gave a fresh interpretation of the laws governing the spiritual life, a fresh message concerning the meaning and the purpose of religion, a new illumination of the sense and the object of the old prophetic utterances. Here lay his genius and originality." *A Jewish View of Jesus* (New York: Macmillan, 1920) 17.

123. *Jesus the Jew*, 89–90.

124. *Encyclopedia Judaica*, 10:14; *Jesus*, 99.

125. *Jesus of Nazareth*, 410. S. Cohon also notes that Jesus was not concerned with this world and thus classifies Jesus with the apocalyptic rather than the prophetic tradition. "The Place of Jesus in the Religious Life of His Day," 86.

126. *Bruder Jesus*, 15.

127. *The Origins of the Synagogue and the Church* (New York: Macmillan, 1929) 230. J. Jacobs also calls attention to the divergent sense of authority that sets Jesus apart from the prophets. *Jewish Encyclopedia* 7:163.

128. As Montefiore is able to admit. *Some Elements of the Religious Teaching of Jesus*, 115.

categories, it is also insisted upon by Jewish scholars that he was mistaken. It will also become clear in what follows that when any of these designations are accepted, they are understood as not meaning what the church takes them to mean.

Messiah. It is remarkable that the majority of modern Jewish scholars conclude that Jesus believed himself to be the Messiah. Montefiore puts it very clearly:"At some period of his career the conviction seems to have come to him that he was yet more than a prophet, that he was in fact none other than he of whom prophets had spoken and for whose coming so many generations had yearned, the Anointed One, the Messiah."[129]

Admitting the difficulty of knowing Jesus' conception of his messiahship, Montefiore nevertheless argues for the probability that he held a view similar to that of the apocalyptic writers. Thus Jesus probably believed that the Messiah was someone greater than the figure of Isaiah 11; more than a mere man inaugurating a new earthly kingdom, he was the proclaimer and leading character of the imminent kingdom of God, which would replace the old order. According to Montefiore, apocalypticism influenced the rabbis and Pharisees so that many believed in a more than human Messiah.[130] "Jesus as the Messiah *in posse* felt that he possessed greater power, and claimed a more personal allegiance, than any prophet before him."[131] In this conclusion, however, Montefiore goes considerably beyond his Jewish colleagues.

Montefiore notes that the idea of a dying and rising Messiah who would only afterward inaugurate the kingdom and be glorified was entirely foreign to the Jews of Jesus' day. The conception of the Messiah's work as a lowly service culminating in death "may have been the special development made by Jesus to the conception of the Messiah."[132] Furthermore, although there is evidence in later rabbinic literature for the idea of the Messiah suffering for his people, "any idea of his death as an atonement or as a 'ransom' was unknown to the Rabbis."[133]

In Klausner's view, Jesus was "obsessed by his idea that he was the Messiah."[134] It is Jesus' messianic consciousness that best explains his

129. *Synoptic Gospels*, 1:cxxii.

130. "Though less than and distinct from God, he was conceived by some as more divine than the ordinary man." *Some Elements of the Religious Teaching of Jesus*, 127.

131. *Some Elements of the Religious Teaching of Jesus*, 120.

132. *Synoptic Gospels*, 1:17. *Some Elements of the Religious Teaching of Jesus*, 135.

133. *Rabbinic Literature*, 305.

134. *Jesus of Nazareth*, 253.

eccentricities and the remarkable paradox of what Klausner perceives as the un-Jewishness of Jesus' teaching.[135] Klausner denies, however, that Jesus anticipated his own suffering or attributed any atoning significance to it.

Cohon also accepts Jesus' messianic consciousness, "in view of the persistence of the testimony," concluding that from it "sprang his entire mode of conduct, his sense of special authority in healing and teaching, his peculiar attitude towards sinners and his apocalyptic teaching."[136] Schoeps is similarly insistent that Jesus can only be understood as claiming to be the Messiah/Son of Man. Referring to Matt 11:27, he writes: "Here Jesus affirms an entirely unique union with God and a knowledge of God's will, as that which could be had only by the one sent by God, the Messiah himself."[137] This, continues Schoeps, is the explanation of his absolute power and authority and his call to discipleship. Sandmel too, though agnostic concerning the Jesus of history, ventures to say "I believe that he believed himself to be the Messiah, and that those scholars who deny this are incorrect."[138]

Perhaps the most common analysis among Jewish scholars who conclude that Jesus thought himself to be the Messiah, is that which stresses the political nature of the messianic expectation, whether in terms of an intended literal revolt or an apocalyptic inbreaking. Lapide and Maccoby regard Jesus as a political messiah; Trattner and A. H. SILVER lean more to Jesus' apocalyptic expectation.[139]

Flusser, on the other hand, is ambivalent concerning the question of Jesus' own claim to be the Messiah. Flusser regards Jesus' continual reference to the Son of Man in the third person as evidence that "Jesus actually did not believe himself to be the Messiah."[140] More recently, however, Flusser has written that "on the basis of the statements of Jesus in the

---

135. *Jesus of Nazareth*, 405. Elsewhere Klausner refers to Jesus' exaggerated Judaism, which brought about a non-Judaism, bringing with it "the ruin of national culture, the national state, and national life." 347, 393, 405.

136. "The Place of Jesus," 86.

137. "Jesus," 73.

138. *We Jews and Jesus*, 109. Only much later, however, was the idea of the Messiah "transformed from something involving specific and temporal characteristics into something involving more suprahuman abstractions," 33.

139. Lapide, *Der Rabbi von Nazareth*, 25-27; Maccoby, *Revolution in Judaea*, 114, 123, 132; Trattner, *As A Jew Sees Jesus*; A. H. Silver, *Where Judaism Differed* (New York: Scribner, 1931).

140. "The Son of Man," 228.

synoptic Gospels it is possible to ascertain that the strong self-consciousness of Jesus, the concept of sonship, and very probably his messianic mission are authentic and go back to the 'historical' Jesus."[141]

Some Jewish scholars remain unconvinced that Jesus ever claimed to be the Messiah. Ben-Chorin attributes the claim to the influence of the kerygmatic tradition.[142] According to Vermes, the Synoptic portrait of Jesus critically interpreted gives "every reason to wonder if he really thought of himself as such."[143] Vermes denies that Jesus conceived of his role along any of the various lines of contemporary messianic speculation. Although Jesus refused the title of a Davidic King Messiah, his followers adopted the title for him by transferring the reign of Messiah to the post-Easter era, producing a theological synthesis of several strands of messianic speculation.[144]

We have now come as far as most Jewish scholars are willing to go in their analysis of Jesus in the Gospels. To many of them it is conceivable that Jesus may have claimed to be the Messiah—as understood in contemporary Jewish expectation—and that he was deluded, though with the best of Jewish intentions. Again the pattern is clear: to the extent that the Jesus of the Gospels is reclaimable, or at least not fundamentally incompatible with Judaism, the Gospel accounts are given credence; to the extent that he appears not to be reclaimable, the evidence is attributed to the theologizing of the post-resurrection church. Thus other possible designations of Jesus such as Lord, Son of Man, Son of God—since they move decidedly away from traditional Jewish acceptability—are ordinarily not considered at all. Vermes is the exception at this point. He gives full consideration to these titles and "salvages" them from kerygmatic mutation.

Lord. Vermes provides a full discussion of the philological background of the word lord in the Aramaic spoken by Jews in the New Testament era. and concludes that "the designation '(the) lord', is appropriate in connection with God, or a secular dignity, or an authoritative teacher,

---

141. "Das Schisma zwischen Judentum und Christentum," *EvTheol* 40 (1980) 219. Elsewhere Flusser suggests that Jesus thought of himself as the Messiah only toward the end of his life (*Encyclopedia Judaica,* 10:13–14). Cf. Kohler, who regards the entry into Jerusalem as the turning point in Jesus' self-understanding. "Jesus of Nazareth—In Theology," 169.

142. *Bruder Jesus,* 13.

143. *Jesus the Jew,* 149.

144. According to Vermes, the Gentile church preserved the title because of its "psychological and polemical value in the Jewish-Christian debate" (*Jesus the Jew,* 153–56).

or a person renowned for his spiritual or supernatural force. The field in fact—and contrary to the opinion generally held by New Testament experts—is entirely open."[145] A survey of the data of the Gospels with "fresh eyes" shows that the use of the appellation "lord" is historically authentic, in Vermes's opinion. In Matthew and Mark it refers to a miracle-worker; in Matthew it is extended to apply to a teacher and religious leader, and this becomes the predominant usage in Luke.[146]

Son of Man. According to Vermes, this expression is never used as an autonomous title but is primarily a circumlocution for the first personal pronoun. All occurrences of the phrase in the Gospels that are not connected directly with Daniel 7:13 mean simply "I"; those that are connected with Daniel 7:13, directly (Mark 13:26; 14:62) or indirectly (Mark 8:38; Luke 12:8), Vermes regards as not explainable within the reconstructed historical background and hence as necessarily "the product of Christianity." If such references go back to Jesus, Vermes admits, "the necessary prerequisite of full Messianic consciousness on the part of the speaker" would have to be accepted.[147] Thus Vermes defends the historical authenticity of the expression in the Gospels as far as his presuppositions will allow him to go, but he finds it necessary in the last analysis to appeal to the pressure of the kerygmatic tradition of the early church.

Flusser is one of the few Jewish scholars to allow the possibility that Jesus did speak of himself as "Son of Man," understood as a messianic title. In his opinion, some "apparently authentic sayings of Jesus can be understood only if it is assumed that Jesus thought himself to be the Son of Man."[148] When Jesus referred to the Son of Man seated at the right hand of the power of God (e.g., Luke 22:69), it was an "indirect admission of his Messianic dignity." Thus, according to Flusser, "In the end, the conviction gained strength that he himself was the coming Son of Man."[149]

---

145. *Jesus the Jew*, 121.

146. Vermes ignores the fact that the evangelists write to and are themselves members of the believing community that confesses Jesus as Lord in the fullest sense of the word, and thus that this meaning is never far below the surface in their narratives, even when a lesser meaning may have been meant by individuals encountering the Jesus of history.

147. *Jesus the Jew*, 183. In circular fashion, Vermes refers to his negative conclusions about Jesus' messianic self-consciousness as evidence why such a prerequisite cannot be accepted.

148. *Encyclopedia Judaica*, 10:14.

149. *Jesus*, 103.

Son of God. Vermes also defends the historical authenticity of the title Son of God as applied to Jesus. A first-century Palestinian Jew, however, upon hearing the title would have thought "first of all of an angelic or celestial being; and secondly, when the human connection was clear, of a just and saintly man."[150] Vermes denies that Jesus defined himself as the Son of God. He attributes passages such as Mark 13:32 and Matt 11:27 to the faith of the primitive church.[151] According to Vermes, in the earliest historical stratum of the Gospels, the title Son of God refers to the miracle-worker exorcist. Later developments come in succession: Son of God as Messiah by adoption, preexistent Son of God, and ultimately Son of God by nature, thus producing "the final amalgam."[152] But these later developments, alien to Judaism, occur only in a Gentile-Christian context in the larger environment of pagan Hellenism.

Vermes has moved beyond most Jewish scholars in the very fact that he discusses the titles of Jesus, but the result is not significantly different. In Vermes's reconstruction, the full sweep of the data of the synoptic Gospels is reduced to the single category of the charismatic Hasid. What does not square with this hypothesis is consistently relegated to the creative faith of the church, leaving the impression that a predetermined conclusion has been successfully reached.

When all is said and done, there remains a uniqueness about Jesus that bars restricting him within the limits and boundaries established by modern Jewish scholarship. As we have noted, Jesus places himself in a strategic place as far as the relationship between humanity and God is concerned. It is the centrality of Jesus in all that God is doing and will do that must be faced. For Jesus, as for Paul, a new and critically important stage of development in the history of the Jewish faith—what could be described as the fulfillment of Judaism's hope, though not its consummation—had been reached.

Jewish scholars have in the modern period been able to say quite remarkable things concerning Jesus. Yet the modern Jewish picture does not do justice to the portrait of him contained in the Gospels. The result of Jewish study and the a priori limits it imposes is a picture of Jesus that is incongruent with the only historical sources about Jesus that we

---

150. *Jesus the Jew*, 200.

151. Elsewhere Vermes allows that these verses may be "in part representative of Jesus' thought," but that all the latter verse suggests is "an ideal reciprocity between Father and son" that "does not entail equality" (*Jesus and the World of Judaism*, 48).

152. *Jesus the Jew*, 212.

possess. In the last analysis, the Jewish reconstruction of Jesus is no more faithful to the historical sources than is that of the old liberal lives of Jesus or the newer radical-critical scholarship. In each of these we are left with a picture of Jesus that raises more questions than answers and one that may be likened to a jig-saw puzzle from which several key pieces are missing.

With Matt 11:25–27 in mind, Schoeps perceptively comments: "There can well be no doubt that one can only speak thus and force men into decision—note well: into decision with regard to his person—who has a most elevated messianic mission-consciousness. It remains beyond understanding how it could ever be doubted in liberal theology."[153]

When confronted with the inescapable uniqueness of Jesus in the Gospels, the Jewish scholar finally demurs and with an undue confidence insists that Jesus cannot have transgressed certain boundaries of "Jewishness." But since it is true that in the final analysis the teaching of Jesus is inseparable from his personal claims, Jewish scholars find themselves hard pressed to understand and account for much of that teaching on any other grounds. That he was a prophet, or that he claimed to be the Messiah, is not necessarily denied. But these admissions in themselves are not sufficient to explain his teaching. Jesus came announcing the presence of the kingdom of God in his own ministry. Obedience to the kingdom became a matter of personal loyalty to him. It was no accident that Jesus became the object of faith, for through his deeds and teaching the challenge to faith is continually present. The main question in the end, therefore, centers not in the teaching of Jesus, but in his person.

V. CONCLUSION

The synoptic Gospels as they stand assert the uniqueness of Jesus repeatedly and in a variety of ways. As we have seen, an examination of the teaching Jesus shows him again and again speaking as no rabbi, however exceptional, could have spoken. He claims an unparalleled authority, providing not only definitive interpretation of the true meaning of the Torah, but acting toward the law with an authority that astonishes and offends his contemporaries. He not only overthrows Pharisaic oral law, while acknowledging in principle the authority of the Pharisees, but

---

153. "Jesus," in *Gottheit und Menschheit*, 73. To be sure, Schoeps goes on to separate sharply this messianic consciousness from the later "church dogma" of his divine sonship.

also transcends the written Torah, while acknowledging its authority and arguing that his teaching is in full accord with that authority. These paradoxes are possible only on the assumption of a supreme authority on the part of Jesus. Jesus proclaims the kingdom as present in and through his ministry and proclaims an ethical tradition as part of the announcement that is so sovereign in its demands that it presupposes movement to a new level of existence. The kingdom that dawns by God's gracious gift brings with it an ethic of response that transcends all ordinary ethics. But the kingdom, and therefore the ethics, is inseparable from the bringer of the kingdom, the person of Jesus. In the same astonishing way, Jesus is himself central to his religious teaching. His death has atoning significance and he possesses a unique relationship with his Father and occupies a unique position of mediation in the relationship between God and humankind. In short, we confront in Jesus one who is without parallel in the authority he assumes, the claims he makes about himself, and the central position he assigns himself in the accomplishment of God's purposes for Israel and the nations.

In addition to this, the silence of Jesus on certain matters is notable, for this too marks him off from his Jewish contemporaries. Thus Jesus is not nationalistic and has nothing to say about a literal realization of Israel's national-political hopes. He gives no place in his teaching to the importance of the land. Nor, finally, does the temple or the cult assume a position of any great significance; instead, he speaks quite readily of its demise. J. NEUSNER has called attention to this important difference between Pharisaism and the Gospels. For the Pharisees the metaphor of the cult is of central significance, whereas for the Gospels it is the historical event of Jesus that is of greatest importance.[154]

If we fully grant the Jewishness of Jesus, as indeed we must, it is also immediately obvious that we cannot force him into a rabbinic mold, unless every passage unamenable to the hypothesis is rejected from the beginning as unreliable. But to do this is to be unfair to the evidence of the Gospels. Among recent Jewish scholars, who are increasingly aggressive in reclaiming the Jesus of the synoptic Gospels, Sandmel alone has called sufficient attention to this fact: "True, Jesus was a Jew. True, there are Jewish presuppositions in virtually every paragraph of the Gospels. Yet

---

154. "The Use of the Later Rabbinic Evidence for the Study of First-Century Judaism," in *Approaches to Ancient Judaism: Theory and Practice*, ed. W. S. Green (Missoula, MT: Scholars, 1978) 224–25.

it is a Jesus at variance with, or over against, Judaism and Jews that constitutes not all, but a great deal of the warp and woof of the Gospels."[155]

The consistency in the "Jewish" Jesus reconstructed by Jewish scholars is possible only by an inconsistent approach to the synoptic Gospels. Material that supports this reconstruction is accepted; material which does not is rejected. The appeal to *Gemeindetheologie*, the theology of the post-resurrection community, is not made judiciously, but seemingly at the convenience of the interpreter, i.e., at every juncture where Jesus seems to violate his "Jewishness." Sandmel's virtual agnosticism concerning the historical Jesus is at least not as arbitrary as this practice of accepting what is congruent with a particular conclusion and rejecting what is not. But in its irresponsibility toward the historical question, the latter position is as unrealistic as Sandmel's agnosticism. It is worth asking again how the evangelists have been so reliable whenever they speak about Jesus as a Jew and yet so unreliable at every point where they describe him as something more.

Does the Jewish research on Jesus give us a better understanding of Jesus than we otherwise would have had? An affirmative answer can be given concerning the illumination of some details in the Gospels—that is, only in matters of peripheral importance, involving such things as background and context. The problem is that Jewish scholars have not truly confronted the Jesus of the Gospels.

Probably the greatest obstacle to a correct understanding of Jesus is the inability of Jews to accept that a new stage in the history of salvation has been reached. The key to understanding the Gospels is in the announcement of the dawning of the kingdom of God. With this key everything forms a coherent pattern; without it much remains strangely enigmatic. The earliest Christians believed both that Jesus was the Messiah and that the kingdom of God had come in advance of the final eschatological events. In no sense were these conclusions felt to be un-Jewish or disloyal to the promises of scripture. But Jewish scholars begin with the denial that anything new can have occurred without the realization of Israel's national-political expectations and the transformation of the world order. For the Jews nothing new seems to have happened, and therefore the Gospels are approached as though they were timeless, frozen texts analogous to the rabbinic writings and containing no significant forward motion. Neusner, however, senses the important

---

155. *Judaism and Christian Beginnings* (New York: Oxford University Press, 1978) 342.

difference. Whereas for the rabbis "regularity, permanence, recurrence, and perpetual activity" are the basis of an "enduring system," what is presupposed in the Gospels is:

> an ontology quite distinct from that of the cult, an ontology which centers . . . on a profoundly disruptive historical event, one which has shattered all that has been regular and orderly. So far as history stands at the center of being, so that the messiah and the conclusion of history form the focus of interest, the ontological conception of Christianity scarcely intersects with that of Pharisaism. So, I think it is clear, the two kinds of piety, the one with its effort to replicate eternity and the perpetual order, the other with its interest in the end of an old order and the beginning of a new age of history, scarcely come into contact with one another.[156]

If this is true, then it is a mistake to be content with a simple comparison and paralleling of rabbinic and Gospel texts. It is just here that we again see the paradox: Jesus inevitably stands in continuity with the past, but insofar as he is also the fulfillment of what preceded, he also manifests an astounding newness.

The Jewish approach to Jesus attempts to bypass this newness and thereby falls considerably short of the mark. The Jewish reclamation of Jesus is thus at best only partially successful. It is in fact only the reclamation of that which fits with an a priori conclusion and is therefore only the reclamation of Jewish ideas and not of the Jesus of the synoptic Gospels. Not even the teaching of Jesus can be fully reclaimed, however, since the teaching, as we have argued, cannot be understood apart from the person of Jesus.

The contributions that Jewish scholars have made to the understanding of Jesus' teaching have been possible because of the Jewishness of these scholars. It is a sad irony that their Jewish perspective also hinders them from a true perception of Jesus and his teaching. What is an invaluable aid in interpreting the Gospels becomes at the same time an unfortunate obstacle. And thus tragically, as in the New Testament era itself, those who in many ways are the closest to Jesus, the Christ, are at the same time the farthest away from him.

---

156. "The Use of the Later Rabbinic Evidence for the Study of First-Century Pharisaism," in *Approaches to Judaism*, 225. See now his *Jews and Christians: The Myth of a Common Tradition* (London/Philadelphia: SCM/Trinity Press International, 1991).

2

Radical Gospel Criticism and the Modern Jewish Study of Jesus

WHEN A JEWISH SCHOLAR writes about Jesus it is an event that captures wide attention. Jews, it is thought, have an inside track in understanding Jesus, and there is surely truth in such a conclusion. Jesus himself was a Jew, after all, and his thorough Jewishness is hardly to be doubted. Thus those familiar with the Jewish literature of the time before, during, and after Jesus, and with Jewish religion and culture of the first century— those who know these things from the inside—have a distinct advantage in understanding the Jesus of history.

For all of its truth, however, such an easy conclusion presupposes that with Jesus we have to deal only with matters of continuity with his context. It would be difficult to deny that Jesus was distinctive. Most Jewish scholars are willing to admit this. But with the increasing appreciation of the diversity of Judaisms[1] in the first century, this constitutes little problem for them. It is a fact, however, that they tend to play down what in the Gospels is distinctive—not to say unique—in comparison to what we know of first-century Judaism, even granting all its diversity. There are certain things from their point of view that Jesus cannot have said or done.

Jewish scholars can point to a long tradition of liberal Christian scholarship that has arrived at conclusions similar to their own. The

---

1. The plural is deliberate. The diversity of first-century Judaism is increasingly emphasized. See, e.g., the SBL centennial volume, *Early Judaism and Its Modern Interpreters,* eds. R. A. Kraft and G. W. E. Nickelsburg (Atlanta: Scholars, 1986).

modern Jewish study of Jesus has not been done in a vacuum. The present essay will trace the impact of radical Gospel criticism on the Jewish approach to the Gospels, summarize the modern Jewish estimate of Jesus, and finally look at the implications of Jewish scholarship for Christian scholarship today.

RADICAL GOSPEL CRITICISM

Radical Gospel criticism is a child of the Enlightenment. At the root of that criticism is a view of the world that has no room for a God who acts in history, no room for events that cannot be explained naturalistically—in short, a universe consisting of a closed system of cause and effect, all within the power of human reason to explain. And with the exhilarating freedom from authority that characterized the Enlightenment came a particularly sharp attack on established religion and orthodox Christian beliefs.

With the Enlightenment began the so-called quest for the historical Jesus, indeed with the underlying presupposition that the real Jesus *cannot* have been like what the church affirms concerning him. This approach exists right down to the present in the so-called Jesus Seminar, which is equally a child of the Enlightenment perspective. The historicity of the Gospels was under attack by the English Deists and certain philosophers early in the period of the Enlightenment. In Germany the earliest important representative of the new study of Jesus was H. S. Reimarus,[2] whose writings or "fragments" were published only posthumously by the dramatist and philosopher Lessing in 1778.[3] For Reimarus, Christianity was built on a fraud. Jesus was no more than a man who deluded himself and others into thinking that he was the Messiah. The disciples of Jesus stole the body from the tomb in order to be able to make the claim that he had risen from the dead (as though in fulfillment of the fear expressed in Matt 27:64!). The Gospels were unreliable historical sources and Christianity was a hoax through and through.

Less than a century later, in 1835, David Friedrich Strauss published what would become the most famous and influential book on Jesus in

---

2. Albert Schweitzer's scintillating book *The Quest of the Historical Jesus* (German original, 1906) had as its original title "Von Reimarus zu Wrede."

3. A modern edition of the Reimarus fragments in English translation can be found in C. H. Talbert, ed., *Reimarus Fragments* (Philadelphia: Fortress, 1970). The relevant fragment is entitled "On the Intention of Jesus and His Disciples."

the 19th century, *Das Leben Jesu*.[4] Here again we encounter a full-blown naturalism and hence a deep skepticism concerning the historical worth of the Gospels.[5] A second highly influential book on Jesus was published by Ernest Renan in 1863. Although very different from Strauss's treatment of the subject, Renan's book was equally skeptical about the history recounted in the Gospels.[6] Here again we find naturalistic presuppositions dominant.

Albert Schweitzer's famous book reviewing the history of the study of Jesus, *The Quest of the Historical Jesus*, effectively points out the weaknesses of the nineteenth-century lives of Jesus. As was soon to be said about the Gospels (unfairly), these writings tell us more about the authors themselves than they do about the Jesus of history. To paraphrase the famous similitude of Alfred Loisy, at the bottom of the well into which their research peered, these scholars saw only the reflection of their own face. As Schweitzer pointed out, these writers succeeded in making Jesus into a polite, nineteenth-century moralizing gentleman.

My colleague Colin Brown notes that Schweitzer called attention to three major crises in the critical study of Jesus.[7] These were posed in terms of stark opposites: a purely historical or a purely supernatural approach; John or the Synoptics; and an eschatological or non-eschatological Jesus. New Testament scholarship long ago agreed on the superiority of the Synoptics over John as historical sources, and until the recent, strong challenge from the Jesus Seminar, that Jesus is to be understood as an apocalyptic figure. On the first point, however, New Testament scholars continue to disagree, although not all would like the alternative posed so starkly. Many would like to think of a historical approach with an openness to the supernatural— historical method which is better, and more adequate to the subject matter, just because of that openness.

---

4. An English translation was made by the famous George Eliot (Marian Evans) in 1846, *The Life of Jesus Critically Examined*.

5. It is hardly surprising that members of the Jesus Seminar dedicated their first main book, *The Five Gospels*, to Strauss along with Jefferson and Galileo. Their description of Strauss as the one "who pioneered the quest of the historical Jesus," however, *is* surprising.

6. Ernest Renan, *Vie de Jesus* (1863); ET, *Life of Iesus* (1890).

7. Colin Brown, "Historical Jesus, Quest of," in *Dictionary of Jesus and the Gospels*, ed. J. B. Green et al. (Downers Grove, IL: InterVarsity, 1992) 332. See also his large book on the subject, *Jesus in European Protestant Thought 1778-1860* (reprint, Grand Rapids: Baker, 1988).

In the middle of the twentieth century, the skepticism about the historical reliability of the Gospels reached a climax in the work of the highly influential Rudolf Bultmann. Like the giants of the study of the Jesus in the nineteenth century, Bultmann strictly ruled out the possibility of the supernatural. In his opinion, it was not possible to live in the modern scientific world and believe in the miraculous. The Gospels are so corrupted by the faith of the resurrection experience overlaid upon them that we cannot penetrate behind them to the real Jesus. Bultmann concluded in a famous statement that we could know "almost nothing concerning the life and personality about the historical Jesus."[8]

Neither the "new quest" of the historical Jesus, begun by Bultmann's disillusioned students in the 1950s, nor the more recent, so-called third quest—for all the good things one might care to say about it—has overcome the bias against the supernatural. What is most disappointing about the modern study of Jesus is exactly this closed-mindedness. How indeed shall the Bible be made sense of when it is the story of God acting in history and that possibility is ruled out from the beginning? And the irony is that science departed some time ago from the closed system of Newtonian physics that underlies the pre-judgment against anything that cannot be explained naturalistically! Developments in quantum mechanics and chaos theory point to the inadequacy of the simple cause and effect determinism that radical critical biblical scholars since the late eighteenth century have so dogmatically insisted upon.

In any event, modern Gospel criticism has redefined what is "historical" as only that which can be explained without recourse to anything transcendent. Incarnation and resurrection—two of the central realities of Christianity, testified to by the New Testament—are simply regarded as impossibilities. And thus the Jesus of the Gospels, whose uniqueness is a main point of these narratives, must be made to fit fully, and more or less comfortably, into his context.

The result of modern Gospel criticism is that a large question mark is put over much of the content of the Gospels. Here indeed we come to one of the true oddities of the radical critical perspective: the shift in the burden of proof. So thorough is the doubt about the historical reliability of the Gospels, that now what requires "proof" is anything in the New Testament that is claimed to be historical. In other words, the material of the Gospels is unhistorical unless shown otherwise. In this regard the

---

8. *Jesus and the Word* (German, 1926; ET: New York: Scribners, 1958) 14. As if to contradict his own statement, Bultmann wrote this book about Jesus!

New Testament is treated differently from the way historians treat ancient sources, and this is the cause of much astonishment on the part of classicists who rightly indicate that if such a procedure were generally practiced on ancient sources we would know next to nothing about the ancient world.

Reflecting the same pessimism concerning the trustworthiness of the Gospel tradition are the widely-accepted criteria of authenticity.[9] The main criterion, "dissimilarity," insists that before something may be confidently taken as historical it must be distinctive, that is, dissimilar to the beliefs of the early Christians and also to contemporary Judaism. Otherwise the Gospel writers may be thought to have borrowed material from their context and put it into the mouth of Jesus.

Two further factors, quite separate but very important, must also be mentioned: the Holocaust and the affirmation of pluralism as requisite in the modern world. These have had a distinct impact on recent approaches to Jesus and the Gospels. Many have claimed that it is Christian theology that is the root of anti-Semitism, and indeed, that anti-Semitism is to be found in the pages of the New Testament itself.[10] Christology has actually been called "the left hand of anti-Semitism."[11] It is not surprising then to hear calls for the complete redoing of Christian theology, and to encounter the desire for a view of Jesus that will not be divisive, a view that Jews and Christians can agree upon and a common scholarship that will draw Jews and Christians together. This is only in keeping with the tenor of our time with its insistence that the truth question remains open, and that triumphalism must give way to an acceptance of the pluralism that characterizes our world.

In light of the remarks I have made about radical Gospel criticism in the preceding paragraphs, I must add one more paragraph to indicate that I do not advocate an uncritical or fundamentalist approach to the Gospels.[12] Although I am myself an adherent to the view of Professor Birger Gerhardsson that the oral tradition underlying the Synoptic

---

9. For an excellent discussion, see C. A. Evans, "Authenticity Criteria in Life of Jesus Research," *Christian Scholars Review* 19 (1989) 6-31.

10. Against such a conclusion, see C. A. Evans and D. A. Hagner, eds., *Anti-Semitism and Early Christianity: Issues of Polemic and Faith* (Minneapolis: Fortress, 1993).

11. Thus Rosemary Reuther, *Faith and Fratricide* (New York: Seabury, 1974; reprint, Eugene, OR: Wipf & Stock, 1996).

12. I am reminded of the not very friendly review of my *The Jewish Reclamation of Jesus* by Brad H. Young, in the journal *Immanuel*. Despite my excursus on "The Use of Gospel Criticism," Young tended to dismiss my book as uncritical and fundamentalistic.

Gospels was a holy tradition, handed on in ways similar to the practice of first-century rabbis and their disciples, and thus highly reliable, at the same time I do not deny the theological overlay upon the Synoptic narratives (nor does Gerhardsson) caused by the post-resurrection perspective of the evangelists. I only believe that the reality of this overlay does not subvert the basic trustworthiness of the narratives as historical accounts.[13] I furthermore believe that it is extremely important for New Testament scholars to be open to the possibility of the supernatural in history.[14] I of course agree that the Holocaust demands a new sensitivity to how we handle certain New Testament texts that speak negatively about the Jews, although I do *not* think that a complete redoing of Christian theology is required. I too accept the reality of pluralism and would reject triumphalism, yet I cannot in faithfulness to the New Testament witness subscribe to a comfortable two-covenant theory that makes Jesus Christ relevant only to the Gentiles, and not the Jews.

THE MODERN JEWISH ESTIMATE OF JESUS

The modern Jewish study of Jesus is a twentieth-century phenomenon undertaken almost exclusively by liberal or reform Jews. Given the history of the persecution of the Jews and the centuries of hostility, it is truly remarkable to find Jews now writing positively about Jesus. This appreciation of Jesus, it goes without saying, is *as a Jew*. It is the *Heimholung Jesu*, the bringing home of Jesus, not as a heretic, but as a representative of the best of Judaism.[15]

---

13. Birger Gerhardsson's classic treatment of the subject, together with a second small book, has recently been reprinted: *Memory and Manuscript: Oral Tradition and Written Transmission in Rabbinic Judaism and Early Christianity* and *Tradition and Transmission in Early Christianity* (Grand Rapids: Eerdmans, 1998). The book contains a new preface by the author and a most interesting foreword by Jacob Neusner. In the latter, Neusner indicates that whereas he had reviewed the original edition of Gerhardsson's book negatively, he has now reversed his opinion and come to the conclusion that Gerhardsson is right. See too Gerhardsson's extremely helpful *The Reliability of the Gospel Tradition* (Peabody, MA: Hendrickson, 2001).

14. On this important issue, see the very helpful treatment discussion in C. Stephen Evans, *The Historical Christ and the Jesus of Faith: The Incarnational Narrative as History* (Oxford: Clarendon, 1996). Also insightful is I. Howard Marshall, *I Believe in the Historical Jesus* (Grand Rapids: Eerdmans, 1977).

15. I have described this fully in Hagner, *The Jewish Reclamation of Jesus: An Analysis and Critique of the Modern Jewish Study of Jesus* (Grand Rapids: Zondervan, 1984; reprint, Wipf & Stock, 1997).

Now it is clear that all that we have discussed above plays well into the hands of Jewish scholars who write about Jesus. Indeed, it could be said that modern Protestant scholarship has made this positive Jewish approach to Jesus possible. The skepticism of radical scholarship concerning the historical reliability of the Gospels allows Jewish scholars under the semblance of scholarly propriety to pick and choose what they will accept as historical in the Gospel narratives. Naturally what is picked by them is that which is consonant with the view that Jesus was no more than an extraordinary teacher/healer. Most of the scholars engaged in the Jewish reclamation of Jesus would share the naturalistic presuppositions of the radical Gospel criticism we have described above. Whether or not they do, however, they welcome the conclusion that Jesus cannot be what the church alleges concerning him. The resurrection of Jesus is of course a crucial dividing point since it is a vindication of the claims made by Jesus and the mainspring of the church's christology.[16]

Thus when liberal Protestantism departed from the church's understanding of Jesus, turning him into little more than a wonderful teacher, the way was prepared for Jewish writers to write appreciatively of Jesus. For they too can appreciate the teaching of Jesus and can discern its authentic Jewishness more effectively than others. Jewish scholars who write about Jesus focus solely on the Synoptics and ignore the rest of the New Testament. Here too they reflect the view of liberal Christian scholarship which has driven a wedge between Jesus and the early church. Paul in particular is regarded as the founder of a new religion—a religion quite out of keeping with the religion of Jesus.

An unavoidable conclusion emerges from what we have been observing. The Jewish reclamation of Jesus focuses only on what is in relative continuity with Judaism. Even on many of these matters the reclamation process is not successful, in my opinion. The reason for this is that the teaching of Jesus is itself so closely linked with the person of Jesus that it cannot finally be understood by those who do not face

---

16. Journalists looking for an Easter story have in the past taken delight in reporting that the Jewish scholar Pinchas Lapide believes in the resurrection of Jesus. They fail, however, to distinguish between resurrection and resuscitation. Lapide apparently believes in the latter only, namely that Jesus was raised from the dead to die again some years later, not that Jesus was raised to a new, eschatological order of existence.

squarely the claims of Jesus concerning himself,[17] and in particular his announcement of the coming of the Kingdom of God in his ministry.[18]

Indeed, it is here that we come to what may be the most important point of all, the supreme point of discontinuity that governs all: the fundamental assertion of the New Testament writers that a definitive fulfillment of the promises of Scripture has occurred and that a turning point in the ages has been reached in the coming of Jesus is unanimously denied by Jewish scholars. For them nothing significant, let alone unique, has occurred in the history of salvation. And for this supreme reason the approach of Jewish scholars to the Gospels is flat and unexciting. Gone is the excitement in the texts about the fulfillment that has come. Gone is the mystery about this person Jesus, and who he is that can do and say such things. Gone is the electrifying realization that the Messiah is present among his people. Gone in short is the gospel, the "good news" itself. Instead, Jewish scholars treat the texts as though they were timeless and frozen, and they find in Jesus a rabbi/prophet with interesting or unusual refinements of halacha.

In fact it is the clear discontinuity with Judaism (which I hasten to add does not cancel out the obvious continuity) that is the Achilles' heel of the modern Jewish study of Jesus. The very wise Samuel Sandmel saw this when he wrote: "True, Jesus was a Jew. True, there are Jewish presuppositions in virtually every paragraph of the Gospels. Yet it is a Jesus at variance with, or over against, Judaism and Jews that constitutes not all, but a great deal of the warp and woof of the Gospels."[19]

Jacob Neusner, too, has called attention to the huge difference: "So, I think it is clear, the two kinds of piety, the one with its effort to replicate eternity and the perpetual order [Pharisaism], the other with its interest in the end of an old order and the beginning of a new age of history [Christianity], scarcely come into contact with one another."[20]

---

17. See D. A. Hagner, "Jesus' Self-Understanding," in *Encyclopedia of the Historical Jesus*, ed., Craig Evans (New York: Routledge, 2008) 324–33.

18. This is the thesis of my book *The Jewish Reclamation of Jesus*. Some reviewers faulted me for making this claim, but I still maintain that those who ignore or reject the personal claims of Jesus will get only so far in understanding his teaching.

19. *Judaism and Christian Beginnings* (New York: Oxford University Press, 1978) 342.

20. "The use of the Later Rabbinic Evidence for the Study of First-Century Pharisaism," in W. S. Green, ed., *Approaches to Judaism: Theory and Practice* (Missoula, MT: Scholars, 1978) 225. See too Neusner's *Jews and Christians: The Myth of a Common Tradition* (London: SCM, 1991).

In the final analysis, Jewish scholarship has repeated what occurred in the nineteenth-century lives of Jesus. It has reconstructed a Jesus in its own image. It has not brought us to the real Jesus simply because it is either unwilling or unable to address the main parts of the Gospel tradition. Where is the discussion of the present dawning .of the Kingdom of God? Where do we read of Jesus' unparalleled authority, the central position he assigns himself in God's salvific activity, or his self-claims? And what of the fact that he seems to have an agenda that transcends national-political aspirations, the land, and even the temple?

All that Jewish scholars can do, in agreement with their liberal Christian counterparts, we again emphasize, is to attribute a large portion of the Gospel narratives to *Gemeindetheologie,* the theology of the post-resurrection Christian community, with the implication that the early Christians either misunderstood Jesus terribly or are guilty of a fraud of stupendous proportions.

IMPLICATIONS OF THE MODERN JEWISH STUDY OF JESUS FOR CHRISTIAN SCHOLARSHIP

Although we have been critical of the modern Jewish study of Jesus—and we would be equally critical of radical non-Jewish scholarship such as represented by the Jesus Seminar—there can be no doubt that Christian scholars can learn much from these Jewish scholars.

Undeniably the Jesus of history was fully Jewish, as indeed were all the first Christians. The Christian faith, like its Lord, who was "born under the law" (Gal 4:4), came to life in an intensively Jewish environment. The thorough study of that Jewish context enriches our understanding of both. It can illuminate passage after passage in the Gospels. We should not underestimate the significance of what is to be learned about Jesus and early Christianity from Jewish scholars. New Testament Christianity is far more Jewish than the average Christian imagines, and it is well worth rediscovering this.

It is no small irony that Jewish scholars tend to respect the historical reliability of the Gospels more than their radical Protestant counterparts. This is often because they recognize the authentic Jewishness of specific data in the Gospels. These ring true to what they know of the first-century Jewish context. Jewish scholars have immediately seen the absurdity of that part of the criterion of dissimilarity that requires rejection of views similar to what one can find in the first-century Jewish context. Why anyone should think that the real Jesus cannot reflect his Jewishness and Jewish background is astounding.

But it is perhaps equally astounding that anyone should reject as unhistorical anything in Jesus that sounds like the early church, thus denying *a priori* that there could be any continuity between the faith of the Church and the Jesus of history. If we allow that the faith of the early church has had an impact on the Gospel narratives, as indeed we must in my opinion, that hardly invalidates the entire historical tradition. If we are able to see that Jesus resembled the Jewish context out of which he came, may it not also be the case that there is substantial continuity between him and the faith of his early followers? Is it not worth pondering how the evangelists can be so reliable when they speak of the Jewish Jesus and so utterly unreliable when they describe him as something more, as the one who was to become the Lord of the church.

What must be avoided is the reductionism, of which Jewish scholars are commonly guilty, that says that Jesus can be fully and completely explained by his Jewishness. It is not a matter of an absolute alternative: that either Jesus was fully Jewish *or* he was the Lord proclaimed by the Church. There is no choice to be made here. On the contrary, he was both fully Jewish and at the same time the Lord who created the Church. Similarly, it is not a matter of the continuity or discontinuity of Jesus with Judaism. We have to face the reality of both continuity *and* discontinuity, which is another way of saying that we must face the reality of something new. The early Jewish church had to do just that. It affirmed the new and, by its fresh reading of the scriptures, was able to see the elements of discontinuity as included under a larger umbrella of continuity. The radically new and surprising things that they discovered in Jesus, for example in the death and resurrection of the Messiah, or the inclusion of Gentiles as full members of the people of God, they now saw as the intended plan of God from the beginning and as indicated already in the scriptures.[21]

What they would not have comprehended is the attempt to understand Jesus by essentially denying his uniqueness and denying that any significant turning point in God's working with Israel had been reached, for these were fundamental convictions of these Jewish Christians. They furthermore would have been incredulous at any suggestion that the Jewishness of Jesus was incompatible with what they were now affirming

21. See D. A. Hagner, *How New Is the New Testament? First Century Judaism and the Emergence of Christianity* (Grand Rapids: Baker Academic, 2018).

concerning the risen Christ, the Lord of the Church. They would have been aghast at the idea of two covenants, one for Israel and one for the Gentile church. No, for them the covenant with Israel had come to its intended goal and fulfillment in the new covenant and the Church.

It will remain important for Christian scholars to keep abreast of what Jewish scholars write about Jesus, not only for the positive knowledge about Jesus and his context that can be acquired in this way, but also for the sake of informed and mutually informing dialogue. There is, however, probably no way around the differences that will remain in the assessment of Jesus. Here Christians must hold their ground, professing loyalty to the Jew from Nazareth whom they confess as their Lord, while at the same time exploring the common ground they have with the Jews and, indeed, coming to an appreciation of the Jewishness of the Christian faith, rightly understood. It is from the Jews that the Messiah has come (Rom 9:5), and that Messiah, Jesus, was meant to be "for glory to your people Israel" (Luke 2:32). Our deep and abiding disagreements with the conclusions of modern Jewish scholarship must never cause us to forget this.

3

The Jesus Quest and Jewish-Christian Relations

THE POINT OF CONTENTION that has always been decisive in the Jewish-Christian dialogue has been the person of Jesus. If we have now begun to see through historical Jesus studies that Jesus Christ binds Jews and Christians together, it is also clear that he remains the main dividing point between Jews and Christians.[1] It is understandable that Jews and Christians have always shared a very large amount of their theology—in fact, a much greater amount than is usually expected. The first Christians, all of whom were Jewish, believed that their faith was the fulfillment of the Jewish scriptures and that they were beginning to receive what had been promised in the covenants and the prophets. They thought of their faith not as a new religion but as the true Judaism. There was nevertheless a key dividing point between the earliest Christians and the Jews, and it centered in the Christian confession of the crucified Jesus as both Messiah and Lord, as the one who had inaugurated a new era in the history of salvation, an era of eschatological fulfillment. The situation was effectively captured in the aphorism of Schalom Ben-Chorin, himself the author of a book entitled *Brother Jesus*: "The faith of Jesus unites us—faith in Jesus separates us."[2] If the estimate of Jesus is the fundamental

---

1. *The Common Bond: Christians and Jews—Notes for Preaching and Teaching* (Vatican Commission for Religious Relations with the Jews, 1986).

2. *Bruder Jesus: Der Nazarener in jüdischer Sicht* (Munich: List, 1967), now available in English translation, *Brother Jesus: The Nazarene through Jewish Eyes*, trans. J. S. Klein and M. Reinhart (Athens: University of Georgia Press, 2001).

cause of disagreement between Jews and Christians, one may well ask whether or not the quest of the "historical Jesus," assuming it arrives at something other than the traditional Christian view of Jesus, might not be a boon for Jewish-Christian dialogue. Without doubt the quest has been an ameliorating factor in the dialogue, as we shall see, but one could hardly call it a boon. We will explore the reasons for this conclusion in this essay. We begin with a brief look at the history of the Jewish study of Jesus that parallels the liberal Protestant quest, proceed to an analysis of some of the specific conclusions of the quest that bear upon our subject, follow this with a discussion of the obstacles posed by the quest, and conclude with some comments about the dialogue itself.

THE JEWISH STUDY OF JESUS AND THE QUEST

The nineteenth-century quest for the historical Jesus, as documented in Albert Schweitzer's famous book, was—from Reimarus to Wrede— almost exclusively a Gentile undertaking. Nevertheless, already with Reimarus (1778),[3]—anticipated by the English Deists—and with a considerable number of the others described by Schweitzer, the Jewishness of Jesus began to emerge with striking clarity, and concomitantly the disjuncture between Jesus and the Christ who was the center of the church's faith. Influential scholars such as Ferdinand Christian Baur[4] and William Wrede[5] drove a great wedge between Jesus and Paul, stressing the discontinuity between the two, and making Paul the de facto creator of Christianity. This is a viewpoint that would eventually be taken up by Jewish scholars in the late nineteenth and twentieth centuries.

Apart from the scandalous *Toledot Yeshu*, an ancient folk-tale based partly on Talmudic anecdotes about Jesus, written down first in the tenth

---

3. German available in Paul Rilla, ed., *Gotthold Ephraim Lessing: Gesammelte Werke*, vols. 7 and 8 (Berlin: Aufbau-Verlag, 1956); ET: *Reimarus Fragments*, trans. R. S. Fraser, ed. C. H. Talbert (Philadelphia: Fortress, 1970).

4. *Paulus, der Apostel Jesu Christi. Sein Leben und Wirken, seine Lehre: Ein Beitrag zu einer kritischen Geschichte des Urchristentums*, 2nd ed., ed. by Eduard Zeller, 2 vols. (Leipzig: Fues, 1866); ET: *Paul the Apostle of Jesus Christ, His Life and Work, His Epistles and His Doctrine: A Contribution to a Critical History of Primitive Christianity*, 2nd ed., trans. A. Menzies, 2 vols. (London: Williams & Norgate, 1876), reprinted as *Paul the Apostle of Jesus Christ: His Life and Works, His Epistles and Teachings* (Peabody, MA: Hendrickson, 2003).

5. *Paulus*, 2nd ed., Religionsgeschichtliche Volksbücher 1. 5/6 (Tübingen: Mohr Siebeck, 1907); ET: *Paul*, trans. E. Lummis (London: Green, 1907; reprint, Lexington: American Theological Association, 1962).

century, but still read by orthodox Jews in the nineteenth century, Jews wrote little about Jesus until the twentieth century. The emancipation of the Jews from the ghettoes of Europe over a two-hundred-year period, ending in 1933, and the birth of the *Haskalah* (the Jewish "Enlightenment") movement among the Jews in the eighteenth century, enabled the Jews to escape their isolation and to enter, and adapt themselves to, the world of modern thinking. The changes occurring for the Jews in this period were enormous and had highly significant results. Not least, the new situation was responsible for the emergence of Reform Judaism. And it was primarily in Reform Judaism that the critical thinking spawned by the Enlightenment began to be applied to the study of Judaism in what became known as *die Wissenschaft des Judentums*, "the science of Judaism." Now Jews began to defend Judaism as a religion in the face of the Enlightenment's rationalistic polemic against all established religion. Gradually, but inevitably, the Pharisees and the Judaism of the New Testament came under scrutiny, and then, at long last, Jesus himself.

Although there were some nineteenth-century pioneers, such as Joseph Salvador, Abraham Geiger, and Heinrich Graetz (all ignored by Schweitzer, except for a brief note about Salvador that misspells his name), it was the twentieth century that brought the flowering of the Jewish study of Jesus, with such notable scholars as Claude Goldsmid Montefiore, Israel Abrahams, Joseph Klausner, Samuel Sandmel, Schalom Ben-Chorin, David Flusser, Pinchas Lapide, and Geza Vermes. There is no need here to review this interesting history.[6] But it will be useful to summarize the general results of the modern Jewish study of Jesus. Enough is held in common by these scholars, in my opinion, to speak of them collectively. The first and most important conclusion of these scholars is that Jesus was a Jew, through and through. There is a surprising amount of openness to

---

6. This history has been reviewed by Gösta Lindeskog, *Die Jesusfrage im neuzeitlichen Judentum: Ein Beitrag zur Geschichte der Leben-Jesu-Forschung* (Uppsala: Almquist & Wiksells, 1938), reprinted with new postscript (Darmstadt: Wissenschaftliche Buchgesellschaft, 1973); and D. A. Hagner, *The Jewish Reclamation of Jesus: A Critique and Analysis* (Grand Rapids: Zondervan, 1984). See too, the two volumes of Jacób Jocz, *The Jewish People and Jesus Christ: A Study in the Relationship between the Jewish People and Jesus Christ* (London: SPCK, 1949; 3rd ed. Grand Rapids: Baker, 1979) and *The Jewish People and Jesus Christ after Auschwitz: A Study in the Controversy between Church and Synagogue* (Grand Rapids: Baker, 1981). Reviews from the Jewish side can be found in Schalom Ben-Chorin, *Jesus im Judentum* (Wuppertal: Brockhaus, 1970), an English distillation of which is found in *Journal of Ecumenical Studies* 11 (1974) 401-30; and Pinchas Lapide, *Ist das nicht Josephs Sohn? Jesus im heutigen Judentum* (Munich: Calwer, 1976; ET: *Israelis, Jews, and Jesus* [New York: Doubleday, 1979]).

concluding that he may have claimed to be the Messiah (thus Montefiore, Hyman Enelow, Klausner, Samuel Cohon, Sandmel, Hugh Schonfield) although it is also clear to these scholars that if he made such a claim he was mistaken, since the messianic age did not come and he died as a common criminal. He was faithful to the Law in his life and teaching, and the seriousness of his concern about its meaning qualifies him, in the minds of some, to be considered as a Pharisee or at least Pharisee-like, or rabbi-like (thus, e.g., Klausner, Geiger, Martin Buber, Paul Winter, Ben-Chorin, and Hyam Maccoby). Others have categorized Jesus as an Essene (Heinrich Graetz; several others see Essenic traits in Jesus without identifying him as an Essene), a Zealot (Joel Carmichael, Lapide), or as a charismatic, miracle-working *hasid* (Kaufmann Kohler, Flusser, Vermes). One of the most interesting designations is that of prophet, since it confers a special dignity upon Jesus that would separate him from his contemporaries (thus Montefiore, Hyman Enelow, Flusser). Although there is obviously little agreement as to what is the most appropriate category in which to position Jesus, it is also clear that all of these categories are eminently Jewish.[7] We may further note that Jewish scholars generally give little or no attention to the classic Christological titles, except in the case of Vermes, who finds the minimum content in each: Lord (an address of respect), Son of Man (a circumlocution for "I"), Son of God (a term applied to a wide variety of individuals). Now the extent to which these results overlap with those of the quest outlined by Schweitzer, and of the twentieth century more particularly, is remarkable. For all of the uncertainty about exactly where to place Jesus in the spectrum of first-century Judaism, it is the Jewishness of Jesus that eventually emerges with striking clarity. Furthermore, equally important is the conclusion that Jesus was very different from the Christ that became the center of Christian faith. The "real" Jesus is not the Jesus of the church. The gospels are documents so colored with the patina of Christian faith that, as they stand, they are historically untrustworthy.

What relationship, if any, is there between this flowering of the Jewish study of Jesus and the Jesus quest of Christian scholars? From the beginning there seems to have been no direct dependence of Jewish scholarship upon Christian scholarship; the former was capable of generating its own momentum. In this field of study Jewish scholars had no need of Christian scholars to assist them. The similarity in conclusions

---

7. For a fuller and more precise discussion, see Hagner, *The Jewish Reclamation of Jesus*, 227–71.

we have noted was rather the result of a common predisposition against the usual convictions of Christianity, caused on the one side by religious reasons[8] and on the other by the demands of critical historiography. Eventually, however—indeed already in the case of Montefiore—it becomes more and more evident that Christian scholarship begins to exert an influence upon Jewish writers. Reform Jews, who were not threatened by the rationalism of the Enlightenment, realized that the scientific historiography practiced by liberal Protestant scholarship could become a helpful ally in showing the error of Christianity. It was hardly discouraging to Jewish scholars that liberal Protestant scholarship continued to assert that the gospel accounts of Jesus reflected *Gemeindetheologie*, the theology of the church, more than it did actual history. The conclusions of Christian scholarship seemed eminently reasonable to Jewish scholars and to square with their reading of the gospels. The result was that the Christian questers became increasingly influential upon Jewish scholarship, as the twentieth century progressed.[9] Indeed, eventually Jewish scholars writing about Jesus become nearly indistinguishable from others involved in the quest as, for example, in the case of Vermes (who goes out of his way to note that he writes as a historian rather than a Jew) and Paula Fredriksen. It would seem now that the Jewish reclamation of Jesus has fully merged with the quest of the historical Jesus.[10] "Und auf jüdischer Seite hat die 'Heimholung Jesu ins Judentum' heute den Wind der historischen Jesusforschung nicht gegen sich, sondern im Rücken."[11]

---

8. See W. Riggans, "The Jewish Reclamation of Jesus and Its Implications for Jewish-Christian Relations," *Themelios* 18 (1992) 9–16.

9. E. Bammel may overstate the matter, however, when he writes: "And when Jewish scholars started to develop an interest in Jesus they based their interpretation on the concepts of liberal German scholarship" ("Christian Origins in Jewish Tradition," *NTS* 13 [1966–67] 317).

10. H. D. Betz concludes: "Modern Jewish interpretations [of Jesus] are again different in that they interact with or are part of historical-critical scholarship of the 19th and 20th century. These contributions also share in the shifts and changes, the loyalties and animosities of modern scholarship, and they must therefore be carefully assessed within the history of scholarship and the cultural and political circumstances in which they came into existence" ("Wellhausen's Dictum 'Jesus was not a Christian, but a Jew' in Light of Present Scholarship," *Studia Theologica* 45 [1991]) 83–110, at 97).

11. K. Haacker, *Versöhnung mit Israel: Exegetische Beiträge*, Veröffentlichungen der Kirchlichen Hochschule Wuppertal, N.F. 5 (Neukirchener: Foedus, 2002) 201.

POSITIVE RESULTS OF THE QUEST FOR JEWISH-CHRISTIAN DIALOGUE

The primary underlying concern of Jewish-Christian dialogue—of supreme and self-evident importance—has been to counteract the kind of misinformed, hateful thinking that ultimately caused the Holocaust. Christians and Jews have accordingly worked together on two fronts: to bring about a better understanding of Judaism, on the one hand, and a better understanding of Jesus, on the other. The quest of the historical Jesus in its recent manifestations[12] has been of great help on both fronts.

One of the distinguishing marks of the so-called, but misnamed, third quest, is the amount of attention given to *Second Temple Judaism as the context in which the historical Jesus must be understood.* Here we encounter influence in the opposite direction: Christian scholars have benefited greatly from the work of Jewish scholars, as one might well expect. There is much agreement between the two on fundamental matters. A great amount of helpful knowledge has been compiled concerning such things as the social conditions, politics, economics, and religious life of first-century Palestine, and there is a unified conviction that if the historical Jesus is to be explained, he must somehow be placed squarely into this context.[13] At the same time, we have acquired a better understanding of Judaism as a religion marked by covenantal nomism, a religion of grace and not merit.[14] Judaism then appears not so much as a foil for the Christian gospel of grace, but rather a parallel expression of a divinely ordained religion. If Jews are saved by the grace of God as much as Christians, then it would seem unnecessary for Christians to proselytize Jews.

---

12. For helpful surveys, see W. R. Telford, "Major Trends and Interpretive Issues in the Study of Jesus," in B. Chilton and C. A. Evans, eds., *Studying the Historical Jesus: Evaluations of the State of Research*, 2nd ed., NTTS 19 (Leiden: Brill, 1994) 33-74; and David A. du Toit, "Redefining Jesus: Current Trends in Jesus Research," in Michael Labahn and Andreas Schmidt, eds., *Jesus, Mark and Q: The Teaching of Jesus and Its Earliest Records*, JSNTSS 214 (Sheffield: Sheffield Academic, 2001) 82-124.

13. An exception that may be said to prove the rule is Burton L. Mack, who regards Jesus as a Hellenistic Cynic sage with little or no concern with things Jewish. See his *A Myth of Innocence: Mark and Christian Origins* (Philadelphia: Fortress, 1988).

14. Fully articulated first by E. P. Sanders in his *Paul and Palestinian Judaism: A Comparison of Patterns of Religion* (London/Philadelphia: SCM/Fortress, 1977), and developed in various later publications.

In 1905 Julius Wellhausen articulated the now famous dictum "Jesus was not a Christian, but a Jew."[15] It is clear that the great accomplishment of the quest, general though it is, is the establishment of *the Jewishness of Jesus*.[16] When Jewish scholars look at the Jesus of the gospels they are able immediately to recognize his intense Jewishness in a wide-ranging variety of respects that need not be reviewed here,[17] and that Jesus belongs as much, if not more, to the Jews as he does to the Christians. The realization of the Jewishness of Jesus may not at first seem to be much of an accomplishment, until one realizes that as the early church became more and more Gentile, and focused more and more upon the risen Lord, the Jewishness of Jesus began to recede, and indeed virtually disappeared from Christian consciousness. Christians lost any sense of their Jewish heritage and this loss soon produced fertile ground in which anti-Semitism could and did flourish.[18] A corollary to the conclusion that Jesus was fully Jewish is that to be Jewish is therefore something good.[19]

Furthermore, and perhaps more importantly for dialogue, it is widely concluded by the quest and by Jewish scholars that *the historical Jesus is of necessity to be separated from the later church's understanding of him*. The faith of the church, it is usually argued, apparently transformed Jesus into something he was not, and something that was very far from his mind. Here we encounter head-on the high Christology of the New Testament documents. There is obviously an affirmation and heightening of the divinity of Jesus in the New Testament that necessarily goes beyond the actuality of the historical Jesus. Rosemary Ruether is famous for her

---

15. *Einleitung in die drei ersten Evangelien* (Berlin: Reimer, 1905) 113; see H. D. Betz, "Wellhausen's Dictum."

16. See Tom Holmén, "The Jewishness of Jesus in the 'Third Quest,'" in *Jesus, Mark and Q*, 143–62. Holmén points out that "Jewishness," as widely defined, has become too broad to be helpful in understanding Jesus. He suggests the need for an "essentialist" approach that specifies core elements of Judaism, against which Jesus can be measured.

17. See J. H. Charlesworth, ed., *Jesus' Jewishness: Exploring the Place of Jesus within Early Judaism* (New York: Crossroad, 1991); Charlesworth, *Jesus Within Judaism: New Light from Exciting Archaeological Discoveries* (New York: Doubleday, 1988).

18. See R. T. Olson, "The Christian Blasphemy: A Non-Jewish Jesus," in J. H. Charlesworth, ed., *Jews and Christians: Exploring the Past, Present, and Future* (New York: Crossroad, 1990) 211–38, reprint of an article that appeared originally in *JAAR* 53 (1985).

19. L. E. Keck notes that "theologically the Jewishness of Jesus has made this disagreement about him rather like a family quarrel": *Who Is Jesus? History in the Perfect Tense* (Columbia: University of South Carolina Press, 2000) 63.

description of anti-Semitism as "the left hand of christology,"[20] meaning that the Christology of the church is a primary cause of anti-Semitism. It is well known that the admirable desire to avoid anti-Semitism has led to frequent calls for a major overhaul of Christian theology in general and Christology in particular. If, as the quest maintains—at least as it does for the most part—that the historical Jesus is to be understood as some type of Jewish teacher, healer, and reformer, then he need no longer be the great dividing point between Jews and Christians. But, as we will see below, such a minimalist conclusion is problematic for the explanation of the rise of Christianity, and therefore, problematic precisely from the perspective of sound historical method.

Furthermore, *Jesus did not intend to create a new faith*. The historical Jesus is fundamentally about Judaism, not about Christianity. He came, it is commonly argued, as a reformer of Judaism. Jesus thus did not intend—on the contrary, would have been offended by—the creation of a new community of faith, over against the Jewish faith, and especially one that made him the center of its theology and worship. It is, rather, the disciples of Jesus who are the creators of Christianity. It is they who transform Jesus into something he was not, and they who are responsible for the separation from Judaism. Jesus of course did not have as his purpose the creation of a new religion. Such a platitude, however, fails to reckon with the complexity of the fulfillment stressed by the New Testament, which involves continuity as well as discontinuity. Christianity entails newness, but the first generation of Christians thought of their faith as the true form of Judaism, not as a new religion.

As the obverse of the preceding claim, *in no way was Jesus disloyal to the Jewish faith*. Quite the contrary, the gospels provide abundant evidence that despite his criticism of the Pharisees, Jesus remained fundamentally loyal to the faith of the Jews. "Instead, there is substantial evidence that *Jesus accepted all of the major tenets of the Jewish faith*: the unity and sovereignty of God, the value and sanctity of the Temple of Jerusalem, the authority of the Jewish Scriptures, the election of the people of Israel, and the hope of Israel's redemption."[21]

---

20. *Faith and Fratricide: The Theological Roots of Anti-Semitism* (New York: Seabury, 1974; reprint, Eugene, OR: Wipf & Stock, 1996) 64–65.

21. Craig A. Evans, "The Jesus of History and the Christ of Faith: Toward Jewish-Christian Dialogue," in P. Copan and C. A. Evans, eds., *Who Was Jesus? A Jewish-Christian Dialogue* (Louisville: Westminster John Knox, 2001) 59–72, at 61, italics are Evans's.

Jesus accepted the Torah and never intended to overthrow its authority. "Do not think that I have come to abolish the law or the prophets; I have not come to abolish but to fulfill" (Matt 5:17). The teaching of Jesus in the gospels is not meant to undermine the law, but rather to fulfill it, in the sense of bringing to expression its intended meaning.

PROBLEMATIC ASPECTS OF THE QUEST FOR JEWISH-CHRISTIAN DIALOGUE

If there are, as we have seen, undeniably some positive results of the quest of the historical Jesus for Jewish-Christian dialogue, there are also problematic aspects. Some of these have to do with the intrinsic methodological weaknesses of the quest, others with results of the quest. We turn now to look at these.

The quest *has shed more light on the context of Jesus than on Jesus himself.* The immense amount of attention given to the socio-cultural milieu of first-century Palestine and Second Temple Judaism has produced a richer understanding of the context of Jesus than ever before, and it has thereby opened up numerous options for the classification of Jesus. At the same time, however, there is little agreement concerning how to understand Jesus himself. Indeed, the current quest has produced as many Jesuses as did the old quest described by Schweitzer.[22] And despite the clear advances in scholarship, it seems no less true today than in the nineteenth century that scholars tend to see in Jesus a reflection of their own image. Which historical Jesus, if any, is the "real" Jesus?

Furthermore, better knowledge of the context has itself brought other new problems. The quest has revealed how complex first-century Judaism was. It seems that we must now speak of a variety of Judaisms.[23] What sort of Judaism does Jesus reflect? Was the Jewish background

---

22. "Thus, the major disputed issue in the 'Third Quest' is what kind of person Jesus was and what the essence of his message, ministry, and intention was." M.E. Boring, "The 'Third Quest' and the Apostolic Faith," in J. D. Kingsbury, ed., *Gospel Interpretation: Narrative-Critical and Social-Scientific Approaches* (Harrisburg, PA: Trinity, 1997) 237–52 (at 240); reprint of an article that first appeared in *Interpretation* 50 (1996) 341–54 (at 343–44).

23. The classic example nowadays of a diverse Judaism is that of the Dead Sea Scroll community. See C. A. Evans, "The New Quest for Jesus and the New Research on the Dead Sea Scrolls," in *Jesus, Mark and Q*, 163–83.

against which Jewish scholars have understood Jesus accurate? Did it possibly make the explanation of Jesus too easy?[24]

The main criteria used by the quest to decide authenticity have not proved to be very effective. In particular, *the criterion of double dissimilarity as classically employed cuts Jesus off not only from his followers but also from the Jewish context in which he lived.* According to this criterion, only that which is unparalleled in the New Testament and in contemporary Judaism can be trusted as reliable history. The result is a Jesus who is totally isolated from his context. What is accepted as authentic concerning the historical Jesus becomes that which marks him out as eccentric and idiosyncratic. As a consequence the Jewishness of Jesus—an element of great importance for the Jewish-Christian dialogue—recedes into the background. According to Theissen and Winter, the theological motive behind this criterion is "anti-Judaism"—namely "the theological rejection of the Jewish religion, expressed especially in a strongly negative portrayal of Jewish faith and life," a portrayal that functions as "a negative foil for the advent of Jesus and/or Christianity."[25]

In recent years, however, a growing dissatisfaction with the dissimilarity criterion has developed. Theissen and Winter comment: "It is therefore time to replace the criterion of dissimilarity with a new criterion, in the process keeping its legitimate elements and correcting its distortions and one-sidedness."[26] They advocate the "criterion of historical plausibility," giving more positive consideration to contextual plausibility on the Jewish side, and to the plausibility of historical effects, on the Christian side. This new criterion will bring with it a positive and a negative result for Jewish-Christian dialogue: it will help establish the Jewishness of Jesus, but it will also help build connections with the Christian view of Jesus.

---

24. D. J. Harrington raises the problem of the variety of Judaisms in the time of Jesus: "The Jewishness of Jesus: Facing Some Problems," *CBQ* 49 (1987) 1-13, reprinted in J. H. Charlesworth, ed., *Jesus' Jewishness: Exploring the Place of Jesus within Early Judaism* (New York: Crossroad, 1991) 123-36. See also J. Neusner et al., eds., *Judaisms and Their Messiahs at the Turn of the Christian Era* (Cambridge: Cambridge University Press, 1987); and T. Holmén, "The Jewishness of Jesus in the 'Third Quest'," in *Jesus, Mark and Q*, 150-52.

25. G. Theissen and D. Winter, *The Quest for the Plausible Jesus: The Question of Criteria*, trans. M. E. Boring (Louisville: Westminster John Knox, 2002) 67.

26. Ibid., 172. For a similar critique, see T. Holmén, "Doubts About Double Dissimilarity: Restructuring the main criterion of Jesus-of-history research," in B. Chilton and C. A. Evans, eds., *Authenticating the Words of Jesus*, NTTS 28.1 (Leiden: Brill, 1999) 47-80.

The determination of Jesus' self-understanding remains an important aspect of the quest. Thus far, however, the quest has not been very successful here. In the opinion of Craig Evans, "probably no feature of Jesus research has been more divisive than the question of the claims that Jesus made for himself."[27] Nevertheless, this is an issue that can have extremely important implications for Jewish-Christian dialogue. It is clear that Jesus was unique in some respects. One of the immediate impressions one gains from the synoptic gospels is that Jesus was perceived as possessing a unique authority. Both in his deeds and his words, Jesus constantly amazed those around him. That pattern of authority stems from personal claims, explicit or implicit. A range of possibilities confronts the interpreter, as we have already seen. Some of these, e.g., proto-rabbi, charismatic healer, reformer, or prophet,[28] are not necessarily problematic for the Jewish-Christian dialogue. Other options—those that move toward a "high" Christology—such as Messiah, Messianic Son of Man, unique Agent of God, one who is uniquely the Son of God, and the personification of Wisdom—since they accord more with the Christian estimate of Jesus, can complicate the dialogue.

The quest, armed with the criterion of dissimilarity, has essentially put a question mark over the perspective of the gospel writers, and seems, thus far, unable to come to a conclusion concerning Jesus' self-perception. But we may well see more progress on this issue in the future,[29] and the implications for Jewish-Christian dialogue are significant.

Another issue that is of the greatest interest to Jews is *the cause of, and the responsibility for, the death of Jesus*. This is crucial for Jewish-Christian dialogue since blaming Jews for the death of Christ— the crime of deicide, as it has unfortunately been called—is perhaps the root cause of anti-Semitism. The dominant Jewish point of view is that Jesus was put to death by the Romans for fomenting political revolt. Since crucifixion

---

27. "The Jesus of History and the Christ of Faith: Toward Jewish-Christian Dialogue," 63.

28. See Markus Öhler, "Jesus as Prophet: Remarks on Terminology," in *Jesus, Mark and Q*, 125-42.

29. As examples of encouraging directions, see Marinus de Jonge, *God's Final Envoy: Early Christology and Jesus' Own View of His Mission* (Grand Rapids: Eerdmans, 1998); and Ben Witherington III, *The Christology of Jesus* (Minneapolis: Fortress, 1990); cf. C. A. Evans, "The Jesus of History and the Christ of Faith," 63-66. See too D. A. Hagner, "Jesus' Self-Understanding" in *Encyclopedia of the Historical Jesus*, ed. C. A. Evans (New York: Routledge, 2008) 324-33.

was a Roman, and not a Jewish, form of punishment, this is obviously true at one level. But is it the whole story?

The role of the Jews in the death of Jesus seems clear from the gospels. But if there is Jewish complicity in the death of Jesus, it is to be limited primarily to the Jewish leadership,[30] rather than to the Jewish people as a whole. Furthermore, the Jewish mob who yelled for the crucifixion of Jesus with the words "Let his blood be upon us and upon our children," is hardly representative of the totality of the Jewish people. Certainly the Jews of later generations down to the present had nothing to do with the death of Jesus. A further point that gospel scholarship has made clear is that the New Testament's hostility toward the Jews is heightened by, and a reflection of, the increasing animosity between Jews and Christians as the first century wore on. This undoubtedly has had its impact upon the passion narrative, as well as other parts of the gospel narratives.

What was it about Jesus that drew forth the wrath of the Jewish leadership? The gospels call attention to Jesus' stance towards two pillars of Judaism, the Law and the Temple.[31] The controversy stories in the early chapters of Mark illustrate the opposition of the leadership stirred up by Jesus' attitude toward typical Sabbath observance (e.g., Mark 3:6). Jesus does appear to have a transcendent authority concerning the law ("the Son of Man is Lord even of the Sabbath," Mark 2:28). Nevertheless, Jesus must finally be judged as being fundamentally loyal to the Law (Matt 5:17). The quest has turned to the Temple as a more promising explanation, for Jesus not only prophesied its destruction (though some doubt this), but he also acted with uncharacteristic violence in ousting the money-changers from the Temple area (Mark 11:15-17 and parallels). The Markan account is followed by the notice that "the chief priests and the scribes heard it and sought a way to destroy him" (Mark 11:18). This revolutionary attack against the establishment could hardly have been overlooked by the Jewish authorities—certainly not at Passover time, and

---

30. One must balk, however, at the excessive portrayal of the Jewish leadership in Mel Gibson's much-discussed movie, *The Passion*.

31. "Torah and temple, it is often correctly said, were the two foci of Judaism, and Jesus either threatened or was perceived as threatening both": W. D. Davies and E. P. Sanders, "Jesus: From the Jewish Point of View," in W. Horbury et al., eds., *The Cambridge History of Judaism*, vol. 3 (Cambridge: Cambridge University Press, 1999) 618-77, at 674. Davies and Sanders conclude that four factors were responsible for the death of Jesus: the question of who speaks for God; proclamation of the kingdom with the implication that Jesus was a king; the political situation that posed danger for a charismatic leader; and the temple incident (675).

not by one who had previously entered the city to the sound of messianic acclamation (Mark 11:1-10 and parallels).[32]

It is clear that the question concerning the reason for the death of Jesus can hardly be answered if he is understood as only an unusual teacher, with unusual interpretations of the commandments. The more solidly scholars place Jesus comfortably into his Jewish context the more difficult it becomes to explain his death. H.-D. Betz rightly faults Wellhausen for his inability to provide a plausible explanation for the crucifixion of Jesus.[33] Why, it is normally and correctly asked, would anyone bother to crucify an exceptional teacher? In response to a similar question, about why anyone would crucify a charismatic hasid and healer, Vermes writes "He died on the cross for having done the wrong thing (caused a commotion) in the wrong place (the Temple) at the wrong time (just before Passover). Here lies the real tragedy of Jesus the Jew."[34] Jesus was thus ultimately crucified for political reasons, as the authorities tried to keep control of a potentially inflammatory situation. Here again we find a concordance between the conclusions of the quest and those of Jewish scholarship.

At the same time, Jesus' stance toward both the Law and the Temple clearly implies a unique authority, an authority in which messianic claims are implicit. The irony of the inscription on the cross, "King of the Jews," is remarkable for several reasons. What is meant as a parody ironically conveys truth. The death of Jesus was probably due to a combination of things, but it is difficult to rule out the unique personal authority and implicit claims of Jesus as major factors in the mix. The reference to blasphemy in the scene of Jesus' "trial" or hearing before the Sanhedrin seems connected with the unacceptable personal claims either made or implied by Jesus.

The trend today seems more and more to underline the Jewishness of Jesus and to fit him into his Jewish context. To the extent, however, that the conclusions of some questers point to the authority of Jesus vis-à-vis the Law and the Temple, and to the extent that personal claims are also regarded as implied, the more the quest provides an obstacle to Jewish-Christian dialogue.

---

32. For a full study of the crucial temple incident, see Jostein Ådna, *Jesu Stellung zum Tempel: Die Tempelaktion und das Tempelwort als Ausdruck seiner messianischen Sendung*, WUNT 2.119 (Tübingen: Mohr Siebeck, 2000).

33. "Wellhausen's Dictum," 86.

34. G. Vermes, *The Religion of Jesus the Jew* (Minneapolis: Fortress, 1993) x.

A final, key issue that confronts the quest is how to frame *an adequate explanation of the faith of the first Christians and the birth of the church.* Here again, the more "ordinary" Jesus is made to appear, the more he fits into his context, the more unconvincing the explanation becomes. Any construal of the evidence that fails to provide a plausible account of Christian origins can hardly be regarded as acceptable.[35]

To begin with, the matter of the resurrection experience of the disciples must be considered. The resurrection itself, of course, has traditionally been regarded as off-limits for historical study. The historian *per se* has no access to that which is outside the normal, closed system of cause and effect.[36] Recently, however, from one deeply involved in the Jesus quest, the issue of the resurrection has been addressed head on. In a bold, path-breaking book, N.T. Wright argues that the resurrection is both a legitimate and necessary subject for historical inquiry.[37] At the end of his long investigation, he concludes: "We are left with the secure historical conclusion: the tomb was empty, and various 'meetings' took place not only between Jesus and his followers (including at least one initial sceptic) but also, in at least one case (that of Paul, possibly, too, that of James), between Jesus and people who had not been among his followers."[38] In Wright's view, "the combination of empty tomb and appearances of the living Jesus forms a set of circumstances which is itself *both necessary and sufficient* for the rise of early Christian belief. Without these phenomena,

---

35. Betz points out that "Wellhausen has no explanation of a historical connection between Jesus and the early church" ("Wellhausen's Dictum," 87).

36. Cf. J. P. Meier, who at the beginning of his multi-volume study of the historical Jesus writes: "a treatment of the resurrection is omitted not because it is denied but simply because the restrictive definition of the historical Jesus I will be using does not allow us to proceed into matters that can be affirmed only by faith" (*A Marginal Jew: Rethinking the Historical Jesus* [New York: Doubleday, 1991], 1.13). Volume 4 thus promises no discussion of the resurrection, but rather a treatment of why Jesus was crucified, "the starkest, most disturbing, and most central of all the enigmas Jesus posed and was" 3:646 (2001).

37. *The Resurrection of the Son of God* (Minneapolis: Fortress, 2003). The empty tomb and the resurrection appearances "took place as real events . . . they are, in the normal sense required by historians, provable events; historians can and should write about them" (709). "Provable" here means reaching the high probability that is within the province of the historian. Cf. J. D. G. Dunn, *Jesus Remembered* (Grand Rapids: Eerdmans, 2003) 102-5. "In historical scholarship the judgment 'probable' is a very positive verdict" (103). See, too, W. P. Alston, "Biblical Criticism and the Resurrection," in S. T. Davis et al., eds., *The Resurrection: An Interdisciplinary Symposium on the Resurrection of Jesus* (Oxford: Oxford University Press, 1997) 148-83.

38. He adds: "I regard this conclusion as virtually certain, as the death of Augustus in AD 14 or the fall of Jerusalem in AD 70" (*Resurrection*, 710).

we cannot explain why this belief came into existence, and took the shape it did. With them we can explain it exactly and precisely."[39]

If the resurrection is taken as a historical datum, what are the implications for the understanding of Jesus? Wright addresses this question in the final chapter of his book, concluding that it points not merely to Jesus as being the Messiah, but as being uniquely the Son of God. Wright's perspective is bound to be controversial among those questing after the historical Jesus, but his argument is not easy to dismiss.

Another factor that must be explained in the quest is the surprisingly early devotion to Jesus in the early church, a topic now taken up fully in the recent book by Larry Hurtado.[40] Devotion to Jesus, writes Hurtado, does not appear at a secondary stage, but "emerges phenomenally early," an occurrence without contemporary religious analogy, and "this intense devotion to Jesus, which includes reverencing him as divine, was offered and articulated characteristically within a firm stance of exclusivist monotheism."[41] Hurtado examines the fact of this devotion to Jesus from the beginning, and not its cause. But lying behind it must be an adequate explanation—one that undoubtedly goes back not only to the impact made by Jesus but also to the resurrection. There are many interesting ramifications of Hurtado's book that we cannot go into here— e.g., when can we first speak of "Christianity" and when does the "parting of the ways" between synagogue and church begin? Perhaps some currently popular conclusions will need revision. Another recent and remarkable book makes a similar point, but pushes the question of the faith of the disciples back into the ministry of Jesus itself. J.D.G. Dunn presents a compelling argument that the faith of the early Christians goes back to the earliest encounters of the disciples with Jesus, and does not begin with or after the resurrection.[42] Dunn finds the essence of the synoptic tradition as already the product of the pre-Easter impact of Jesus and the resultant faith of the disciples.

---

39. *Resurrection*, 696.

40. *Lord Jesus Christ: Devotion to Jesus in Earliest Christianity* (Grand Rapids: Eerdmans, 2003). The earlier work of Franz Mussner along these lines should be noted, as well as his treatment of other themes pertinent to the present essay. See now his collected essays, *Jesus von Nazareth im Umfeld Israels und der Urkirche*, ed. Michael Theobald, WUNT 111 (Tübingen: Mohr Siebeck, 1999); and, of course, his classic *Tractate on the Jews*, trans. L. Swidler (Philadelphia: Fortress, 1984).

41. *Lord Jesus Christ*, 2-3.

42. J. D. G. Dunn, *Jesus Remembered*.

Inevitably the attempt to explain the origin of the faith and worship of the earliest Christians drives us back to the person of Jesus and inevitably we are brought back to an early and very "high" Christology. Insofar as that is the case, it is clear that the results of the work of Wright, Hurtado, and Dunn will be problematic for Jewish-Christian dialogue.

Two further matters—now concerning the methodology of the quest—deserve mention here. The first is the well-known *problem of the inadequacy of the historical method*. Because of the self-imposed limitations of the method, Jesus will always be more than the historians can describe or analyze.[43] The quest for the historical Jesus must play by the rules, but the problem is that the rules predetermine the outcome in a way that may not be fair to reality. With no room for the possibility of recognizing God at work in the historical process, thereby negating the very assertion of the gospels, the method is seemingly bound to produce a severely diminished Jesus, at least so far as those of Christian faith are concerned. "It is precisely in the material that is most problematic to the secular historian (for example, the birth and resurrection stories) that this acknowledgment of the true scope and significance of the event of Jesus' life is most clearly manifested."[44] The gospel portraits of Jesus continually challenge the adequacy of the historical method. As a result, the historian's Jesus is necessarily an artificial Jesus. John P. Meier begins his monumental multi-volume study of the historical Jesus with the paradoxical words: "The historical Jesus is not the real Jesus. The real Jesus is not the historical Jesus."[45] M.E. Boring has called attention to the problem with these words: "If, however, one wishes to engage in the perfectly legitimate, perhaps for us in our time even theologically necessary, enterprise of reconstructing a historian's Jesus that can be argued about by historians limiting themselves to historical methods, the Jesus so reconstructed will always be less than the 'real Jesus.'"[46]

---

43. Cf. *Jesus Remembered*, 125–26.

44. Francis Watson, "The Quest for the Real Jesus," in M. Bockmuehl, ed., *The Cambridge Companion to Jesus* (Cambridge: Cambridge University Press, 2001) 156–69, at 165. Cf. L. Keck: "What must not be missed is that by deleting from Jesus' history all references to divine action, critics set aside precisely those parts of the gospels by which the Evangelists expressed the most explicitly their understanding of the ongoing significance of Jesus, his perfect tense" (*Who Is Jesus?*, 5).

45. *A Marginal Jew: Rethinking the Historical Jesus*, vol. 1 (New York: Doubleday, 1991) 21.

46. "The 'Third Quest' and the Apostolic Faith," 249. Boring rightly adds, "Even so, there must also be lines of continuity between the reconstructed historian's Jesus and

Once one is required by the historical method to reject the interpretive framework and perspective of the gospel writers, the possible interpretations quickly multiply, as has happened in the third quest, and the resultant Jesus necessarily becomes the reflection of the interpreter's image, even as Schweitzer demonstrated in his review of the nineteenth-century quest.

Insofar as the basic method of the quest by its nature can say nothing about items central to the Christian faith, its results remove a traditional obstacle to dialogue and are accordingly looked upon favorably by Jewish scholars. The resultant predicament of Christian scholars, however, is that "having been deprived of the pivotal figure of Jesus, Christianity is left either without a historical foundation or with the extremely difficult task of finding another way to relate to the historical Jesus."[47]

For those thoroughly bogged down in this quandary, Wright's approach to the resurrection (see above) holds considerable promise. Can the historical method, in any meaningful sense, deal responsibly with the miracles of Jesus?[48] At this point, not unexpectedly, many will decline the invitation. And this brings us to our second observation concerning methodology.

There is no need here to go into the vagaries of post-modernism.[49] Nevertheless, it is worth calling attention again to *the impossibility of a*

---

the 'real Jesus'—these cannot be utterly discontinuous, or one of them is wrong" (249).

47. H. D. Betz, "Wellhausen's Dictum," 98.

48. Cf. N. T. Wright: "But one cannot rule out *a priori* the possibility of things occurring in ways not normally expected, since to do so would be to begin from the fixed point that a particular worldview, namely the eighteenth-century rationalist one, or its twentieth-century positivist successor, is correct in postulating that the universe is simply a 'closed continuum' of cause and effect" (*The New Testament and the People of God* [Minneapolis: Fortress, 1992] 92). Cf. Dunn: "the question remains whether a viable concept and practice of 'historical method' can also be retrieved from the blinkered historicist and positivist perspectives of modernity, from the narrowing rationalist and scientific assumptions of the Enlightenment" (*Jesus Remembered*, 29). Particularly helpful on the subject is C. S. Evans, *The Historical Christ and the Jesus of Faith: The Incarnational Narrative as History* (Oxford: Clarendon, 1996). Cf. Graham H. Twelftree, "The History of Miracles in the History of Jesus," in S. McKnight and G. R. Osborne, eds., *The Face of New Testament Studies: A Survey of Recent Research* (Grand Rapids: Baker, 2004) 191–208: "No less than in the nineteenth century, the fluctuating fortunes of the way the miracles of Jesus are treated has remained theologically driven and often philosophically shackled by rationalism or naturalism. It cannot be otherwise until historiographers are able to challenge successfully this ascendant paradigm of reality supposed by most Jesus questers" (208).

49. Dunn is one of the few who address the matter head-on: *Jesus Remembered*, 92–97.

neutral history. We are much more sensitive now, than earlier in the last century, to the biased character of all our observation and knowledge. We have no access to pure facts; there is no escape from interpretation. The hermeneutical circle, which no-one fully escapes, means that all of us incline to see things the way we have been taught to see them, and the way our respective communities see them. The positivist ideal of objective facts has had to give way to the reality of socially constructed, and community-influenced, knowledge.

Those who have the eyes of faith will, of course, tend to deal with the historical evidence differently from those who are skeptical. Christians will see the Jesus of history one way; Jews will see him in a different way. There is no neutral ground from which to decide who is right and who is wrong. This is not a counsel of despair. All can make the attempt to step outside their prior understandings. All can take a new look at the evidence. There is still room for the use of reason, evaluation of evidence, and the presentation of arguments. But under the circumstances there will also be plenty of room for humility and charity.

In fact, we cannot give up on the importance of historical research and the rational consideration of evidence. We simply cannot do without it unless we choose the comfort of solitude and silence and cut ourselves off from the realm of public discourse. Because we cannot have absolute knowledge does not mean that we cannot have knowledge.[50]

THE QUEST AND JEWISH-CHRISTIAN DIALOGUE

Having looked at the positive and negative aspects of the quest for Jewish-Christian dialogue, we may now turn to some concluding remarks on the subject. Given the mixed results that we have noted, what can we say about the quest of the historical Jesus and its impact upon Jewish-Christian relations? How far have we come? How much further can we go? What can we realistically expect?

To begin with, we must be grateful for what has been accomplished, which at least deserves the evaluation *so far, so good*. If we had only the two main achievements of the quest, namely, our increased knowledge of Second Temple Judaism, and the firm establishment of the Jewishness of

---

50. See Alan G. Padgett's helpful article, "Advice for Religious Historians: On the Myth of a Purely Historical Jesus," in Davis, et al., eds., *The Resurrection*, 287-307.

Jesus, our gratitude would be justified. These are indeed significant contributions that have had a positive effect on Jewish-Christian dialogue.

The quest to this point has focused on areas upon which Jews and Christians can often readily agree, and to this extent we may judge the quest as helpful. But how far has the quest come, and how successfully?

Since it is widely agreed that thus far the quest can itself hardly be called an unalloyed success, *the potential of the quest for Jewish-Christian relations remains unclear.* The trouble is that the quest has not been able to get very far in arriving at its announced goal. Focusing more on the context than on Jesus himself, the quest, as we have noted, has failed to address the ultimately decisive questions. The historical method has seemed ill-suited to its subject matter in this case. Perhaps with the recent works of Wright, Dunn, and Hurtado, however, this may have begun to change.

Problems remain even with some agreed-upon positive conclusions mentioned above that have importance for Jewish-Christian dialogue. Thus, the quest's insistence that Jesus was fundamentally loyal to the Jewish faith and did not intend to create a new religion, while true enough on the one hand, can also conceal the newness that is implicit in so much of Jesus, his message and the new community of faith. It is clearly wrong to speak of that newness in terms of the creation of a new religion or of disloyalty to the Jewish faith. The only adequate word is "fulfillment," with all the continuity (and discontinuity) implied by that word, but "fulfillment" is not exactly a term that will promote positive responses from Jewish scholarship, or enhance Jewish-Christian relations. Not unexpectedly, "fulfillment" has the ring of supersessionism to Jewish ears. Supersessionism, however, we must insist, cannot be an option to any Christian who has read Romans 11.

In the final analysis, it would appear that *the "historical" Jesus arrived at through the historical method as traditionally practiced, cannot finally become a bridge strong enough to cross the chasm that divides Jews and Christians.* ". . . . Christians and Jews have drawn different conclusions and can stay together regarding Jesus' identity only part of the way. At some point along that way we necessarily confront the theological issues . . ."[51] This should not be a distressing conclusion. The limited agreement that the quest has been able to provide has been helpful, but

---

51. D. J. Harrington, "The Jewishness of Jesus: Facing Some Problems," 13.

productive dialogue and good relations do not depend on the ability to agree on everything.

In fact, Jewish and Christian scholars who look at Jesus will continue to disagree, and therefore we must learn how to face and cope with our disagreements. "Why are we so reluctant, in this age of dialogue, to emphasize those things that *separate* or *differentiate* Jews and Christians?" asks Isabel Wollaston.[52] The point of dialogue, after all, is not to erase disagreements or to overcome all differences, but rather to come to a better understanding and to learn to respect those with whom we disagree. Post-holocaust sensitivities, as highly appropriate as they are, have unfortunately made it difficult—indeed, sometimes nearly impossible—for Christian scholars to arrive at any negative conclusions about the Judaism of the New Testament, or things Jewish, such as the Pharisees or the Law, without being considered anti-Semitic, or at least potentially so.

For that very important reason, however, one very important caveat must be insisted upon at this point. Christians can disagree with Judaism only if they remain highly vigilant against any semblance of anti-Semitism. Here we are required to speak in absolute, non-negotiable, terms: Christians cannot and will not tolerate anti-Semitism.

Dialogue must finally take place within the framework of the faith of the other, as defined by the other. Jacob Neusner has called attention to the futility of Christians defining Judaism, and Jews defining Christianity, in such ways as to minimize the differences between the two.[53] In this way the distinctive character of each is compromised. One of the most common instruments used in this regard is the historical Jesus, who is seen more and more as the common denominator that can pull together the two religions. Neusner refers to the minimalist or "Judaic Christology" of the Jewish Jesus as the product of what he calls a "dual monologue."

Similarly, Christians who in their eagerness to build bridges or repair the damage to relations caused by the holocaust, appeal to the "historical" Jesus, and speak of a Jesus fully explainable within Jewish categories, hardly recognizable as the Lord of the church, do no service to dialogue. Facing the differences candidly, Neusner concludes "'the

---

52. "Responses to anti-Judaism and anti-Semitism in contemporary Christian-Jewish relations," in D. Cohn-Sherbok, ed., *The Future of Jewish-Christian Dialogue* (Lewiston, NY: Mellen, 1999) 31–48, at 44.

53. *Telling Tales: Making Sense of Christian and Judaic Nonsense: The Urgency and Basis for Judeo-Christian Dialogue* (Louisville: Westminster John Knox, 1993). See his earlier *Jews and Christians: The Myth of a Common Tradition* (New York: Trinity, 1990).

historical Jesus' is simply inconsequential when it comes to a dialogue between Judaism and Christianity. Either Judaism addresses Jesus Christ God Incarnate (or equivalently critical formulations of Christian theology) or it fails to address Christianity at all."[54]

New Testament scholar David Catchpole articulates a similar perspective when he argues that Christians who participate in Jewish-Christian dialogue "must be more careful than they have sometimes been to work *to* and then *from* a clear definition of the essence of Christianity."[55] "This pattern of faith," he continues, "does not invest in the historical Jesus as such, nor in Jesus the Jew, nor in the Jesus who confined his mission to the Jewish people, nor in the Jesus who worked within the parameters of the Mosaic law and thus understood the 'boundary markers' of the people of God to be circumcision, food laws, and sabbath."[56]

Catchpole nevertheless does not dismiss the importance of the historical Jesus. He calls attention to the importance of historical elements within the Niceno-Constantinopolitan creed itself. One of the central elements in that creed is the crucifixion of Jesus, which already points to what remains a remarkable tension within the historical Jesus.

> Himself *a member of* the Jewish people, [Jesus] was in his mission *in conflict with* the Jewish people, and in the end he believed he was *dying for* the Jewish people. That essential identification with, and at the same time critical distance from, his people represents a tension in the mission of the historical Jesus

---

54. *Telling Tales*, 89. "On the Jewish side, by focusing upon the man Jesus—presenting him, for example, as a Reform rabbi or a marginal Jew or a Galilean pietist (Hasid) or in numerous other this-worldly Christologies—Jews have avoided stating forthrightly what in the Middle Ages, under different circumstances, they found the courage to state on pain of death: he was not and is not what the Christians say he was and is" (103).

55. "The role of the historical Jesus in Jewish-Christian dialogue," in Dan Cohn-Sherbok, ed., *The Future of Jewish-Christian Dialogue* (Lewiston, NY: Mellen, 1999) 183–216, at 211. "My suggestion is that the absolutely crucial and essential core of that position is to be found in post-historical-Jesus realities: the resurrection itself, the inclusive and corporate Christ who is the eschatological Adam and the embodiment of a new humanity; the worldwide community, drawing into itself persons of any and every ethnic background without distinction; the one baptism which makes legally binding and determinative the faith experience of the one God who is the God of the whole world, and whose sovereignty over that one world is effected through the lordship of the risen one."

56. "Role of the Historical Jesus," 211.

which, I submit, the Jewish-Christian dialogue at any and every later time must not relax.[57]

CONCLUDING THOUGHTS

It is clear that we have reason to be grateful for the significant achievements of the quest of the historical Jesus. We have been deeply enriched by an increased knowledge of Second Temple Judaism and the emphasis upon the Jewishness of Jesus. At the same time, however, we have had to criticize the quest at points and to deem its method as, in the last analysis, inadequate to the task. It remains to be seen whether the historical-critical method can be refined, as some are attempting to do, so as to make it a more effective tool in understanding the Jesus of history.

In light of the calls of Betz, Neusner and Catchpole for the necessity of Jewish-Christian dialogue to come to terms with the full Christology of the church, some might conclude that the quest of the historical Jesus is not merely impossible, but unnecessary too. This would be a grave mistake, however, since it would result in the heresy of docetism, wherein the humanity of Jesus becomes a mere illusion. The creeds, like the New Testament itself, affirm with equal vigor the humanity *and* the deity of Jesus. This fact alone warrants the robust study of Jesus as a man set fully in his own historical context.

It is clear that dialogue worthy of the name cannot succeed if it works with the severely reduced data base that the quest of the historical Jesus provides. But, as Catchpole and others have indicated, even within the criteria normally mandated of the historical Jesus there are surprising indicators that do not fit the Jewish context well—the unusual, the unexpected, the problematic. We cannot expect the historical Jesus to correspond exactly to the Christology of the church, impacted—but not created by!—the experience of the resurrection. The post-resurrection perspective of the church has its inevitable effect upon the gospel narratives. But if we cannot look for a one-to-one correspondence between the historical Jesus and the Jesus believed upon in the early church, we can at least establish a degree of continuity between the two.[58] And that

---

57. "Role of the Historical Jesus," 212. On the death of Jesus, see Peter Balla, "What Did Jesus Think about His Approaching Death?" in *Jesus, Mark and Q*, 239–58.

58. There will, of course, always be those who dissent, such as Geza Vermes who, having concluded that Jesus the Jew "does not reflect, but rather clashes with,

continuity is of the greatest importance, since without it the Christian faith becomes like a vaporous cloud, nothing more than the phantasm of deluded minds.

The quest of the historical Jesus has much importance for Jewish-Christian relations. It is not, however, a panacea. True dialogue will always have to go beyond the historical Jesus to consideration of the Jesus confessed by the faith of the church. But there are positive contributions of the quest that can and ought to lead not merely to tolerance, but also to mutual respect, good will, and, yes, even love for the other. After all, Christians are, because of Jesus, kinsfolk of the Jews—indeed, Gentiles come into the larger family through adoption—even if at the same time they remain members of different families.[59]

We end where we began, with the comment that Jesus Christ is paradoxically the one who divides and unites Jews and Christians. Jewish scholar Lewis John Eron makes the point in the following words:

> Jesus, the Jew, neither binds us nor separates us. He is historically interesting. Jesus, the Christ of the Church, is the one who brings us together and draws us apart. It is because of Christ that religious Jews can meet with religious Christians, realize the depth of our experiences, and learn that we are truly not the same but refreshingly different.[60]

---

traditional, dogmatic, Christocentric, Trinitarian Christianity" and that "historic Christianity is not the religion of Jesus the Jew, nor the religion taught by him," speaks of the serious questions "awaiting Christian answers": "Jesus the Jew: Christian and Jewish Reactions" in Ernst-Wolfgang Böckenförde and Edward Shils, eds., *Jews and Christians in a Pluralistic World* (New York: St. Martin's, 1991) 25–42, at 39.

59. As Keck points out, "that Jesus links Gentiles to Israel is as true today as it was in the first century": *Who is Jesus?*, 63.

60. "Jesus and Judaism," in Leonard Swidler et al., *Bursting the Bonds? A Jewish-Christian Dialogue on Jesus and Paul* (Maryknoll, NY: Orbis, 1990) 108.

4

Matthew: Apostate, Reformer, Revolutionary?

ONE OF THE MOST conspicuous of recent trends in NT scholarship is the new and widespread emphasis on the Jewishness of the NT, its writers and its contents. The quest for the historical Jesus, for example, has shed a great amount of fresh light on the specifically Jewish background of Jesus and the Gospels. In Pauline studies these days the full Jewishness of Paul and his theology has begun to emerge with new clarity, involving fresh conclusions that challenge traditional interpretations. Now, even for the Gospel of Matthew, the Jewishness of which has only seldom been doubted (notable exceptions arguing for a Gentile author or final redactor: K. W. Clark, P. Nepper-Christensen, W. Trilling, G. Strecker, J. Meier),[1] we encounter a new stress on its Jewishness. Indeed, the new claim goes so far as to conclude that Matthew's community is most accurately described not in the traditional way, as a Jewish form of Christianity, but rather as a Christian form of Judaism. That is, for these scholars—the most important are Andrew Overman,[2] the late Anthony

---

1. For a useful *Forschungsbericht*, see B. Repschinski, *The Controversy Stories in the Gospel of Matthew: Their Redaction, Form and Relevance for the Relationship between the Matthean Community and Formative Judaism*, FRLANT 189 (Göttingen: Vandenhoeck & Ruprecht, 2000) 13-61.

2. Andrew Overman, *Matthew's Gospel and Formative Judaism: The Social World of the Matthean Community* (Minneapolis: Fortress, 1990); *Church and Community in Crisis: The Gospel According to Matthew*, The New Testament in Context (Valley Forge, PA: Trinity International, 1996).

Saldarini,[3] and David Sim[4]—Matthew's community is not a group that has in any significant sense broken with Judaism, but rather one which in its own way continues in full loyalty to the synagogue.

It is this claim that I intend to address in the present paper. My thesis is that there is a radical newness in the Gospel of Matthew that continually moves beyond the bounds of Judaism and requires the conclusion that Matthew's community be described as a form of Christianity.

1. SOME PRELIMINARY COMMENTS

In assessing Matthew the question is not whether Matthew is Jewish *or* Christian. The truth is that Matthew is both Jewish *and* Christian. Nearly everyone is willing to admit this. Neither Overman, Saldarini, nor Sim, for example, deny the Christian aspects of the Gospel of Matthew. On the other hand, it does not seem to me that anyone can fairly deny that Matthew is exceptionally Jewish and is making a deliberate attempt to stress continuity with the old as much as possible. If it is true that in one sense there is no Christianity that is not Jewish, it is also the case that Matthew is as Jewish as, or more Jewish than, perhaps any other manifestation of Christianity that we find in the NT.

Given the truth on both sides, one may be excused for thinking that perhaps the issue involves merely looking at the same thing from different perspectives: a classic example of the glass that can be described as either half empty or half full, depending on one's inclination. Matthew's community is thus equally Jewish and Christian, and one may choose to focus on one or the other aspect. But in my opinion this is not the case, nor would such an egalitarian conclusion do justice to the perspective of Matthew. To my mind, Matthew decidedly reflects a Christianity rather than a Judaism.

---

3. Anthony Saldarini, *Matthew's Christian-Jewish Community* (Chicago: University of Chicago Press, 1994); "The Gospel of Matthew and Jewish-Christian Conflict," in *Social History of the Matthean Community: Cross-Disciplinary Approaches*, ed. D. L. Balch (Minneapolis: Fortress, 1991) 38–61; "Boundaries and Polemics in the Gospel of Matthew," *Biblical Interpretation* 3 (1995) 239–65.

4. David Sim, *The Gospel of Matthew and Christian Judaism: The History and Social Setting of the Matthean Community* (Edinburgh: T. & T. Clark, 1998); "Christianity and Ethnicity in the Gospel of Matthew," in *Ethnicity and the Bible*, ed. M. G. Brett, Biblical Interpretation Series 19 (Leiden: Brill, 1996) 171–95; "The Gospel of Matthew and the Gentiles," *JSNT* 57 (1995) 19–48.

One of the reasons for confusion and disagreement is the matter of definitions. What do we mean by 'Judaism' or 'Jewish' and what do we mean by 'Christianity' or 'Christian'? On the one side, first-century Judaism is now known to have been very diverse indeed. This is admitted by all. Judaism was able to encompass many different perspectives, ranging from the Qumran community and the Pharisees to the Zealots and the Sadducees—even perhaps to Christianity, according to the view argued against here.[5] At the same time, however, even if we have to speak of Judaisms in the plural, there remain some common elements shared by any group that would claim to be a Judaism.[6] There remains, in short, a "common Judaism," as E. P. Sanders puts it,[7] or a "complex Judaism," in M. Hengel's terms.[8] J. D. G. Dunn mentions four such common elements: monotheism, election, Torah, and temple.[9] Jacob Neusner indicates three general aspects: a worldview, a way of life, and a social group,[10] and it would not be difficult to relate these to Dunn's specifics. Maurice Casey identifies eight aspects of Second Temple Judaism: ethnicity, scripture, monotheism, circumcision, sabbath observance, dietary laws, purity laws, and major festivals.[11] If there is a dominant marker among these

---

5. The view that first-century Christianity is to be regarded as a type of Judaism is set forth by G. Boccaccini, *Middle Judaism: Jewish Thought, 300 BCE to 200 CE* (Minneapolis: Fortress, 1991). Especially interesting in connection with our topic are the reservations expressed by J. H. Charlesworth in the Foreword to the book, xviii.

6. On this point N. J. McEleney was right, regardless of the objections raised by D. E. Aune. McEleney, "Orthodoxy in Judaism of the First Christian Century," *JSJ* 4 (1973) 19-42; D. E. Aune, "Orthodoxy in First Century Judaism? A Response to N. J. McEleney," *JSJ* 7 (1976) 1-10; see McEleney's rejoinder: "Orthodoxy in Judaism of the First Christian Century," *JSJ* 9 (1978) 83-8; cf. L. L. Grabbe, "Orthodoxy in First Century Judaism: What Were the Issues?" *JSJ* 8 (1977) 149-53.

7. E. P. Sanders, *Judaism: Practice and Belief, 63 BCE-66 CE* (London: SCM, 1994).

8. M. Hengel and R. Deines, "E. P. Sanders' 'Common Judaism': Jesus and the Pharisees: Review Article of *Jewish Law from Jesus to Mishnah* and *Judaism: Practice and Belief* by E. P. Sanders," *JTS* 46 (1995) 60-67.

9. See J. D. G. Dunn, *The Partings of the Ways Between Christianity and Judaism and their Significance for the Character of Christianity* (London: SCM, 1991).

10. Jacob Neusner, "What Is a 'Judaism'?," in *Judaism in Late Antiquity*, ed. A. J. Avery-Peck et al. (Leiden: Brill, 2001) 3-21. In another place, Neusner refers to three elements of "the common religion in pre-70 Israel: the Hebrew scriptures, the temple, and the 'accepted practices of the ordinary folk" ("The Formation of Rabbinic Judaism: Yavneh (Jamnia) from AD 70 to 100," in *ANRW* II.19.2, 21). See B. D. Chilton and J. Neusner *Judaism in the New Testament: Practices and Beliefs* (New York: Routledge, 1995), where it is concluded that any group that values scripture and Torah is to be regarded as a Judaism (4-8).

11. Maurice Casey, *From Jewish Prophet to Gentile God* (Cambridge: James Clarke,

various elements, it would have to be Torah, which itself includes most of the other items.

As for 'Christianity', there are those who would say that the word should not be used to describe anything prior to the second century. Only then, it is argued, in such writers as Ignatius and Barnabas, do we have a sufficiently unified and independent identity over against Judaism to warrant its use. Luke, of course, writing perhaps in the 80s, gives us the first occurrence of the word, noting that it was in Antioch (in the 40s) that 'the disciples were for the first time called Christians' (Acts 11:26). Although the use of the name indicates a contrast to Judaism, it says little concerning the extent of the differences with Judaism. Already by the 80s, however, Paul was able to speak of "Judaism" as distinct from his Christian faith (Gal 1:14) and to differentiate between Jews, Greeks and the church of God (1 Cor 10:32). If by Christianity we mean the Great Church, self-conscious of its identity and place in the history of salvation, we may have to wait until at least late in the first century to use the word. But if we have in mind communities who believed in the basic constellation of ideas such as is found, for example, in Paul's letters, then we need wait no longer than the middle of the first century, if that long.

Further deserving our attention, of course, are the expressions "Jewish Christianity" and "Christian Judaism." It is difficult to find an actual definition of Christian Judaism in Overman, Saldarini, or Sim. For them it points to Jews who have come to faith in Jesus as Messiah and who continue in their living as faithful Jews, participating in the synagogue and the sacrificial cult of the temple, and marked above all by faith obedience to the Torah.[12] To frame a parallel definition of Jewish Christianity[13] that draws out the differences, perhaps we could say the following: Jewish Christianity refers to Jews who have come to faith in Jesus as the divine

---

1991) 12.

12. Phillip Segal had earlier spoken of "Christian Judaism" in similar terms. *The Emergence of Contemporary Judaism*, vol. 1, pt 1: "From the Origins to the Separation of Christianity" (Pittsburgh: Pickwick, 1980) 431-33.

13. On this much discussed subject, see R. A. Kraft, "In Search of 'Jewish Christianity' and Its Theology: Problems of Definition and Methodology," *RSR* 60 (1972) 81-92; A. F. J. Klijn, "The Study of Jewish Christianity," *NTS* 20 (1973/74) 419-31; B. J. Malina, "Jewish Christianity or Christian Judaism: Toward a Hypothetical Definition," *JSJ* 7 (1976) 46-57; R. Murray, "Jews, Hebrews and Christians: Some Needed Distinctions," *NovT* 24 (1982) 194-208; J. E. Taylor, 'The Phenomenon of Early Jewish-Christianity: Reality or Scholarly Invention?," *VigChr* 44 (1990) 313-34; J. Carleton Paget, "Jewish Christianity," in *The Cambridge History of Judaism*, vol. 3, ed. W. Horbury et al. (Cambridge: Cambridge University Press, 1999) 731-75.

kyrios, who affirm their faith as the fulfillment of the scriptures, whose experience involves a degree of newness that transcends the synagogue and temple, and who believe that by following the teaching of Jesus, their Messiah-Teacher, they fulfill the righteousness of the Torah.

On the latter question, we may recall Raymond Brown's analysis of four types of Jewish Christianity (which he more exactly described as "Jewish Christians and their Gentile converts"). He ranked these according to the extent of their commitment to the Mosaic Law. Thus, group 1 held to its "full observance, including circumcision"; group 2 did not require circumcision of Gentiles but only the keeping of "some religious observances"; group 3 also did not require circumcision, nor the observance of the dietary law; and group 4 "saw no abiding significance in Jewish cult and feasts."[14] David Sim goes so far as to put the Matthean community in group 1, as equivalent to the Judaizers opposed by Paul, despite the fact that there is no mention of circumcision in Matthew, even where one might expect it, on this hypothesis, in the commission to preach the gospel to the Gentiles at the end of the Gospel. But is Matthew's community really a group such as described in Acts as "the party of the circumcision" (11:2), or "the party of the Pharisees" (15:5)? Brown is probably right in implying that Matthew would fit into category 2. But this classification is not really adequate to handle the unique perspective of Matthew. Although Matthew's community very probably continued in a distinctly Jewish mode of existence, *it treasured a perspective that was dramatically new compared to anything previously known in Judaism.*[15]

The problems we are concerned with here are, of course, a subset of the larger question of the parting of the ways between Judaism and Christianity. Although we cannot go into this challenging problem here, I must at least make the following comments. It seems clear that the operative phrase for this subject must be *gradual transition*. The parting of the ways between Judaism and Christianity involved a transition that took place gradually and with varying rapidity in different places. It is

---

14. R. E. Brown and J. P. Meier, *Antioch and Rome* (New York: Paulist, 1983) 2-8. For a similar analysis, see S. G. Wilson, *Related Strangers: Jews and Christians, 70-170 C.E.* (Minneapolis: Fortress, 1995) 148-59.

15. This is underappreciated by those who speak of Matthew's community as a sect within Judaism. Saldarini, for example, characterizes Matthean Christianity as "the rearrangement of the Jewish symbolic world according to the teachings of Jesus." "Reading Matthew without Anti-Semitism," in *The Gospel of Matthew in Current Study*, ed. David E. Aune (Grand Rapids: Eerdmans, 2001) 166-84, here 178. Such a description hardly does justice to the content of the Gospel.

impossible to give it a specific date. At the beginning, the disciples of the early Jerusalem church could not yet realize the full significance of the events that had so recently happened. They could hardly have yet anticipated the consequences that were to follow or that they would necessarily take on an identity that would separate them so sharply from the Judaism of the synagogue. But with the passing of perhaps less time than many scholars suppose, the differences became increasingly apparent and unavoidable. By the time Matthew was written, regardless of what date one chooses, things would have been quite different than in those first years in the Jerusalem church.

A classic and much disputed question in Matthean studies is whether or not Matthew's community is to be understood as having broken with the synagogue or not. Although this is not exactly the question being asked in this paper, it is of course directly related to it. If Matthew's community was a Christian Judaism, then presumably it had *not* broken with the synagogue; if it was a Jewish Christianity, then it *may*, although not necessarily, have broken with the synagogue. My own conviction is that Matthew's community *had* broken with the synagogue,[16] but that it remained in proximity to the synagogue and inescapably in an ongoing situation of debate and controversy with it. This is an issue that can be decided only on the basis of the content of the Gospel itself. Given the widely recognized uncertainties about the work of the rabbis at Yavneh and the addition of the *Birkath Ha-Minim* (as the twelfth) to the Eighteen Benedictions,[17] this should no longer be appealed to either in the question of the dating of the Gospel or concerning the matter of the separation

---

16. Thus too, e.g.: E. Schweizer, D. R. A. Hare, S. H. Brooks, R. Walker, J. D. Kingsbury, B. Przybylski, J. T. Sanders, P. Luomanen, U. Luz, G. N. Stanton; against R. Hummel, P. Richardson, B. Repschinski, and W. D. Davies and D. C. Allison, Jr. More than one scholar has changed his mind on the question. Thus notably G. Bornkamm, who initially argued against the break, was later inclined to see a break ("The Authority to 'Bind' and 'Loose' in the Church in Matthew's Gospel," in *Jesus and Man's Hope*, ed. D. G. Miller [Pittsburgh: Pittsburgh Theological Seminary, 1970] 1.37–50). More recently, H. Frankemölle, who had earlier argued *for* a break, now concludes *against* a break (*Jüdische Wurzeln christlicher Theologie: Studien zum biblischen Kontext neutestamentlicher Texte*, BBB 116 (Bodenheim: Philo, 1998] 343). S. von Dobbeler argues that Matthew's community is just on the verge of departing from Judaism. "Auf der Grenze: Ethos und Identität der matthäischen Gemeinde nach Mt 15, 1–20," *BZ* 45 (2001) 55–78.

17. See P. Schäfer, "Die sogennante Synode von Jabne: Zur Trennung von Juden u. Christen im ersten/zweiten Jh. n. Chr.," *Judaica* 31 (1975) 54–64, 116–24; G. Stemberger, "Die sogenannte 'Synode von Jabne' und das frühe Christentum," *Kairos* 19 (1977) 14–21.

of the church from the synagogue.[18] As we have already indicated, there was no specific point when either the church was put out of the synagogue or when Jewish persecution of Christians began. Rather, we are on more solid ground to think of a long process of separation and growing hostility taking place from almost the beginning, again varying in different places and times, with the events of AD 70 surely being of key importance.

Another preliminary question to be considered is whether we are here concerned with Matthew's and Matthew's community's view of its identity, with how contemporary Jews may have perceived it, or how *we* perceive that identity from our perspective.[19] It seems quite probable that Matthew's community thought of *itself* as Judaism—not as *a* Judaism, but as the *true* Judaism that brought the fulfillment of the promises to Israel.[20] It also seems probable that the Jews regarded Matthew's community as apostate. At the same time, paradoxically, it may be that from our retrospective perspective we may be in a better position to understand Matthew's identity vis-a-vis Judaism, as long as we are careful to think historically and not to read our own understandings into the first century.[21]

Much recent study of Matthew has employed sociological insights to help understand Matthew's community.[22] We are becoming familiar with the language of sects and sectarianism, social conflict, dissidence,

---

18. There seems to be no relation between the Gospel of Matthew and Yavneh, despite the claims of Davies and Allison. Luz writes: "Thus it has become clear that the Gospel of Matthew is not a Christian answer to 'Jamnia.' Rather it is a Christian answer to Israel's no to Jesus or the attempt to cope with this no in a fundamental definition of a position," *Matthew 1-7: A Commentary*, Continental Commentaries (Minneapolis: Augsburg, 1989) 88.

19. See the cautionary remarks of R. A. Kraft, "The Multiform Jewish Heritage of Early Christianity," in *Christianity, Judaism, and Other Greco-Roman Cults*, ed. J. Neusner (Leiden: Brill, 1975) 3.174-99; cf. Judith Lieu, "'The Parting of the Ways': Theological Construct or Historical Reality?," *JSNT* 56 (1994) 101-19.

20. So too, S. Sandmel: "Christianity in Matthew's View Is the Authentic Judaism." *Anti Semitism in the New Testament?* (Philadelphia: Fortress, 1978) 70.

21. P. Luomanen, rightly: "Matthew's community was not yet in a position to ponder its 'Christian' essence apart from its relation to Judaism." *Entering the Kingdom of Heaven: A Study on the Structure or Matthew's View of Salvation*, WUNT 2/101 (Tübingen: Mohr Siebeck, 1998) 266. Matthew's community thought of its faith, for all its newness, as the completion of Judaism, not an alternative to it.

22. R. K. McIver concludes that sociology has become the "dominant methodology used in research into the Matthean community since 1990." "Twentieth Century Approaches to the Matthean Community," *AUSS* 37 (1999) 23-28 (at 37).

identity markers, boundaries, group cohesion, legitimizing and delegitimizing, fictive kinship, and so forth. Without question these approaches have helped us to understand the dynamics that must have come into play as Matthew's community sorted out its identity over against the synagogue. It is not difficult to recognize in Matthew, for example, the processes of delegitimizing and legitimizing going on with considerable intensity.[23]

In a recent analysis of the 'sociology of sectarianism', Petri Luomanen appeals to the work of Stark and Bainbridge[24] in concluding that it is more appropriate to designate Matthew's community as a 'cult' than as a 'sect'.[25] In this framework, the designation 'cult' emphasizes not merely schism from the parent body, but the importance of the new ideas that cause the formation of a new group. Luomanen, rightly in my opinion, finds 'so much new to [the Jesus cult] that it can be regarded as a religious innovation', and thus Matthew is to be regarded as much more a cult than a sect.[26]

Sociological studies are helpful, but in the end nothing can replace the attempt to understand the text and the information it provides. And this inevitably at last brings us to theological matters.[27]

---

23. S. Freyne refers to the "rhetoric of vituperation." "Vilifying the Other and Defining the Self: Matthew's and John's Anti-Jewish Polemic in Focus," in *To See Ourselves as Others See Us: Christians, Jews, "Others" in Late Antiquity*, ed. J. Neusner and E. S. Frerichs (Chico, CA: Scholars, 1985) 129. There can be little doubt that the intensity of Matthew's language is caused by his need to defend his Christianity against non-Christian Judaism. Thus, too, Stanton: "Matthew's anti-Jewish polemic should be seen as part of the self-definition of the Christian minority which is acutely aware of the rejection and hostility of its 'mother', Judaism." *A Gospel for a New People: Studies in Matthew* (Edinburgh: T. & T. Clark, 1992) 157.

24. R. Stark and W. S. Bainbridge, *A Theory of Religion*, Toronto Studies in Religion 2 (New York: Lang, 1987).

25. Petri Luomanen, "The 'Sociology of Sectarianism' in Matthew: Modeling the Genesis of Early Jewish and Christian Communities," in *Fair Play: Diversity and Conflicts in Early Christianity: Essays in Honour of Heikki Räisänen*, ed. I. Dunderberg (Leiden: Brill, 2002) 107-30. I am indebted to Professor Graham Stanton for this reference.

26. Luomanen, "The 'Sociology of Sectarianism' in Matthew." 129. Cf. R. Scroggs's description of a sect as a group that "rejects the view of reality taken for granted by the establishment," and that "intends to create a reality, in so far as is possible, totally different from that of establishment society." "The Earliest Christian Communities as Sectarian Movement," in *Christianity, Judaism, and Other Greco-Roman Cults*, ed. J. Neusner (Leiden: Brill, 1975) 2:1-23.

27. In a time when some call for a turning away from theological issues, it is refreshing to read these words from the well-known Matthean scholar Donald Senior:

2. OLD AND NEW IN MATTHEW

As if knowing that his readers would need some help on the question, Matthew has some direct and informative things to say about the vexing question of old and new. In a quite remarkable passage unique to Matthew, at the end of the parable discourse, he says "every scribe who has been trained for the kingdom of heaven is like a householder who brings out of the treasure box new things and old things" (13:52). His affirmation of both new and old indicates that there is some truth on both sides of the argument. There is *both* continuity *and* discontinuity with the old. Matthew is both Jewish *and* Christian, and this would have constituted no problem for him or his community. To be noted, however, is that unexpectedly the *kaina* are mentioned first, and thus may be presumed to have a degree of priority over the *palaia*. At least it is the *kaina*—those things that have to do with the dawning of the kingdom of God— that get the reader's attention, since we would normally expect the scribes to occupy themselves with the *palaia*—things such as the Torah, the prophets, the promises and hope of Israel. Matthew's Gospel is above all an announcement of the *kaina*. Just here we have the puzzle of Matthew: that such newness is so boldly proclaimed precisely in a document that attempts to establish and honor continuity with the old.

In a second well-known passage, Matthew illustrates the impossibility of simply combining the new with the old. The new in fact is simply not compatible with the old, at least not unless significant necessary adjustments are made. You cannot put a new patch of cloth upon an old garment without negative consequences, Jesus says, nor can you put new wine into old wine skins without losing both (9:16–17; Mark 2:21–2; Luke 5:36–9). In this triple tradition passage, Matthew alone makes note of the fact that when new wine is put into new skins, *both* the wine *and* the skins are preserved. The new skins that are preserved symbolize a new mode of righteousness which from Matthew's perspective is consistent with the new things that have come and which more adequately reflects the righteousness of the Torah. In this novel way both the gospel and the law are preserved. The new wine of the gospel is analogous to, and takes up, the righteousness of Torah, albeit in a new and revolutionary way.

"Attempting to decipher Matthew's literary and rhetorical strategies without fully engaging the Gospel's theological convictions will lead interpreters in the wrong direction." "Directions in Matthean Studies," in *The Gospel of Matthew in Current Study*, ed. David E. Aune (Grand Rapids: Eerdmans, 2001) 5–21 (at 17).

Matthew's Christianity, then, is not simply the addition of something new to Judaism, leaving Judaism essentially intact. On the contrary, the new has dramatic consequences that cannot be avoided.

It is obvious that for Matthew's Jewish Christians this is necessarily an issue of very great importance. The Gospel is filled with new things that are, mildly put, problematic for Judaism, and a Jew reading the Gospel for the first time would have been repeatedly amazed, not to say offended, by what he encountered:[28] for example, the eschatological announcement that the Messiah and the kingdom had come,[29] bringing fulfillment albeit short of the judgment of the wicked that would occur at the consummation of the age; that God's Messiah was somehow a manifestation of God and uniquely so; that God's Messiah had to die the death of a criminal,[30] as one cursed by God thereby making possible the forgiveness of sins;[31] that obedience to God now centered upon Jesus rather than upon the law; that participation in the new kingdom of God would involve suffering; that a new community, the *ekklēsia*,[32] called out of Israel, was now the center of God's salvific activity; and that the new community of the kingdom was to include Gentiles on an equal basis with Jewish Christians.[33] In what follows, we will focus on one crucial area, that of law and Christology.

---

28. For an elaboration of the following, see D. A. Hagner, "New Things from the Scribe's Treasure Box (Mt 13:52)," *ExpT 109* (1998) 329-34.

29. Cf. Davies and Allison: "No interpretation which does not recognize the messianic-eschatological character of Jesus and the movement which he inaugurated can do justice to our Gospel." *A Critical and Exegetical Commentary on the Gospel according to Saint Matthew*, ICC (Edinburgh: T. & T. Clark, 1988-97) 3.707.

30. Craig Evans finds the root causes of the separation of Christianity from Judaism in the shameful death of Jesus and the failure of the promised kingdom to materialize. "Root Causes of the Jewish-Christian Rift from Jesus to Justin," in *Christian-Jewish Relations through the Centuries*, ed. S. E. Porter and B. W. R. Pearson (Sheffield: Sheffield Academic, 2000) 20-35.

31. "The Eucharist and Jesus' blood have replaced the Temple sacrifices." Luomanen, *Entering the Kingdom of Heaven*, 283.

32. See G. N. Stanton, "Revisiting Matthew's Communities," in *SBL 1994 Seminar Papers* (Atlanta: Scholars, 1994) 9-23, esp. 16-18.

33. On the last point, see esp. B. Holmberg, "Jewish *versus* Christian Identity in the Early Church," *RB* 105 (1998) 397-425. "The original idea about what God's 'messianic' mission among the Jews would look like had to be expanded, almost exploded, by the fact forced upon the Jewish-Christian church that the Gentiles belonged in the church as well" (421).

3. TORAH AND CHRISTOLOGY

A. The centerpiece of the case made by Overman, Saldarini, and Sim that Matthew's community should be regarded as a sect of Judaism is the striking statement of 5:17-19:

> Do not think that I have come to abolish the law or the prophets; I have come not to abolish but to fulfill. For truly I tell you, until heaven and earth pass away, not one letter, not one stroke of a letter, will pass away from the law until all is accomplished. Therefore, whoever breaks one of the least of these commandments, and teaches others to do the same, will be called the least in the kingdom of heaven; but whoever does them and teaches them will be called great in the kingdom of heaven.

According to Overman, during the first century "the law became perhaps *the* central means by which . . . sectarian communities attempted to establish the truth of their claims and discredit the claims and position of their opponents."[34] To Overman and others, Matt 5:17-20 qualifies Matthew's community to be considered as a sect within Judaism. Torah, after all, is at the very heart of Judaism, and if Matthew upholds the Torah this indicates that his community has not left the fold.

Now it can hardly be regarded as surprising that Jewish Christians of Matthew's community would hold the law in high regard. One of the distinctive ways Matthew presents Jesus is as the definitive interpreter of the law. The meaning of *plērōsai* in 5:17 is "to bring to its intended meaning." Jesus in effect becomes the rabbi of the Jewish Christians and provides them with the correct meaning of Torah. The Sermon on the Mount can be regarded as an exposition of the righteousness of the law. Jesus is the teacher of the law *par excellence*: "you are not to be called rabbi, for you have one teacher (*didaskalos*) . . . neither be called masters, for you have one master (*kathēgētēs*), the Christ" (23:8-10).[35] Jesus alone brings the correct, authoritative understanding of Torah, and he can do so because he is the promised Messiah. Law is an important issue in the Gospel, without question.

---

34. Overman, *Matthew's Gospel and Formative Judaism*, 30. Cf. Saldarini, *Matthew's Christian Jewish Community*, 124.

35. On this see S. Byrskog, *Jesus the Only Teacher: Didactic Authority and Transmission in Ancient Israel, Ancient Judaism and the Matthean Community*, ConBNT 24 (Stockholm: Almqvist & Wiksell, 1994).

Nevertheless, Sim overstates the matter, in my opinion, when he writes: "The Mosaic law occupies a central place in the Gospel of Matthew."[36] On the contrary, it is Jesus the Messiah, not the law, that is at the center of Matthew. This is clear throughout the Gospel. The unparalleled authority of Jesus is apparent wherever the meaning of the law is in question. The reaction of those who heard Jesus is revealing: "the crowds were astonished at his teaching, for he taught them as one who had authority, and not as their scribes" (7:28; cf. 13:54; 22:33).

The interpretation of the law by Jesus according to Matthew has a new and radical character about it that lifts it to a different level compared with contemporary teachers of the law. Jesus has an incomparable authority, an authority that transcends that of Torah. In the famous antitheses of 5:21-48, as in Jesus' teaching concerning the sabbath or divorce, Jesus is not *disloyal* to the law of Moses. Rather, it is much more a matter of an incomparable, authoritative interpretation of the law that relativizes the law in the presence of the Messiah, who alone can bring it to its definitive interpretation.

Everyone will admit that Torah is one of the pillars of Judaism and that faithful obedience to the commands of Torah is of central importance to Jewish identity. Similarly it is clear that for Matthew obedience to the law remains important. What is of crucial significance, however, is that it is not the law in itself that is Matthew's concern, but only the law *as mediated through the teaching of Jesus*. The focus constantly shifts to Jesus. Where one might have expected a reference to Torah, Jesus says "Where two or three are gathered in my name, there am I in the midst of them" (18:20).[37] It is finally the words of Jesus, not Torah, that are of ultimate authority: "Heaven and earth will pass away, but my words will not pass away" (24:35). At the end of the Gospel Jesus calls his disciples to teach new disciples "to observe all that I have commanded you" (28:20). They are finally called to obey not Torah, but Jesus.[38]

---

36. Sim, *The Gospel of Matthew and Christian Judaism*, 123. The section heading is "The Centrality of the Law."

37. In the Mishnah (Abot 3:2) a similar, but also very different, statement occurs: "If two sit together and words of the Law [are spoken] between them, the Divine Presence [=the Shekinah] rests between them."

38. Klyne Snodgrass attempts to avoid an either/or by arguing that Matthew puts his emphasis on both Christ *and* Torah. "Matthew and the Law," in *Treasures New and Old: Contributions to Matthean Studies*, ed. D. R. Bauer and M. A. Powell (Atlanta: Scholars, 1996) 99-127, here 126. In my opinion, it is fairer to Matthew's perspective to say that Christ is the center of Matthew, and that Torah is *in effect* preserved only

There is thus an important shift in Matthew that explains the newness of its perspective on the law. To be sure, the law remains significant for these Jewish Christians, but *only as it is taken up in the teaching of Jesus*. It is hardly the case, however, that Matthew's words in 5.17–20 necessitate the conclusion that his community is to be regarded as a sect of Judaism.[39]

B. It is well known that we encounter in Matthew one of the highest christologies of the NT.[40] We can deal with it here only very briefly. Jesus is the Jewish Messiah, but not merely a human Messiah. He is the Son of God—not, however, like others who have been called "son of God." For Matthew Jesus is "Emmanuel" (1:23), "God with us"—now not only in the sense of one who represents God, but directly, as one who *is* God with us.[41] Matthew also presents Jesus as the divine Son of Man who at the end of the age will act as judge of the nations (25:31–2; cf. 16:27–8). In keeping with this exalted view of Jesus are the remarkable words of 11:27, "All things have been delivered to me by my Father; and no one knows the Son except the Father, and no one knows the Father except the Son and any one to whom the Son chooses to reveal him"; we may compare with this the words of the risen Jesus at the end of the Gospel: "All authority in heaven and on earth has been given to me" (28:18). It is thus in "the name of the Father and of the Son and of the Holy Spirit" that the disciples are to baptize their converts (28:19). This Jesus furthermore promises to be with them "always, to the close of the age" (28:20).

Nothing less than astonishing is the central, mediatorial position Jesus assigns himself in the relationship between humanity and God: "So everyone who acknowledges me before others, I will acknowledge before my Father who is in heaven; but whoever denies me before others, I also will deny before my Father who is in heaven" (10:32). In short, Jesus is an

---

through Christ's teaching.

39. So too, in an insightful article, Douglas R. A. Hare: Those few verses that seem to require strict conformity with the ritual requirements of the Torah can be understood in a very different way; they do not validate the hypothesis [that Matthew was written for a Law-observant Jewish sect]. "How Jewish Is the Gospel of Matthew?," *CBQ* 62 (2000) 264–77, here 277. Hare concludes that "for Matthean Christians Jesus has replaced Torah as the key to a right relationship with the God of Israel" (277).

40. See Birger Gerhardsson, "The Christology of Matthew," in *Who Do You Say that I Am? Essays on Christology*, ed. M. A. Powell and D. R. Bauer (Louisville: Westminster John Knox, 1999) 14–32; C. Tuckett, *Christology and the New Testament: Jesus and His Earliest Followers* (Louisville: Westminster John Knox, 2001) 119–32.

41. See David Kupp, *Matthew's Emmanuel: Divine Presence and God's People in the First Gospel*, SNTSMS 90 (Cambridge: Cambridge University Press, 1996).

exalted figure in Matthew far beyond any others who have been sent from God in the history of Israel—there is something "greater than Solomon" here (12:42), indeed, something even "greater than the Temple" (12:6).[42]

In Matthew, then, *Jesus Christ is at the very center of the story*. All revolves around him.[43] Saldarini has to admit as much: "Matthew hopes to unite all within a Jesus-centered Israel."[44] So, too, Overman refers to Matthew's community as standing "within Jesus-centered Judaism."[45] At least from a later perspective these statements sound oxymoronic. Saldarini admits the shift in Matthew: "As a consequence of this focus on Jesus as central authority and symbol, Torah becomes subordinate to both Jesus and his interpretation of its provisions, as articulated in a unique way by Matthew."[46] Such a conclusion hardly seems congruent with Saldarini's hypothesis.

What above all defines first-century Israel, and later Israel too, is that it is Torah-centered. Can there be a Jesus-centered Israel that has not departed from the very essence of Judaism? In Matthew Christ has taken the place of Torah. Where this has happened, one may wonder how Matthew's community can fairly be described as a sect within Judaism, despite that community's own distinctive way of loyalty to the Torah. Robert Gundry makes the point effectively in a response to Saldarini (and Alan Segal): "This high Christology of Matthew and its fundamental difference from anything known to Judaism, including the

---

42. In light of all of this, Saldarini's comment is very misleading: "Though Christology quickly became a problem for Jewish believers-in-Jesus, when Matthew wrote, there was no articulated and theologically sophisticated set of claims for Jesus that could be called a Christology, with all the Trinitarian overtones that term implies." *Matthew's Christian Jewish Community*, 286 n. 7. Granted we are not at Nicea or Chalcedon, but Matthew does articulate a very high Christology and even with an implied Trinity at the end of his Gospel.

43. Davies-Allison: "The distinctiveness of Matthew's thinking over against that of his non-Christian Jewish contemporaries was the acceptance of Jesus as the centre of his religion: it was around him as a person that his theological thinking revolved. The fact is crucial." *Commentary on Saint Matthew*, 3.709. So too W. Stegner: "Actually the whole center of gravity seems to have shifted from Law to Jesus." "Breaking Away: The Conflict with Formative Judaism," *BibRes* 40 (1995) 7–36, here 27. Cf. K. Pantle-Schieber, "Anmerkungen zur Auseinandersetzung von ekklesia und Judentum in Matthäusevangelium," *ZNW* 80 (1989) 145–62.

44. Saldarini, *Matthew's Christian-Jewish Community*, 202.

45. Overman, *Church and Community in Crisis*, 20.

46. Saldarini, "The Gospel of Matthew and Jewish-Christian Conflict," in *Social History of the Matthean Community: Cross-Disciplinary Approaches*, ed. D. L. Balch (Minneapolis: Fortress, 1991) 50.

two powers doctrine, is almost bound to have fixed a great gulf between Matthew's community and Judaism."[47]

Despite the statement in 5:17ff., the status of Torah in Matthew is highly problematic for Judaism. There are, of course, several other aspects of Matthew that are highly problematic for the conclusion that Matthew's community was a sect within Judaism. We can only mention them here. The high Christology itself constitutes a problem noticed by many.[48] But other elements vital to Judaism are also seriously affected by the message of Matthew, such as the election of Israel, ethnicity, the land, and the temple.[49] The radical stance of the Gospel on these and other issues strengthens our conclusion that Matthew's community is more a Christianity than a Judaism.

4. ANTI-SEMITISM?

Unfortunately, one occasionally gets the impression that to conclude that Matthew's community was a form of Christianity rather than a sect within Judaism is somehow anti-Semitic. The fear of anti-Semitism, indeed, has caused an increasing number of scholars to ignore or explain away the strong marks of discontinuity with Judaism in Matthew. The abhorrence of anti-Semitism, admirable in itself, has thus caused scholars to

---

47. Robert Gundry, "A Responsive Evaluation of the Social History of the Matthean Community in Roman Syria," in *Social History of the Matthean Community*, 64. David Kupp, too, in his study of Matthew's Christology, concludes that Christology is a dividing point: "It is probably not excessive to claim . . . that this christological development functioned as a clear parameter between Matthew's communities and his Jewish counterparts" (*Matthew's Immanuel*, 221). Luz concludes: 'Der Konflikt war unausweichlich, denn für Matthäus und seine Gemeinde ist die Autorität des Menschensohns Jesus so überragend und seine Geschichte in Israel derart grundlegend, daß nur die Gestalt und die Botschaft Jesu die Grundlage Israels sein können.' *Das Evangelium nach Matthäus*, EKK (Neukirchen-Vluyn: Neukirchener, 2002) 1/4.467.

48. For further helpful treatment of the topic, focusing on Matthew's answer to Jewish claims that Jesus was an imposter or deceiver in league with the prince of demons, see Stanton's chapter, "Christology and the Parting of the Ways," in *A Gospel for a New People: Studies in Matthew* (Edinburgh: T. & T. Clark, 1992) 169–91.

49. On these points see the very helpful discussion provided by John K. Riches in *Conflicting Mythologies: Identity Formation in the Gospels of Mark and Matthew* (Edinburgh: T. & T. Clark, 2000). Riches offers insightful critique of Saldarini, Overman, and Sim. On the issue of temple, see esp. R. Bauckham, "The Parting of the Ways: What Happened and Why?," *StudTheol* 47 (1993) 135–51.

change their minds on the interpretation of Matthew and continues to affect the understanding of many texts.⁵⁰

Some scholars, to be sure, have concluded that Matthew's Gospel is itself anti-Semitic, not just because of its well-known anti-Jewish polemic, but particularly because of specific infamous statements. Only in Matthew's passion narrative do we read that "the people said: 'His blood be upon us and upon our children'" (27:25). To take another prime example, Matthew's statement at the end of the parable of the vineyard tenants that "the kingdom will be taken away from you and given to a nation producing its fruits in their seasons" (21:43) sounds terribly like supersessionism. So, too, Matthew indicates that Gentiles will enjoy the kingdom of God with the patriarchs while "the sons of the kingdom will be cast into the outer darkness" (8:11); and Jesus makes this statement following his lament over Jerusalem: "Behold, your house is left to you desolate" (23:38). For Matthew, the church of Jesus (*mou ekklēsia*) takes the place of the synagogue (*synagōgai autōn*). Many scholars, whether rightly or wrongly, regard this as supersessionism, and supersessionism is widely regarded as one of the wellsprings of anti-Semitism.

A distinction between anti-Semitism and anti-Judaism can be useful, the latter referring to theological disagreement, but without the racial hatred of the former.⁵¹ But for some the distinction is not significant since anti-Judaism has often led to anti-Semitism. The unfortunate result is that any disagreement with Judaism, whether in the early church, or today, is castigated as anti-Semitic. Clearly Matthew cannot fairly be called anti-Semitic, however, if only because Matthew and his community were Jewish. The key to understanding Matthew on this matter is that we are dealing with an internal dispute.⁵² In Gentile hands, by contrast, the Gospel of Matthew can, and often has, become anti-Semitic.

---

50. It is moving, for example, to see how D. Georgi's argument on our subject is influenced by his deep concern about anti-Semitism. "The Early Church: Internal Jewish Migration or New Religion?," *HTR* 88 (1995) 35-68. In the same way, one is impressed by the similar motivation that has caused H. Frankemölle to change his views (see n. 16) and to develop new hermeneutical sensitivities. "Antijudaismus im Matthäusevangelium?', in *"Nun steht aber diese Sache im Evangelium...": zur Frage nach den Anfängen des christlichen Antijudaismus*, ed. R. Kampling (Paderborn: Schoningh, 1999) 73-106.

51. See C. A. Evans and D. A. Hagner, eds., *Anti-Semitism and Early Christianity: Issues of Faith and Polemic* (Minneapolis: Fortress, 1993).

52. This has been pointed out by many. For excellent treatments of the subject, see B. Przybylski, "The Setting of Matthean Anti-Judaism," in *Anti-Judaism in Early Christianity*, vol.1, *Paul and the Gospels*, ed. P. Richardson with D. Granskou (Waterloo, ON: Wilfrid Laurier University Press, 1986) 181-200; S. McKnight, "A Loyal Critic:

But is Matthew anti-Judaic? There can be no question but that Matthew opposes the Jews who have not believed in Jesus as the Christ, and articulates a theology that is startlingly new and in considerable tension with Judaism. To this extent at least Matthew must be seen as anti-Judaic. At the same time, however, the designation is hardly appropriate since, as we have already argued, Matthew would have regarded his Christianity as itself "Judaic," the fulfillment of Judaism.[53] In an important sense, then, Matthew is not anti-Judaic. The problem is that the effect of his belief that Christianity is the true Judaism results in apparently anti-Judaic statements. There can be little doubt, on the other hand, that Matthew is convinced that Jews need to believe in Jesus. They too are included in the *panta ta ethnē* of 28:19. They too will see Christ and proclaim "Blessed is the one who comes in the name of the Lord" (23:39). For all his heated disgreement with the Jews who have not accepted the gospel of the kingdom, Matthew continues to love his kinsfolk. In this sense Matthew is not a supersessionist.

Given the sad history of the "Christian" persecution of Jews, today all Christian scholars of the NT are required to guard against any semblance of anti-Semitism. That does not mean, in my opinion, that we can no longer disagree with Judaism or the Jews, or that we cannot let Matthew say what he says. It does mean, however, that we must go out of our way to indicate what potentially anti-Semitic texts of the NT do *not* mean and how those texts *must not* be used. Matthew knows better than any that the Jews to whom Jesus came are the covenant people of God and that the gospel is for them in the first instance, and only subsequently for the Gentiles. Gentile Christians, who owe their salvation to the Jews, should honor, love and defend the Jews even when they may disagree strongly with them.

5. CONCLUSION

There can be no doubt that Matthew is an exceptionally Jewish document. Overman, Saldarini, and Sim have effectively brought us a new

---

Matthew's Polemic with Judaism in Theological Perspective," in *Anti-Semitism and Early Christianity: Issues of Faith and Polemic*, 55–79.

53. "Matthean anti-Judaism deals with the problem of the correct interpretation of Judaism. Jewish Christians insist that the acceptance of Jesus as the Messiah is part of true Judaism. What is at stake is this interpretation of what is Jewish, not the wholesale rejection of Judaism and Jews." Przybylski, "The Setting of Matthean Anti-Judaism," 199.

appreciation of this fact. The case is much overstated, however, in the flat, unwarranted conclusion that "the religion of the Matthean community was not Christianity but Judaism."[54]

The appeal to 5:17–20. and the exclusivist sayings will not bear the. weight of the hypothesis. There is plenty of continuity with Judaism in Matthew, but that does not mean Matthew's community is properly regarded as a Jewish sect. As I have tried briefly to show, there is far too much newness in Matthew to sustain such a conclusion. The differences are far too significant to be described as mere "deviance" from other Jewish groups. To my mind, Overman, Saldarini, and Sim seriously underestimate the degree, character, and significance of the newness. Matthew reflects a *new community* with a *new focus* of a revolutionary kind that puts it in strong contrast with all other contemporary Jewish communities. An eschatological turning point has been reached and this requires a radical reorientation of previous perspectives.

It is of course true that Matthew would never have thought of Christianity as a *new religion*. Such a conclusion would be anathema to any Jewish Christian, including Paul. For Matthew, Jewish Christianity is the perfection and fulfillment of Judaism. It is important to note, however, that a thoroughly *Jewish* Christianity is still Christianity and not Judaism. Matthew's community regarded itself as *in its own way* faithful to the Mosaic law, as it followed the teaching of Jesus. And it is of course true that these Christians never stopped thinking of themselves as Jews.

Matthew, in short, represents not Judaism without Christianity, nor Christianity without Judaism, nor an indiscriminate blend of the two. Because of the "new things" affirmed by Matthew's community, it is best described *not* as a Christian form of Judaism, but as a Jewish form of Christianity. There is no reason why the full Jewishness of Matthew cannot be given its due emphasis without denying the fully Christian identity of his community.

Matthew, therefore, is not adequately described as a *reformer* of Judaism. Matthew's Jesus is concerned with far more than a restorationist eschatology and a prophetic-like call for the people to turn more earnestly to *dikaiosynē*. On the other hand, Matthew certainly cannot correctly be described as an *apostate* from Judaism, though quite probably he was regarded as such by the Jews. In no sense would he have thought of himself or his community as disloyal to Israel, its scriptures

---

54. Thus Sim, *The Gospel of Matthew and Christian Judaism*, 163.

or its heritage. The word *revolutionary* is the most accurate of the three descriptive words, in that without denying the strong aspects of continuity, it points to a radical alteration of affairs of the kind we encounter in the message of fulfillment that is at the heart of the Gospel of Matthew.

5

New Things from the Scribe's Treasure Box (Matt 13:52)

Professor Birger Gerhardsson has written the following:

> A sure way to cut oneself off from any possibility of understanding the structure of Jesus' and early Christianity's ethos is to begin with the slogan "Behold I make all things new." Our sources speak an altogether different language. Nowhere in the New Testament documents is it said that Jesus came to the people of God in order to do something fundamentally new.[1]

These are wise words, with which the evangelist would heartily agree. An adequate understanding of the Gospel of Matthew must value the old and not only the new. Indeed, the new things must be held in balance with the old. If one stresses only the new things, or only the old things, one is bound to misunderstand the Kingdom of God and the Christian faith. One will, indeed, also misunderstand the Gospel of Matthew, as some recent studies do, in my opinion.[2] The student of these things, the

---

1. Birger Gerhardsson, *The Ethos of the Bible*, trans. S. Westerholm (Philadelphia: Fortress, 1981) 33. See the same point made in reference to the Kingdom of God in "The Seven Parables in Matthew XIII," *NTS* 19 (1972–73) 74, reprinted in *The Shema in the New Testament* (Lund: Novapress, 1996) 74.

2. A recent trend in Matthean studies stresses the old to the extent that insufficient importance is assigned to the new and the discontinuity with Judaism entailed in the Gospel. In my view the result is a distorted view of Matthew. See especially A. J. Saldarini, *Matthew's Christian-Jewish Community* (Chicago: University of Chicago Press, 1994); cf. J. A. Overman, *Matthew's Gospel and Formative Judaism: The Social World of the Matthean Community* (Minneapolis: Fortress, 1990), and Overman, *Church and*

scholar trained in the things of God, must have full awareness of the old and the new, and know how they fit together. For Matthew the new, for all of its newness, always finds its meaning as the fulfilment of the old.

The Christian scribe brings out of the box of treasures, Matthew says, not only *kaina,* "new things," mentioned first by the evangelist because of their importance, but also *palaia,* "old things." It is not difficult to comprehend what the "old things" are. They must be, to begin with, the Law of Moses and the prophets, which are explicitly said to be fulfilled by Jesus (5:17). In Matthew, Jesus is fully loyal to the law, although that loyalty is the loyalty of a sovereign interpreter who, as the one Teacher, can penetrate behind the letter of the law to its spirit and intent. At the same time, Jesus is clearly the One to whom the prophets pointed and he has come to inaugurate the last days foretold by them. The *palaia,* therefore, must encompass the promises to Israel and the hopes of Israel which are contained in the scriptures. The "old things" must also, for Matthew, include the righteousness of the Torah.

But what more precisely is meant by the *kaina*? In order to arrive at some understanding of this, I decided to read the Gospel of Matthew once again, putting aside—as much as I could—my pre-understanding of the text. Indeed, I attempted something more difficult: I tried to pretend I was a first-century Jew reading the Gospel for the first time. But then, with a full awareness of the diversity of first-century Judaism, I had to ask myself what kind of Jew I would be. I decided that to be a Pharisee or an Essene was far too demanding; to be a zealot was too dangerous; to be a Sadducee too repugnant. I decided my temperament suited me best to be an *Am ha-Aretz,* by which I mean an ordinary Jew, with no noticeable special agenda, a person sharing the basic viewpoint and beliefs of the Jewish people, but without the time or energy for much more. My *Am ha-Aretz* is perhaps a little unusual in that he is able to read Greek tolerably well, but that is the result of his business dealings with Hellenists in the area where he lives.

Rather than now reporting my reactions by means of a verse by verse, or chapter by chapter, reading of the Gospel, which would be tedious and time-consuming, I here take a synthetic approach and condense my collected material under several headings.

Community in Crisis. The Gospel According to Matthew (Harrisburg, PA: Trinity, 1996).

PART ONE | JESUS

1. THAT THE MESSIAH AND THE KINGDOM OF GOD HAVE COME

The first shock comes already from the opening line of the Gospel. There my Jewish reader notes that the book he is about to read concerns one named Jesus Messiah, who is the son of David and the son of Abraham. From the start, then, the reader encounters the idea of *fulfilment*, an idea that he will encounter repeatedly throughout the Gospel. For Matthew, fulfilment of the prophecies has begun. At the climactic end of the genealogy (1:16, 17), in which he will have noted a number of surprising names, he will again read that this Jesus was called "Messiah." From 1:18 (cf. 2:4) it will be clear that it is being alleged that the Messiah has come into the world. At a climactic point in the Gospel, the confession of Peter on behalf of the disciples concerns the identity of this man named Jesus *as the Messiah*, a confession readily accepted by Jesus. My Jewish reader will note a little later that this Jesus entered Jerusalem toward the end of the narrative (ch. 21) and accepted the Hosannas of the crowds and children (21:26) in their affirmation that here was the Son of David, i.e. the Messiah. He will also observe near the end of the story that before the high priest Jesus answers the direct question, "Are you the Messiah?" Somewhat obliquely, but that he does not deny it. But it remains an oddity to our Jewish reader that Jesus did not allow his disciples to tell others that he was the Messiah (cf. 16:20). That oddity, as we shall see, is caused by the surprising work this Messiah has come to do.

Consonant with this conviction that the Messiah has come, is the announcement of John the Baptist, Jesus, and his disciples (3:2; 4:17; 10:7), that the kingdom of God had drawn near (*eggizein*). The Messiah, our Jewish reader thinks, is of course to bring the kingdom; where the Messiah is, the kingdom is surely soon to follow. But then, more surprisingly, Jesus seems to say, indeed, that the kingdom has already come, then and there: "If I cast out demons through the Spirit of God, then the kingdom of God has come (*phthanein*) upon you" (12:28). This strange notion of the presence of the kingdom is found again very strongly in the statement to the disciples: "Blessed are your eyes for they see, and your ears for they hear. Truly I tell you, many prophets and righteous people longed to see what you see, but did not see it, and to hear what you hear, and did not hear it" (13:16–17). That is, the witnesses to .Iesus' ministry see the kingdom in the deeds of Jesus and they hear the kingdom in the words of Jesus.

This man, John the Baptist, who is identified by Jesus with Elijah (11:14), the one who comes before the day of the Lord (cf. Malachi 3:1; 4:5), appears later to have had justifiable doubts, as he sat in prison, concerning whether Jesus was in fact the Messiah. But Jesus sent back a message describing his own work, using the language of the prophets where they speak of the great things that are to occur at the end of the age (11:2–6).

Thus the first and indeed the major surprise in this book is the very affirmation of the arrival of the time of fulfilment. This point is made very strongly in the ten or eleven quotations of the Hebrew scriptures that are introduced with formulae using the verb *plēroun*, "to fulfill." We may note that our Jewish reader was not so surprised with the way the scriptures were interpreted—the underlying hermeneutic was similar to the midrashic approach he had seen among the *sopherim*—as he was just at the idea that this author and those Christians really believed that any fulfilment had occurred at all. Indeed, that these people seemed to accept the message and the messianic claims, indirect as they were, of this strange Jesus. The ready response of so many to Jesus was astounding.

In fact, however, the objections of our Jewish reader to the idea of the presence of fulfilment were squarely faced by the evangelist, as we now shall see.

2. BUT, THE KINGDOM OF GOD BRINGS FULFILLMENT WITHOUT CONSUMMATION

The middle of the five discourses, which occurs at nearly the middle of the Gospel, contains parables that have to do with *ta mystēria tēs basileias tōn ouranōn*, "the mysteries of the kingdom of heaven" (3:11).[3] The mysteries being explicated in these parables point particularly to (1) the inconspicuous nature of the kingdom, and (2) the delay of the judgment usually associated with the coming of the kingdom. For our Jewish reader these are difficult matters. That the kingdom should come and not overwhelm the world is a great surprise. How can the kingdom be as apparently insignificant as a mustard seed (13:3), or unseen leaven in lumps of dough (13:33), or treasure hidden in a field (13:44), or a

---

3. See Gerhardsson, "Illuminating the Kingdom: Narrative Meshalim in the Synoptic Gospels," in *Jesus and the Oral Tradition*, ed. H. Wansbrough, JSNTSup 64 (Sheffield: Sheffield Academic, 1991) 286.

small pearl one can carry in one's pocket (13:45)? To put it mildly, this is a very strange kingdom, i.e. a strange expression of the sovereignty of God, granted even that the mustard seed will grow, the leaven will have its effect, and the value of the treasure and pearl will come to light.

Not only, however, is the blessing of the righteous veiled, but other parables in this discourse point to the fact that the judgment of the wicked is to be delayed. Thus the weeds are to be allowed to grow together with the wheat until the harvest, i.e. the end of the age (13:39). Similarly, the net of the kingdom contains both good fish and bad, with the separation not occurring until the end of the age (13:49). The kingdom will be present, but without the anticipated judgment of the wicked.

The shocking point, for our Jewish reader, is that evil will continue to coexist with the kingdom. To put it another way, the kingdom will come without bringing the end of the age. We have to reckon, then, with the presence of eschatological reality prior to the Eschaton itself. There is a remarkable complexity here which the Jewish reader must learn to assimilate. Parenthetically, it is amazing how the Jew, Paul, was able to affirm this paradox and to work out a rich theological exposition of it.

3. THE MESSIAH NOT AN ORDINARY NOR EVEN EXTRAORDINARY HUMAN AGENT

There are also some surprises concerning the Messiah himself, for our Jewish reader. The Messiah was to be the human agent of God, a special human to be sure—of the line of David and even a king, but simply human nevertheless. Regardless of how or what Jesus may have thought of himself—a difficult question, at best—the evangelist, in retrospect, presents Jesus as more than even an extraordinary human being.[4]

Again from virtually the beginning, he presents Jesus as unique. Jesus is named Emmanuel, and the evangelist informs us that this means "God is with us." Taken alone, it is conceivable that this could mean simply that God was with us through a chosen, special human being. It means at least that much. But Matthew means that somehow this language is to be taken with more literalness than one might ordinarily

---

4. On this subject, see B. Gerhardsson, "Monoteism och högkristologi i Matteusevangeliet," *SEÅ* 37/38 (1972/73) 125-44, found also in *'Hör, Israel!' Om Jesus och den gamla bekännelsen* (Lund: Liber Läromedel, 1979) 171-90. See too, "Sann Gud och sann människa. Om kyrkans bild av Jesus Kristus," in *Kristen människosyn* (Lund: Liber Läromedel, 1979) 69-94.

expect. This becomes clear from two other related passages. In 18:20 the evangelist reports Jesus as promising to the church that "where two or three are gathered in my name, I am there among them" (cf. the rabbinic idea that where two or three study Torah together, the Shekinah glory is there among them [m. Abot 3:2]). And, of course, at the very end of the Gospel, the risen Jesus associates his name, the name of the Son, with that of the Father and the Holy Spirit, as he calls his disciples to baptize others in that name, tells them to teach others all that he (not Torah) has commanded them, and finally promises them, "I am with you always, to the end of the age" (28:19–20).

When historically a number of characters in Matthew's narrative referred to Jesus as *kyrios,* they may have meant the word as an address of respect, something like "sir" (e.g., 8:2, 6, 8; 15:22; 17:15). Matthew's readers, however, know that *kyrios* is to be understood as "Lord," that is, as an ascription of deity. Indeed, for the evangelist the word has become a confessional title and it is never found on the lips of those who resist or oppose Jesus.

Already from 3:3 our Jewish reader may have noted with surprise that the prophecy concerning the preparing of the way of 'the Lord' (i.e. Yahweh) in Isaiah 40:3 was applied to the Baptist who prepared the way for Jesus.

Similarly, our Jewish reader would undoubtedly have been struck with the absolute use of the title "Son of God." He might well have thought of himself as a son of God, just as he would have been familiar with the reference to corporate Israel as the Son of God. But the use of the title, "(the) Son of God," in reference to Jesus would have been surprising, as it is found for example in 4:3, 5 (cf. 27:40, 43); 16:16; 26:63; the two references to "my beloved Son" in 3:17 and 17:5; and especially the trio of references in 14:33; 16:16; and 27:54. This one is the Son of God in a unique sense: Jesus mysteriously manifests deity— and yet Matthew does not relinquish his monotheism.[5] Most astonishing to our Jewish reader would have been the statement reported in 11:27: "All things have been handed over to me by my Father; and no one knows the Son except the Father, and no one knows the Father except the Son and anyone to whom the Son chooses to reveal him."

---

5. Referring to Matt 28:16–20, Gerhardsson writes: "Here we note that the inherited monotheism is maintained without reduction, but that it now has been enriched with a high and clear christology" ('*Hör, Israel!*', 189).

Particularly revealing along this line, and no doubt intriguing to our Jewish reader, would have been the passage in 22:41–45, where Jesus asks whose son the Messiah is. When the Pharisees answer "the Son of David," Jesus says: "How is it then that David by the Spirit calls him Lord, saying: 'The Lord said to my Lord, "Sit at my right hand, until I put your enemies under your feet"'? If David thus calls him Lord, how can he be his son?" The point seems to be that more than a merely human descendant of David is in view. The Messiah, the one already present in their midst, is referred to by David as his *kyrios*.

4. THE FATE OF GOD'S MESSIAH

We have a good indication within Matthew's narrative about something that was totally surprising to the disciples and something that would have been surprising not only to the Jews then, but also to Jewish readers today. The initial, shocking revelation of the necessity for God's Messiah to die[6] is deliberately announced by Jesus immediately after Peter's confession at Caesarea Philippi that Jesus was the Messiah.

The disciples, and presumably the Jewish populace as a whole, expected the Messiah to drive out the Romans and re-establish the state of Israel together with the Davidic monarchy, thus bringing about the expected era of fulfilment. The coming of the kingdom of God was hardly conceivable apart from this. Jesus' triumphal entry into Jerusalem seemed to encourage such thinking, even if, in agreement with Zechariah 9:9, he entered the city in the manner of a humble king. At the same time, the disciples have on their minds only what wonderful things they were soon to receive (see especially, the request of the sons of Zebedee through their mother in 20:20–21; cf. 19:27).

The idea of Jesus' imminent death was a total surprise to Peter and the disciples. Peter strongly reacted to the suggestion of Jesus's death. The Greek is not easy, but it amounts to something like, "God forbid it, Lord. May this not happen to you" (16:22). Peter, indeed, is said to rebuke Jesus

---

6. See Gerhardsson, "Sacrificial Service and Atonement in the Gospel of Matthew," in *Reconciliation and Hope: New Testament Essays on Atonement and Eschatology, Presented to Leon Morris on His 60th Birthday*, ed. R. Banks (Grand Rapids: Eerdmans, 1974) 25–35; reprinted in *The Shema in the New Testament*, 98–108; see too, "Gottes Sohn als Diener Gottes. Messias, Agape und Himmelsherrschaft nach dem Matthäusevangelium" (*Studia Theologica* 27, 1973, 73–106); later version, "Guds son som Guds tjänare: Messias, agape och himlens herravalde enligt Matteusevangeliet," in *'Hör, Israel!'*, 114–46.

for such thinking. But Peter, in turn, receives an equally strong response from Jesus. So contrary to the purpose and will of God is his reaction to the idea of the death of the Messiah that Jesus addresses him as "Satan" (cf. the tempter and his designs in ch. 4) and accuses him of setting his mind on "human things" (16:23).

Without question the idea of the death of God's Anointed was unthinkable to the Jews of the first century.[7] In Matthew, as in the other Gospels, the puzzle of this apparent contradiction is buttressed by the insistence that the death of the Messiah is both the fulfilment of the scriptures and nothing less than the will of God (26:31; and especially at the point of his arrest, in denying himself angelic rescue: "How then would the scriptures be fulfilled, which say it must happen (*dei genesthai*) in this way?" (26:54); followed by the indicative statement that "all this has taken place, so that *(hina)* the scriptures of the prophets may be fulfilled" (26:56); so too 20:28; 26:39, 42).

The degree to which the idea of a crucified Messiah was objectionable to the Jews becomes crystal clear in the Apostle Paul's handling of the problem. What was undoubtedly a major reason for his initial rejection of Christianity was the very idea of the Messiah being crucified. But after the Damascus road encounter, when he began to understand the divine logic, he turned the objectionable element—that one who is hanged upon a tree is cursed by God—into a positive element in his elaboration of the significance of that death: Christ became a curse for us (Gal 3:13). It was this central mystery—the death of the Messiah—that then became the cornerstone of his kerygma, as it was also of the church before him: "We preach Christ crucified, a stumbling block to the Jews and foolishness to the Greeks" (1 Cor 1:23). What Paul described as a stumbling block to the Jews would have been no less so to our Jewish reader. It took the early church, which was entirely Jewish, no small effort to understand that the Messiah had been ordained by God to fulfil the work of Isaiah's suffering Servant. It would take no less effort on the part of our Jewish reader.

---

7. Cf. Gerhardsson, "Utlämnad och övergiven: Till förståelsen av passionshistorien i Matteusevangeliet" (in "*Hör, Israel!*," 90, originally published in *SEÅ* 32 [1967] 92–120).

5. THE NATURE OF DISCIPLESHIP: ORIENTATION TOWARDS JESUS AND NOT THE LAW

The question of how one is to live one's life would naturally be of great interest and importance to our Jewish reader. Here too, however, there would be new and strange things to consider. Perhaps most shocking is the fact that life is oriented not to the performance of Torah—at least not specifically—but to the person of Jesus himself. This fact is undoubtedly related in a close way to the point made under 3 above.

The expectation of our reader is that the Messiah will call the people to the obedience of Torah and provide its definitive interpretation. Matthew's Jesus clearly does the latter, and he also indicates in good Jewish fashion the permanence of the Torah, down to the last detail (5:17–19). But the *focus* of everything is not upon the Torah as such, but upon relationship and obedience to Jesus himself. For example, he calls people not to Torah, but to himself, not to the yoke of Torah, but to his own yoke which he describes as easy (11:28–30). At the end of the Sermon on the Mount, the call is to obey "these words of mine" (7:24, 26). And at the end of the Gospel we again encounter the command to obey "everything I have commanded you" (28:20).

Indeed, Jesus puts himself in a position of indispensable importance: "Everyone who acknowledges me before others, I also will acknowledge before my Father in heaven; but whoever denies me before others, I also will deny before my Father in heaven" (10:32). A few lines later in the same discourse (10:37), he audaciously says that commitment to him must precede that to one's own parents and family (at one point he even calls a disciple to follow him to the neglect of attending to his father's burial [8:21]). Very strange to our Jewish reader are the subsequent words: "whoever does not take up the cross, and follow me is not worthy of me; those who find their life will lose it, and those who lose their life for my sake will find it" (10:38). In short, the constant egocentrism of this Jesus can only surprise our Jewish reader. The life of the disciples of Jesus is to be oriented to Jesus and not to the Torah, although paradoxically, following the teaching of Jesus brings the disciple to the righteousness of the Torah.

A. The Higher Righteousness

The content of Jesus' description of righteousness in Matthew[8] surprises our Jewish reader. Quite shocking is Jesus' statement that "unless your righteousness exceeds that of the scribes and Pharisees, you will never enter the kingdom of God" (5:20). At first, one might think that Jesus calls his disciples to beat the Pharisees at their own game. It becomes clear, however, that Jesus has in mind a qualitatively higher kind of righteousness. There is in fact a startling difference between the ethical teaching of Jesus and that of the rabbis. By comparison, Jesus' ethic is idealistic and even perfectionist. The content of Jesus' ethical teaching is inseparable from the message that surrounds it and provides its context, namely the dawning of the kingdom of God. It is an ethic with an inescapably eschatological aspect.

Our Jewish reader of course knew that the intention or motive of a deed was important, and not merely the deed itself—that is, that the inner dimension of an act was important as well as the outward.[9] But the contrasts stated in the antitheses of the Sermon on the Mount are nevertheless quite surprising to him. The standard set forward there seems to him to be both unrealistic and utopian. Our Jewish reader would perhaps have heard the rabbinic teaching that one should not do to others what one does not want others to do to oneself (cf. *b. Shabb.* 31a). But a further example of the unrealistic tone in the teaching of Jesus is his casting of this command into the positive: "In everything do to others as you would have them do to you," to which Jesus adds the remarkable words "for this is the law and the prophets" (7:12).

Our Jewish reader, unfortunately, has no access to the key to the understanding of the ethical teaching of Jesus: namely, the reality of the gift of grace embodied in the announcement of the kingdom. For righteousness, as Matthew sees it, has both the aspect of demand *and* gift, and the demand presupposes the gift. For the same reason, our Jewish reader would have been confused by Jesus' statement that "I have come to call not the righteous but sinners" (9:13), and he would not have been particularly happy with the freedom with which Jesus associated with tax collectors and sinners (9:10-11; 11:19). Nor would he have found familiar or comfortable the parable of the workers in the vineyard (20:1-16).

---

8. On this, see Gerhardsson, "Urkristendoms ethos enligt Matteus," in *Med hela ditt hjärta*, 35-62.

9. See Gerhardsson, "Den judiska gudsstatens ethos," in *Med hela ditt hjärta*, 22-34.

B. Suffering Required of the Disciples

What Jesus required of his disciples would no doubt have deeply surprised our Jewish reader. The motif of self-denial he would have found indeed strange and objectionable. A part of that self-denial was the willingness to die for Jesus, if necessary. Thus when Jesus sprang upon his disciples that greatest of surprises—the fact that he would soon be put to death—he immediately noted that the disciples were to be prepared to follow in his footsteps. In words we have already quoted: "If any want to become my followers, let them deny themselves and take up their cross and follow me. For those who want to save their life will lose it, and those who lose their life for my sake will find it" (16:24–25). Earlier in Matthew Jesus had spoken very similar words (10:38–39) and had indicated the sufferings that the disciples could expect (10:16–22; cf. even more gloomily, 24:9–10). In 5:11 the theme is similar, and surely foreign to our Jewish reader: "Blessed are you when people revile you and persecute you and utter all kinds of evil against you falsely on my account."

Rather than getting immediate advantages and rewards for being disciples, as they had earnestly hoped, they were asked if they were willing to drink the cup (of death) that Jesus was to drink (20:20–23). To follow Jesus in the present, despite the dawning of the kingdom, would not seem an attractive option to our Jewish reader, unless he could develop a larger perspective.

6. THE LENGTHENING INTERIM PERIOD

Acquainted with the problem of the mystery of the kingdom discussed above in section 2, concerning the coming of fulfilment without consummation, our Jewish reader would undoubtedly have been as surprised as were the disciples about the delay of the consummation. From his perspective, he might well conclude (like many scholars of the modern era) from the increasing time of the delay that Jesus and the Christians were fundamentally mistaken. The coming of fulfilment naturally implies the imminence of consummation.

Several things about the interim period, indeed, would have surprised our Jewish reader. We cannot mention the Christian Pentecost, that which marks the interim period most distinctively, since Matthew does not refer to it except in a prophetic and allusive way, when John the Baptist says that the one coming after him "will baptize you with the Holy

Spirit and fire" (3:11). But two things in particular would have been quite surprising to our Jewish reader.

A. The Church (and Israel)

The statement of Jesus that he was going to build a new community of faith, what he calls "my ekklesia." upon the confessing Peter (16:18; 18:15), would have probably been surprising to our Jewish reader. He might well have thought of the separatist community of the Essenes at Qumran as a kind of parallel. But would not the Messiah be concerned for the whole of Israel? Was not his work to be directed to the entire community of Israel and not to a select group within it? Furthermore the exclusivity of this group would have bothered our reader: they, Peter and the disciples, have the authority to bind and loose—in effect, to decide on who was within and who was without the community of salvation.

What Matthew has to say about Israel would again have been surprising to our Jewish reader. He would have been struck by the apparent hostility to Israel in the Gospel. To be sure, the hostility is primarily directed toward the leadership of Israel, but often the statements have wider implications. Our Jewish reader would have been surprised, not to say shocked, when Jesus says: "Therefore I tell you, the kingdom of God will be taken away from you and given to a people that produces the fruits of the kingdom" (21 :43). The idea of the transference of the kingdom from Israel to the church would have jolted our Jewish reader.

Also shocking to our Jewish reader would have been Jesus' prophecy concerning the destruction of Jerusalem in 24:2 and the desecration of the temple in 24:15. Again like the disciples of Jesus, he would have found it impossible to contemplate such things apart from the end of the age (cf. the question in 24:3). Surely the fall of Jerusalem and the demise of the second temple would also entail the appearance of the Messiah and the inauguration of the promised kingdom of David. The end of Jerusalem was to come, however, apart from the consummation of the ages, thus leaving Judaism during the interim period in a kind of suspended animation. That this interim period should last two thousand years would have been unthinkable to our reader.

B. The Gentile Mission

Our Jewish reader would have felt quite comfortable with the statements of Jesus concerning the limitation of the messianic mission to the house of Israel. Thus in sending out the twelve, Jesus tells them: "Go nowhere among the Gentiles, and enter no town of the Samaritans, but go rather to the lost sheep of the house of Israel" (10:5–6). When implored by the Canaanite woman to heal her daughter, Jesus responds: "I was sent only to the lost sheep of the house of Israel" (15:24).

But there are also statements in Matthew that stand in considerable tension with the limitation of the work of Jesus and the disciples to Israel. Indeed, for our Jewish reader, the Gentiles seem to hold an altogether too important place in the Gospel of Matthew. He would have been very surprised at the statement, for example, in 8:11–12, made in reference to the faith of a Gentile centurion, ."In no one in Israel have I found such faith. I tell you, many will come from east and west and will eat with Abraham and Isaac and Jacob in the kingdom of heaven, while the heirs of the kingdom will be thrown into the outer darkness, where there will be weeping and gnashing of teeth." Nor would our Jewish reader have been very happy with the parable of the wedding banquet, where it is said that "the wedding is ready, but those invited were not worthy. Go therefore into the main streets and invite everyone you find to the wedding banquet" (22:8–9). As he proceeds to the end of the Gospel, our Jewish reader notes first the prophecy that "this good news of the kingdom will be proclaimed throughout the world, as a testimony to all the nations; and then the end will come" (24:14) and then the commission itself at the end of the Gospel: "Go therefore and make disciples of all nations" (28:19).

While our Jewish reader would have been well aware that the Gentiles were not out of the picture altogether in God's plan, they were in fact only on the edge of the picture, as the recipients of the overflow of the blessing that was to come to Israel. It would have been both surprising and shocking to see the Gentiles taking central stage in the drama of God's redemptive history.

CONCLUSION

It is difficult to know precisely what the evangelist meant by the *kaina* in 13:52. If we restrict ourselves to the context of the statement, it would seem to refer to the unexpected aspects of the kingdom discussed in ch.

13, referred to as the 'mysteries of the kingdom' (and discussed above in 2). But because all the new things of the Gospel are necessarily interconnected, we have here cast a wide net to see what might strike a typical Jewish reader as surprising and new.

The evangelist is aware that much in the gospel involves what might be described as *kaina*. As it is put in one passage, "For all the prophets and the law prophesied until John came" (11:13). One cannot begin to talk about Jesus without facing the reality of the dramatically new. And yet, as the honorand of this symposium has taught us so well, the new for Matthew is ever at the same time in continuity with, and the fulfilment of the old.

In an important passage for our subject, the evangelist refers to the new situation caused by the presence of the bridegroom. He then points to two new things whose newness must be recognized or else there will be trouble: a piece of unshrunk cloth and new wine. To take the latter metaphor, what the evangelist narrates in his book, the story of Jesus, is like new wine. It cannot be contained in old skins without itself being lost. No, new wine because of its nature must be put in new skins. And Matthew, ever the conserver, uniquely adds "and so both are preserved" (9:17).

This is something our friendly Jewish reader would have to understand—just as the disciples themselves had to do—if ever he hoped truly to comprehend the meaning of Matthew's narrative and Matthew's Lord.[10]

---

10. This paper was originally given at a symposium on the Gospel of Matthew held at the University of Lund, Sweden, in September, 1996, given in honor of the seventieth birthday of Professor Birger Gerhardsson.

PART TWO
Paul

6

Paul in Modern Jewish Thought

IN HIS RECENT BOOK on Paul, Professor F. F. Bruce writes:

> Although [Paul] was rabbinically trained, his reappraisal of the whole spirit and content of his earlier training was so radical that many Jewish scholars have had difficulty in recognizing him as the product of a rabbinical education. They have found it easier to appreciate the Prophet of Nazareth (who, indeed, was not rabbinically trained) than the apostle to the Gentiles. Paul presents an enigma with which they cannot readily come to terms.[1]

Our century has indeed witnessed the amazing phenomenon of the Jewish reclamation[2] of Jesus. Jewish writing on Jesus continues to increase,[3] with the conclusion concerning Jesus' Jewishness gaining ever more forcefulness.[4] Building upon the results of radical Protestant Christian

---

1. *Paul: Apostle of the Free Spirit* (Grand Rapids: Eerdmans, 1977) 462.

2. See the essay by Harry A. Wolfson, "How the Jews Will Reclaim Jesus," *The Menorah Journal* (1962) 25–31, reprinted in *Judaism and Christianity*, ed. J. B. Agus (New York: Arno, 1973). Wolfson's answer is: as a rabbi among rabbis, as a part of Israel's literary heritage.

3. The best survey of this research, G. Lindeskog, *Die Jesusfrage im Neuzeitlichen Judentum* (Uppsala: Almqvist & Wiksell, 1938), has now been reprinted with an epilogue on more recent Jewish study of Jesus (Darmstadt, Wissenschaftliche Buchgesellschaft, 1973). See also Pinchas E. Lapide, "Jesus in Israeli Literature," *Christian Century* 87 (1970) 1248–53; Schalom Ben-Chorin, "The Image of Jesus in Modern Judaism," *JES* 11 (1974) 401–30.

4. The following important works may be noted: C. G. Montefiore, *Some Elements of the Religious Teaching of Jesus According to the Synoptic Gospels* (London: Macmillan,

scholarship, Jewish writers argue that the Jesus of the Gospels is to a very large extent the product of the faith of the later Church. The actual Jesus of history, on the other hand, is regarded as belonging with Judaism rather than Christianity. The real Jesus is a reformer of Judaism, a new Amos or Isaiah who calls his people back to the faith of their fathers, a loyal Jew from whose mind nothing was further than the idea of a new religion with himself at the centre. For modern Jews, Jesus has indeed come home.

But what of Paul? He is, of course, regarded as the founder of the new religion, the person largely responsible for turning Jesus, the proclaimer of the kingdom, into the one who is himself proclaimed as Lord, and finally, as the person who takes this new message to the Gentiles of the Mediterranean world with an astonishing degree of success. But to say all this is not to account for Paul. How in fact did this amazing Jew, who so strongly emphasizes his Jewish (indeed Pharisaic) background, come to such apparently bizarre conclusions? Jewish scholars have no small fascination for Saul of Tarsus, who became the Christian Paul. He is somehow at the root of the difference between Judaism and Christianity, it is believed, and thus he demands Jewish analysis. If Jesus has been brought home, Paul has remained a stranger. Therefore several Jewish scholars (e.g. Montefiore, Klausner, Ben-Chorin), having written about Jesus, subsequently turned to write about Paul. The number of Jewish writers on Paul has increased in the last few decades[5] and will continue to increase in the future. Can there be a Jewish reclamation of Paul, even if partial, paralleling the Jewish reclamation of Jesus? What are the ingredients of the enigma which Paul presents to Jewish scholars?

The purpose of the present essay is to examine the direction taken by Jewish writers in accounting for Paul. In particular the focus of attention is on Paul's background since above all this is regarded as the ultimate source of his idiosyncratic views in such crucial areas as the Law, soteriology, christology, sacraments and mysticism. Paul's views are fairly

---

1910) and *Rabbinic Literature and Gospel Teachings* (London: Macmillan, 1930); J. Klausner, *Jesus of Nazareth*, trans. H. Danby (New York: Macmillan 1925); S. Sandmel, *We Jews and Jesus* (New York: Oxford University Press, 1965); S. Ben-Chorin, *Bruder Jesus* (Munich: List, 1967); D. Flusser, *Jesus*, trans. R. Walls (New York: Herder & Herder, 1969); G. Vermes, *Jesus the Jew* (New York: Macmillan, 1973); P. E. Lapide, *Der Rabbi von Nazaret* (Trier: Spee, 1974).

5. For surveys of this research, see Halvor Ronning, "Some Jewish Views of Paul," *Judaica* 24 (1968) 82–97; Wolfgang Wiefel, "Paulus in jüdischer Sicht," *Judaica* 31 (1975) 109–15, 151–72; J. Blank, *Paulus und Jesus*, SANT 18 (Munich: Kosel, 1968) 106–23.

well agreed upon; it is rather the explanation of how Paul the Jew could come to such views that interests Jewish scholars. In Paul's background and experience must lie the key that accounts for the origin of Pauline Christianity.

Before we begin our review, however, we must note the silence of Jews on the subject of Paul until the modern period.[6] Two main factors, not of equal importance, account for this silence. First, Jews at the beginning had little reason to concern themselves with Paul, this eccentric heresiarch so important to the development of Christian theology. His views were not only wrong, but also patently dangerous, as the success of his missionary endeavors made abundantly clear. It seemed the best course of action for Jews to ignore Paul as they did Christianity and even Jesus, although with less success in the last instance.[7] Far more important, however, in explaining the silence was the precarious situation of the Jews under a Christian tyranny that existed from the fourth century to the nineteenth-century Emancipation—the ultimate, but slowly realized, fruit of the Enlightenment. As long as this oppression continued, Jews were unable to speak publicly and objectively about Jesus, Paul or Christianity. Thus the history of the Jewish study of Paul is closely parallel to the history of the Jewish study of Jesus. With the new climate of freedom produced by the gradual acceptance of Jews into European society came the first scholarly assessments of Jesus and Paul from Jewish writers. A pioneer in this early scholarship was the historian Heinrich Graetz who in the second half of the nineteenth century authored the first comprehensive history of the Jews[8] and who in many ways anticipated the di-

---

6. For the possibility that Paul is alluded to by R. Eleazar in the Mishna (Abot 3:12), see G. Kittel, "Paulus im Talmud," in *Rabbinica*, Arbeiten zur Religionsgeschichte des Urchristentums 1, 3 (Leipzig: Hinrichs, 1920). The passage refers to one who "profanes the Hallowed Things and despises the set feasts and puts his fellow to shame publicly and makes void the covenant of Abraham our father, and discloses meanings in the Law which are not according to the *Halakah*." *The Mishnah*, trans. H. Danby (Oxford: Oxford University Press, 1933) 451. A further possible reference is found in *b. Šabb.* 30b where a pupil of Gamaliel is said to have exhibited "impudence in matters of learning." Klausner accepts the view that the pupil is Paul (*From Jesus to Paul,* 311).

7. See H. Laible, "Jesus Christ in the Talmud" in G. Dalman, *Jesus Christ in the Talmud, Midrash, Zohar, and the Liturgy of the Synagogue* (Cambridge: Deighton, Bell, 1893; reprint, New York: Arno, 1973) 1–98; R. Travers Herford, *Christianity in Talmud and Midrash* (London: Williams & Norgate, 1903; reprint, Clifton, NJ: Reference Book Publishers, 1966), summarized in Hastings' *Dictionary of Christ and the Gospels* II, 877–78; cf. also J. Klausner, *Jesus of Nazareth,* 18–47.

8. *Geschichte der Juden von den ältesten Zeiten bis zur Gegenwart,* 11 vols. (Leipzig: Leiner, 1853–1870). A condensation of this work was published in English in six

rection future Jewish scholarship was to take concerning both Jesus and Paul. Paul is regarded as the founder of the new religion Christianity, which he was able to create by virtue of his Hellenistic background and his consequent unfamiliarity with authentic Judaism. Indeed, were it not for Paul's transformation of the faith of the early messianic movement into Christianity, that movement would have come to its end like other messianic movements before and after. Already with Graetz it becomes apparent that Paul is more difficult to explain and more alien to Judaism than Jesus.

In the twentieth century important Jewish writings on Paul have appeared from such scholars as Claude Goldsmid Montefiore,[9] Kaufmann Kohler,[10] Joseph Klausner,[11] Martin Buber,[12] Leo Baeck,[13] Samuel Sandmel,[14] Hans Joachim Schoeps,[15] Schalom Ben-Chorin,[16] and Rich-

---

volumes, *History of the Jews* (Philadelphia: Jewish Publication Society, 1891–95). A section of volume three of the original work, on the subject of Jesus and Christian origins, appeared as a separate monograph in French translation, *Sinai et Golgotha* (Paris: Levy, 1867).

9. *Judaism and St. Paul: Two Essays* (London: Goschen, 1914; reprint, New York: Arno, 1973); "Rabbinic Judaism and the Epistles of Paul," *JQR* 13 (1901) 162–217, reprinted in *Judaism and Christianity*, ed. Jacob B. Agus (New York: Arno, 1973).

10. "Saul of Tarsus," *JE* 11 (1905) 79–87; *The Origins of the Synagogue and the Church* (New York: Macmillan, 1929; reprint, New York: Arno, 1973) 260–70.

11. *From Jesus to Paul*, trans. from Hebrew original of 1939 by W. F. Stinespring (London: Macmillan, 1943; reprint, Boston: Beacon, 1961).

12. *Two Types of Faith*, trans. N. P. Goldhawk (London: Routledge & Kegan Paul, 1951).

13. "The Faith of Paul," *JJS* 3 (1952) 93–110; the essay appears also in German translation in *Paulus, die Pharisäer und das Neue Testament* (Frankfurt: Ner-Tamid, 1961) 7–37.

14. *The Genius of Paul: A Study in History* (New York: Farrar, Straus & Cudahy, 1958; reprint, with new introduction, New York: Schocken, 1970); "Paul Reconsidered" in S. Sandmel, *Two Living Traditions* (Detroit: Wayne State University Press, 1972) 195–211; "Judaism, Jesus, and Paul: Some Problems of Method in Scholarly Research," in *Vanderbilt Studies in the Humanities*, vol. 1 (Nashville: Vanderbilt University Press, 1951) 220–48, reprinted in *Two Living Traditions*; see also *A Jewish Understanding of the New Testament* (Cincinnati: Hebrew Union College Press, 1956), reprinted in an "augmented edition," New York: Ktav/Anti-Defamation League of B'nai B'rith, 1974, 37–104; and *Judaism and Christian Beginnings* (New York: Oxford University Press, 1978) 308–36.

15. *Paul: The Theology of the Apostle in the Light of Jewish Religious History*, trans. H. Knight (Philadelphia: Westminster, 1961).

16. *Paulus: Der Volkerapostel in jüdischer Sicht* (Munich: Paul List, 1970), with annotated bibliography, 223–30.

ard L. Rubenstein.[17] Despite certain differences between these writers, there is perhaps enough basic agreement among them to enable us to recognize an emerging modern Jewish perspective on Paul.[18]

Although the issue takes on a special importance for Jewish scholars, since for them particularly Paul's relation to Judaism demands explanation, the struggle over the question of Paul's background is of course shared by New Testament scholarship generally. Because it is important to the initial formation of a Jewish perspective on Paul, we begin with a brief review of the modern discussion of the problem.

In the first decades of our century, NT scholarship largely came under the domination of *Religionsgeschichte*, a discipline which saw Christianity as one among many religions in the Hellenistic world and which in "strictly historical" fashion attempted to account for similarities by arguing for primitive Christianity's dependence upon these Hellenistic religions. A most impressive scholarly tradition emerged, including such noteworthy names as Pfleiderer, Heitmüller, Gunkel, Reitzenstein, Bousset and Bultmann.[19] Inevitably their attention was focused on Paul, for it was above all he among the NT writers who exhibited Hellenistic influence. The Mystery Religions and Gnosticism provided a rich source of striking parallels to Paul's theology and much energy was expended in combing through literary remains, such as the Hermetic and Mandaic corpora, in search of similarities. The widespread conclusion drawn from this approach was that Paul had combined Jewish and Hellenistic ideas, with a preponderance of the latter, into a new syncretism and had thereby created a new religion. He had borrowed freely from a variety of Hellenistic sources; his sacramental views, his mysticism, his Christology and soteriology and more, were fundamentally derived from the Mystery Religions, the kyrios cult, and Gnosticism (particularly the myth of the cosmological redeemer). In this hellenization of Christianity Jesus thus

---

17. *My Brother Paul* (New York: Harper & Row, 1972).

18. Note should also be taken of D. Flusser, "Paul of Tarsus," in *Encyclopedia Judaica* 13:190–92; E. I. Jacob, "Paul" in *The Universal Jewish Encyclopedia* 8 (1939–43) 415–17; and H. J. Schonfield, *The Jew of Tarsus: An Unorthodox Portrait of Paul* (London: MacDonald, 1946).

19. A convenient survey of the History-of-Religions School may be found in W. G. Kümmel, *The New Testament: The History of the Investigation of Its Problems*, trans. S. M. Gilmour and H. C. Kee, from German original of 1970 (Nashville: Abingdon, 1972) 206–25, 245–80.

became another mystery-god and Paul perhaps the greatest of all the Gnostics.[20]

Together with this new explanation of Paul came the emphatic conclusion that Paul's religion was a radical departure from what Jesus had preached. The differences between Jesus and Paul had of course been noted much earlier. The modern debate of this problem goes back to F. C. Baur, who regarded Paul as an innovator and who was followed in this by others among whom Wendt, Goguel, Wrede and Bultmann deserve special mention.[21] These scholars drew the contrast between Jesus and Paul much more sharply than had Baur, and their viewpoint continues to have influence.[22] The newer knowledge of Hellenistic religion brought by the early twentieth century served to widen the chasm that already existed between Jesus and Paul.

Thus from Christian writers with massive scholarly erudition came conclusions that Jews had long felt to be true. Paul, importing Greek notions intrinsically foreign to Judaism, had invented a new religion quite out of sympathy with the intent of Jesus. Whereas Jesus had come to reform Judaism, Paul had subverted it; Jesus, more than ever, seemed to belong on the side of Judaism against Paul who belonged on the side of Christianity. To have such views uttered not out of a context of religious polemics or apologetics, but from what could be claimed to be "objective," "scientific" Christian scholarship was indeed a boon to the Jewish perspective.

Jewish scholars were not slow to make use of these conclusions in their own evaluation of Paul. At the same time, Jews are too aware of an authentic Jewishness in Paul amidst all that seems unfamiliar to be satisfied to account for him solely on the basis of Hellenism. It is particularly to a Hellenistic Judaism that they have in large measure resorted in seeking to explain Paul. But Paul the Hellenist remains Paul the Jew, and the most recent writers, as we shall see, stress Paul's Jewishness more than ever.

We begin with the influential writer of the early part of this century, Claude Goldsmid **Montefiore**, whose writings on Paul have as a major purpose to demonstrate that Paul's Judaism was vastly different

---

20. So R. Reitzenstein, *Die hellenistischen Mysterienreligionen* (Leipzig: Teubner, 1910) 55-56. The quotation is found in Kümmel, op. cit., 270.

21. For a thorough survey, see V. P. Furnish, "The Jesus-Paul Debate From Baur to Bultmann," *BJRL* 47 (1965) 342-81.

22. The debate, however, is hardly at an end. Cf. F. F. Bruce's recent defense of Paul as a faithful interpreter of Jesus in *Paul and Jesus* (Grand Rapids:Baker, 1974).

from Rabbinic Judaism. From Montefiore's point of view, the difference is a key to understanding Paul. As he puts it repeatedly, "there is much in Paul which, while dealing with Judaism, is inexplicable by Judaism."[23] When Solomon Schechter began his sympathetic study of Rabbinic theology, he admitted that the results would not square with Paul's account of the same subject, and that this would make the Apostle to the Gentiles seem "quite unintelligible."[24] Montefiore avoids this dilemma by denying that Paul ever knew an authentic Rabbinic Judaism.[25] Paul was not, as Wellhausen had described him, "the great pathologist of Judaism."[26] On the contrary, the Judaism Paul knew was markedly different from Rabbinic Judaism and, moreover, his thinking had been affected by alien, non-Jewish influences.[27]

Montefiore's earlier essay on Paul is to a large extent a refutation of certain Christian statements bearing on Jewish theology and more particularly the book of the Christian scholar Ferdinand Weber, entitled *Jüdische Theologie auf Grund des Talmud und verwandter Schriften*.[28] It is especially the distortion of the Rabbinic teaching on the Law that Montefiore seeks to correct. Here, as well as in his later essay, Montefiore draws a sharp contrast between the Rabbinic Judaism of AD 500 (which he regards as not essentially different from that of AD 50) and the Judaism which Paul attacks in his epistles. The radical discrepancy between the two suggests to Montefiore that either Paul "was never a Rabbinic Jew at all, or he has quite forgotten what Rabbinic Judaism was and is."[29]

In his most forceful presentation of these differences, Montefiore explores eight areas of Paul's theology which are impossible to explain on the basis of Rabbinic Judaism.[30] According to Montefiore, the first two of these, Paul's view of Christ as a divine being and his commitment to the

23. "Rabbinic Judaism and the Epistles of St. Paul," 167, 207.

24. *Aspects of Rabbinic Theology* (New York: Macmillan, 1909; reprint, New York: Schocken, 1961) 18.

25. *Judaism and St. Paul*, 12, 17.

26. *Prolegomena to the History of Ancient Israel*, trans. J. Sutherland and A. Menzies (Cleveland: World, 1957) 425. See "Rabbi Judaism and the Epistles of St. Paul," 167 and *Judaism and St. Paul*, 21. Montefiore allows that Jesus may legitimately be called a pathologist of Judaism.

27. *Judaism and St. Paul*, 18.

28. For a contemporary refutation of the same book, see E. P. Sanders, *Paul and Palestinian Judaism* (Philadelphia: Fortress, 1977).

29. "Rabbinic Judaism and the Epistles of St. Paul," 206.

30. *Judaism and St. Paul*, 58–60.

mission to the Gentiles, although not paralleled in the Rabbinic Judaism of AD 500, can be explained from first-century Jewish (even Palestinian) backgrounds without difficulty—the former on the basis of expectations of Jewish apocalyptic, the latter as a reflection of an active Jewish proselytism. But in the remaining six items Paul departs altogether from Rabbinic Judaism (whether of 500 or 50): his pessimism, his theory of Law (as in Romans), his neglect of the idea of repentance, his peculiar mysticism, soteriology and religious psychology.

Montefiore is content to stress these differences and to assert the unrabbinic character of Paul's theology. He offers no constructive account of Paul other than to designate Paul's Jewish background as a "particular sort of cheap and poor Hellenistic Judaism."[31] Diaspora Judaism is regarded by Montefiore as decidedly inferior; its religion was "colder and more sombre"; its God was more remote and less approachable than the Rabbis' God; its outlook was gloomy, anxious and defensive; it saw the Law negatively rather than positively; it became concerned with sin and salvation; it was theoretical and systematic.[32] Here it appears that Montefiore attributes to Diaspora Judaism every quality of Paul he dislikes.

It is obvious for Montefiore that Paul's Diaspora background is the key to understanding his theology. As for NT data which could be taken as referring to Paul's contact with Palestinian Judaism, Montefiore follows the critical opinion of some Christian scholars that Acts is not to be trusted as history (he cites Loisy); he does not accept the reference in 22:3 where Paul refers to being brought up in Jerusalem at the feet of Gamaliel.[33] According lo Montfiore the reference in Phil. 3:5–6 concerning Paul's Pharisaic background and his blamelessness according to the righteousness under the Law could have been spoken by a Hellenistic Jew as easily as a Palestinian Jew, although he adds that the passage has "no genuine Jewish ring."[34]

Montefiore was by no means the first Jewish scholar to explain Paul by appealing to the Hellenistic Judaism of the Diaspora, nor of course

---

31. *Judaism and St. Paul*, 153, cf. 164. Montefiore never undertook a detailed study of how Hellenistic Paul's Judaism actually was. Cf. his avoidance of this question in "Rabbinic Judaism and the Epistles of St. Paul," 174.

32. *Judaism and St. Paul*, 93–101. The quoted words are on 94.

33. *Judaism and St. Paul*, 90. Montefiore shows his acquaintance with critical scholars at several points. It may also be noted here that in an appendix (pp. 221–40) he has quoted a number of passages from Loisy (on Paul's dependence upon the MysteryReligions) drawn from the *Revue d'histoire et de littérature religieuses* 3 (1912) 556–67; 573–74; 4 (1913) 477–80; 486.

34. Ibid., 94.

was he the last to do so. Kaufmann **Kohler** was one of the earliest and most forceful proponents of Paul's Hellenism in his influential article in the *Jewish Encyclopedia*. Despite Paul's own claims about his Jewishness, from his epistles Kohler can only conclude that he was "entirely a Hellenist in thought and sentiment."[35] There is no indication of rabbinic influence in Paul's writing or argumentation, according to Kohler. Therefore it is impossible that Paul could ever have been a disciple of Gamaliel; rather, the source of his theology is to be found in the literature of Hellenistic Judaism and the influence of Greek mystery cults. An additional factor in accounting for Paul's strange doctrines is his susceptibility to ecstatic visions (caused by epilepsy) and the accompanying mental paroxysms, to which may be attributed certain irrational and pathological elements in his writings.[36] All of this, argues Kohler, contributes to the decidedly un-Jewish character of Paul: "The conception of a new faith, half pagan and half Jewish, such as Paul preached, and susceptibility to its influences, were altogether foreign to the nature of Jewish life and thought."[37] Paul's christology and his view of the Law are regarded as influenced by Gnosticism; his mysticism and sacramentalism are traced to Hellenistic Mystery Religions. Yet for all of Paul's dependence upon Hellenism, he himself remained recognizably Jewish.

When Joseph **Klausner** turned his attention to Paul, he too stressed the significance of Hellenistic influence upon Paul. The primary datum is that Paul was born, raised, and lived almost all of his life, in a Hellenistic environment. Klausner does not deny that Paul had been at one time a student of Gamaliel in Jerusalem and that he therefore had some knowledge of Palestinian Judaism. But this was not sufficient to overcome Paul's basic orientation. Paul's soul, according to Klausner, was in fact "torn between Palestinian Pharisaism ... and Jewish Hellenism—and in a certain measure also pagan Hellenism."[38] It was this divided loyalty that ultimately brought about the betrayal of Judaism by Paul.

The message which Paul proclaimed involved a world-view "completely foreign to Palestinian Jews."[39] Appealing to the abundant parallels to Paul discovered by the *Religionsgeschichte* school, Klausner argued that the un-Jewish character of Paul's teaching was the result of his religious

35. "Saul of Tarsus," 79; cf. *Origins*, 261.
36. "Saul of Tarsus," 79, 82.
37. "Saul of Tarsus," 79.
38. *From Jesus to Paul*, 312.
39. *From Jesus to Paul*, 354.

syncretism.⁴⁰ It was indeed just this accommodation to and adaptation of pagan ideas that enabled Paul to produce a Christianity that became a world religion. There was a kind of Christianity before Paul, but only in its Pauline metamorphosis could it conquer the pagan world.⁴¹

Paul's message is not only new and un-Jewish, for Klausner, but fundamentally an "anti-Judaism, the complete antithesis of Judaism."⁴² Paradoxically, however, Klausner can also say that "there is nothing in the teaching of Paul—not even the most mystical elements in it—that did not come to him from authentic Judaism."⁴³ This last statement seems incompatible with the dominant argument of the book that Paul's religion is the result of his Diaspora background with its pagan influences wherein "he was detached from the authentic, living Judaism which was rooted in its own cultural soil."⁴⁴ But this is a tension frequently encountered in Jewish writing on Paul.

In the work of Martin **Buber** we again find the familiar polarization between Judaism, the Pharisees and Jesus⁴⁵ on the one hand, and Paul, Hellenistic Judaism and Christianity on the other. Buber sees here two different types of faith: the former represented by *Emunah*, an existential trust wherein the person finds himself in association with community (i.e. nation); the latter represented by *Pistis*, an intellectual assent to truth whereby an individual is converted.⁴⁶ Paul must be regarded as "the real originator of the Christian conception of faith," which he arrived at through the transformation of Israel's original notion of faith.⁴⁷ Paul's new faith arises "from a Greek attitude."⁴⁸

---

40. *From Jesus to Paul*, 461. "In place of a dying and rising *god*, such as was common in the various pagan religions of that time, he added to this attenuated Judaism a dying and rising *Messiah*" (449).

41. *From Jesus to Paul*, 580–81, 590.

42. *From Jesus to Paul*, 443; cf. 591.

43. *From Jesus to Paul*, 466. He describes this as "a deep conviction" arrived at through "intensive research over many years," and refers to personal letters from G. F. Moore in agreement with this view. Cf. Klausner's statement that Paul "was firmly rooted in Pharisaic Judaism in spite of himself" (606).

44. *From Jesus to Paul*, 465.

45. Buber poignantly writes, "From my youth onwards I have found in Jesus my great brother." *Two Types of Faith*, 12.

46. *Two Types of Faith*, 7–11, 170–74.

47. *Two Types of Faith*, 44, 48–49.

48. *Two Types of Faith*, 172.

Buber accounts for Paul's departure from classical Judaism by the Greek influence which he received through Hellenistic Judaism. At the outset of his book, Buber rejects Schweitzer's assessment that Paul's roots lie in the Jewish rather than the Greek world, adding that he "can connect the Pauline doctrine of faith . . . only with a peripheral Judaism, which was actually 'Hellenistic.'"[49] Buber does not go into detail concerning Paul's Hellenistic-Jewish background or the degree to which Paul was influenced by it. In discussing Paul's theology, however, he does refer to "the Gnostic nature of the essential features," viz., belief in powers which rule the world, the enslavement of man and the cosmos, and the consequent need of liberation.[50] Buber argues that the idea of the resurrection of Jesus found its preparation in Hellenism's Mystery Religions with their doctrine of dying and rising gods.[51] The perception of Jesus as deity was in turn made possible through "the crystallizing of the mythical element lying ready in the hearts of those influenced by Hellenism . . . until the new binitarian God-image was present."[52] When Buber contemplates Paul's theology, and in particular his doctrine of God, he writes "I no longer recognize the God of Jesus, nor his world in this world of Paul's."[53]

Paul's view, in short, is a "Gnostic view of the world."[54] At a key point, in the notion of the fatalistic domination of this world by evil powers, Paul was under the influence of "hellenistic Judaism of a popular variety."[55] It is particularly this notion of "demonocracy" with its stress on fate and the concomitant need for a mediator and redeemer that is seen by Buber to be the essence of Paulinism. Christian history, indeed, is classifiable according to the degree of influence of this Paulinism which by its very nature is antithetical to the perspective of Pharisaic Judaism.[56]

Without question Samuel **Sandmel** is the most prolific representative of the view that the key to understanding Paul is to be found in

---

49. *Two Types of Faith*, 14.
50. *Two Types of Faith*, 83.
51. *Two Types of Faith*, 100. Buber stresses that the resurrection of an individual person "does not belong to the realm of ideas of the Jewish world" (128).
52. *Two Types of Faith*, 109.
53. *Two Types of Faith*, 89.
54. *Two Types of Faith*, 148.
55. *Two Types of Faith*, 140. Hellenistic Judaism is characterized by Buber as "an eclecticsm from an attenuated Biblical tradition and a not less attenuated Stoic philosophy" (145).
56. *Two Types of Faith*, 162, 149–54. Buber finds this Paulinism outside Christianity, for example in the pessimism of Kafka (162–69).

his Greek background. The Greek environment in which he lived "had worked on him intensely,"[57] indeed to the extent that Pauline Christianity can be described as "a completely Grecian phenomenon."[58] Sandmel repeatedly compares Paul to Philo, another Hellenistic Jew— that is, one for whom "the purpose, perplexities, quests, and sense of achievement of Greek religion were accepted, harmonized, and assimilated."[59] Paul's Hellenistic ideas are said to "have as much or as little a Jewish matrix as Philo's own thought."[60]

At the same time, Sandmel stresses that Paul always thought of himself as a loyal Jew and his message as the purest Judaism.[61] He *was* loyal to his Hellenistic Judaism; yet, argues Sandmel, "the content of his Judaism, like that of other Greek Jews, had undergone a subtle, but radical shift," involving not merely new definitions of old words but "a change in the fabric of religious suppositions and in the goal of the religious quest."[62] Sandmel, who more than any other of the Jewish writers discussed in this essay employs the methodology of radical biblical criticism, regards the Acts of the Apostles as possessing little historical value and denies that Paul had any contact with the Pharisaic Judaism of Palestine.[63] Fundamental to Sandmel's perspective is his insistence that "Pauline Christianity and rabbinic Judaism share little more than a common point of departure, the Bible."[64] Indeed, the two are antithetical and this is ultimately due to the fact that Hellenistic Judaism, adapting to the Greek world, is itself "the blending of antitheses."[65]

While not going into detail, Sandmel refers to the specifically Hellenistic influence in Paul's doctrine through the pagan cults, philosophy and mythology of his environment. Like Buber, he finds of basic importance Paul's Greek notion of the individual human predicament and the

57. *The Genius of Paul*, xvi.

58. *A Jewish Understanding of the New Testament*, 104. "Paul is a Greek Jew, remote in thought and feeling from Palestinian Jews of his time." *Ibid.*, xxxiii (from the 1974 preface).

59. *The Genius of Paul*, 23.

60. *The Genius of Paul*, 70.

61. *The Genius of Paul*, xvi, 15, 21.

62. *The Genius of Paul*, 15.

63. *The Genius of Paul*, 12–15. Cf. *A Jewish Understanding of the New Testament*, xxxiii.

64. *The Genius of Paul*, 59. So far as religious experience is concerned, "Paul and rabbinic Judaism are poles apart" (60).

65. *The Genius of Paul*, 9.

necessity of escape from the body.⁶⁶ With a background common to Philo and the Stoics, Paul finds the solution in mystical experience, especially union with God resulting in the possibility of becoming a divine man, the transformation of a material being into a spiritual one.⁶⁷ This is the content through which Paul transmuted the comparatively Jewish Christianity which preceded him into a "gentilized Christianity" which itself made the Gentile mission a possibility and a success.⁶⁸ In Sandmel's view, Paul in this way recreated Christianity; it did not begin with him, but through him received new impulse sufficient to be regarded as a second beginning.⁶⁹

Note may finally be made of Sandmel's Montefiore Lecture of 1969, "Paul Reconsidered."⁷⁰ Here Sandmel suggests that Goodenough's work on Philo's Judaism provides a key for the positive explanation of Paul which Montefiore did not attempt. Sandmel, while still finding Hellenistic Judaism the best background against which to understand Paul, does not believe this enables him to account for the genesis of Paul's religion. Unlike the majority of Jewish writers on Paul, Sandmel regards the background of Paul as "unimportant"; Paul is "so individualistic that conceivably he could have come from any kind of a background."⁷¹

We may turn next to Leo **Baeck,** who more than any scholar thus far considered stresses Paul's Jewishness. Baeck does not for a moment deny the influence of Hellenistic ideas upon Paul; what he does do, however, is to point out the large extent to which these ideas were at home in the genuinely Jewish Diaspora. The fundamental shift from the horizontal perspective of the prophets (future oriented) to the vertical perspective of apocalyptic (the disclosure of the "above" in the present) that was crucial to Christianity and Paul (cf. his vision of Christ) had already found expression in Jewish apocalyptic (e.g. Daniel) influenced by Alexandrian Greek philosophy.⁷² Paul found much that was appealing in Hellenism;

---

66. *The Genius of Paul*, 22, 80, 89.

67. *The Genius of Paul*, 84, 92, 97. Cf. *Jewish Understanding*, 51, 99; *Judaism and Christian Beginnings* (New York: Oxford University Press, 1978) 335.

68. *The Genius of Paul*, 114-16. In Paul's Hellenism there is "a resounding echo of popular philosophy, popular religion, and both the attitudes and the sense of arrival which characterized the Greek mysteries" (114).

69. *The Genius of Paul*, 97, 113, 116. *Understanding*, 104.

70. In *Two Living Traditions*.

71. *Two Living Traditions* 210. See also *The First Christian Century in Judaism and Christianity: Certainties and Uncertainties* (New York: Oxford University Press, 1969) 127-28.

72. "The Faith of Paul," 98.

but, as Baeck puts it, since much of it was reminiscent of Jewish wisdom speculation, "no Jew could resist such aspects of Hellenism."[73] Paul's Hellenism is easily traceable; his sacramental teaching especially is influenced by the mystery cults. But much of his Greek, Stoic philosophical terminology may also be seen to be "within the Jewish compass."[74] Paul should not be regarded as a "Hellenist" at all since "his approach to the Hellenistic world was the same as that of some Palestinian teachers."[75] To be sure, Paul was "captivated by the analogies" offered by the mystery cults to the Christ-centered faith he proclaimed. Indeed analogy is basic to Paul's whole theological method.[76] Paul did not, however, create a new type of mystery religion. Rather, he saw and took advantage of the abundant means available in the Hellenistic world in order to carry out the essentially Jewish mission of gathering in the Gentiles.[77] In his missionary task and in his theology, Paul never wavered in his basic Jewish loyalty, down to and including the special election of the Jewish people. Thus while affirming Paul's Hellenism, Baeck also emphasizes Paul's Jewishness, and in this regard Baeck serves as an appropriate transition to the most recent Jewish trend in explaining Paul's background. Here it is argued that Paul's Judaism is indeed to be understood as a Palestinian Judaism.

Hans Joachim **Schoeps**' lengthy monograph on Paul is in some respects the most impressive of Jewish works devoted to Paul yet to appear. At the beginning of his book, Schoeps gives a full summary of Pauline research, reviewing in turn Hellenistic, Hellenistic-Judaistic, Palestinian-Judaic, and Eschatological approaches to the understanding of Paul. Regarding the Hellenistic-Judaistic approach, and in response particularly to Montefiore's structuring of the problem of Paul, Schoeps cautions that the rabbinism even of Palestine contained some exponents of Hellenistic ideas and that apocalypticism (neglected by Montefiore) also flourished in Palestine. Our present state of knowledge, moreover, "does not justify us in concluding that there was an irreconcilable opposition between Hellenistic and rabbinic Judaism."[78] There were, of course,

---

73. "The Faith of Paul," 101.
74. "The Faith of Paul."
75. "The Faith of Paul."
76. "The Faith of Paul," 104, 109.
77. "Nor did Paul, by stressing his apostolate to the Gentiles, deviate from the genuine Jewish creed." "The Faith of Paul," 108.
78. *Paul*, 26. Montefiore's procedure was an attempt "to replace one unknown quantity—the theology of Saul—by another unknown quantity, the theology of the

differences between the two;⁷⁹ nevertheless, there was also considerable overlap between the two.

What is remarkable in Schoeps' portrayal of Paul is his insistence upon Paul's contacts with Palestinian Judaism. He accepts the account in Acts concerning Paul's discipleship under Gamaliel, and takes note also that Paul was able to speak Aramaic when the occasion demanded it (Acts 21:40).⁸⁰ Indeed, only from Paul's contact with Pharisaic Judaism can the general character of Paul's thought be explained, and more especially his rabbinic argumentation and exegesis.⁸¹ "The fact that Paul was a 'rabbinist,' that his religion is to be approached as a 'radicalized Pharisaism' . . . may be accepted without further discussion."⁸² Further, writes Schoeps, "rabbinic connections and parallels may be discovered for most of Paul's doctrines and expressions of faith, without its being necessary to exploit in a prejudiced way the criterion of 'Hellenistic Judaism.'"⁸³ Even more striking is Schoeps' insistence that in ascertaining the derivation of Paul's thought "every explanation proceeding from rabbinism deserves *a limine* preference over all other explanation."⁸⁴

This is not to say that Schoeps finds the problem of Paul easy⁸⁵ or that he is oblivious to the reality of Hellenistic influence on Paul, or to those aspects of Paul that seem particularly non-Jewish (e.g. what he regards as sacramental mysticism).⁸⁶ In his summarizing remarks, Schoeps says that all of the schools of interpreting Paul "are relatively right."⁸⁷ Nevertheless it remains true that Schoeps is at odds with the Jewish scholars

---

Pharisaic Diaspora" (ibid.).

79. Hellenistic Judaism, for example, possessed a heightened consciousness of a missionary purpose, tended to ethicize Judaism, and viewed the Torah as a pedagogical book for all of humanity. *Paul*, 28-32.

80. *Paul*, 36-37.

81. *Paul*, 37-40. Paul, it is pointed out, was familiar with the seven hermeneutical rules of Hillel. Further, "as an allegorizing midrashist Paul became great among his contemporary rabbis" (39).

82. *Paul*, 37-38.

83. *Paul*, 40.

84. *Paul*, 40.

85. Schoeps describes the problem as "uncommonly difficult to solve" (*Paul*, 47). He also indicates the need for great caution when he writes of Pauline doctrine that "no sure genealogies . . . can be established" (43).

86. *Paul*, 42.

87. *Paul*, 47.

previously discussed,[88] and that he stresses Paul's authentic Jewishness even as measured by the standards of Palestinian Rabbinism. In keeping with this viewpoint, Schoeps argues for continuity between pre-Pauline Palestinian Christianity and Paul's Christianity: "The talk of Paul's acute Hellenization of Christianity which has sprung up in consequence of the Tübingen school must, however, be rejected."[89]

A recent full-length Jewish book on Paul is the very interesting contribution of Schalom **Ben-Chorin**. The burden of Ben-Chorin's book is found in his repeated insistence that Paul was and remained a Jew. Paul's argumentation, his exegesis, theology (even christology) are essentially Jewish—indeed at many points Pharisaic.[90] Paul is repeatedly dependent upon rabbinic teaching materials, as Ben-Chorin points out in the major chapter of his book, where he examines the theology of Paul's letters seriatim.[91] He disagrees with Buber's argument that Paul's concept of faith excluded the Hebrew notion of *Emunah*, siding rather with Schweitzer's opinion that "Paulus in der jüdischen, nicht in der griechischen Gedankenwelt wurzelt."[92] Even when Paul's teaching is in opposition to the views of Judaism, "er kann gar nicht anders denken, sprechen und schreiben als jüdisch, denn er ist und bleibt 'ein Pharisäer von Pharisäern.'"[93]

Paul's fundamental Jewishness traces back to his youth, to the days of his tutelage under Gamaliel. Unlike some of the Jewish scholars already discussed, Ben-Chorin accepts and affirms as of first importance Paul's time in Jerusalem at the feet of Gamaliel.[94] The young Paul was a "Talmid-Chacham," a "Jeschiva-Schüler," and the later Paul sounds again and again like a man who could not forget his earlier training.[95] The persistent Jewishness of his thought and speech, his deeply Jewish soul can only be explained by a firm rootage in Pharisaic Judaism in the

---

88. Cf. his criticism of Klausner for neglecting the eschatological dimension in Paul (*Paul*, 47–48). See also his criticism of Montefiore, 25f.

89. *Paul*, 48. Cf. also the following: "ideas of faith cherished and taught by the Jerusalem church were taken over by the neophyte Paul and are reflected in his letters" (62). In these passages Schoeps takes a deliberate stance against the Tübingen school, otherwise so influential upon Jewish scholars (e.g. Montefiore and Sandmel).

90. *Paulus*, 9.

91. "Theologie in Briefen," 106–81; cf. 39.

92. *Paulus*, 13.

93. *Paulus*, 168; cf. 174, 179.

94. As an aid to understanding Paul, Ben-Chorin devotes an entire chapter to Gamaliel as "Die Lehrer des Paulus," 189–203.

95. Ibid., 121, 152, 178.

days of his formal training—and only in the light of these can Paul be truly understood.

Yet Paul was also undoubtedly a Diaspora Jew in the fullest sense. Like other Diaspora Jews, he had drunk deeply of Hellenism. Paul indeed is best described as a "wanderer between two worlds"; it was his goal—and proved in no small measure his success—to be "a Jew to the Jews and a Greek to the Greeks" (1 Cor 9:20). It is here that Ben-Chorin finds the explanation of Paul. Far from downplaying the Hellenistic dimension in Paul, Ben-Chorin calls attention to it again and again. Thus, like many of the scholars considered above, Ben-Chorin contrasts Paul the Diaspora Jew with Jesus' Palestinian Jewishness, and Paul with the original disciples.[96] Paul's transformation of Jesus and his theology in general are so Hellenistic that the original disciples could not understand him.[97] In his christology Paul employs the apocalyptic tradition of Hellenistic Judaism; for his concept of baptism he is dependent on the mystery cults.[98] His world is abstract and also dualistic (e.g. flesh and spirit).[99] For his preaching, in short, he has "das unendliche Reservoir der Heidenwelt vor sich."[100]

Paul is the prototype of the assimilated Jew who in speech and thought conforms to his Diaspora environment, but who though he appears to repress his Judaism, actually mediates it to his environment.[101] Paul indeed may be said to have had another teacher in Philo. Like Philo from whom he is said directly to have derived his allegorical interpretation of the Bible, he attempted to synthesize Jewish and Greek ideas.[102] Paul, like Philo, in the last analysis can only be understood in terms of Hellenistic Judaism.

For Ben-Chorin, then, both Palestinian and Hellenistic Judaism are vitally important to the understanding of Paul. The blend is the result of

---

96. Ibid., 43, 48.

97. "Er ist nicht einfach ein hellenistisch assimilierter Jude, sondern er benutzt Elemente des Hellenismus zur Darstellung des Judentums, *seines* Judentums, aber dieses Judentum ist wiederum so hellenistisch durchsetzt, dass es Gedankengänge und Gedankenreihen enthält, die die ... könnten" (ibid., 56; cf. 48).

98. Ibid., 48, 52.

99. Ibid., 49, 52.

100. Ibid., 52.

101. Ibid., 100.

102. The fundamental difference between the two is that while Paul wanted to be a Jew to the Jew and a Greek to the Greek, Philo tried to be a Greek to the Jew and a Jew to the Greek. Ibid., 198.

Paul's understanding of his mission to the Gentiles, itself the outworking of a Jewish universalism. What he took to them was fundamentally Jewish, but Hellenized for the sake of the mission. Inevitably Paul was misunderstood and became a tragic figure. Contrary to Paul's best intention, the Jew perceived him as a lawless, pagan Greek, and the Greek perceived him as a strange Pharisaic rabbi.[103] In attempting to bring Judaism to the Gentiles by means of Christianity, he experienced rejection both from Judaism and from early Christianity.[104] Thus without denying Paul's Hellenism, Ben-Chorin has given one of the strongest affirmations of Paul's Jewishness, insisting especially on Paul's deep rootage in Pharisaic Judaism.

Ben-Chorin was able to entitle his book on Jesus, *Bruder Jesus;*[105] now **Richard L. Rubenstein** has given us a book entitled *My Brother Paul*. In this interesting and unusual book, Rubenstein studies Paul primarily from the perspective of Freudian psychology, attempting to demonstrate the extent to which Pauline insights parallel and anticipate those of Freud. In the course of reaching this goal, however, Rubenstein engages in biblical and theological analysis important and insightful in its own right and this is the subject matter which we focus upon, to the neglect of the major purpose of the book.

Rubenstein stresses Paul's Jewishness and Pharisaic background.[106] He is of course aware of Hellenistic influence on Paul,[107] but regards this influence as minimal. He points to the influence of Hellenism upon first-century Judaism and the great difficulty of distinguishing between the Hellenistic and Jewish influence upon early Christianity.[108] He is therefore pessimistic about resolving the question of Paul's background; yet he writes "I have come to believe that Paul's thought and religious life were far more Jewish than Greek."[109]

---

103. Ibid., 213.

104. Ibid., 209.

105. See above, n. 4. To be fair to Ben-Chorin, he does refer to "der brüderlichen Gestalt des Juden Paulus" (ibid., 217). But it is significant that he did not entitle his book "Brüder Paulus."

106. Paul derived the training necessary for his mission, his interpretive skills and methodology from the Pharisees (*My Brother Paul*, 141).

107. *My Brother Paul*, 90, 105, 156.

108. *My Brother Paul*, 19, 145.

109. *My Brother Paul*, 19. In a bibliographical note he mentions his conviction that "contemporary interpretations of Paul must build largely upon the foundations laid by Davies" (in the latter's book *Paul and Rabbinic Judaism* [London: SPCK, 1955²]).

Paul always thought of himself as a faithful Jew, loyal to the religion of his fathers.[110] Rubenstein takes "most emphatic exception" to the opinion that "no one misunderstood Judaism more profoundly than Paul."[111] Rubenstein, like several other Jewish scholars, refers to Paul's plight vis-à-vis his Jewish brethren as a "tragedy."[112] The root of the disagreement concerned Jewish messianic expectation: for Paul fulfillment had begun. It was as a result of his Jewishness and his conviction of the dawning of fulfillment that Paul turned to the Gentile mission. "Nowhere is Paul more prototypically Jewish" than in this enterprise, which he saw as the necessary precondition of the eventual consummation of God's purposes for Israel.[113]

Nevertheless, in his message of Christ crucified and risen, as in his sacramentalism, Paul "understood clearly how profoundly Judaism had been 'stood on its head.'"[114] More than anyone, "Paul of Tarsus stood at the crossroads of rabbinic Judaism and Christianity."[115] But the surprise is that Rubenstein rejects the widespread view of Jewish scholars that Paul is the virtual creator of Christianity: "In reality it was not Paul but Jesus who instituted the irreparable breach with established Judaism."[116] Rubenstein also denies that there was a radical disagreement between the views of Paul and those of the primitive Jerusalem church.[117]

The unusual character of much of Rubenstein's perspective is no doubt to be explained by his own relativism. He rejects both Judaism and Christianity as normative solutions to the problem of mankind.[118] In the last analysis, when Rubenstein refers to Paul as his brother, he affirms not Paul's religious heritage, but Paul's existential humanness. He

110. *My Brother Paul*, 6, 114.

111. *My Brother Paul*, 198. The words expressing the opinion (wrongly attributed to Loewe by Rubenstein) are C. G. Montefiore's in *A Rabbinic Anthology*, eds. C. G. Montefiore and H. Loewe (New York: Schocken, 1974) xiii.

112. *My Brother Paul*, 127. "Rejection of Pharisaism was not equivalent to rejection of Judaism" (117).

113. *My Brother Paul*, 129.

114. *My Brother Paul*, 103.

115. *My Brother Paul*, 23.

116. *My Brother Paul*, 121, following Johannes Munck, *Paul and the Salvation of Mankind*. Rubenstein notes the "watchword of much of the thoughtful Jewish New Testament scholarship in modern times"—"Jesus, yes; Paul, never!"—adding that "I have never been able to share that judgment" (114).

117. *My Brother Paul*, 122–23.

118. *My Brother Paul*, 20, 138.

has empathy with Paul's conflicts and their eventual resolution through the authority of a personal experience.[119] With this in mind, one may question the fairness of representing Rubenstein, the self-proclaimed "psychological man" as truly Jewish in outlook.[120]

The above survey shows that Jewish scholars have increasingly stressed Paul's authentic Jewishness. The trend is to locate Paul's background not primarily in Hellenistic and Diaspora Judaism as Montefiore had done,[121] but in Rabbinic and Palestinian Judaism.[122] This trend of course is consonant with the recent realization of some scholars that it is no longer possible to make a facile dichotomy between Hellenism and Judaism and thus between Diaspora and Palestinian Judaism.[123] Even the Judaism of Palestine was subject to a high degree of Hellenistic influence, and thus much that was previously described as Hellenistic and alien may now be designated as Rabbinic

It is nevertheless to be noted that despite the new willingness to perceive Paul as a Rabbinic Jew, at key junctures Jewish scholars still appeal to Hellenistic influence upon Paul. That is, when Paul as a Rabbinic Jew draws conclusions that do not fit the preconceived model of Rabbinic Judaism, his position is explained by appealing to something external to that Judaism. W. D. Davies has thus criticized Schoeps for presenting a Paul who is a "split personality" in whose mind Jewish and Hellenistic concepts "never come to terms," and who therefore may be "psychologically incredible."[124] Ben-Chorin, who also has recourse lo the Hellenistic explanation of Paul at the most important points, indicates his awareness of the difficulty when he deliberately describes Paul as a "wanderer between two worlds."[125]

---

119. *My Brother Paul*, 4-6.

120. *My Brother Paul*, 21.

121. Sandmel is the most notable exception to this statement. He still regards Paul as a Hellenistic Jew but without alleging that this can account for the genesis of Paul's religion. "Paul Reconsidered," 210.

122. To the scholars discussed above we may add David Flusser, who also identifies Paul's Judaism as Pharisaic in form. "Paul of Tarsus," 190-92.

123. See M. Hengel, *Judaism and Hellenism*, 2 vols., trans. J. Bowden (London: SCM, 1974); W. D. Davies, *Paul and Rabbinic Judaism*, 1-16. For a criticism of this dichotomizing as applied to the study of early Christianity, see I. H. Marshall, *NTS* 19 (1973) 271-87.

124. In his review of Schoeps' book on Paul in *NTS* 10 (1963-64) 293-304.

125. The title of chapter five in *Paulus*.

The key areas are obvious: Paul's view of the Law, his soteriology and christology, his mysticism and doctrine of sacraments. What explanation of Paul's background is most compatible with Paul's teaching on these subjects? This is the quandary of Jewish writers on Paul.

Paul's view of the law is widely regarded by Jewish scholars as unacceptable even within the Hellenistic Judaism of the Diaspora (Montefiore, Klausner) and as indeed attributable to Gnostic (Kohler, Buber) or more generally Diaspora (Friedländer,[126] Sandmel) influence. In his important essay Leo Baeck argues that Paul's attitude toward the Law was authentically Rabbinic and is to be explained by his conviction that the eschatological age was already present because the Messiah had appeared, and therefore that the aeon of Torah was at an end.[127] This explanation of Paul's view of the Law is accepted by Schoeps who regards Paul as adhering to an aeon-theology although he still finds it necessary to see much of Paul's perspective in this area as essentially Hellenistic, especially where Paul reveals a legalistic or moralizing view of the Law.[128] Only Ben-Chorin does not appeal to Hellenistic influence in explaining Paul's view of the Law. For him the notion of suffering under the burdensome yoke of Torah is conceivable within Pharisaic Judaism[129] and Paul's personal frustration need not be attributed to Hellenistic influence. Paul's attitude toward the Law, according to Ben-Chorin, is paradoxical but "keinen Ausbruch aus den Judentum darstellt."[130]

Jewish scholars thus stress as far as they can Paul's Jewishness in his view of the Law. All agree in pointing out that Paul himself remained an observer of the Law and encouraged other Jewish Christians to do so; that even when Paul spoke about freedom from the Law, he did not mean

---

126. "The 'Pauline' Emancipation From the Law: A Product of the PreChristian Jewish Diaspora," *JQR* 14 (1902) 265–302, reprinted in *Judaism and Christianity*, ed. Jacob B. Agus (New York: Arno, 1973).

127. "The Faith of Paul," 106. (Baeck, it will be recalled, does not deny a degree of Hellenistic influence upon Paul.) See the full discussion of this subject in W. D. Davies, *Torah in the Messianic Age and/or the Age to Come*, SBLMS 7 (Philadelphia: SBL, 1952).

128. Thus on the one hand Schoeps can write: "we have here in Paul's abolition of the Law a purely Jewish problem of saving history, not a Hellenistic one" (*Paul*, 173); but on the other: "Paul succumbed to a characteristic distortion of vision which had its antecedents in the spiritual outlook of Judaic Hellenism" (213), so that "the Christian church has received a completely distorted view of the Jewish law at the hands of a Diaspora Jew" (261–62).

129. He likens Saul the Pharisee to zealous Yeshiva students in modern Jerusalem. *Paulus*, 66.

130. Ibid., 69.

the moral Law; and that it was exactly this attitude of freedom toward the ceremonial and purity laws that made possible the mission to the Gentiles to which Paul felt called, and which itself is rightly regarded as a Jewish enterprise.

The apparent necessity of the appeal to Hellenistic influence upon Paul's theology is of course even more obvious when it comes to the areas of christology, soteriology, mysticism and sacraments. Here even those who most stress Paul's Palestinian Jewishness (such as Schoeps and Ben-Chorin) turn to Hellenistic influence whether direct or indirect, via Hellenistic Judaism, to explain Paul. Yet with due recognition of Paul's appropriation of Hellenistic vocabulary for his own purposes, his theology is capable of being explained as a whole on the basis of what was available to him within Palestinian Judaism[131]—that is, if we are able to add his experience of Christ on the Damascus road as the dynamic responsible for his theology.

The irony is that the more Jewish Paul is seen lo be, the more difficult it becomes to explain him when one denies the truth of his major premise, viz. that the crucified, risen Jesus is Lord of all, the fulfillment of the promises of God. If Paul is basically a syncretist, combining Hellenistic ideas derived from the Mystery Religions or Gnosticism with ideas from Judaism, then Paul may properly be regarded as the creator of a new religion, something neither Jewish nor Greek. But if, on the other hand, Paul is an exponent of fundamentally Jewish ideas, then his theology can at least conceivably reflect, as he says it does, the fulfilment of the Old Testament.

If a consistently Jewish explanation of Paul is undertaken, as in the trend of Jewish scholarship, what must be faced is Paul's major premise which for him in turn depends upon his experience on the Damascus road. The reality of that experience as well as its central importance is affirmed by Jewish scholars (especially Baeck, Schoeps and Ben-Chorin). It is admitted that only an objective reality of some kind is able lo account for the dramatic transformation of Paul and the christocentric character of his theology.[132] Damascus is clearly the watershed that is

---

131. See especially W. D. Davies, *Paul and Rabbinic Judaism*; cf. E. P. Sanders, *Paul and Palestinian Judaism*; and more generally H. Ridderbos, *Paul: An Outline of His Theology*, trans. J. R. DeWitt (Grand Rapids: Eerdmans, 1975); and F. F. Bruce, *Paul: Apostle of the Free Spirit = Paul: Apostle of the Heart Set Free*.

132. "If we wish to understand what happened at this point in the life of the apostle, and what were its consequences, then we must accept fully the real objectivity of the encounter as it is testified in the letters and in Acts." Schoeps, *Paul*, 55.

responsible for the work and thought of the Apostle.[133] What the experience actually was is not so clear. The older view that Paul was an epileptic (e.g. Kohler, Klausner) is strongly rejected by Sandmel and Ben-Chorin,[134] as is any suggestion of mere hallucination. The virtually unanimous Jewish explanation is that Paul experienced some kind of vision analogous to the psychic phenomena referred to in 2 Cor 12:2-4, 7. Because of indications of Paul's mystic and ecstatic bent (1 Cor 14:6, 18), he is regarded as having been especially susceptible to extraordinary visions. Several Jewish authors (Kohler, Buber, Baeck, Ben-Chorin) also refer to a Hellenistic context or influence as pertinent to understanding Paul's experience. Thus the Damascus experience of Paul is not regarded as a fabrication, but as an objective event to be explained naturalistically on the basis of Paul's psychic personality.[135] What actually happened on the Damascus road, as Ben-Chorin puts it, "bleibt letzlich das Geheimnis der Seele des Paulus."[136]

We may now make some general summarizing comments about the modern Jewish study of Paul. (1) Jewish scholars are making a genuine effort to understand Paul. They evidence a new openness to Paul and a repudiation of the old stereotypes. (2) There is a conscious attempt to bring Paul within the sphere of Judaism as far as this is possible. Explanation of Paul on the basis of Hellenism, or even Hellenistic Judaism, is giving way to the assertion of Palestinian Judaism as Paul's background. This Jewish reclamation of Paul, however, is still hindered at important points by the appeal to Hellenism to explain what is regarded as non-Jewish.[137] (3) From the Jewish perspective Paul's teaching is eccentric but

---

133. "Was Paulus formte, lag vor Damaskus, was ihn unformte, erfolgte in Damaskus, in der Vision vor den Toren der Stadt." Ben-Chorin, *Paulus*, 178-79.

134. Ben-Chorin refers to a refutation of this idea in a paper read by a Jewish physician (Dr. Arthur Stern) at a neurology congress in Jerusalem in 1955 entitled "Zum Problem der Epilepsie des Paulus," later published in *Psychiatria et Neurologia*, 133.5 (Basel, 1957).

135. Rubenstein explains Paul's Damascus experience in Freudian terminology as the result of Paul's yearning to regain the infant's feeling of omnipotence. *My Brother Paul*, 50.

136. *Paulus*, 37.

137. We have not included in this essay the highly eccentric view of Hyam Maccoby, who argued that Paul was a Greek proselyte to Judaism and the creator of Christianity. For a full review, see my essay, "The Making of a Myth: Hyam Maccoby's View of Paul," in *The Cradle of Christianity: Judaism, Jesus and the New Testament. Essays in Honor of Craig A. Evans*. Thomas R. Hatina and Stanley E. Porter, eds. (Leiden/Boston:

nevertheless it is attributed ultimately to his Jewishness in that it is the result of his great burden for the Gentiles and his desire to make Judaism a truly universal religion. He thus may be said to have created a Judaism for Gentiles. Even Kohler, who minimizes Paul's Jewishness and regards him as an out-and-out Hellenist, is able to write: "He was an instrument in the hand of Divine Providence to win the heathen nations for Israel's God of righteousness."[138] That Paul remained loyal to Israel and thus never finally abandoned his Jewishness, despite this preoccupation with the Gentiles, is noted by frequent appreciative reference to Romans 9–11. (4) Jewish writers are able to speak admiringly of Paul as a great and influential theologian. Insofar as Paul is regarded as authentically Jewish he is praised.[139] A distinction of course is generally made between Paul and Paulinism. The latter is regarded as the exaggeration of certain of Paul's insights and the neglect of others, resulting in the opposite of what Paul actually held. It is Paulinism that is responsible for the widespread distortion of Paul which has concealed his true and abiding Jewishness. (5) Despite all the energy expended by Jewish scholars to uncover Paul's authentic Jewishness and to approach him positively and appreciatively, it is all the more remarkable that his theology is rejected *in toto*. His christology, his view of the Law, his soteriology with its pessimism concerning man's moral capability, his doctrine of sacraments, and many of his social and ethical teachings are considered objectionable.

It must be said then that although Paul's Jewishness is increasingly seen and appreciated, Jewish scholarship has not been able to reclaim Paul. The impasse that confronts Jewish scholarship at this point, though more formidable, is not dissimilar to that which is met in the Jewish reclamation of Jesus: Whence the undeniable newness, the strange, the unexpected? If the source of that newness in Paul is alien to the authentic religion of the Jews, and stems from Gnosticism or the Mystery Religions, then the Jewish argument stands and Paul the syncretist is properly regarded as the creator of Christianity. If, on the other hand, that newness is, so to speak, a Jewish newness, the result of the initial fulfilment of the

---

Brill, 2024) 236–57.

138. "Saul of Tarsus," 86.

139. Sometimes this appreciation can be very individualistic. Thus, for example, Montefiore admires Paul to the extent that Paul supports the perspective of Liberal Judaism; Ben-Chorin as a Diaspora Jew who has lived in Jerusalem identifies with Paul in his attempt to find a bridge between two worlds of existence; Rubenstein, on the other hand, finds psychological empathy with Paul as one who opts for the authority of his own experience over against the tradition in which he stands.

promises of the Old Testament to Israel, then Paul is the recipient of truth and the rejection of Paul's theology by Jewish scholars is unwarranted. If Paul on the Damascus road really received a revelation from the resurrected Christ, then we have the dynamic that can explain Paul's theology with its newness within a fully Jewish framework, viz. as the culmination of the history of Israel and the inaugurated consummation of the Old Testament tradition.

Certain trends in Jewish scholarship on Paul seem to suggest the propriety if not the plausibility of the latter interpretation: that Paul exhibits thorough (Palestinian) Jewishness (contra the Hellenistic explanation); that Paul himself viewed his theology as nothing other than the true Judaism (and not something alien); that Paul stands in a degree of continuity with the Jerusalem apostles (rather than in total discontinuity);[140] and that Paul's Damascus road experience is to be understood as an objectively real event (not hallucination or deliberate fraud). All of this can be accounted for, and the whole of Paul's theology can be integrated satisfactorily into a fully Jewish framework, when the truth oJ his gospel is accepted. If the promised messianic age is somehow present in and through the crucified, risen Jesus, the surprising, required newness that even Paul had to learn before he gave it expression can be conceived. But if this possibility—the key to Paul's theology, as is correctly recognized by many Jewish scholars—is denied from the beginning, then Paul can only remain an enigma. There is much to appreciate in the stress on Paul's Jewishness in recent Jewish scholarship, but the extent of Paul's true Jewishness—its depth, its joy, and its vision—is grasped only when Paul's central premise is accepted: that "all the promises of God find their Yes in him [Christ] and that is why we utter the Amen through him, to the glory of God" (2 Cor 1:20).

---

140. Of the items mentioned here, admittedly this has the weakest support from Jewish scholars. But despite dissenters, support is found in Klausner (limited), Schoeps and Rubenstein.

7

Balancing the Old and the New

The Law of Moses in Matthew and Paul

FEW WOULD CHALLENGE THE statement that one of the most interesting—and, to be sure, most challenging—aspects of New Testament theology is the problem of continuity and discontinuity between the old and the new. Exactly here lies the potential for exceptional richness of understanding but also for considerable perplexity. A proper, that is, *biblical*, understanding of most if not all important theological themes of the New Testament requires determining the proper balance between the old and the new. Unless one sees the New Testament as the fruition of the Old Testament, one will come to a true understanding of neither. But equally important, unless one at the same time allows in the New Testament what is truly new, one will be unable to gain a proper understanding of the relationship between the two Testaments. The challenge of biblical theology is to give proper heed to both the old and the new—not just the old, not just the new, but finding the right balance between the two.

There is thus an admirable wisdom in Augustine's famous dictum *the new lies latent in the old and the old is made patent in the new.*[1] The richest understanding of the theological themes of the Old and New Testaments begins by exploring the lines of connection between promise and fulfillment. The New Testament student must know the Old

---

1. *In vetere novum lateat, et in novo vetus pateat* (Migne, *Patrologia Latina* 34.625).

Testament and the Old Testament student must know the New Testament, and both indeed should also know the literature of the Second Temple period.

Virtually every major theme of the New Testament comes into sharp focus by an examination of the extent of its continuity and discontinuity with the Old Testament. This is true of such important themes as law (as we shall see below), gospel, covenant, the person of Christ, salvation, the people of God, and eschatology, to mention only a few. The New Testament never tires of stressing that what it is describing is the fulfillment of the Old Testament. But, as all who have studied the quotations for even a short time know well, it is the Old Testament as interpreted by the New Testament writers! Thus it is a matter of old *and* new The old is seen through the lens of the new. In a similar way, Jesus clearly comes as the fulfiller of the old, not on its own terms, without any significant forward motion in the history of salvation, but as, and by virtue of being, the bringer of the new, the dramatic *novum* of the gospel. With the new comes new and deeper understanding of the old. But where old and new are juxtaposed in this way, we should not be surprised to encounter tensions, complexity, and paradox.

The Gospel of Matthew provides exceptionally fruitful ground for exploring this matter since the question of how the gospel relates to the scriptures of the Old Covenant was far from theoretical for its Jewish Christian readers. Indeed, one main reason the evangelist wrote was to demonstrate the continuity of the new with the old, as the famous fulfillment quotations alone indicate. And yet, as Matthew knows well, this fulfillment contains within it undeniably new dimensions. The key to understanding the well-known tensions within Matthew thus is an appreciation of the importance of the statement in 13:52 "And he said to them, 'Therefore every scribe who has been trained for the kingdom of heaven is like the master of a household who brings out of his treasure what is new and what is old.'" It hardly need be said that the old remains important. The new, however, is not only *also* important, It is *indispensable* to a true knowledge of God's purposes in their totality. A Christian scribe—that is, one trained in the understanding of the work of Jesus in proclaiming the kingdom—must therefore find the balance that does justice to both old and new.

The need to discern the proper balance between old and new is stressed also by Paul, who is often wrongly put at the opposite pole from Matthew on virtually every subject. Paul too knows the importance of understanding the new from the old and the old from the new. He can write that "in him [Christ] every one of God's promises is a 'Yes'" (2 Cor 1:20), knowing full well that this "yes" could make sense only if one took into account the new dimensions of what God had disclosed in Christ. Thus he soon refers to the need of the Jews to read the old with new understanding: "But their minds were hardened. Indeed, to this very day, when they hear the reading of the old covenant, that same veil is still there, since only in Christ is it set aside. Indeed, to this very day whenever Moses is read, a veil lies over their minds, but when one turns to the Lord, the veil is removed" (2 Cor 3:15–16).[2] Matthew and Paul would have agreed on the necessity of a new understanding of the old, while continuing to maintain the importance of the fact that it is precisely the old that comes to fulfillment in the new.

In what follows, I intend to show that this perspective can help us to understand the notoriously difficult subject of the law in both Matthew and Paul. In the process, I hope also to show that Matthew and Paul are not nearly as far apart on this subject as is often claimed.

MATTHEW AND THE LAW

The Gospel of Matthew is well known for the statement in 5:17–18, which marks Jesus' loyalty to the law in the following words, "Do not think that I have come to abolish the law or the prophets. I have not come to abolish but to fulfill. For truly I tell you, until heaven and earth pass away, not one letter, not one stroke of a letter, will pass from the law until all is accomplished." Although Matthew has probably reformulated the material and perhaps added some emphasis in adapting it to his readership, I find little reason to doubt that Jesus said something quite like this. We have, on the contrary, every reason to believe that Jesus considered his work and his teaching to be in continuity with, and thus loyal to, the scriptures of Israel generally, and the law specifically. His quotation of those scriptures and the extent to which his own ethical teaching depends on them are clear evidence of this loyalty.

At the same time, however, it is clear that for Matthew Jesus is anything but merely another interpreter of the law. Immediately following the passage quoted above come the well-known antitheses, where Jesus

---

2. On this passage, see the probing study by Scott J. Hafemann, *Paul, Moses and the History of Israel: The Letter/Spirit Contrast and the Argument from Scripture in 2 Corinthians 3* (Peabody, MA: Hendrickson, 1996).

deals with the sacred tradition of the law with an unparalleled sovereign freedom and authority: "You have heard [such and such about the meaning of the law], but *I* say to you." In the third, fourth, and fifth of these antitheses he goes against the normal interpretation of the Torah. The note at the end of the Sermon on the Mount, that "the crowds were astounded at his teaching, for he taught them as one having authority, and not as their scribes" (7:28-29), is therefore no surprise. And for all of Matthew's conservatism, as reflected for example in his redaction of Mark 7:19 (where he omits Mark's comment that thus Jesus declared all foods clean), he still presents Jesus as one who by his interpretation of the law transcends the usual understandings of it. Thus Jesus still declares that "it is not what goes into the mouth that defiles a person" (15:11), and the implications for the dietary laws are not far below the surface of this statement. He transcends the usual understanding of the sabbath commandment (12:1-14). His teaching concerning the grounds for divorce (5:31-32; 19:3-12) also transcends the normal understanding of the law. By refusing to allow a would be disciple to bury his father. he violates in a shocking way the contemporary understanding of the commandment to honor one's father and mother (8:21-22).

This authority of Jesus with respect to the law is inseparable from his announcement of the dawning of the kingdom of God and his own personal claims in that connection. For Matthew, Jesus is not one teacher among others. He is the "one teacher," the "one tutor, the Messiah" (23:8, 10).[3] Jesus' announcement of the kingdom brings a turning point in the ages, and Matthew's emphasis on the fulfillment of the scriptures has this in view. He furthermore records Jesus' saying that "all the prophets and the law prophesied until John came" (11:13). The day of messianic fulfillment has come (11:2-6), the time longed for by "many prophets and righteous people," and blessed are the eyes of the disciples because *they* see and hear the good news (13:17). The day of the bridegroom has come, the time of the new cloth and the new wine (9:14-17). It is in this dramatic newness that we will find the key to understanding the statements of Matthew concerning Jesus and the law. That is, it is a mistake to attempt to understand 5:17-18 as if it were spoken by a teacher who could be ranked with others, even at the head of others, and as if nothing

---

3. For a fruitful drawing out of the meaning of this passage, see Samuel Byrskog, *Jesus the Only Teacher: Didactic Authority and Transmission in Ancient Israel, Ancient Judaism and the Matthean Community*, ConBNT 24 (Stockholm: Almquist & Wiksell, 1994).

dramatically new were being announced. The teaching of Jesus will not make sense apart from this context of newness.

We have, then, both old and new here. The old cannot be understood on its own terms because the times have changed. And yet the new is by no means to be understood apart from the old. It is, rather, in continuity with the old, but as its fulfillment and not merely its perpetuation.

This insight informs our approach to Matthew's view of the law as expressed in the difficult 5:17–19. Matthew's Jesus calls his disciples to the righteousness of the law. He does so, however, as the eschatological Messiah, who is by definition the supremely authoritative interpreter of the law. He comes to fulfill the law (and the prophets)[4] through his definitive interpretation of it. It is obvious that the resultant pattern of righteousness taught by Jesus has a high congruence with the righteousness taught by the law As we have seen, however, at a number of points his teaching transcends the usual reading of the law This is a part of the newness he brings. The effect of this newness, and the accompanying definitive authority, is such that Jesus' interpretation of the law *is* the ultimate meaning of the law. He brings the law to its intended meaning.[5] It is this fact alone that makes intelligible the reference to the permanent validity of the tiniest detail of the law and the importance of "the least of these commandments" (5:19). To be faithful to Jesus' exposition of the law is to be loyal to the entirety of the law. To put It differently, not even the law's slightest detail is lost within the definitive interpretation provided by the Messiah, who brings newness—indeed, the turning of the ages.[6]

This is the meaning of Jesus affirmation of unshakable loyalty to the law. Not for a moment will Matthew allow that Jesus or his teaching was untrue to the law. In a context that does not allow for the new, it may well appear that Jesus was not loyal to the law; however, the placement of 5:17–18 just prior to the antitheses, guards against such a misunderstanding. The *key* to a correct understanding is the realization that the new has an effect on how the old is preserved. The redaction of Mark

---

4. Four out of the eight occurrences of *nomos* ("law") in Matthew (5:17; 7:12; 11:13; 22:40) link the word with *prophētai* ("prophets"). The law, for Matthew, cannot be understood without attention to the fulfillment of the prophets.

5. For the exegesis of the passage, see D. A. Hagner, *Matthew 1–13*, WBC 33A (Dallas: Word, 1993) 102–10.

6. To be sure, hyperbole is part of the rhetoric of 5:18–19. Cf. Klyne Snodgrass, "Matthew and the Law," in SBLSP (Atlanta: Scholars, 1988) 549. Now available in *Treasures New and Old*, eds. D. R.Bauer and M. A. Powell (Atlanta: Scholars, 1996) 99–127.

2:22 in Matt 9:17 is revealing. According to Matthew, following Mark, new wine (i.e., the gospel) is put into new wineskins (i.e., new modes of conduct appropriate to the new wine). But then Matthew uniquely adds the statement "and so both are preserved," indicating that the skins themselves remain important. To be noted, however, is the fact that the skins are *new*. The old skins— the traditional interpretation of the law—are not compatible with the newness entailed by the gospel. The law is indeed preserved, but *as interpreted by Jesus*. New wine requires new skins. For Matthew, the one who follows the teaching of Jesus has in effect fulfilled the slightest aspects of the law.

PAUL AND THE LAW

The recent flurry of books and articles on the subject of Paul and the law indicates well the difficulty of the subject. Some scholars even deny that Paul could conceptualize with any degree of complexity; they then draw the rather desperate conclusion that he was either confused on the subject or could not make up his mind.[7]

Although there is no need for us to review the discussion here, a crucial factor affecting all recent writing on the subject must be mentioned, namely the more positive understanding of first-century Judaism propagated especially by E. P. Sanders.[8] Sanders's view, now widely held in the scholarly world, is that first-century Judaism is not to be understood as being legalistic—that is, merit based, so that one had to earn acceptance with God by means of righteous deeds. Instead, Judaism is to he understood as a "covenantal nomism," in Sanders's phrase; that is, a religion *centered on obedience to the law*, but within the larger framework of grace provided by the covenant (and its basis, election). If, however, there were no Jews in Paul's day who were legalists in this sense, the questions arise: Against whom does Paul argue in Galatians and Romans? And what does his polemic against the law mean? The result has been the development of the so-called "new perspective" on Paul, in which it is further argued that justification by faith is not central to Paul's theology, but rather a pragmatic way of facilitating the gentile mission.

---

7. E. g . Heikki Räisänen, *Paul and the Law*, WUNT 29, 2nd ed. (Tübingen: Mohr Siebeck, 1987). E. P. Sanders, *Paul, the Law and the Jewish People* (Philadelphia: Fortress, 1983).

8. E. P. Sanders, *Paul and Palestinian Judaism* (Philadelphia: Fortress, 1977).

We must begin, however, with a very brief look at the problem posed by Paul's statements concerning the law in the context of the gospel. The major difficulty is that Paul makes both positive and negative statements. Positively, for example, he writes with forceful words, "Do we then overthrow the law by this faith? By no means! On the contrary, we uphold the law" (Rom 3:31). Elsewhere he writes, "Is the law then opposed to the promises of God? Certainly not" (Gal 3:21). He can describe the law, and specifically the commandments, with the adjectives "holy and just and good" (Rom 7:12). And, commenting on the purpose of the work of Christ, he says that the goal was "that the just requirement of the law might be fulfilled in us" (Rom. 8:4).

On the other hand, Paul's gospel is disclosed "apart from the law" (Rom 3:21), with the result that "a person is justified by faith apart from works prescribed by the law" (Rom 3:28; cf. Gal 2:16). By contrast, "all who rely on the works of the law are under a curse," and "Christ redeemed us from the curse of the law" (Gal 3:10, 13; cf. 4:4–5). Christians are described as people "discharged from the law, dead to that which held us captive" (Rom 7:6). Similarly, "the law was our disciplinarian until Christ came, so that we might be justified by faith. But now that faith has come, we are no longer subject to a disciplinarian" (Gal. 3:24–25). Most dramatic of all, Paul writes in Romans 10:4 that "Christ is the end of the law so that there may be righteousness for everyone who believes."

Of course, it is one thing to quote texts; it is another to understand them correctly. Exegesis is everything, and the question remains: What do these texts mean? In the effort to reconcile the apparent contradiction in the above paragraphs, the texts have recently been subject to widely varying interpretations. We will here focus on the work of those who adhere to the new perspective on Paul. The positive view of Judaism as a religion of grace, and not of merit based on righteous deeds, now provides the backdrop against which all discussion of Paul must be conducted. We cannot for a moment doubt the basic correctness of this conclusion concerning the essential nature of Judaism. But if this conclusion is correct, then about what, or against whom, is Paul arguing? Advocates of the new perspective deny that Paul had any quarrel with Judaism or the law per se.[9] What Paul opposes, for them, is not obedience to the law or righteousness based on the law. The "works of the law" against which Paul

---

9. On this subject, see Hagner, "Paul's Quarrel With Judaism," in *Anti-Semitism and Early Christianity: Issues of Polemic and Faith*, eds. C. A. Evans and D. A. Hagner (Minneapolis: Fortress, 1993) 128–50.

argues are instead the badges of identity that mark out the people of God from the gentiles. The issue is thus one of national righteousness—not grace but race.[10] This view of the law Paul had to resist for the sake of the gentile mission to which he was called.

James D. G. Dunn, the leading advocate of the new perspective, in his important Romans commentary, denies that Paul carries on a basic polemic against the law in his insistence on justification by faith.[11] This is judged by Dunn as "too Lutheran" a reading of Paul. According to Dunn, Paul has no problem with the law, but only with a "too narrowly Jewish perspective" that puts emphasis on the law as the establishment of boundary markers excluding gentiles from grace. Only such a view, according to Dunn, enables one to do justice to both the positive and negative statements of Paul concerning the law.

Does Dunn's approach result in a satisfying exegesis of the negative statements of Paul concerning the law? This is not the place to explore this question. Readers of the Romans commentary will have to decide for themselves. I am afraid I am not persuaded. In my opinion, the exegesis often seems forced. The fact that Dunn can make as strong a case as he does is due to the undeniable degree of truth in his main point. That is, it is obviously true that the law does specify boundary markers that mark out Israel from the nations, and that Paul as the missionary to the gentiles is naturally opposed to the law understood in this sense. The question is whether that is *all* Paul finds wrong with the law.

Dunn does better with Paul's positive statements about the law, which after all is what his proposal aims to do. To my mind, the exegesis of Paul in the tradition of the Protestant reformation is basically correct, despite the fact that Paul's positive statements about the law need more attention. But this can be done without the drastic rereading of Paul found in Dunn's approach. It is not necessary to abandon Paul's basic soteriology—which is, for Paul, the same for Jew and gentile—in order to give proper heed to his positive statements about the law. Before we attempt to understand these positive statements, however, we must look again at the question of legalism in the first century.

---

10. This is the language of N. T. Wright. See his *The Climax of the Covenant: Christ and the Law in Pauline Theology* (Minneapolis: Fortress, 1992), and *The New Testament and the People of God*, Christian Origins and the Question of God (Minneapolis: Fortress, 1992).

11. James D. G. Dunn, *Romans 1–8* and *Romans 9–16*, WBC 38A-B (Dallas: Word, 1988). See too his collected essays, with valuable additional notes, *Jesus, Paul and the Law: Studies in Mark and Galatians* (Louisville: Westminster John Knox, 1990).

The starting point for the new perspective is the conclusion that first-century Judaism was not legalistic; that is, it did not attempt to establish merit before God on the basis of righteous deeds. The result of this conclusion is that if we still accept the traditional Protestant exegesis of the texts, there appear to be no people to correspond to those being criticized by Paul. In that case, the Pauline polemic obviously must be understood in a new way. I have already indicated above that I accept the essential correctness of the case made by E. P. Sanders for regarding Judaism as a covenantal nomism. Without question, grace is the fundamental bedrock in the Old Testament texts. A few mitigating points must immediately be noted, however: (1) there are also legalistic-sounding statements alongside the texts concerning covenant and election; (2) in the frustration of the post-exilic period, stress on the importance of obeying the law be came ever greater; (3) even if the stress on works was in actuality related to "staying in" rather than "getting in," as Sanders maintains, the line between the two can become very thin; and (4) adherents to a religious faith often do not live by its best articulated theology.

In short, it is not at all difficult to believe that there were large numbers of Jews in Paul's day who did not fully appreciate the foundations of grace upon which their religion was based. Going against the best of their theology, they lost the balance between law and covenant, and became *de facto* legalists. There indeed appears to be something in all of us that finds the freeness of grace difficult to believe, and legalistic Christians, who try to earn their way with God, are not all that rare. This conclusion makes the best sense of the Pauline texts. Paul is not simply protesting an overly nationalistic understanding of the law, but warning against a mistaken idea of righteousness altogether. The contrast is between a supposed "righteousness of my own that comes from the law" and "one that comes through faith in Christ, the righteousness from God based on faith" (Phil 3:9; cf. Gal 2:16).

If we assume that Paul's polemic against the righteousness of the law, as traditionally understood, has some basis in reality, what are we then to make of his positive statements about the law? What is immediately striking is Paul's ability to put negative and positive statements about the law together without hesitation. This surely is not the result of confusion or indecision. Paul finds it natural to say in nearly the same breath both that the law has been done away with for the Christian and yet that the law is fulfilled in the life of the Christian (cf. Rom 3:28 and 3:31; Rom 7:6 and 7:12; Gal 3:21 and 3:24–25). Indeed, it is often exactly in contexts where he stresses freedom from the law that he stresses the importance of righteousness (see Rom 7:1–6; Gal 5:13). For all his emphasis on freedom from the law, Paul continues to stress the importance of righteousness and tirelessly calls his readers to it.

How is it, then, that Paul's law-free gospel does not overthrow the law? The answer is that response to the gospel entails obedience to a pattern of teaching that corresponds remarkably to the righteousness of the law. The paradox, and the secret to Paul's doctrine of sanctification, is that when one is justified by faith and set free from the law ("dying to it," in the Pauline idiom), one really begins to manifest the righteousness of the law! Of course, this obedience to the law is to be distinguished from that of the previous era. It is, in fact, not an obedience oriented to the law at all, but an obedience oriented to Christ. Although based upon grace, it cannot be described as a "covenantal nomism." It is not nomism because it is not law-centered. The upholding of the law, the obedience to its standard of righteousness, is not direct, but indirect—the result of discipleship oriented to Christ. Paul's Christianity is christocentric, not nomocentric.

Probably it is the congruity of the righteousness of Christian discipleship with the righteousness of the law that enables Paul to speak as he does in the difficult passage of Romans 2:6–10, 13–16.[12] Paul believes that Christians *will* "do good," and *will* be "doers of the law" and not merely "hearers only."[13] From the context of Rom 1:18—3:20, however, it is clear that such righteousness, despite its key importance, cannot be the ground of salvation.

It should be obvious that all this cannot be understood without allowing for the newness brought by Christ. This is indicated in verses that are important for our subject: "For God has done what the law, weakened by the flesh, could not do: by sending his own Son in the likeness of sinful flesh, and to deal with sin, he condemned sin in the flesh, so that the just requirement of the law might he fulfilled in us, who walk not

---

12. Dunn points out the difficulty of integrating Romans 2 into the negative assessment of the law in traditional Protestant exegesis *(Romans 1–8,* lxvi) For a critique of the new perspective on Paul, see Donald A. Hagner, "Paul and Judaism: Testing the New Perspective," in Peter Stuhlmacher, *Revisiting Paul's Doctrine of Justification* (Downers Grove, IL: InterVarsity, 2001) 75–105.

13. As Klyne Snodgrass rightly points out, "Pauls defense of his mission would not have had the slightest chance with Jews or Jewish Christians had he rejected this cardinal belief of the biblical and Jewish tradition" ("Justification by Grace—to the Doers: An Analysis of the Place of Romans 2 in the Theology of Paul," *NTS* 32 [1986] 72–93).

according to the flesh, but according to the Spirit" (Rom 8:3–4). Here Paul indicates that the way to righteousness is through Christ and not the law. The death of Christ, according to this passage, had the goal not only of atoning for sin, but also of enabling the redeemed to arrive at the righteousness of the law.

It is in this sense that I would understand the meaning of the much debated Romans 10:4. When Paul says that Christ is the *telos* of the law, does he mean "end" or "goal"? Usually, in cases like this, the exegete does not want to accept the possibility of a double entendre. Here, however, given the argument of Paul in Romans, we may have one of the few such deliberate double meanings in the New Testament. Here Paul may well mean both that Christ has brought the law to an end and that through Christ the law reaches its intended goal. In Christ the era of the law has come to an end. The law has achieved its limited purpose, and Christians are discharged from obedience to it. Salvation does not lie down this road, as some mistakenly imagined. Saving righteousness comes not from good deeds, but from God as a gift through justification by faith. On the other hand, as we have seen, the faithful Christian will in effect do the righteousness of the law by obedience to the teaching of the Lord and thus, paradoxically, arrive at the goal of the law.

MATTHEW AND PAUL

Despite their different readers—mainly Jews for Matthew, mainly gentiles for Paul—both Matthew and Paul manifest a deep commitment to continuity with the law, or more specifically with the righteousness articulated by the law. To be sure, Paul can write things that Matthew would find unacceptable, and perhaps vice versa. Yet at bottom their concerns are very similar.[14] Neither would be happy with any suggestion that the real meaning of the law has been abandoned in Christianity. Neither would abandon the ongoing importance of righteousness.

Not by accident, both writers independently refer to Jesus' summary of the law. Matthew records Jesus' answer to a lawyer of the Pharisees concerning the greatest commandment: One is to love God with one's whole being (an allusion to the *Shema* of Deut 6:4–5) and one's neighbor as oneself. To this Jesus adds, "On these two commandments hang all

---

14. This has been shown very clearly by Roger Mohrlang, *Matthew and Paul: A Comparison of Ethical Perspectives*, SNTSMS 48 (Cambridge: Cambridge University Press, 1984).

the law and the prophets" (Matt 22:37-40).[15] Expounding this saying, which he knew from the oral tradition, Paul writes, "the one who loves another has fulfilled the law," and all the commandments "are summed up in this one word, 'Love your neighbor as yourself.' Love does no wrong to a neighbor; therefore, love is the fulfilling of the law" (Rom 13:10). For both Matthew and Paul, Jesus as the Messiah is the supremely authoritative interpreter of the law. For both, to follow Jesus as Lord is to embody the pattern of righteousness found in the Old Testament and thereby to fulfill the law.

Common to both, of course, is the stress on the fulfillment of the Old Testament scriptures and the affirmation of the new era inaugurated by the work of Christ. A turning of the ages has been reached and the establishment of the old is not by mere perpetuation, but in what is necessarily a new way. New understanding is therefore required. The old is not displaced by the new, but it is transposed to a higher key.

But the point to be noticed is that not even Paul's law-free, grace-centered gospel abandons the righteousness of the law. Although for him the role of the law per se is very different from what it was in the era before Christ, the call to a righteousness that paradoxically corresponds to the law is as serious as ever.

Righteousness is not merely an option for the Christian; it is a requirement. Any suggestion that Paul's law-free, grace-centered gospel leads to antinomianism—a life devoid of righteousness—therefore consistently receives the immediate, strong protest: *mē genoito*, "By no means!"

On the other hand, Matthew's insistence on absolute fidelity to the law is not to be understood as merely an intensification of the old, nor even as a new nomism. It must always be remembered that Matthew's clarion call to righteousness is given in the context of the gospel of the kingdom. For all its seriousness about the matter of righteousness, Matthew does not advocate a salvation dependent on good works.[16] In fact,

---

15. See Birger Gerhardsson, "The Hermeneutic Program in Matthew 22:37-40," in his *The Shema in the New Testament: Deut 6:4-5 in Significant Passages* (Lund: Novapress, 1996) 202-23. He describes the love commandments as a hermeneutical key to unlock the divine intention of the law. See also T. L. Donaldson, "The Law that Hangs (Matthew 22 40): Rabbinic Formulation and Matthean Social World," *CBQ* 57 (1995) 689-709.

16. See Donald A. Hagner, "Righteousness in Matthew's Theology," in *Worship, Theology and Ministry in the Early Church: Essays in Honor of Ralph P. Martin*, eds. M. J. Wilkins and T. Paige, JSNTSup 87 (Sheffield: JSOT Press, 1992) 101-20.

both of our writers can make statements which, if taken out of context (both immediate and larger), can sound as though they advocated salvation by works (for Paul, see not only Rom 2:6–11, 13–16, but also Gal 5:19–21; 6:7–8). In both cases, the writers in this way indicate their seriousness about the matter of righteousness. But this is not the heart of their soteriology, which in both cases centers on the announcement of the grace of God in Christ.[17]

Thus, while not saying exactly the same thing, Matthew and Paul are by no means far apart. Their thought is bound together by the common acceptance of Jesus of Nazareth as God's Anointed One—the one who has inaugurated the new era of the reign of God and the fulfillment of Israel's scriptures, a fulfillment that brings righteousness to the people of God.

---

17. Snodgrass writes that "for Matthew and his readers the center of their relation with God is Jesus. They do not gather around the Torah, they gather in the name of Jesus There they experience the presence of God and live in accordance with his will" ("Matthew and the Law," 554).

8

Paul as a Jewish Believer—According to His Letters

It is a mere platitude to state that Paul was a Jewish believer in Jesus. Almost no one contests this and no defense of the statement is required. Paul himself is as clear about it as he could be. In fact, he is emphatic about his Jewishness: "If anyone else has reason to be confident in the flesh, I have more: circumcised on the eighth day, a member of the people of Israel, of the tribe of Benjamin, a Hebrew born of Hebrews; as to the law a Pharisee; as to zeal, a persecutor of the church; as to righteousness under the law, blameless" (Phil 3:4–6);[1] "I myself am an Israelite, a descendant of Abraham, a member of the tribe of Benjamin" (Rom 11:1); "Are they Hebrews? So am I. Are they Israelites? So am I. Are they descendants of Abraham? So am I" (2 Cor 11:22). In addition to these autobiographical statements, Paul's thorough Jewishness is manifest throughout his letters in such things as his theology, his esteem for the Torah, his concern for the righteousness of the Torah, his use of the Scriptures and his method of interpreting them, his abiding love for Israel, his soteriology, his eschatology, and even his Christology. This is only to say that Christianity is itself essentially a Jewish faith. Nothing is to be understood of Christianity without a knowledge of the Hebrew Scriptures and without taking for granted their basic perspectives.[2]

---

1. Quotations throughout are from the NRSV, unless otherwise noted.
2. Martin Hengel rightly insists that Paul's theology "cannot be understood as Christian theology without attention to its Jewish roots, indeed I would venture to say its latent 'Jewish' character. Knowledge of Saul the Jew is a precondition of understanding

Yet behind the simple statement that Paul was a Jewish believer in Jesus lies a nest of difficult questions. These questions center on both the relationship between Paul's pre-Christian Judaism and his Christianity, and also the relationship between Paul's Christianity and the Judaism of those who did not accept the gospel that he preached.[3] Another way of putting the matter is in terms of continuity and discontinuity. How much continuity is there between Saul's Judaism and Paul's Christianity? How much discontinuity? Where specifically are the points of continuity and discontinuity to be found? What implications can be drawn from these points of continuity and discontinuity, and what are their significance?

These are the questions we will focus upon in this essay. Questions such as these are exceptionally complicated, of course. We will have to face the reality of both continuity and discontinuity; and perhaps even of a discontinuity within a larger continuity and vice versa. In addition, we may well expect the degree of continuity and discontinuity to vary on different subjects.

To put ourselves in position for our study, we begin with a brief overview of the modern study of Paul. Then we shall turn to the question of continuity and discontinuity on some key subjects, and conclude with some final remarks about the old and the new in Paul's theology.

I. THE CHANGING UNDERSTANDING OF PAUL

We have seen a remarkable trend over the past century in the understanding of the Apostle to the Gentiles. At the beginning of the twentieth century, it was common for Paul to be explained mainly in terms of Hellenism and his identity as a Diaspora Jew. The popular *religionsgeschichtliche Schule* saw in Paul a Hellenistic Jew who borrowed deeply from his Diaspora religious environment. Paul's syncretism produced an odd

---

Paul the Christian. The better we know the former, the more clearly we shall understand the latter." *The Pre-Christian Paul* (London: SCM, 1991) xiii.

3. The use of the terms "Judaism" and "Christianity" in reference to the first century is nowadays regarded as problematic. Neither term means what it will come to mean in the centuries following the time of Paul. Judaism is in a highly formative stage in the first two centuries (especially before the destruction of Jerusalem in 70). Similarly, first-century Christianity is not what it will become in the second century. But this terminological debate anticipates the discussion that follows. We will continue to use the terms for the sake of convenience.

combination of Jewish and pagan ideas, derived mainly from the mystery religions of Asia Minor and the influence of Gnosticism.[4]

A number of Jewish scholars who have studied Paul[5] also found this explanation attractive. C. G. Montefiore, for example, concluded that it was the influence of Diaspora Hellenism that explained what seemed aberrant in Paul's theology, when considered from a Palestinian or Rabbinic Jewish standpoint.[6] Several other Jewish scholars also found the Hellenistic explanation of Paul convincing. Thus, Kaufmann Kohler,[7] Joseph Klausner,[8] Martin Buber,[9] Samuel Sandmel,[10] and Hyam Maccoby,[11] all come to similar conclusions.

The impact of Hellenism upon the New Testament and Paul in particular was promoted not only by these Jewish scholars and the *Religionsgeschichte* scholars mentioned above, but also by other Gentile scholars, among whom we may mention Edwin Hatch, Arthur Darby Nock, W. L. Knox, and Kirsopp Lake.

A turn in the tide of opinion may be said to have begun around the middle of the century with the publication of the first edition of W. D. Davies's seminal *Paul and Rabbinic Judaism*.[12] Davies was able to show

4. Among those who looked in this direction for the explanation of Paul, we may mention the following: R. Reitzenstein, W. Bousset, O. Pfleiderer, W. Heitmüller, A. Eichhorn, H. Windisch, H. J. Holtzmann, and R. Bultmann.

5. For a comprehensive treatment, see Stefan Meißner, *Die Heimholung des Ketzers: Studien zur jüdischen Auseinandersetzung mit Paulus*, WUNT 2/87 (Tübingen: Mohr Siebeck, 1996). See too D. A. Hagner, "Paul in Modern Jewish Thought," in *Pauline Studies: Essays Presented to Professor F. F. Bruce on His 70th Birthday*, ed. D. A. Hagner and M. J. Harris (Exeter: Paternoster, 1980) 143-65.

6. See C. G. Montefiore, *Judaism and St. Paul: Two Essays* (London: Goschen, 1914; reprint, New York: Arno, 1973); Montefiore, "Rabbinic Judaism and the Epistles of Paul," *JQR* 13 (1901) 162-217; reprint in *Judaism and Christianity*, ed. Jacob Agus (New York: Arno, 1973).

7. In his influential article "Saul of Tarsus," in *Jewish Encyclopedia*, 11:79-87.

8. *From Jesus to Paul*, trans. W. F. Stinespring (London: Macmillan, 1943; reprint, Boston: Beacon, 1961).

9. *Two Types of Faith*, trans. N. P. Goldhawk (London Routledge & Kegan Paul, 1951).

10. *The Genius of Paul: A Study in History* (New York: Farrar, Straus & Cudahy, 1958; repr., Philadelphia: Fortress, 1979); Sandmel, "Paul Reconsidered," in *Two Living Traditions*, ed. S. Sandmel (Detroit: Wayne State University Press, 1972) 195-211.

11. *The Mythmaker: Paul and the Invention of Christianity* (New York: Harper & Row, 1986); Maccoby, *Paul and Hellenism* (London: SCM, 1991). See D. A. Hagner, "The Making of a Myth: Hyam Maccoby's View of Paul," in *The Cradle of Christianity: Judaism, Jesus.and the New Testament. Essays in Honor of Craig A. Evans*. Thomas R. Hatina and Stanley E. Porter, eds. (Leiden: Brill, 2024) 236-57.

12. (London: SPCK, 1948). The book appeared in a 4th ed. (Philadelphia: Fortress,

that many key aspects of Paul's theology widely regarded as explainable only on the basis of Hellenistic thought actually had a background within Palestinian Judaism. At about the same time the Dead Sea Scrolls were coming to light, and they also began to reveal that certain perspectives hitherto regarded as Hellenistic were in fact equally at home in at least one form of Palestinian Judaism.

It has become increasingly clear that the supposed dichotomy between Diaspora and Palestinian Judaism, upon which the earlier explanations of Paul rested, is a false one. This was already beginning to emerge when it was given a definitive statement in the masterful work of Martin Hengel.[13] With great erudition Hengel demonstrated that Judaism had been interpenetrated by Hellenism not only in the Diaspora, but also even in Palestine. There was no such thing as a "pure" Judaism. On the other hand, Hellenism itself was influenced by Judaism. Davies summarizes the resultant conclusion as it bears on Paul especially well in the following words: "In Paul Athens and Jerusalem are strangely mixed . . . because the Judaism within which he grew up, even in Jerusalem, was largely Hellenized, and the Hellenism he encountered in his travels largely Judaized."[14]

Another point that has emerged with great clarity is the fact that Palestinian Judaism itself was anything but monolithic. It soon became clear that to be accurate it may perhaps be necessary to speak of first century Judaisms in the plural. The Judaisms of Paul's day furthermore were intensely complex. The mysticism of Paul, previously attributed to the influence of the mystery religions, was now seen to have a possible background in Rabbinic Judaism. Apocalyptic, so crucial to Paul's entire perspective, was no longer seen as antithetical to his earlier Pharisaism. There was, in short, no "normative" Judaism but only what could be described as a "formative" Judaism, i.e., a variegated Judaism in the process of formation.

Thanks to this emerging, more adequate knowledge of Palestinian Judaism, the Hellenistic explanation of Paul's theology thus necessarily gave way to an increasing appreciation of the continuing Jewishness of Paul. This change becomes apparent in the approach of Jewish scholars

---

1980) with a new introduction(= reprint of an article written in 1964 titled "Paul and Judaism since Schweitzer") and a new preface taking into account the work of E. P. Sanders.

13. *Judaism and Hellenism* (Philadelphia: Fortress, 1974).
14. *Paul and Rabbinic Judaism*, xi.

such as Leo Baeck,[15] Hans Joachim Schoeps,[16] Schalom Ben-Chorin,[17] Richard L. Rubenstein,[18] Alan F. Segal,[19] Daniel Boyarin,[20] and Mark D. Nanos.[21] In contrast to the earlier Jewish writers who saw Paul's thought as essentially determined by Hellenistic ideas, these authors see an authentic Jewishness in him with which they are able to identify. Some of them will still appeal to Hellenistic influence at strategic points, but the trend is to explain Paul more and more as one who thoroughly reflects Rabbinic and Palestinian Judaism.[22]

The trend to explain Paul entirely through his Jewish background, a background of Palestinian Judaism(s), has grown stronger in recent years. By all standards, Paul is now thought by many to have had no essential problem with Judaism, even after the Damascus Road experience, but rather to have continued as a faithful Jew all his life.[23] The one thing

15. "The Faith of Paul," *JJS* 3 (1952) 93–110; the essay appears in German in Baeck's *Paulus: Die Pharisäer und das Neue Testament* (Frankfurt: Ner-Tamid, 1961).

16. *Paul: The Theology of the Apostle in the Light of Jewish Religious History*, trans. H. Knight (Philadelphia: Westminster, 1961).

17. *Paulus: Der Volkerapostel in jüdischer Sicht* (Munich: List, 1970).

18. *My Brother Paul* (New York: Harper & Row, 1972).

19. *Paul the Convert: The Apostolate and Apostasy of Saul the Pharisee* (New Haven: Yale University Press, 1990).

20. *A Radical Jew: Paul and the Politics of Identity* (Berkeley: University of California Press, 1994).

21. *The Mystery of Romans: The Jewish Context of Paul's Letter* (Minneapolis: Fortress, 1996); *The Irony of Galatians: Paul's Letter in First Century Context* (Minneapolis: Fortress, 2002).

22. This is true of current scholarship generally as will be seen in W. D. Davies's article, "Paul: From the Jewish Point of View," in *The Cambridge History of Judaism*, ed. William Horbury, W. D. Davies and John Sturdy, vol. 3; (Cambridge: Cambridge University Press, 1999) 678–730.

23. See Markus Barth, "St. Paul-A Good Jew," *Horizons in Biblical Theology* 1 (1979) 7–45; Lloyd Gaston, *Paul and the Torah* (Vancouver: University of British Columbia Press, 1987); Edwin D. Freed, *The Apostle Paul, Christian Jew: Faithfulness and Law* (Lanham, MD: University Press of America, 1994); Brad H. Young, *Paul the Jewish Theologian: A Pharisee among Christians, Jews, and Gentiles* (Peabody, MA: Hendrickson, 1997); J. Gager, "Re-Inventing St. Paul: Was the Apostle to the Gentiles the Father of Christian Anti-Judaism?," in *A Multiform Heritage: Studies on Early Judaism and Christianity in Honor of Robert A. Kraft*, B. G. Wright, ed., Homage Series 24 (Atlanta: Scholars, 1999) 49–63; Jacob Jervell, *The Unknown Paul: Essays on Luke-Acts and Early Christian History* (Minneapolis: Augsburg, 1984) 52–67 ("The Unknown Paul"). A common weakness of these writings is that they tend to neglect the Pauline passages that are not in accord with their conclusions (e.g., the negative statements concerning the law dealt with below under 4.1.1). See too, the interesting dialogue volumes on Paul: Pinchas Lapide and Peter Stuhlmacher, *Paul: Rabbi and Apostle* (Minneapolis:

that made him peculiar at points was his calling to preach the gospel to the Gentiles. This caused Paul to shape a gospel free of circumcision, kashrut, and Sabbath observance for the Gentiles, and if he criticized Judaism it was only insofar as its law had been made a barrier to Gentile salvation. Indeed, even with respect to the Gentiles, some now allege that in good Jewish fashion Paul maintained that much of the law was mandatory for the Gentiles.[24]

This rediscovery of the full Jewishness of Paul was paralleled by the earlier rediscovery of the Jewishness of Jesus, led too by Jewish scholars,[25] but now commonplace among Gentile scholars. The Gospel of Matthew, the Jewishness of which has never been questioned, is now regarded by some as reflecting not a Christian community, so much as a sect within Judaism.[26] The entire trend is salutary in that it gives heed to the fully Jewish character of our New Testament and of the Christian faith of its authors. But the subject is often pursued in such a manner as to ignore or downplay the discontinuities caused by the dramatic newness of Christianity itself. Contrary to the frequently heard claim, the Christianity of the New Testament is not simply a reformed Judaism or a Judaism applied to Gentiles. The tensions and discontinuities between Judaism and Christianity should not be swept under the carpet even for the good motive of wanting to avoid anti-Semitism, as important as that is.

Augsburg, 1984); and G. Sloyan and L. Dean, "A Jewish-Christian Dialogue on Paul," in *Bursting the Bonds? A JewishChristian Dialogue on Jesus and Paul*, ed. L. Swidler et al. (Maryknoll, NY: Orbis, 1990) 125-216.

24. Peter J. Tomson, *Paul and the Jewish Law: Halakha in the Letters of the Apostle to the Gentiles*, CRINT 3.1 (Minneapolis: Fortress, 1990); Tomson, *"If This Be from Heaven...": Jesus and the New Testament Authors in Their Relationship to Judaism* Biblical Seminar 76 (Sheffield: Sheffield Academic, 2001); Markus Bockmuehl, *Jewish Law in Gentile Churches: Halakha and the Beginning of Christian Public Ethics* (Edinburgh: T. & T. Clark, 2000). More on this below.

25. See Gösta Lindeskog, *Die Jesusfrage im Neuzeitlichen Judentum* (Darmstadt: Wissenschaftliche Buchgesellschaft, 1973); D. A. Hagner, *The Jewish Reclamation of Jesus* (Grand Rapids: Zondervan, 1984; reprint, Eugene, OR: Wipf & Stock, 1997).

26. See the work especially of Anthony J. Saldarini, *Matthew's Christian-Jewish Community* (Chicago: University of Chicago Press, 1994); J. Andrew Overman, *Matthew's Gospel and Formative Judaism: The Social World of the Matthean Community* (Minneapolis: Fortress, 1990); and David C. Sim, *The Gospel of Matthew and Christian Judaism: The History and Social Setting of the Matthean Community*, Studies of the New Testament and Its World (Edinburgh: T. & T. Clark, 1998). For a critical response, see Donald A. Hagner, "Matthew: Apostate, Reformer, Revolutionary?," *NTS* 49 (2003) 193-209.

Yes, Paul is fully Jewish and his Christianity is characterized by great continuities with Judaism.[27] At the same time, however, a close reading of Paul, as we now hope to show, points also to striking discontinuities which must not be minimized.[28] The issues are complex[29] and a fairness to all the data necessitates complex conclusions. But to be stressed here is that if we disallow the complexity, and in reductionistic fashion explain Paul solely in terms of continuity, we will misrepresent Paul.

2. STUDIES IN CONTINUITY AND DISCONTINUITY

We turn now to the specific issues raised by Paul's Jewishness together with his new Christian identity as the Apostle to the Gentiles. It will be necessary to try to examine all the relevant data, even if we must do so with the greatest of brevity. There is a risk in this, but also a benefit in seeing the various parts in light of the whole. This is the purpose in bringing together texts from different Pauline letters. Paul is not being treated here as though he were systematic in his thinking. The only implication is that all the texts need to be heard, and that given the chance they can be seen as coherent.

2.1. Call or Conversion?

We must begin with a preliminary question that has caused a fair amount of discussion.[30] Is it proper to speak in Paul's case of a call (emphasis on continuity) or a conversion (emphasis on discontinuity)? It should not be difficult to see that since a good argument can be made on both sides,

---

27. For the similarities between Paul and the Pharisaic document the Psalms of Solomon, see Dieter Lührmann, "Paul and the Pharisaic Tradition," *JSNT* 36 (1989) 75–94.

28. For a general treatment of the subject, see D. A. Hagner, "Paul's Quarrel with Judaism," in *Anti-Semitism and Early Christianity: Issues of Polemic and Faith*, ed. C. A. Evans and D. A. Hagner (Minneapolis: Fortress, 1993) 128–50.

29. As Heikki Räisänen has reminded us, but without allowing Paul the capability of maintaining a complex view of anything. *Paul and the Law* (Philadelphia: Fortress, 1986).

30. See, for example, Krister Stendahl, *Paul Among Jews and Gentiles* (Philadelphia: Fortress, 1976) 7–23 ("Call Rather than Conversion"); and James D. G. Dunn, "Paul's Conversion—A Light to Twentieth Century Disputes," in *Evangelium—Schriftauslegung—Kirche: Festschrift für Peter Stuhlmacher zum 65. Geburtstag*, ed. O. Hofius (Göttingen: Vandenhoeck & Ruprecht, 1996).

the question rests on an artificial dichotomy. In fact, there is a sense in which both are true.

From one point of view it is clear that we should speak of Paul's calling rather than conversion. It is surely true that Paul does not believe that he has left one religion for another. Indeed, he uses the word "called" when he describes what happened to him, deliberately using words that refer to a prophet's calling (Isa 49:1; Jer 1:5): "But when God, who had set me apart before I was born, and called me through his grace, was pleased to reveal his Son to me, so that I might proclaim him among the Gentiles, I did not confer with any human being" (Gal 1:15-16; cf. Rom 1:1). The very idea of moving to a new religion would have been anathema to him. Christianity is for him rather the fulfillment of his Jewish faith.

At the same time, however, that fulfillment involves a dramatic enough shift that conversion is also an appropriate word.[31] In the words just prior to the ones quoted above, Paul speaks of his life in Judaism as something in the past, something now left behind: "You have heard, no doubt, of my earlier life in Judaism. I was violently persecuting the church of God and was trying to destroy it. I advanced in Judaism beyond many among my people of the same age, for I was far more zealous for the traditions of my ancestors" (Gal 1:13-14). Similarly, after he has listed his impressive Jewish pedigree in Phil 3:4-6 (quoted above), he writes: "Yet whatever gains I had, these I have come to regard as loss because of Christ. More than that, I regard everything as loss because of the surpassing value of knowing Christ Jesus my Lord. For his sake I have suffered the loss of all things, and I regard them as rubbish, in order that I may gain Christ and be found in him, not having a righteousness of my own that comes from the law, but one that comes through faith in Christ, the righteousness from God based on faith" (Phil 3:7-9). There is sufficient discontinuity in this shift in allegiance from Torah to Christ to warrant speaking also of a conversion of Paul.[32] Paul has not changed religions, but he now has a new center: the crucified and resurrected Messiah, who has inaugurated a new era in salvation history and brought

---

31. See B. Corley, "Interpreting Paul's Conversion—Then and Now," in *The Road from Damascus: The Impact of Paul's Conversion on His Life, Thought, and Ministry*, ed. R. N. Longenecker (Grand Rapids: Eerdmans, 1997) 1-17; cf. Segal, *Paul*.

32. James D. G. Dunn thus rightly speaks of a conversion of Paul from Judaism and zeal for the law, "Paul's Conversion." Where he is wrong, in my opinion, is in saying that what Paul was converted to was the necessity of taking the gospel of Christ to the Gentiles. This does not do justice to the personal significance of what happened to Paul himself, entirely apart from the Gentile mission to which God called him.

a new dynamic to his existence. He could no longer have felt comfortable in his former Judaism.³³

2.2. The Law and Salvation

We come directly to what undoubtedly is the central issue in this debate about Paul. It is bound up, of course, with the questions of the nature of salvation in Judaism, and particularly, the function of the law in Judaism, subjects given much careful study in recent years.³⁴

As background we must briefly review the revolution in the study of first-century Judaism that has taken place especially in the last twenty-five years, although the viewpoint was hardly unknown earlier. It was the great virtue of E. P. Sanders's now famous book, *Paul and Palestinian Judaism*,³⁵ to correct the widespread misunderstanding of Judaism as a religion of works righteousness wherein salvation is something earned by one's conduct. As is well known, Sanders demonstrated that Judaism was a religion based upon grace, best described as a "covenantal nomism." This ideal characterization of Judaism seems correct to me, although whether the balance between covenant and law was always able in fact to be maintained is another question. Given the great preoccupation with the law in the post-exilic period, the possibility of widespread *de facto* legalism that virtually occluded the covenant seems not unlikely.³⁶

---

33. John M. G. Barclay notes that Paul was repudiated as an apostate by his Jewish contemporaries. Barclay rightly objects to the reinstating of Paul "in hindsight as a 'legitimate' Jew." "Paul among Diaspora Jews: Anomaly or Apostate?" *JSNT* 60 (1995) 89–120. For a thorough examination of Paul's references to his Jewishness and their significance to his purposes in the letters, see Karl-Wilhelm Niebuhr, *Heidenapostel aus Israel: Die jüdische Identität des Paulus nach ihrer Darstellung in seinen Briefen*, WUNT 62 (Tübingen: Mohr Siebeck, 1992). Niebuhr focuses on four passages: Gal 1:13–14; Phil 3:5–6; 2 Cor 11:22–23; and Rom 11:1.

34. The quantity of literature on the subject is immense. See Mark Adam Elliott, *The Survivors of Israel: A Reconsideration of the Theology of Pre-Christian Judaism* (Grand Rapids: Eerdmans, 2000); and especially James D. G. Dunn, ed., *Paul and the Mosaic Law* (Grand Rapids: Eerdmans, 2001) which contains a bibliography covering the years 1980–1994. For more recent literature, see Peter Stuhlmacher with D. A. Hagner, *Revisiting the Pauline Doctrine of Justification: A Challenge to the New Perspective* (Downers Grove, IL: InterVarsity, 2001).

35. Philadelphia: Fortress, 1977.

36. Because of Sanders's book, it is now taken for granted by many New Testament scholars that there could have been no Jews in the first century who thought that they had to earn their salvation by works of the law. It is this that has caused the current revisionist reading of Paul. Friedrich Avemarie has shown, however, that in rabbinic

The understanding of Judaism as a covenantal nomism meant that the traditional reading of Paul had promoted a misunderstanding of Judaism as a merit-based religion. Paul, it was now argued, had been read through "Lutheran" eyes, aligning law with works and gospel with grace. It therefore now became incumbent to read Paul afresh, in a way that was more consistent with an understanding of Judaism as a religion of grace. Paul, it is alleged, cannot have been polemicizing against Jews who were attempting to earn their salvation, since in fact there were no such Jews. This emphasis gave rise to the so-called new perspective on Paul, vigorously promoted by James D. G. Dunn.[37] Fundamental to the new perspective is not only that Judaism is a religion of grace, but also that justification by faith, regarded (with Schweitzer and Wrede) now as not the center of Paul's soteriology, was stressed by Paul only for the sake of the Gentile mission. Paul's theology concerns, therefore, not a universal human problem, but specifically the salvation of Gentiles.

Paul accordingly had no fundamental problem with the law except for the single fact that it constituted an obstacle to the Gentile mission. He opposes "works of the law" only insofar as they constitute badges of Jewish identity that exclude the Gentiles. The issue is not grace, but race, as N. T. Wright puts it.[38] Not legalism, but nationalism. Paul has no criticism of the religion of Judaism as such. Thus, the oft-quoted statement of Sanders: "In short, *this is what Paul finds wrong in Judaism: it is not Christianity.*"[39]

With this background of the new perspective in view, we may now turn to look at the main issues more closely.[40] The key issue remains Paul's

---

soteriology grace and merit stand with equal importance in an unresolved tension, and that the focus can often be upon merit. "Erwählung und Vergeltung. Zur optionalen Struktur rabbinischer Soteriologie," *NTS* 45 (1999) 108-26; Avemarie, *Torah und Leben. Untersuchungen zur Heilsbedeutung der Torah in der frühen rabbinischen Literatur*, TSAJ 55 (Tübingen: Mohr Siebeck, 1996). The words ascribed to Akiba in Abot 3:20 point in the same direction: "The world is judged by grace, and yet all is according to the amount of work." Where such a viewpoint prevails, the existence of a *de facto* legalism should hardly be surprising.

37. "The New Perspective on Paul," *BJRL* 65 (1983) 95-122, also found in Dunn's *Jesus, Paul and the Law: Studies in Mark and Galatians* (Louisville: Westminster John Knox, 1990).

38. *The Climax of the Covenant: Christ and the Law in Pauline Theology* (Minneapolis: Fortress, 1991) 168.

39. *Paul and Palestinian Judaism*, 552.

40. For a more detailed argument against the new perspective, see Stuhlmacher with Hagner, *Revisiting*, 75-105, and especially Seyoon Kim, *Paul and the New Perspective:*

view of the law. It is, of course, a defining question. If for Paul Christ has brought the law to an end, then by the usual standard of judgment Paul has broken with Judaism. If, as the new perspective maintains, Paul continues to uphold the law, then he remains fully within Judaism.

2.2.1. Paul and the Law

The subject is complex and the literature is extensive. A primary difficulty is that Paul makes both negative and positive statements concerning the law. Paul is either confused and unable to gain clarity on the matter,[41] or he knows what he is doing and has reasons for making the two kinds of statements. If we give Paul the benefit of the doubt, can we make sense of his perspective?

(1) Negative statements concerning the law. We may begin with the well known passages in Galatians. In Gal 3:15-29 Paul makes the following points: (a) the law was a parenthesis, not something permanent, in God's purposes, coming 430 years after the Abrahamic Covenant, and being in effect only "until faith would be revealed," i.e., "until Christ came" (3:23-24); (b) the people of that parenthetical period were "imprisoned and guarded under the law" (3:23); (c) the law functioned as a "disciplinarian" (*paidagōgos*) and was unable to "make alive" or produce righteousness (3:21); (d) the result is that now "we are no longer subject to (*hypo*) a disciplinarian" (3:25). With the coming of "the fullness of time (*to plērōma tou chronou*)" (4:4), came redemption for those who were "under the law" (4:5). "Christ redeemed us from the curse of the law" (3:13).[42] "But if you are led by the Spirit you are not subject to [*hypo*, 'under'] the law" (5:18). Paul writes fervently: "For freedom Christ has set us free" and therefore we should not submit "to a yoke of slavery;" "yoke" being a well known metaphor for the law (5:1; cf. Acts 15:10). He describes the Sinai covenant as bringing slavery in comparison to the freedom of the heavenly Jerusalem (4:21-31).

Determinative for Paul on this issue is the point he makes in Gal 2:21: "I do not nullify the grace of God; for if justification (*dikaiosynē*) comes through the law, then Christ died for nothing." So too, the

---

Second Thoughts on the Origin of Paul's Gospel (Grand Rapids: Eerdmans, 2002).

41. H. Räisänen's well-known counsel of despair (see n28).

42. See F. F. Bruce, "The Curse of the Law," in *Paul and Paulinism*, ed. M. D. Hooker and S. G. Wilson (London: SPCK, 1982) 27-36.

argument in Gal 3:11-12 has a powerful effect on the significance of the law: "Now it is evident that no one is justified before God by the law . . . the law does not rest on faith."

To be sure, the incident at Antioch referred to in Gal 2:11-14 concerns the matter of the imposition of the law upon Gentile converts by so-called Judaizers, Jewish (or in some instances Gentile) Christians who wanted to impose the law upon Gentile Christians. That is the immediate issue addressed in Paul's letter to the Galatian churches. But for a Jew like Paul the law was a unity, and he does not limit himself to that specific problem in the remarks about the law that follow. Instead, he addresses the matter of the law more generally, in a way that includes but goes beyond the question of whether Gentile Christians must obey the law. The passage is supremely relevant to Jewish Christians.

It is obvious from the delegation sent from James that there were Jewish Christians who continued to hold the law in high esteem, that is, as obligatory, not only for themselves but also for the Gentiles.[43] And it is clear that Paul must argue on behalf of the Gentiles in order to fulfill his commission as the Apostle to the Gentiles. What is of the highest importance to note, however, is that Paul has a single soteriology, namely that there is only one way of salvation through Christ for both Jew and Gentile.[44] What he argues concerning the law in connection with his Gentile converts therefore holds true also for the Jews. That the Christian Jews were no longer under the law seems to have been understood by Peter, until he became intimidated by those sent from James. This seems to be the point of the criticism expressed in 2:14: "If you, though a Jew, live like a Gentile and not like a Jew, how can you compel the Gentiles to live like Jews?" Peter apparently understood his freedom, but under pressure his courage failed.

There are two passages in Romans that deserve special attention. The much disputed meaning of Rom 10:4, "For Christ is the *telos* of the law so that there may be righteousness for everyone who believes," turns

---

43. Raymond E. Brown finds in the New Testament four different groups of "Jewish Christians and their Gentile converts," ranging from full acceptance of the entire Mosaic law to those who "saw no abiding significance in Jewish cult and feasts." Raymond E. Brown and John P. Meier, *Antioch and Rome: New Testament Cradles of Catholic Christianity* (New York: Paulist, 1983) 2-8; see also his "Not Jewish Christianity," 74-79. Brown puts Paul in the third group (those not insisting on circumcision and *kashrut*), whereas my reading of Paul would put him in the fourth, most radical, group.

44. Some do not agree with this assessment. See, e.g., Lloyd Gaston, *Paul and the Torah* (Vancouver: University of British Columbia Press, 1987).

upon the meaning of *telos*. Is it to be taken in the sense of "end" or "goal"? In the immediate context the most natural meaning, in my opinion, is "end." In the preceding verse, Paul describes his own people as zealous but not enlightened (both words perfectly fit Saul the Pharisee), adding without mincing words: "being ignorant of the righteousness that comes from God, and seeking to establish their own, they have not submitted to God's righteousness" (10:3). How did they seek to establish their own righteousness other than by the law? The NRSV translates 10:4 appropriately, "For Christ is the end of the law so that there may be righteousness for everyone who believes." The verses that follow also draw a contrast between two kinds of righteousness, that which comes "from the law (*ek tou nomou*)" and that which comes "from faith (*ek pisteōs*)" (10:5-6). In the verses that follow, Paul turns the words of Moses on their head when he interprets what is "near you, on your lips and in your heart" (Deut 30:14) as referring not to the commandments of the Torah, but rather to the confession of Jesus as Lord (Rom 10:8-9).

It is of course true, as Paul would affirm, that Christ is also the goal of the law. If we understand *nomos* (Torah) as the Scriptures, Christ is their goal: "For in him every one of God's promises is a 'Yes.'" (2 Cor 1:20). Even if we keep to the meaning of *nomos* as "law" in the sense of commandments, Paul could still affirm that Christ is the goal in that he embodies and calls his disciples to righteousness.[45]

The character of the law as an interim matter—something we have seen in Galatians—is also apparent in Rom 5:20, where the translation "law came in" (thus RSV, NRSV) hardly does justice to the verb *pareisēlthen*, which means "slipped in" or "sneaked in." REB catches the idea: "Law intruded into this process." In Rom 5 the pivotal termini are Adam and Christ, with the law coming in as an extraneous element and playing a decidedly minor and temporary role.

A second important passage in Romans concerning the law is Rom 7:1-6, where Paul likens the Christian's freedom from the law to the freedom of a wife whose husband dies. He concludes the analogy with the emphatic affirmation, similar to that of Galatians, that "now we are discharged from the law, dead to that which held us captive, so that we are slaves not under the old written code but in the new life of the Spirit" (7:6). The last clause is important, as Paul already indicated in 7:4: "you have died to the law through the body of Christ, so that you may belong

---

45. For a balanced discussion, see Douglas Moo, *The Epistle to the Romans*, NICNT (Grand Rapids: Eerdmans, 1996) 636-43.

to another, to him who has been raised from the dead in order that we may bear fruit for God." Freedom from the law for Paul never means license to do as we please.

There are other passages in Romans where the law is treated negatively. For example, in 3:20 Paul concludes: "For no human being will be justified in his sight by deeds prescribed by the law, for through the law comes the knowledge of sin." In a way similar to his argument in Galatians, Paul writes: "If it is the adherents of the law who are to be the heirs, faith is null and the promise is void. For the law brings wrath" (Rom 4:14–15).

The contrast between two kinds of righteousness appears again in Phil 3:9, where Paul contrasts his previous viewpoint with his present perception: "and be found in him, not having a righteousness of my own that comes from the law, but one that comes through faith in Christ, the righteousness from God based on faith." A similar contrast is drawn in 2 Cor 3:6–17. The old covenant is described as a letter that kills, "a ministry of death, chiseled in letters on stone tablets," a "ministry of condemnation," and it is set in contrast to the "new covenant" of the Spirit who gives life, "a ministry of justification," and "freedom." Paul notes that "if what was set aside came through glory, much more has the permanent come in glory!" (2 Cor 3:11).[46] We have given the most representative examples of Paul's negative statements concerning the law. We must now look at counterbalancing statements that speak positively of the law. How are they to be taken? Are they compatible with the negative statements? If so, how?

(2) *Positive statements concerning the law.* After the weight of the negative statements about the law reviewed above, it is striking, to say the least, that Paul can also say very positive things about the law. Even in Galatians, where Paul most consistently speaks of the law negatively, he sounds a positive note in 3:21: "Is the law then against the promises of God? Certainly not!" Given the polarities of faith and law in Galatians, one might well have expected Paul to answer the question affirmatively, but he does not.

---

46. On 2 Cor 3, see Scott J. Hafemann, *Paul, Moses, and the History of Israel: The Letter/Spirit Contrast and the Argument from Scripture in 2 Corinthians 3* (Peabody, MA: Hendrickson, 1996). Hafemann labors, unconvincingly in my opinion, to transform the negative language concerning the old covenant (law) in this passage into a positive view of the law (as he also finds in Gal 3–4!).

In Romans Paul speaks more positively about the law than perhaps anywhere else. To the question "Do we then overthrow the law by this faith?" he answers, "By no means! On the contrary, we uphold the law" (Rom 3:31). He describes the law very positively in 7:12: "So the law is holy, and the commandment is holy and just and good."

In 1 Cor 7:19 Paul makes one of his most remarkable statements: "Circumcision is nothing, and uncircumcision is nothing, but obeying the commandments of God is everything." Even if we omit the added "is everything" of the NRSV, for which there is no Greek counterpart, the statement is strange. What are we to make of the fact that circumcision is one of the commandments of God? How can the commandments be kept if circumcision is ignored?

How are we to put together Paul's negative and positive statements concerning the law? One popular way to do so is to conclude that Paul opposes the ritual or ceremonial law but not the moral law. There are two reasons to reject such a hypothesis. First, the law was accepted as a unity by the Jews, all of it equally binding, so that the distinction itself seems artificial. Second, Paul's statements about no longer being "under the law" are too sweeping and absolute to refer only to the ceremonial law. The "works of the law" against which he militates involve more than simply the ceremonial law or the Jewish badges of identity. This is not to deny that for Paul, as for Jesus, it is the moral law that is of primary interest and perpetuated in the church.

Another, more attractive, way of handling the problem is to take the negative statements as referring to *nomos* understood as commandments, and the positive statements as referring to the broader meaning of *nomos*, namely as Scripture. In other words, *nomos* as the commandments is done away with, but *nomos* considered as the whole of Scripture is viewed positively, witnessing ultimately to Christ and justification by faith, as well as containing within it the parenthetical *nomos* whose purpose has now been served. This explanation often works well, but not in every instance, and I believe there is a more satisfactory way to deal with the problem.

If we take the negative statements concerning the law as referring to the commandments, it is possible to take the positive statements as referring simply to the righteousness that is the goal of the law. Thus, although we are no longer "under the law" as commandments, we still are meant to arrive at something approximating the righteousness of the law, so that in this sense the law in effect is finally upheld. If the moral righteousness that is the heart of the law is mediated to the church through the teaching of Christ and the apostles, and followed by Christians, then it can be seen that the gospel does not overthrow the law, but rather it produces what the law was after in the first place. The dynamic, however, is totally different, referring not to being under the law—language which is anathema to Paul—and not to tablets of stone, but to the law of the new covenant written on our hearts (2 Cor 3:3), in the life of the Spirit.[47]

2.2.2. Paul and Salvation

It is not possible to comprehend the complexity of Paul's view of the law without bringing in the issue of salvation, since the two are so intertwined. The negative view of the law is the result of its inability to save. "Works of the law" are consistently contrasted with faith in Paul. The point is made with clarity more than once in Galatians. Thus in 2:15–16: "We ourselves are Jews by birth and not Gentile sinners; yet we know that a person is justified not by works of the law but through faith in Jesus Christ. And we have come to believe in Christ Jesus, so that we might be justified by faith in Christ, and not by doing the works of the law, because no one will be justified by the works of the law." The same contrast is evident in 3:11–12: "Now it is evident that no one is justified before God by the law; for 'The one who is righteous will live by faith.' But the law does not rest on faith; on the contrary, 'Whoever does the works of the law will live by them.'" Paul goes on to say that Christ has delivered us from the curse of the law having become a curse on our behalf. Paul does say in 3:14 that this had occurred "in order that in Christ Jesus the blessing of Abraham might come to the Gentiles." From Paul's perspective this is a crucially important fact, both for his mission to the Gentiles and for the particular argument in Galatians. But this is no warrant for limiting the point of the argument merely to the hindrance to the Gentiles posed by the identity markers that separated them from Israel.[48]

---

47. On the subject of the law, see Dunn, *Paul and the Mosaic Law*; and Dunn's own essays, especially because of his interaction with disagreeing scholars, *Jesus, Paul and the Law*. See too A. Andrew Das, *Paul, the Law, and the Covenant* (Peabody, MA: Hendrickson, 2001); Das, *Paul and the Jews* (Peabody, MA: Hendrickson, 2003).

48. The present essay limits itself to the undisputed letters of Paul. For a helpful discussion of the later letters of the Pauline corpus, see I. Howard Marshall, "Salvation, Grace and Works in the Later Writings in the Pauline Corpus," *NTS* 42 (1996) 339–58. Marshall concludes, "If works are explicitly put in antithesis to faith in the *Hauptbriefe*, the later epistles emphasize the more fundamental implicit opposition between grace

The statements in Romans are equally strong. The first main section of the book (1:18—3:20) presents an unforgettable indictment against all humanity, both Gentile and Jew. After admitting in 3:1 that the Jews have some (limited) advantage over the Gentiles, he comes to his comprehensive conclusion: "What then? Are we any better off? No, not at all; for we have already charged that all, both Jews and Greeks, are under the power of sin." In the last analysis, those who had the law were not benefited by it. After the catena of Scripture quotations that follows (3:10–18), Paul concludes: "Now we know that whatever the law says, it speaks to those who are under the law, so that every mouth may be silenced, and the whole world may be held accountable to God. For 'no human being will be justified in his sight' by deeds prescribed by the law, for through the law comes the knowledge of sin" (3:19–20).

A few verses later, in the section describing the solution to the human predicament (3:21–31), he asserts: "For we hold that a person is justified by faith apart from works prescribed by the law" (3:28). This is followed by the stress that since there is only one God, he is the God of both Jews and Gentiles and that "he will justify the circumcised on the ground of faith and the uncircumcised through that same faith." If we turn the argument around we may say that since Jews and Gentiles are necessarily saved in the same way (3:23–24), Paul's negative conclusions concerning the law apply equally to Jews and Gentiles, at least so far as salvation is concerned, and therefore both Jews and Gentiles need the free salvation brought by Christ.[49]

In Rom 4:4–5, after the quotation of Gen 15:6, where Abraham's faith was reckoned to him as righteousness, Paul criticizes the idea of earning salvation: "Now to one who works, wages are not reckoned as a gift, but as something due. But to one who without works (*mē ergazomenō*) trusts (*pisteuonti*) him who justifies the ungodly, such faith is reckoned as righteousness (*eis dikaiosynēn*)." In the verse that follows, Paul speaks again of the reckoning of "righteousness apart from works (*chōris ergōn*)."

---

and works which is the ultimate basis of the antithesis between faith and works. A question mark is thus placed against the view that Paul was opposed to 'works of the law' simply as the symbols of a Judaism which excluded the Gentiles. Rather Paul was opposed to any view that regards works as something on which people may depend for salvation rather than purely upon divine grace" (358).

49. The equality of Jew and Gentile in their sin and their need of the same salvation is set forth with particular clarity by Daniel Jong-Sang Chae, *Paul as Apostle to the Gentiles: His Apostolic Self-Awareness and its Influence on the Soteriological Argument in Romans* (Carlisle, UK: Paternoster, 1997).

In words reminiscent of Galatians, Paul writes in Rom 5:20–21: "But law came in (*pareisēlthen*), with the result that the trespass multiplied; but where sin increased, grace abounded all the more, so that, just as sin exercised dominion in death, so grace might also exercise dominion through justification leading to eternal life through Jesus Christ our Lord."

The final verses we note on this subject are found in Rom 11:5–6, where Paul, speaking of Jewish believers in Jesus, including himself, writes: "So too at the present time there is a remnant, chosen by grace. But if it is by grace, it is no longer on the basis of works (*ouketi ex ergōn*), otherwise grace would no longer be grace."

From the above cursory review of Paul's thinking on the subject, at least the following points are clear. (1) The law had a temporary role to play, and that role was not to bring the kind of righteousness that would enable one to stand before God justified, but rather to heighten sin and the awareness of sin; (2) Jews and Gentiles alike are sinful and unable to fulfill the law. Therefore, they are in the same dire situation: without hope apart from the grace of God; (3) salvation for both Jews and Gentiles is available only through faith in Christ and not works of the law, and for that reason the gospel must be preached to both Jews and Gentiles.

This is the heart of Paul's theology and he argues it with such energy that it is very difficult, in my opinion, to read him otherwise. Those statements in Paul that can be seized upon as seeming to point in a different direction must be held in tension with what we have seen, and not be taken as canceling out the main emphases in Paul. With this in mind, we turn to look at two well known difficult passages in Rom 2. The first is Rom 2:6–11: "For he will repay according to each one's deeds: to those who by patiently doing good seek for glory and honor and immortality, he will give eternal life; while for those who are self-seeking and who obey not the truth but wickedness, there will be wrath and fury. There will be anguish and distress for everyone who does evil, the Jew first and also the Greek, but glory and honor and peace for everyone who does good, the Jew first and also the Greek. For God shows no partiality." A verse later (v. 13) Paul adds: "For it is not the hearers of the law who are righteous in God's sight, but the doers of the law who will be justified." To put it mildly, this is a puzzling passage since it seems to affirm the works righteousness perspective and the possibility of obtaining such righteousness, which Paul, as we have seen, is so adamant against and which he forcefully opposes in the argument that follows. Indeed, what

Paul says here appears to be the standard Jewish viewpoint commonly held in Paul's day.

The question is, how can this be seen to be compatible with what Paul will say in the chapters that follow? One popular explanation is to say that Paul is speaking only hypothetically in these passages. In other words, if there were any who obeyed the law they would be justified, but in fact there are not any. But Paul does not seem to be speaking hypothetically in 2:14, when he writes: "When Gentiles, who do not possess the law, do instinctively what the law requires, these, though not having the law, are a law to themselves." Here we must observe the very important point that Paul can envisage righteousness quite apart from the commandments of the law. This is a key to understanding the complexity of Paul's thinking concerning the law, salvation and righteousness. And for Paul, Christians will exhibit that righteousness without being under the law.[50]

2.2.3. The Ongoing Importance of Righteousness for Paul

If anyone thinks that Paul's law-free gospel means the abandonment of righteous living, that person has not understood Paul. Justification by faith does not mean that one may live as one pleases. Paul could hardly make this clearer, especially in the repeated *mē genoito*, "absolutely not" of Romans (6:2, 15). The goal of our identification with Christ's death is that "we too might walk in newness of life" (6:4). For Paul the surprising fact is that "sin will have no dominion over you, since you are not under law but under grace" (Rom 6:14). One might be tempted to say that Paul meant that sin will not rule over us because we *are* under law as well as under grace. But that language for Paul would be totally unacceptable. He is absolutely insistent that Christians are no longer under the law. That cardinal principle he will not compromise. Yet, righteousness remains a high priority for Paul.

---

50. In the final analysis, this conclusion is not very different from that argued by K. R. Snodgrass, "Justification by Grace-to the Doers: An Analysis of the Place of Romans 2 in the Theology of Paul," NTS 32 (1986) 72–93; and (somewhat differently) by Kent L. Yinger, *Paul, Judaism, and Judgment According to Deeds* (SNTSMS 105; Cambridge: Cambridge University Press, 1999). My disagreements appear to be mainly semantic, though of course semantics can sometimes be everything. For me there are two Pauline non-negotiables: that Christians are no longer under law and that nevertheless righteousness remains an indispensable priority. See now Simon J. Gathercole, *Where Is Boasting? Early Jewish Soteriology and Paul's Response in Romans 1–5* (Grand Rapids: Eerdmans, 2002).

The paradox can be summed up by saying that those who are free from the law are now in a position to, and called to, pursue a righteousness that remarkably corresponds to the goal of the law. Thus Paul says that having been set free from the slavery to sin Christians "have become slaves of righteousness" and are to present their members as "slaves to righteousness for sanctification" (Rom 6:18–19). The metaphor is carried on in 7:6: "But now we are discharged from the law, dead to that which held us captive, so that we are slaves not under the old written code but in the new life of the Spirit." The same thread is found in Gal 5:13: "For you were called to freedom, brothers and sisters; only do not use your freedom as an opportunity for self-indulgence, but through love become slaves to one another." For Paul then it could hardly be clearer that freedom from the law and the practice of righteousness are not contradictory.

Here then lies the clue to understanding Paul's positive statements about the law and his Jewish-sounding statements concerning good works, in the very books where he champions freedom from the law and repeatedly contrasts the works of the law with faith and grace. Thus Gal 6:7–8 points to the ongoing importance of righteousness in a law-free gospel of grace: "Do not be deceived; God is not mocked, for you reap whatever you sow. If you sow to your own flesh, you will reap corruption from the flesh; but if you sow to the Spirit, you will reap eternal life from the Spirit." The passages from Rom 2, cited above, are to be explained in this way. So too, when Paul writes in Rom 3:31: "Do we then overthrow the law by this faith? By no means! On the contrary, we uphold the law," he refers not to the commandments as such but to the righteousness which was the goal of the law, now arrived at through obedience to Christ apart from the commandments of the law. This too is even the meaning of the reference to "obeying the commandments of God" in 1 Cor 7:19, as can be confirmed by the parallel passage, Gal 6:15, where the counterpart is "a new creation" (cf. Gal 5:6). It is also how Rom 8:3–4 is to be understood: "For God has done what the law, weakened by the flesh, could not do: by sending his own Son in the likeness of sinful flesh, and to deal with sin, he condemned sin in the flesh, so that the just requirement of the law might be fulfilled in us, who walk not according to the flesh but according to the Spirit." The repeated references to the Spirit, the dynamic of Christian sanctification, in this connection are worthy of note.

To repeat the paradox once more, Paul argues that since Christ has come the law is no longer in effect and Christians are therefore no longer under the law. At the same time, however, the righteousness that corresponds to the goal of the law, but not arrived at by obeying the commandments as such, is emphasized by Paul, and it is in this way that his gospel is not the denial of the law but in the last analysis an upholding of the law.[51]

2.2.4. Paul's Own Practice

What was Paul's own personal practice concerning the law? Several writers have recently argued that Paul continued not only to practice but also to promote not merely the moral law but even the ceremonial or ritual law. Thus, combing through the Pauline letters, Peter Tomson detects the presence of *halakoth* at numerous points and concludes that Paul's life was structured by *halaka*.[52] Paul furthermore expected Gentile Christians to obey *halakoth*, including among others the Noachide commandments. Markus Bockmuehl, somewhat more reasonably than Tomson, has also traced the significance of the Noachide commandments for Gentile Christians in Paul.[53] We can hardly do justice to this unusual argument here, but one may wonder whether applied Christian ethics are appropriately defined as *halaka*, even when they are not derived from Torah (Tomson thus speaks of dominical, apostolic, and general *halaka*). No one denies that the New Testament has ethical standards derived from Jesus and ultimately from the Old Testament, but within the framework of Paul's theology of the law it would seem more accurate to say that we have an analogy to *halaka*, rather than *halaka* as usually encountered.

To return to the question of Paul's own practice with respect to the law, we are fortunate enough to have a comment on the subject from Paul himself. In 1 Cor 9:19–23 Paul admits to a deliberate inconsistency. We quote the passage in full:

---

51. A similar view of the matter, with minor variations, can be found in the following: Stephen Westerholm, *Perspectives Old and New on Paul: The "Lutheran" Paul and His Critics* (Grand Rapids: Eerdmans, 2004); Thomas R. Schreiner, *The Law and Its Fulfillment: A Pauline Theology of Law* (Grand Rapids: Baker, 1993); Frank Thielman, *Paul and the Law: A Contextual Approach* (Downers Grove, IL: InterVarsity, 1994)

52. *Paul and the Jewish Law.*

53. *Jewish Law in Gentile Churches.* Along the same line, see too A. F. Segal, "Universalism in Judaism and Christianity," in *Paul in His Hellenistic Context*, ed. T. Engberg-Pedersen (Minneapolis: Fortress, 1995) 1–29. Bockmuehl admits that the Noachide commandments are "not the theological key to New Testament ethics," but argues that they "provide an essential clue to the specific *rationale and content* of early Christian ethics" (*Jewish Law in Gentile Churches*, 173; his italics). I think this ascribes an exaggerated importance to the Noachide commandments.

> For though I am free with respect to all, I have made myself a slave to all, so that I might win more of them. To the Jews I became as a Jew, in order to win Jews. To those under the law I became as one under the law (though I myself am not under the law) so that I might win those under the law. To those outside the law I became as one outside the law (though I am not free from God's law but am under Christ's law) so that I might win those outside the law. To the weak I became weak, so that I might win the weak. I have become all things to all people, that I might by all means save some. I do it all for the sake of the gospel, so that I may share in its blessings.

Several things are clear from this statement. Paul regards himself as no longer under the law. One can hardly be described as being "under law" if one only obeys it now and then. Paul thus feels free to identify with the Gentiles and not to remain an observant Jew. Incidentally, how remarkable it is that the Jew Paul can speak of himself as an outsider: "To the Jews I became as a Jew"! The implied break with Judaism here is parallel to the statement in Phil 3:4–9. It is clear, furthermore, that observing or not observing the law is, in a sense, an unimportant issue before God. The position taken by Paul is one of complete expedience: he will or will not observe the law only in relation to its usefulness in the proclamation of the gospel. Before God the issue of obeying the commandments is in the category of *adiaphora*.

There is, of course, an important qualifier in v. 21 that tends to confirm our interpretation of the sense in which Paul continues to affirm the law. When he indicates that when he was among the Gentiles he became as "one outside the law," he then adds the words "though I am not free from God's law but under Christ's law." He had already stated that "I myself am not under the law" (v. 20). Now he says, in an apparent contradiction, that he is "not free from God's law." But in the words immediately added, he specifies the sense in which he still pursues the righteousness of the law, namely through "Christ's law (*ennomos christou*)." It is important to note that despite the translation of NRSV (and RSV), Paul does not use the language of being *under* the law of Christ; nor does he do so in the other reference to "the law of Christ" in Gal 6:2 where he speaks of fulfilling the "law of Christ." It is not as though nothing has changed except that the law of Christ now takes the place of the law of Moses. In fact, the dynamic is entirely different (cf. 2 Cor 3:6, 17). But the main point is that faithfulness to the law of God is arrived at through obedience to the teaching of Christ. At bottom is a faithfulness to the righteousness of the Torah—and it is the righteousness of the Torah for Paul—as mediated through the Messiah and the Holy Spirit. This again points to the eschatological dimension of the turning of the ages, because of which we have the complexity of both continuity and discontinuity.[54]

Although Paul had departed from the structures of his previous Judaism, I have little doubt but that his default conduct, so to speak, was very Jewish, simply by habit if for no other reason. He would probably have continued to say the *Shema* twice daily, and ordinarily to observe *kashrut* and Sabbath. But this would perhaps best be described as expression of his ethnic Jewishness, and as a matter of convenience because of the fact that he moved among Jews so frequently. This conduct no longer had any soteriological significance, however, nor was he under compulsion to obey the commandments. His conduct was now solely under the sway of Christ.

2.3. Paul's Understanding of the Old Testament and His Interpretive Method

We need spend little time on the Jewishness, indeed the rabbinic character, of Paul's interpretive approach to the Scriptures. This has been well established.[55] Along with the continuity afforded by this fact, we have of course to reckon with a major point of discontinuity in the fact that Paul's conviction that Jesus is the Messiah now controls his reading of the Scriptures. Paul, in short, has a christological hermeneutic. The Scriptures of Israel are ultimately about Christ and therefore Christ is the key to understanding them. This is put clearly in 2 Cor 3:14-15, where speaking of the Jews he writes: "But their minds were hardened. Indeed, to this

---

54. See Stanley E. Porter, "Was Paul a Good Jew? Fundamental Issues in a Current Debate," in *Christian-Jewish Relations through the Centuries*, ed. S. E. Porter and B. W. R. Pearson, JSNTSup 192 (Sheffield: Sheffield Academic, 2000) 148-74. The allusion to Markus Barth's essay ("St. Paul—A Good Jew") is deliberate, with the answer being quite different.

55. See Joseph Bonsirven, *Exegese rabbinique et exegese paulinienne* (Paris: Beauchesne, 1939); Joachim Jeremias, "Paulus als Hillelit," in *Neotestamentica et Semitica: Studies in Honour of Matthew Black*, ed. E. E. Ellis and M. Wilcox (Edinburgh: T. & T. Clark, 1969) 88-94; D. Cohn-Sherbok, "Paul and Rabbinic Exegesis," *SJT* 35 (1982) 117-32; Richard N. Longenecker, *Biblical Exegesis in the Apostolic Period* (Grand Rapids: Eerdmans, 1975). See now, however, the cautionary remarks of Richard B. Hays, *Echoes of Scripture in the Letters of Paul* (New Haven: Yale University Press, 1989) 10-14.

very day, when they hear the reading of the old covenant, that same veil is still there, since only in Christ is it set aside. Indeed, to this very day whenever Moses is read, a veil lies over their minds; but when one turns to the Lord, the veil is removed." Paul's approach to the Old Testament is both very Jewish and very Christian! Again the determinative factor is the eschatological event of the coming of the Messiah.

This last point means that the new covenant has taken the place of the old covenant. The 2 Cor 3 passage makes this quite clear. The old is described as the letter that kills, the ministry of condemnation and death. By contrast the new is of the Spirit and gives life, a "ministry of justification" abounding in a glory that immeasurably exceeds that of the old. The old was "set aside"; the new is "the permanent" (v. 11). Then, speaking of the sanctification of believers, Paul concludes "And all of us, with unveiled faces, seeing the glory of the Lord as though reflected in a mirror, are being transformed into the same image from one degree of glory to another; for this comes from the Lord, the Spirit" (2 Cor 3:18).

2.4. The Temple

Since the temple was one of the pillars of pre-70 Judaism, it may be worth pointing out how little Paul has to say about it. In the whole discussion of Paul this is a much neglected subject. In fact, the temple is mentioned by Paul only in the letters to Corinth (with one reference each in the disputed letters, 2 Thess 2:4 and Eph 2:21). In 1 Cor 3:16–17; 6:19, as well as in 2 Cor 6:16, Paul spiritualizes the word so that it refers to the holiness of the Christian's body: the Christian is God's temple. The mention of the temple in 1 Cor 9:13 is made in an incidental allusion to workers in the temple receiving food for their work as a justification for Christian workers to receive material benefits for their work.

Although still functioning in Paul's day, the temple and the ritual purity of the temple play no role in Paul's perspective. The reason for this is transparently clear. Since the sacrifice of Christ is the fulfillment of the temple sacrifices, and it was his sacrifice to which they pointed, his death makes the ongoing sacrificial ritual of the temple a redundancy, something perhaps already seen by Stephen (Acts 6:13–14). Paul writes: "For our paschal lamb, Christ, has been sacrificed" (1 Cor 5:7). Using the language of the temple and the holy of holies, he refers to the justification of Christians "by his grace as a gift, through the redemption that is in

Christ Jesus, whom God put forward as a sacrifice of atonement [these three words translate *hilastērion*, lit. 'place of atonement,' i.e., the lid covering the ark of the covenant] by his blood" (Rom 3:24–25).

For Paul it is the sacrificial death of Christ alone that provides forgiveness of sins. The realization on the Damascus Road that God had sent his Messiah to be crucified, an idea that was previously a stumbling block to Paul, enabled him to proclaim the message of "Christ crucified," who now for Paul took the place of Torah as "the power of God and the wisdom of God" (1 Cor 1:23–24; 2:2). It is fully to be expected that Paul would find little of significance in the temple after the cross. Yet, at the same time, it was only the temple and its ritual that made the death of Christ comprehensible, and it was only in its terms that the meaning of Christ's death could be described.

We may simply add here that another very important element in the Judaism of Paul's day, namely the land, finds no place in Paul's thinking, so far as it can be judged from his letters. Indeed, quite remarkably, in the one instance where we might have expected the word "land" (*hē gē*) we read instead of "the promise to Abraham and his descendants, that they should inherit the world (*ho kosmos*)" (Rom 4:13, RSV). This reflects Paul's understanding of the universality of the Abrahamic covenant, and that the history of salvation transcends the promise of the land.

2.5. Paul's Hope for Israel

As a final subject in our study of continuity and discontinuity, we turn to the question of the relation of the church to Israel and to the question of Israel's future. Our focus, of course, will be that remarkable passage, Romans 9–11.

We begin with the dialectical affirmation that the church has taken the place of Israel, and yet at the same time it has not. With great personal vexation of spirit, Paul begins his discussion lamenting his kinsfolk's unbelief in the gospel of Jesus Christ (9:1–5). He summarizes the strange turn of events in the following words: "What then are we to say? Gentiles, who did not strive for righteousness, have attained it, that is, righteousness through faith; but Israel, who did strive for the righteousness that is based on the law, did not succeed in fulfilling that law. Why not? Because they did not strive for it on the basis of faith, but as if it were based on works. They have stumbled over the stumbling stone" (9:30–32). In 10:3

the same observation is made: "For, being ignorant of the righteousness that comes from God, and seeking to establish their own, they have not submitted to God's righteousness."

The painful and undeniable reality of Israel's unbelief in the gospel inevitably raises the question of God's faithfulness. As he begins to bring his discussion to resolution, Paul puts the question directly: "I ask, then, has God rejected his people? By no means! I myself am an Israelite, a descendant of Abraham, a member of the tribe of Benjamin. God has not rejected his people whom he foreknew" (11:1–2). Paul appeals to a remnant of Jewish believers in Christ, "chosen by grace" (11:5), including himself. This is the outworking of a distinction already made by Paul between ethnic Israel and spiritual Israel (see 9:6–8, 27–29; cf. 2:28–29). The fact that a remnant of Jews have believed in Christ itself satisfies the question of the faithfulness of God.

Nothing more needs to happen for the question of God's faithfulness to be put to rest. The remnant itself is the concrete evidence of that faithfulness. This is not, however, the end of the story. In 11:11 Paul asks "have they stumbled so as to fall? By no means!" He then successively speaks of their future "full inclusion" (11:12), and "their acceptance" (11:15). They, the Jews who have not accepted Christ, are subsequently referred to as part of a holy "batch" of dough, and as holy "branches" of a "holy root" (11:16)

This leads Paul to his famous olive tree analogy. Here the tree no doubt is Israel, the earlier covenant people of God, and the root in particular, if it is specifically to be identified, is probably the patriarchs. Paul likens the Jewish unbelievers to branches that were broken off "because of their unbelief" (11 :20), i.e., in the gospel. God can easily graft these natural branches back into the olive tree, and Paul now announces what lies in the future for these branches: "And even those of Israel (NRSV adds the last two words), if they do not persist in unbelief, will be grafted in, for God has the power to graft them in again." The unbelief referred to here can only be unbelief in Christ. Paul knows only one way of salvation. This is followed directly by Paul's announcement of a "mystery," namely that "a hardening has come upon part of Israel, until the full number of the Gentiles has come in. And so all Israel will be saved" (11:25–26). Paul does not tell us how this will come about, but the assumption seems to be that there will be a turning of Israel ("all" is meant to be comprehensive, but not necessarily universal) to faith in Christ.[56] The sequence revealed in the mystery reverses the order that Paul would have held earlier, namely the Jewish view that after the eschatological salvation of Israel, only then would there be salvation for the righteous Gentiles. Now the sequence is salvation first to the Gentiles and only then to Israel. Paul accordingly could have conceived of his apostleship to the Gentiles as ultimately serving Israel, as a prerequisite to Israel's salvation, and hence as a mark of his loyalty to Israel.

In the best Jewish fashion, Paul says of Israel: "as regards election they are beloved, for the sake of their ancestors; for the gifts and the calling of God are irrevocable" (11:28-29). Paul returns to his fundamental loyalty to Israel, or perhaps better put, to the God of Israel. This he never lost, for all the newness and change in him that one may care to discuss. Israel and the church are, as it will finally turn out to be, part of one great story.[57] Christ is and will be the consummation of Israel's hope.

Following this affirmation of God's unchanging faithfulness, Paul presents one last summary of the great epic of salvation history: "Just as you were once disobedient to God but have now received mercy because of their disobedience, so they have now been disobedient in order that, by the mercy shown to you, they too may now receive mercy. For God has imprisoned all in disobedience so that he may be merciful to all" (11:30-32). This astounding encapsulation of the purpose of God leads Paul, not unexpectedly, to a moving doxology that brings this section of Romans to a climactic end. He can only bow in submission and adoration at the unsearchable and mysterious ways of God: "For from him and through him and to him are all things. To him be the glory forever. Amen."

3. OLD AND NEW IN PAUL

The entirety of Paul's theology is a juxtaposition of old and new, just as Paul himself is a unique combination of old: rabbinically trained Jew; and new: Christian apostle and witness of the resurrected Jesus. This combination is the root of the complex continuities and discontinuities

---

56. See Reidar Hvalvik, "A 'Sonderweg' for Israel? A Critical Examination of a Current Interpretation of Romans 11.25-27," *JSNT* 38 (1990) 87-107; and Scott Hafemann, "The Salvation of Israel in Romans 11:25-32: A Response to Krister Stendahl," *Ex Auditu* 4 (1988) 38-58.

57. See Bruce W. Longenecker, "Different Answers to Different Issues: Israel, the Gentiles and Salvation History in Romans 9-11," *JSNT* 36 (1989) 95-123.

that we have examined.[58] Paul never regarded himself as no longer a Jew. Because Christianity is the fruit and fulfillment of the hope of the Jewish Scriptures there are substantial points of continuity between Paul the Jew and Paul the Christian. For him, being a Christian is not something opposed to being a Jew. At the same time, however, Christianity is not simply a further development of the Old Testament or of Judaism. Nor is it primarily a way for Judaism to become accessible to the Gentiles. The death of Christ is the means of salvation for Jews as well as Gentiles. Paul makes it very clear: the gospel "is the power of God for salvation to everyone who has faith, to the Jew first and also to the Greek" (Rom 1:16). The ultimate conclusion of the argument in Rom 1:18—3:20 is that Jews are as much under the power of sin as are Gentiles, and thus are in need of the same justification, which alone comes through the atoning death of Christ. At the end of Romans, Paul emphasizes that "Christ has become a servant of the circumcised on behalf of the truth of God in order that he might confirm the promises given to the patriarchs, and in order that the Gentiles might glorify God for his mercy" (Rom 15:8-9).

Furthermore, the old and the new are not present in an equal balance. We do not have a situation in which a variety of new perspectives are added to the staple of old things that constitute Judaism, causing only minor readjustments. On the contrary, the new that comes is an eschatological turning point in the ages,[59] of such great consequence that we must be prepared for dramatic shifts. Here is the reason for the striking discontinuities we encounter in Paul. This key fact, that Jesus is the promised Messiah who inaugurates the new, eschatological age, is what is finally determinative for Paul, and it is the one thing that revisionist readings of Paul consistently underestimate. Put very simply: Paul was a Jew who believed that the Messiah had come. That made all the difference in the world.

God had a far more complicated program for his Messiah, however, than Saul the Pharisee could have anticipated. Most unexpectedly, it involved the Messiah's redeeming death on the cross, but also it involved a

---

58. For a helpful discussion, see James D. G. Dunn, "How New Was Paul's Gospel? The Problem of Continuity and Discontinuity," in *Gospel in Paul: Studies on Corinthians, Galatians and Romans for Richard N. Longenecker*, ed. L. A. Jervis and P. Richardson, JSNTSup 108 (Sheffield: Sheffield Academic, 1994) 367-88.

59. See I. Howard Marshall, "A New Understanding of the Present and the Future: Paul and Eschatology;' in *The Road from Damascus: The Impact of Paul's Conversion on His Life, Thought, and Ministry*, ed. R. N. Longenecker (Grand Rapids: Eerdmans, 1997) 43-61.

temporary hardening of Israel—except for the remnant—and it involved the creation of a new community of faith, the church, consisting of not only Gentiles, but also Jews. The era of promise and preparation, when God had focused his attention on Israel and her existence under Torah, had come to an end. Christ and the church were now the focus of God's purposes, but with Israel as a whole still to be incorporated at the approach of the eschaton proper.

With this shift of aeons and all of its related aspects in mind, it can hardly be adequate to characterize Paul's theology as a form of Christian Judaism. It is instead necessarily a new entity: a Christianity that is intimately and inseparably related to Judaism as its fulfillment and consummation (cf. 1 Cor 10:32, which refers to three entities, namely Jews, Greeks, and the church of God). The significance of the special identity of the Jews is relativized: "There is no longer Jew or Greek, there is no longer slave or free, there is no longer male and female; for all of you are one in Christ Jesus" (Gal 3:28). And, as the text in Gal 6:16 is probably to be taken, Paul can refer to the church as "the Israel of God."

Although it grew out of Judaism, and despite undeniable Jewish aspects, Pauline Christianity cannot adequately be described as a sect of Judaism. Two questions are debated by scholars today. First, when can we speak of Christianity? And, second, when did the church break with the synagogue? As for the first, the answer depends on what we mean by the word. Of course institutionalized Christianity as a self-conscious entity came about relatively late. But if we define a Christian as one who believes in the crucified and risen Jesus as Lord, whose atoning death brings the reality of salvation, and if a Christian is one who understands the participation of the Holy Spirit as the mark of the dawning of a new era, then we have Christianity from the day of Pentecost. When the label "Christian" was first used is irrelevant. For the first few years of the Jerusalem church, the Christians were all Jews. Pre-Pauline Christianity was a Jewish phenomenon, and despite some ongoing tensions, Paul found much agreement with those in Jerusalem who had been Christians before him (Gal 2:9).

As for the second question, it would seem wise not to think in terms of a specific date for the break of the church from the synagogue.[60] We undoubtedly have to reckon with a process taking place in different

---

60. On this and other matters addressed in the present essay, see Martin Hengel, "Early Christianity as a Jewish-Messianic, Universalist Movement," in *Conflicts and Challenges in Early Christianity*, ed. D. A. Hagner (Harrisville, PA: Trinity, 1999) 1–41.

locations at different rates of speed. Dating the supposed break circa 85–90 CE, during the work of the Yavneh rabbis and the adding of the "benediction" of the *minim* to the Eighteen Benedictions, to my mind is much too late. Tensions were great virtually from the start, and only increased with the passing of time. Paul knew the reality of Jewish opposition to the message he preached (cf. 2 Cor 11:23-26). There were clear points of vital importance, especially, the destruction of Jerusalem in 70, but it is likely, in my opinion, that the church and synagogue were obviously separate entities before the end of the first century.[61]

From the beginning, Paul knew that his faith in Christ meant a separation from his previous Jewish existence. As we have repeatedly noted, however, his Christian faith was not the nullification of his former Judaism as much as it was its fulfillment. He now spoke of new communities, the churches, consisting of Gentiles and a remnant of Jewish believers among whom he counted himself. The new that brought the old to its intended goal had now come into existence. And in that new reality Paul, the apostle of Christ to the Gentiles, found the meaning and culmination of his Jewish identity.[62]

---

61. On this subject, see especially James D. G. Dunn, *The Partings of the Ways Between Christianity and Judaism and their Significance for the Character of Christianity* (London: SCM, 1991) and *Jews and Christians: The Parting of the Ways A.D. 70 to 135*, ed. J. D. G. Dunn (Grand Rapids: Eerdmans, 1999).

62. A number of important essays germane to the present essay will be found in *Justification and Variegated Nomism*, vol. 2: *The Paradoxes of Paul*, ed. D. A. Carson et al.; WUNT 2/181 (Tübingen: Mohr Siebeck, 2004).

9

Paul's Quarrel with Judaism

THERE CAN BE NO question but that the Holocaust—that ripest and most bitter fruit of anti-Semitism—perpetrated by the leadership of an at least nominally Christian nation, constitutes a fundamental turning point in Jewish-Christian relations. It should no longer be possible for Christians to remain unaware of the evil that can be caused by an improper or insensitive use of the anti-Judaic statements of the New Testament. Christians from now on must be vigilant against every manifestation of anti-Semitism and every misuse of New Testament materials that leads to anti-Semitism. Because of the possibility of misunderstanding these texts, we have reached the point where it is now necessary for every exposition of the anti-Judaic passages of the New Testament to be accompanied by explicit statements concerning what they do not mean. Anti-Judaism is theological disagreement with Judaism, and, as we shall see, this disagreement can become polemical in tone. Anti-Semitism, by contrast, is nothing less than racial hatred of the Jews, a hatred that can take a variety of forms such as prejudice, injustice, slander, abuse, and even physical violence.[1]

---

1. The "criteria of anti-Semitism" listed by M. Barth in his essay "Was Paul an Anti-Semite?" refer really to anti-Judaism. Barth justifies the label by designating what he refers to as "a wolf-in-sheep's-clothing type of anti-Semitism" (*Israel and the Church* [Richmond: John Knox, 1969] 54ff.). This use of terminology, however, results in confusion rather than clarity. W. D. Davies points out that "the use of the term anti-Semitism, strictly so called, for attitudes and conduct in the early church is anachronistic" ("Paul and the People of Israel," NTS 24 [1977–78] 18). S. Sandmel admits that· "anti-Semitism" is "a completely wrong term when transferred to the first and second centuries" and that "anti-Jewish" and "anti-Judaic" "are better because they are correct."

PART TWO | PAUL

It cannot be denied that there are clearly anti-Judaic passages in the letters of Paul and elsewhere in the New Testament. There is of course a sense in which the expression "anti-Judaism" is itself totally inappropriate, since the Jewish Christians responsible for the New Testament, including Paul, regarded Christianity as the fulfillment of Judaism.[2] Rather than being disloyal to the faith of the patriarchs and the Bible in their new-found Christian experience, they believed they had encountered what the promises had pointed toward. It was thus not a new religion they joined but the true and perfect manifestation of their ancestral faith. What they opposed in their polemicizing was in their eyes not truly Judaism, but only a truncated version of it, which tragically rejected its Messiah and which thus remained incomplete. Although "anti-Judaism," strictly speaking, is thus itself a misnomer, the term is nevertheless retained here in its commonly used sense. None of the Jewish Christians of the New Testament, however, would have been comfortable with the expression, least of all Paul.[3]

This essay will explore key passages in Paul's letters in order to ascertain the nature of Paul's anti-Judaism and to differentiate it from anti-Semitism. I do not contest the fact that anti-Judaism can lead to anti-Semitism, as it tragically has so often in the past. What I challenge is that the latter is a necessary outcome of the former. The anti-Judaic

---

He nevertheless decides to use "anti-Semitism" throughout his book while being "aware of how wrong the term is" (*Anti-Semitism in the New Testament?* [Philadelphia: Fortress, 1978] xxi). See too the excellent article of E. H. Flannery, "Anti-Judaism and Anti-Semitism: A Necessary Distinction," *JES* 10 (1973) 581-88.

2. J. Klausner thus correctly notes that while Paul's teaching involved an anti-Judaism, "he considered his teaching as true Judaism, as the fulfillment of the promises and assurances of authentic Judaism" (*From Jesus to Paul*, trans. W. F. Stinespring [New York: Macmillan, 1943] 591). G. Lindeskog writes: "'Anti-Judaism' therefore was from the beginning an opposition within Judaism. This inner-Jewish controversy is therefore not anti-Jewish" (*Das jüdisch-christliche Problem* [Stockholm: Almqvist & Wiksell, 1986] 158). S. Sandmel notes that Paul considered his "new convictions . . . to be the true and sure version of Judaism" (*Judaism and Christian Beginnings* [New York: Oxford University Press, 1978] 336). See also J. D. G. Dunn, *The Partings of the Ways between Christianity and Judaism and Their Significance for the Character of Christianity* (Philadelphia: Trinity, 1991) 148-49.

3. Thus P. Stuhlmacher is correct when he concludes: "However, as long as the apostle is criticized for harboring anti-Judaistic tendencies, without taking into account his situation and his teaching, I consider Paul to have been misinterpreted and unrefuted" (*Paul: Rabbi and Apostle*, with P. Lapide, trans. L. W. Denef [Minneapolis: Augsburg, 1984] 61). Lapide too concludes that Paul "was neither an anti-Semite nor an anti-Judaist" (54).

passages of the New Testament are in my opinion an essential component of New Testament Christianity;[4] anti-Semitism, in contrast, is not.[5]

The problem for many, however, is not simply the anti-Judaic passages of the New Testament, but the absolute claim of Christianity over against all other options, including Judaism. This claim is itself thought to be objectionable because with it seems to come an ecclesiastical triumphalism and imperialism that cannot tolerate the continued existence of Judaism. But such a conclusion greatly exaggerates what is implied by the absolutism of Christianity. In view here is nothing less and nothing more than the question of truth. Paul believed in the absolute and exclusive truth of his gospel. But he no more advocates the overthrow of Judaism and the burning of synagogues than he does of the pagan mystery religions and their sanctuaries. Not that he would ever have put the two on the same level! Indeed, as we shall see, Paul can continue to say good things of Judaism and expect good things for the Jewish people. But to be fair to his teaching, it must be said that as much as we might have liked him to do so, he does not see Judaism as a valid alternative to Christian faith.[6] I shall argue, nevertheless, that this does not mean that Paul can correctly be considered anti-Semitic.

---

4. Here I agree with the conclusion of U. Wilckens in a well-known article in the extensive German discussion of the question ("Das Neue Testament und die Juden," *EvT* 34 [1974] 602-11). Wilckens's conclusion that the anti-Judaic theme in the New Testament is "in essence Christian-theological" and has as its intent the profiling of the Christian faith rather than the defaming of the Jewish faith was formulated as a part of his response to D. Flusser's article "Ulrich Wilckens und die Juden," *EvT* 34 (1974) 236-43, which criticized Wilckens's handling of certain passages in his translation and commentary, *Das Neue Testament* (Zurich: Zwingli, 1970).

5. It is above all Rosemary Ruether who has insisted that anti-Semitism is intrinsic to Christianity, as for example in her famous dictum that anti-Judaism (and hence anti-Semitism) is the left hand of Christology. See her influential book *Faith and Fratricide: The Theological Roots of Anti-Semitism* (New York: Seabury, 1971; reprint, Eugene, OR: Wipf & Stock, 1996). Her analysis of the extent and importance of the New Testament data is, in my opinion, one of the best available. She rightly speaks only of anti-Judaism in the New Testament, but she is convinced that anti-Judaism "constantly takes expression in anti-Semitism" (116).

6. See E. E. Johnson, who in a sensitive article calls attention to arguments that "frequently go beyond Paul himself by claiming in his name that non-Christian Judaism retains abiding validity alongside Gentile Christianity." "That," she adds, "may indeed be true in ultimate theological terms — that is, in the mind of God — but it is exegetically indefensible to say Paul thinks so" ("Jews and Christians in the New Testament: John, Matthew, and Paul," *Reformed Review* 42 [1988] 127 n21).

1 THESSALONIANS 2:14-16

I begin with what is the most notorious anti-Judaic passage in the Pauline corpus, 1 Thess 2:14-16. Paul, it must be said, comes the closest here to sounding like an anti-Semite. He parallels the suffering of the Thessalonians experienced from their compatriots to that of the churches in Judaea at the hands of the Jews (*hypo tōn Ioudaiōn*), describing these Jews further as those "who killed both the Lord Jesus and the prophets, and drove us out; they displease God (*theō mē areskontōn*) and oppose everyone (*pasin anthrōpois enantiōn*) by hindering us from speaking to the Gentiles so that they may be saved. Thus they have constantly been filling up the measure of their sins (*eis to anaplērōsai autōn tas hamartias pantote*); but God's wrath has overtaken them at last (*ephthasen de ep' autous hē orgē eis telos*)."[7]

So repugnant is this passage to the modern mind that although there is no textual evidence supporting the conclusion,[8] many have argued that the passage was not written by Paul, but constitutes a later addition to the authentic epistle.[9]

A fairly strong and attractive case has been made for regarding the passage as an interpolation. Birger Pearson has marshaled arguments from the form and content of the material.[10] According to one plausible analysis, chap. 1 constitutes the opening thanksgiving, and 2:1-12 is the first section of the main body of the letter. The second thanksgiving, beginning in v. 13, is then regarded as a later intrusion together with vv. 14-16 (with vv. 15-16 being particularly irrelevant to Paul's purpose

---

7. Throughout this chapter, biblical translations, with some slight alterations, are from the NRSV.

8. The only concrete evidence of the omission of any material at all, according to the Nestle-Aland apparatus, is of v. 16c, and that in only a single Vulgate MS. Ritschl conjectured that v. 16c was an addition to the Pauline material. A late nineteenth-century Jewish author named Rodrigues argued that vv. 14-15 (and 16?) were a later interpolation. See T. Baarda, "l Thess. 2:14-16: Rodrigues in 'Nestle-Aland,'" *NedTT* 39 (1985) 186-93.

9. B. Pearson, "I Thessalonians 2:13-16: A Deutero-Pauline Interpolation," *HTR* 64 (1971) 79-91; D. Schmidt, "I Thess 2:13-16: Linguistic Evidence for an Interpolation," *JBL* 102 (1983) 269-79. For further support of this conclusion, see N. A. Beck, *Mature Christianity* (Selinsgrove, PA: Susquehanna University Press, 1985) 40-46; H. Boers, "The Form-critical Study of Paul's Letters: 1 Thessalonians as a Case Study," *NTS* 22 (1975-76) 140-58; H. Koester, *Introduction to the New Testament* (Philadelphia: Fortress, 1982) 2.113; J. P. Sampley et al., *Ephesians, Colossians, 2 Thessalonians, the Pastoral Epistles*, Proclamation Commentaries (Philadelphia: Fortress, 1978) 77-79.

10. Pearson, "I Thessalonians 2:13-16."

in the preceding and following material); it is pointed out that one can move smoothly from v. 12 to v. 17 without missing the intervening material and at the same time avoiding the unnatural breaks it causes. Pearson furthermore argues from the content (esp. v. 16, taken as an allusion to the fall of Jerusalem) that the material must be dated after 70 CE, and thus cannot be Pauline. Daryl Schmidt has added linguistic arguments for the inauthenticity of these verses, pointing to stylistic (i.e., especially syntactical) variations from the surrounding authentic material and concluding that the passage is "built around a conflation of Pauline expressions."[11] There is furthermore and perhaps most importantly the problem of the theological incompatibility of this material with the view of Paul in Romans 11, where, far from suggesting the final judgment of the Jews, he speaks concerning the continuing validity of God's covenant with them and indeed of their eventual salvation.

All of these arguments, however, constitute only circumstantial evidence that cannot in the end overcome the total lack of confirming textual evidence. They are well-intentioned attempts to keep Paul from saying what it seems he ought not to have said. Not only can these arguments be answered, but the objectionable material is capable of more than one explanation.[12]

As we shall see, it is not at all historically improbable that Paul could have written this blistering passage. The argument from formal considerations is a precarious one.[13] It is a well known fact that Paul exercised considerable freedom in his letters so far as formal structure is concerned. It is furthermore the case that a number of scholars who have studied the structure of the epistle have had no difficulty in integrating 2:13-16 into

---

11. Schmidt, "1 Thess 2:13-16," 276.

12. See especially the fine article by I. Broer, " 'Antisemitismus' und Judenpolemik im Neuen Testament: Ein Beitrag zum besseren Verständnis von 1 Thess 2,14-16," *Biblische Notizen* 20 (1983) 58-91, as well as his "'Der ganze Zorn ist schon über sie gekommen': Bemerkungen zur Interpolationshypothese und zur Interpretation von 1 Thess 2,14-16," in R. F. Collins, ed., *The Thessalonian Correspondence*, BETL 87 (Leuven: Leuven University Press, 1990) 137-59, and "Antijudaismus im Neuen Testament? Versuch einer Annäherung anhand von zwei Texten (1 Thess 2,14-16 und Mt 27,24f)," in L. Oberlinner and P. Fiedler, eds., *Salz der Erde-Licht der Welt: Exegetische Studien zum Matthäusevangelium* (Stuttgart: Katholisches Bibelwerk, 1991) 321-55. Also against the view that the passage is an interpolation, see the excursus in G. Lüdemann, *Paulus und das Judentum* (Munich: Kaiser, 1983) 25-27.

13. See W. D. Davies's conclusion: "The structural argument is not certain" ("Paul and the People of Israel," 6). It is worth pointing out that yet a third thanksgiving passage occurs in 3:9.

their analyses.¹⁴ The linguistic evidence is in itself also hardly compelling. The irregularity of the syntax may well be accounted for in part by the character of the passage as well as the use of traditional materials.¹⁵ Nor does the content of the passage necessitate the acceptance of a post-70 date. It is thus by no means certain (pace Pearson, following F. C. Baur, who on this basis denied the authenticity of 1 Thessalonians) that the words *ephthasen de ep' autous hē orgē eis telos* at the end of v. 16 are an allusion to the destruction of Jerusalem in 70 CE. Even if one were to insist on the aorist verb as referring to something that had already occurred, other conclusions are possible.¹⁶

Although it is not necessary for our purposes to decide upon the exact meaning of the statement,¹⁷ the following may be said. It is quite possible and in keeping with the language of the passage (especially *eis telos*) to take the aorist as a kind of "prophetic perfect" referring to a final, eschatological judgment expected in the near future.¹⁸ At the same time, however, the aorist probably points to an aspect of judgment already experienced (cf. the practically identical statement in T. Levi 6:11). The context shows that Paul has in mind the unbelief of the Jews that is responsible for their

---

14. E.g., R. Jewett, *The Thessalonian Correspondence: Pauline Rhetoric and Millenarian Piety* (Philadelphia: Fortress, 1986) 72-76; T. Holtz (*Der Erste Brief an die Thessalonicher*, EKKNT (Neukirchen-Vluyn: Neukirchener, 1986] 94) finds a close connection between 2:1-12 and 2:13; C. A. Wanamaker (*The Epistles to the Thessalonians*, NIGTC (Grand Rapids: Eerdmans, 1990) 108-10) regards 2:13-16 as a rhetorical digression with a paraenetic function (on this matter, see also W. Wuellner, "Greek Rhetoric and Pauline Argumentation," in W. R. Schoedel and R. L. Wilken, eds., *Early Christian Literature and the Classical Intellectual Tradition: In Honorem Robert M. Grant* [Paris: Beauchesne, 1979] 177-88).

15. See J. W. Simpson Jr., "The Problems Posed by 1 Thessalonians 2:15-16 and a Solution," *HBT* 12/1 (1990) esp. 52-54.

16. E.g., the expulsion of the Jews from Rome in 49 CE by Claudius, as the anticipation of a broader and final judgment (see E. Bammel, "Judenverfolgung und Naherwartung," *ZTK* 56 [1959] 249-315); the massacre of Jews in the Temple court, after 48 CE (following S. Johnson, see R. Jewett, *Thessalonian Correspondence*, 37-38, where other possibilities are also mentioned: "to someone who lived before that catastrophe [70 CE], several of the other events could easily have appeared to be a final form of divine wrath"). See also J. Coppens, "Miscellanées bibliques LXXX: Une diatribe antijuive dans I Thess. II, 13-16," *ETL* 51 (1975) 90-95.

17. I. H. Marshall summarizes the options for *eis telos* as follows: (1) "at long last" or "finally"; (2) "completely," "to the uttermost"; (3) "for ever," "to the end," i.e., "lasting for ever"; and (4) "until the end" qualifying "wrath," i.e., "the wrath (that leads up) to the End." Marshall opts for "a combination of nuances," namely "fully and finally" (*1 and 2 Thessalonians*, NCB (Grand Rapids: Eerdmans, 1983] 81).

18. Thus, e.g., Dobschütz, Rigaux; see G. E. Okeke's correct rejection of this option, "I Thessalonians 2.13-16: The Fate of the Unbelieving Jews," *NTS* 27 (1980-81) 130.

persecution of Christians and their hindering of the proclamation of the gospel to the Gentiles. In their present unbelief, the wrath of God has in a sense already come upon them (see Rom 1:18 for a similar, present dimension of the wrath of God), this in anticipation of the imminent, final wrath.[19] They are filling up the measure of their sins, and God's wrath has already come upon them in a final or eschatological sense.[20]

There is no compelling reason to conclude that Paul did not write 1 Thess 2:14-16. But how could he have written such vitriolic words, and do they constitute anti-Semitism (and not simply anti-Judaism)? How, furthermore, are we to reconcile the content of this passage with the final optimism of Romans 11, where Paul speaks of the salvation of the Jews in connection with the end of the age?

The language, to begin with, is obviously both polemical[21] and highly emotional. It reflects something of Paul's own personal history as well as his present commission.[22] It is written in a moment of agonizing frus-

---

19. See Wanamaker, *Thessalonians*, 117: "God's wrath has overtaken the unbelieving and disobedient Jews in that they have been hardened by God and no longer experience God's grace. That they had not believed the gospel would have been proof enough of this for Paul." F. F. Bruce, *1 and 2 Thessalonians*, WBC (Waco: Word, 1982) 49: "The language of v. 16c implies that the end-time judgment has come upon them ahead of time." Holtz, *Erste Brief an die Thessalonicher*, 109: "Because the synagogue opposes the eschatological salvation, it has fallen into the eschatological judgment." Broer, "'Antisemitismus' und Judenpolemik," 85: "The present situation is itself the judgment of God," and more explicitly in "Der ganze Zorn," 157: "so Paul sees this judgment in the removal of the fundamental advantage of the Jews over all other human beings." Cf. E. Bammel, "Judenverfolgung und Naherwartung," *ZTK* 56 (1959) 308. Goppelt finds a parallel to 1 Thess 2:15-16 in Rom 9:22; see *Jesus, Paul and Judaism*, trans. E. Schroeder (New York: Nelson, 1964) 159. Cf. now too Dunn, *Partings of the Ways*, 146.

20. Donfried's conclusion that *eis telos* should be taken in the sense of "until the end," although it makes the passage more compatible with Romans 11, unfortunately does not reflect the most natural meaning of the language; see "Paul and Judaism: 1 Thessalonians 2:13-16 as a Test Case," *Int* 38 (1984) 252. A similar argument was earlier set forward by J. Munck in *Christ and Israel*, trans. I. Nixon (Philadelphia: Fortress, 1964) 64.

21. Thus O. Michel: "At stake for the apostle are conflict and argument, not reaction or temper alone" ("Fragen zu 1 Thessalonicher 2,14-16: Antijüdische Polemik bei Paulus," in W. Eckert, N. P. Levinson, and M. Stohr, eds., *Antijudaismus im Neuen Testament? Exegetische und systematische Beiträge* [Munich: Kaiser, 1967] 51).

22. Here I have in mind the persecution suffered by Paul at the hands of Jews in his missionary work (see 2 Cor 11:24-26). See P. Stuhlmacher, "The sharp tone that recurs in Paul's letters, for example, the unfortunately formulated polemic in 1 Thess. 2:14f., can, in my opinion, be explained as a direct result of this situation of personal conflict and suffering" (*Paul: Rabbi and Apostle*, 16). S. Ben-Chorin, however, goes too far in saying that Paul's attitude reflects a deep hatred of himself as a former persecutor of the Christians (Gal 1:13; 1 Cor 15:9) ("Antijüdische Elemente im Neuen Testament," *EvT*

tration as he remembers those who have opposed his work. It partakes furthermore of the intensity and absolutism of the apocalyptic condemnation of the enemies of God.[23] The statement is thus a generalizing one applied to the Jews as a whole, rather than just to those who killed Jesus or hindered Paul's mission.[24] Like the Old Testament prophets, Paul is righteously indignant concerning Israel's opposition to the plan and purposes of God.[25] Indeed, as I. Broer has convincingly argued, it is probable that Paul's words quite consciously reflect a Deuteronomistic-type judgment oracle directed against the Jews in general.[26] The language is furthermore reminiscent of that used in polemic between philosophical schools in the ancient world, being rhetorical in function rather than denotative.[27]

The statement is therefore anything but a calm, reasoned estimate of the present circumstances of the Jews or their possible future. The bitter

---

40 [1980] 205).

23. Thus, correctly, J. C. Hurd, "Paul ahead of His Time: 1 Thess. 2:13-16," in P. Richardson and D. Granskou, eds., *Anti-Judaism in Early Christianity*, vol. 1: *Paul and the Gospels* (Waterloo, ON: Wilfrid Laurier University Press, 1986) 33-35.

24. A common method used to soften the impact of our passage is to see it as directed only against certain Jews, e.g., those who killed the prophets and Jesus or who persecuted Paul. See W. Marxsen, *Der erste Brief an die Thessalonicher* (Zurich, 1979) 48ff.; see O. Michel, "Fragen,"53. Against this conclusion see Broer, "'Antisemitismus' und Judenpolemik," 73-77; Marshall,*Thessalonians*, 83. More recently, F. D. Gilliard has revived this argument by maintaining that in keeping with Paul's common syntactical style, the participial phrase following the noun *Ioudaiōn* is restrictive and should therefore not be set off by a comma ("The Problem of the Antisemitic Comma between 1 Thessalonians 2.14 and 15," *NTS* 35 (1989) 481-502). It is clear from the context (see v. 14) that Paul has the Judaean Jews in mind initially. But the polemical words in vv. 15-16 quickly broaden in their application (with the assistance of the unnecessary *tōn Ioudaiōn*, "the Jews") to include all the Jews who were unreceptive to the gospel and who opposed Paul's missionary work.

25. M. J. Cook points out that one source of the New Testament's anti-Judaism is Judaism's own tradition of self-criticism ("Anti-Judaism in the New Testament," *USQR* 38/2 [1983] 125). For parallel sentiments at Qumran, see 1QM 3:9; 1QS 2:15.

26. Broer, "Der ganze Zorn," 156; Broer, "Antijudaismus im Neuen Testament?" 330.

27. F. Mussner describes 1 Thess 2:14-16 as Paul's working "with the conventional handed-on topoi" (*Tractate on the Jews*, trans. L. Swidler [London: SPCK; Philadelphia: Fortress, 1984] 153). See L. T. Johnson, "The New Testament's Anti-Jewish Slander and the Conventions of Ancient Polemic," *JBL* 108 (1989) 419-41. According to Johnson, "The way the New Testament talks about Jews is just about the way all opponents talked about each other back then" (429). See Wanamaker's description of the passage as an example of ancient rhetoric called *vituperatio* (*Thessalonians*, 118). See too D. Fraikin ("The Rhetorical Function of the Jews in Romans," in Richardson and Granskou, eds., *Anti-Judaism in Early Christianity*, 1.91-105), who concludes that Paul's attitude to Israel was positive.

material is indeed a digression—Paul is on his way to something else in the letter. In passing, then, and in the heat of the moment, he lashes out against his enemies, that is, the gospel's enemies. All of this suggests that it may be a mistake to conclude too much from this passage concerning Paul's view of Israel and its future,[28] as he might care to articulate it on another occasion and in a more reflective mood

Since Paul stands in the critical tradition of the prophets and Jewish apocalyptic, it makes no more sense to call him anti-Semitic in this passage than it does to call the prophets anti-Semitic. There is no racial hatred here. The language, harsh as it is, is spoken by a Jew to Jews and reflects the polemical idiom of an in-house debate[29] on matters of essential importance and of great consequence. It may furthermore be the case, as some have argued, that Paul makes use of traditional elements in formulating the passage.[30] Thus the reference to the Jews killing Jesus probably reflects elements that were already a part of the oral tradition (see Acts 2:23; 10:39; 13:28); the reference to their killing the prophets is found in the Synoptic tradition (Matt 23:37; Luke 13:34) and is found again in Paul in his quotation of 1 Kgs 19:10, 14 in Rom 11:3. The reference to the Jews as those who "displease God and oppose everyone," in contrast, seems to be drawn from the repertoire of anti-Semitic slander common among the Gentiles of that era.[31] It is surprising that Paul would use such language at all. Yet the rhetorical language suited Paul's purpose, and he

28. K. P. Donfried makes effective use of J. C. Beker's notion of "contingent" elements in the Pauline letters in order to diminish the importance of 1 Thess 2:14-16. This approach also enables him to hold this passage together with Romans 11 without having to harmonize them ("Paul and Judaism").

29. I. Broer has rightly called attention to the fact that at the early date when 1 Thessalonians was written Christianity had not yet become separate from Judaism (see, too, Johnson, "Anti-Jewish Slander"). He refers to our passage "as an example of inner-Jewish polemics"("'Antisemitismus' und Judenpolemik," 87–89). W. D. Davies writes: "The discussions of Judaism and Jews in Paul's letters are intramural" ("Paul and the People of Israel," 19). See K. Haacker, "Paulus und das Judentum *Judaica* 33 (1977) 168–69; D. Patte, "Anti-Semitism in the New Testament: Confronting the Dark Side of Paul's and Matthew's Teaching," *CTS Register* 78/1 (1988) 44.

30. For dependence on the Synoptic Gospels or Synoptic tradition, see J. B. Orchard, "Thessalonians and the Synoptic Gospels," *Bib* 19 (1938) 19–42; R. Schippers, "The Pre-Synoptic Tradition in 1 Thessalonians II 13–16," *NovT* 8 (1966) 223–34; D. Wenham, "Paul and the Synoptic Apocalypse," in R. T. France and D. Wenham, eds., *Gospel Perspectives II* (Sheffield: JSOT Press, 1981) 345–75; Davies, "Paul and the People of Israel," 7. See also Lüdemann, *Paulus und das Judentum*, 22ff.

31. See Tacitus, *Hist.* 5.5.2; *Ann.* 15.44.5; and Josephus, *Ag. Ap.* 2.10 §121 and 2.14 §148 (where, as Broer ["'Antisemitismus' und Judenpolemik," 79–80] points out, the words "atheism" and "misanthropy" occur beside each other in reference to the Jews).

makes it his own, ironically turning what was actually anti-Semitic slander into heated polemic against his own unbelieving Jewish brethren.[32]

It is true, finally, that in this passage Paul contemplates no future salvation of the Jews as he does in Rom 11:23, 26, 31. This has been taken by some to mean that Paul could not have written our passage, and thus has been used as important evidence to support the interpolation theory. It may be, however, that Paul changed his mind about Israel in the interim between the writing of the early 1 Thessalonians and the considerably later epistle to the Romans.[33] At least one widely accepted change in Paul—his move from the expectation of an imminent *parousia* to the possibility of a delayed *parousia*—may explain how he could write the words of 1 Thess 2:16c when he did, but not some seven years later. As indicated above, however, we may be right in not taking those words as anything more than a polemical and emotional outburst, consistent with the conventions of time and context, and contingent upon the specific pain experienced by Paul as he contemplated the unbelief of the Jews and their opposition to his mission. And even as strong as they are, these words do not entirely preclude the possibility of any future repentance, should the *parousia* be further delayed.[34] (Romans 11 will be discussed in the fourth section of this essay.)

Although it is perhaps an extreme example, 1 Thess 2:14-16 is hardly the only passage in which Paul used very sharp language against his opponents. In passages such as Gal 5:12; Phil 3:2, 18-19; 2 Cor 11:13-15; Rom 11:8-10 and 16:18, he also engages in harsh denunciation of them. Yet since these passages criticize not Jews but Christians (in the first two instances, Judaizers), no one is troubled by them.

It is, however, not only the language of 1 Thess 2:14-16 that has brought the charge of anti-Semitism against Paul, but perhaps above all

---

32. F. F. Bruce concludes that "such sentiments are incongruous on the lips of Paul; . . . nor can he be readily envisaged as subscribing to them even if they were expressed in this form by someone else" (*Thessalonians*, 47). This together with the fact that Paul here addresses the words not to the ones being denounced, but to Gentiles, leads Bruce to the conclusion that the Pauline authorship of vv. 15-16 "remains sub judice" (49).

33. Opting for this solution are Okeke, "1 Thessalonians 2:13-16," 127-36; Simpson, "The Problems," 42-72; N. Hyldahl, "Jesus og joederne ifolge 1 Tess 2,14-16," *SE* 4 37/38 (1972-73) 238-54. See, too, M. Barth, *Israel and the Church*, 75.

34. See Holtz: "That the perpetrators nevertheless stand under the possibility, indeed, the invitation, to faith, and therewith the repentance from their evil ways, is in no way placed in question" (*Erste Brief an die Thessalonicher*, 111).

it is his repudiation of Judaism that is responsible for the charge. To this subject we must now turn our attention.

PAUL AND THE LAW

The issue of Paul's view of Judaism is increasingly debated today. As the result of a combination of factors such as a new appreciation of Judaism that corrects the stereotyping of it as a religion of legalistic works-righteousness, the exigencies of Jewish-Christian dialogue, and perhaps a desire to protect Paul from the charge of anti-Semitism, Paul is being understood as one who had no quarrel with Judaism in itself. His quarrel was alone with those Jews who opposed his Law-free gospel for the Gentiles. Paul, it is further argued, had no desire to repudiate Judaism or to convert Jews to Christianity. His sole concern was to fulfill his mission of preaching salvation in Christ for the Gentiles apart from the necessity to keep the Law.[35] In this perspective, not only is there no antiSemitism in Paul, there is not even any anti-Judaism,[36] and thus the problem addressed in this essay is circumvented from the start.

---

35. Above all, see the collected essays of L. Gaston, *Paul and the Torah* (Vancover: University of British Columbia Press, 1987); see, too, J. G. Gager, *The Origins of Anti-Semitism: Attitudes toward Judaism in Pagan and Christian Antiquity* (New York: Oxford University Press, 1983) 193–264; Beck, *Mature Christianity*, 39–79; Mussner, *Tractate on the Jews*, 133–53; E. Stegemann, "Der Jude Paulus und seine antijüdische Auslegung," in R. Rendtorff and E. Stegemann, eds., *Auschwitz-Krise der christlichen Theologie* (Munich: Kaiser, 1980); C. M. Williamson, *Has God Rejected His People? Anti-Judaism in the Christian Church?* (Nashville: Abingdon, 1982) 47–63; M. Barth, "St. Paul-A Good Jew," *HBT* 1 (1979) 7–45; M. Barth, *Israel and the Church*, 58–78; see, too, R. Jewett, "The Law and the Coexistence of Jews and Gentiles in Romans," *Int* 39 (1985) 341–56.

36. "All of the positive things Paul has to say about the righteousness of God effecting salvation for Gentiles in Christ need not at all imply anything negative about Israel and the Torah. Indeed, it may be that Paul, and Paul alone among the New Testament writers, has no left hand" (Gaston, *Paul and the Torah*, 34). See F. Mussner: "When looking at . . . passages on the Jews in the Epistle to the Romans, one can in no way speak of an 'anti-Judaism' of Paul" (*Tractate on the Jews*, 145). For a remarkable contrasting statement by G. Baum (whose position represents a radical change of opinion), see the preface to R. Ruether's *Faith and Fratricide*: "What Paul . . . taught is unmistakably negative: the religion of Israel is now superseded, the Torah abrogated, the promises fulfilled in the Christian Church, the Jews struck with blindness, and whatever remains of the election to Israel rests as a burden upon them in the present age" (6). See, too, E. P. Sanders, who concludes that. Paul "denies two pillars common to all forms of Judaism: the election of Israel and faithfulness to the Mosaic law" (*Paul, the Law and the Jewish People* [Philadelphia: Fortress, 1983] 208).

Those who hold this viewpoint deny that Paul broke with the Law in any fundamental way, other than in refusing to impose it upon the Gentiles. They call attention to passages where Paul speaks positively of the Law, arguing that only a position such as theirs can do justice to these passages. Thus, statements in Romans such as, "Do we then overthrow the law by this faith? By no means! On the contrary, we uphold the law" (3:31; cf. Gal 3:21); "For it is not the hearers of the law who are righteous in God's sight, but the doers of the law who will be justified" (2:13); "The law [is] the embodiment of knowledge and truth" (2:20); "Circumcision indeed is of value if you obey the law" (2:25); "So the law is holy, and the commandment is holy and just and good" (7:12)—these are taken as evidence that Paul has not parted with Judaism's view of the Law.

There are, however, many passages where Paul speaks of the Law in a different tone. Thus, "'No human being will be justified in his sight' by deeds prescribed by the law [*ergōn nomou*], for through the law comes the knowledge of sin" (Rom 3:20); "For we hold that a person is justified by faith apart from works prescribed by the law [*ergōn nomou*]" (Rom 3:28); "If it is the adherents of the law who are to be the heirs, faith is null and the promise is void" (Rom 4:14); "You are not under law but under grace" (Rom 6:14-15); "But now we are discharged from the law, dead to that which held us captive, so that we are slaves not under the old written code but in the new life of the Spirit" (Rom 7:6); "For Christ is the end [*telos*] of the law so that there may be righteousness for everyone who believes" (Rom 10:4). To these verses at least the following from Galatians should be added: "We know that a person is justified not by the works of the law [*ergōn nomou*] but through faith in Jesus Christ [*dia pisteōs Iēsou Christou*]. And we have come to believe in Christ Jesus, so that we might be justified by faith in Christ [*ek pisteōs Christou*], and not by doing the works of the law [*ergōn nomou*], because no one [*pasa sarx*] will be justified by the works of the law [*ergōn nomou*]" (2:16); "I do not nullify the grace of God; for if justification comes through the law (*dia nomou*), then Christ died for nothing" (2:21); "Now it is evident that no one is justified before God by the law [*en nomō*]" (3:11); "For if a law had been given ihat could make alive, then righteousness would indeed come through the law [*ek nomou*]" (3:21); "Now before faith came, we were imprisoned and guarded under the law until faith would be revealed. Therefore the law was our disciplinarian [*paidagōgos*] until Christ came, so that we might be justified by faith. But now that faith has come, we are no longer subject to a disciplinarian" (3:23-25); "You who want to be justified by the law [*en nomō*] have cut yourselves off from Christ; you have fallen away from grace" (5:4).

We cannot here go fully into the vexed question of Paul and the Law.[37] Although there is no need to conclude that Paul's view of the Law is simply muddled (pace Räisänen), it is apparent just from the statements quoted above that his view of the Law is complex. While Paul regards himself as in some fundamental sense loyal to the Law, he has at the same time clearly relativized the Law, subordinating it to the gospel. This is plain from his view of the Law as a parenthesis between Abraham and Christ (Gal 3:15-18, 23-29). But more than that, Paul's negative statements about the Law seem to leave little, if any, place for it in the life of the Christian or, more accurately, at least for the gentile Christian.[38] In practically every element of Paul's theology we have to do with aspects both of continuity and discontinuity. Any fair representation of Paul's view of the Law, even if it is unable to synthesize his disparate statements into a comprehensive "system,"[39] must at least hold them in tension and not allow one group to render the other group void.

Since our task centers on the question of anti-Semitism in Paul, we must take seriously Paul's negative statements about the Law. These statements seem to imply something about Judaism and in turn raise the important question of the nature of first-century Judaism. E. P. Sanders's well-known characterization of Judaism as a "covenantal nomism"[40] has had an enormous impact on Pauline studies over the past decade. What he means by this is that Israel's preoccupation with the Law is to be

---

37. Among the spate of recent works, see especially: H. Hübner, *Law in Paul's Thought*, trans. J. C. G. Greig (Edinburgh: T. & T. Clark, 1984); H. Räisänen, *Paul and the Law* (Philadelphia: Fortress, 1986); E. P. Sanders, *Paul, the Law, and the Jewish People*; S. Westerholm, *Israel's Law and the Church's Faith: Paul and His Recent Interpreters* (Grand Rapids: Eerdmans, 1988); J. D. G. Dunn, *Jesus, Paul, and the Law: Studies in Mark and Galatians* (Louisville: Westminster John Knox, 1990); P. J. Tomson, *Paul and the Jewish Law: Halakha in the Letters of the Apostle to the Gentiles*, CRINT 3/1 (Minneapolis: Fortress, 1990). T. R. Schreiner, *The Law and its Fulfillment: A Pauline Theology of Law* (Grand Rapids: Baker, 1993); A useful bibliographical essay is provided by D. Moo, "Paul and the Law in the Last Ten Years," *SJT* 40 (1987) 287-307.

38. It is nevertheless paradoxically true that the Christian fulfills the righteousness of the Law by following the teaching of Jesus (see Rom 6:13, 15, 22; 8:4; Gal 5:13-14).

39. Sanders is of the opinion that Paul is "coherent," in that his divergent statements derive from "an identifiable 'central conviction,'" but not "systematic," in that he does not relate the divergent statements to one another (*Paul, the Law and the Jewish People*, 147-48).

40. See his influential *Paul and Palestinian Judaism: A Comparison of Patterns of Religion* (Philadelphia: Fortress, 1977).

understood as occurring within the framework of election and covenant. Grace thus precedes obligation, Jews have no need to earn their way with God, and consequently the hitherto common idea of Judaism as a legalism—establishing of one's righteousness by works of the Law—is ruled out from the start. At most Judaism is concerned with "staying in," not "getting in." Yet Paul makes statements that seem to take Judaism as involving just such a legalism (e.g., Gal 3:10-12; Rom 9:31-32; 10:3, 5; Phil 3:9).

Despite recent denials,[41] Paul opposes within Judaism what must be described as a legalistic righteousness, that is, a righteousness established by doing the works of the Law.[42] But how is this to be reconciled with the understanding of Judaism as a covenantal nomism? In my opinion, the answer lies in a discrepancy between Judaism as ideally (and correctly) conceived and as generally lived out on a day-to-day basis. Judaism has always been a religion whose strength lies more in praxis than in theory (or theology). As Sanders readily admits, the covenantal framework of Judaism's nomism was most often presupposed and taken for granted, rather than actually being articulated.[43] At the same time, it is a fact that in the Jewish literature a great stress is put upon the importance of works[44] and that frequently one encounters the language of merit. It should not be surprising, bearing these things in mind, if Jews often forgot the framework of grace within which the Law had been given and ended up functioning in a legalistic mode that in reality reflected a misunderstanding of their faith. (Christians too have been known to fall into this trap!) Paul is clearly against any distortion of the Old Testament that leads to the idea that righteousness is the result of our performance of the works of the Law and that it is this that merits our acceptance by God.[45]

---

41. See especially Gaston's chapter, "Israel's Misstep in the Eyes of Paul," in *Paul and the Torah*, 135-50.

42. Thus, correctly, R. H. Gundry: "The use of the law to establish one's own righteousness is what Paul finds wrong in Palestinian Judaism, including his past life" ("Grace, Works, and Staying Saved in Paul," *Bib* 66 (1985) 16). See too the balanced perspective of S. Westerholm, *Israel's Law and the Church's Faith*, esp. 141-73.

43. Thus, e.g., Sanders, *Paul and Palestinian Judaism*, 236.

44. Even on this point there is a contrast with Paul, as Gundry points out: "For Paul good works are only (but not unimportantly) a sign of staying in, faith being the necessary and sufficient condition of staying in as well as of getting in" ("Grace, Works," 35).

45. See C. E. B. Cranfield, *The Epistle to the Romans*, ICC (Edinburgh: T. & T. Clark, 1975-79) 2:851-52.

Paul's disagreement with Judaism, however, seems to have been even more fundamental, so that it appears that he would even have distanced himself from a covenantal nomism. It seems impossible to deny that some of Paul's negative statements about the Law inevitably involve an anti-Judaism. For despite claims to the contrary,[46] Paul at least in some sense regarded the Mosaic Law itself as abolished with the coming of the Messiah.[47] A few of the important passages need to be looked at briefly. In Gal 3:15-29 Paul argues that the Law was intended to be temporary. Promise and faith are the operative realities that remain constant before, after, and even during (see Rom 4:6-8) the dispensation of the Law. The Law was "added because of transgressions" and was never meant to make possible the achievement of righteousness (see Gal 3:21; Rom 5:20; 7:10). With the coming of the Messiah, the Law is no longer binding (see Gal 4:5; 5:1). A new era has dawned in Jesus Christ, who is himself the source of righteousness to all who have faith (see Gal 2:16). All of this stands over against the viewpoint of Judaism wherein the Law remains permanently in force and the *de facto* means to righteousness.

The fact that Paul in Galatians argues against Judaizers (whether Jewish or gentile is of little consequence) by no means necessitates the conclusion that the arguments pertain only to gentile converts and involve no application or reference to Judaism itself.[48] In Paul's view, just as the plight of the Jew is the same as that of the Gentile, so far as the problem of sin is concerned (see Rom 3:9-20), so too the answer to that problem is the same.[49] Paul never countenanced any alternative means of salvation beyond the death of Jesus Christ (Rom 3:22-24; 10:9-13). On

---

46. Dunn attempts to demonstrate that the problem Paul confronts is not the attempted establishment of righteousness by the Law, but the elevation of the boundary markers of Judaism (e.g., circumcision, the food laws, the Sabbath) to the status of criteria that determine one's relation to God. See "The New Perspective on Paul," originally published in *BJRL* 65 (1983) 95-122, now also available in Dunn, *Jesus, Paul, and the Law*, 183-214, including an "Additional Note." See too F. Watson, *Paul, Judaism and the Gentiles: A Sociological Approach*, SNTSMS 56 (Cambridge: Cambridge University Press, 1986).

47. See T. R. Schreiner ("The Abolition and Fulfillment of the Law in Paul," *JSNT* 35 [1989] 47-74), who, however, makes a questionable distinction between the moral and ritual Law, arguing that only the latter is abolished by Paul. See Sanders, *Paul, the Law, and the Jewish People*, 4.

48. The view that the arguments of Galatians concerning the Law apply only to gentile converts and not to Judaism is held by many. See Gaston, "Paul and the Law in Galatians 2 and 3," in *Paul and the Torah*, 64-79; Gager, *Origins*, 230-41; Mussner, *Tractate on the Jews*, 144.

49. See C. H. Talbert, "Paul on the Covenant," *RevExp* 84 (1987) 310 n23.

the contrary, the gospel is the message of salvation to be offered "to the Jew first" (Rom 1:16; see 1 Cor 1:24). In this sense Paul's gospel involves a distinct and undeniable element of anti-Judaism.

Even apart from the preceding discussion of the material in Galatians, the interpretation of Rom 10:4, when taken in its context, points most naturally to the understanding of *telos* as "end." There is no question but that for Paul, Christ is also the goal of the Law, and this is one reason why the translation "goal" is favored by many. But in the immediately preceding verse Paul is contrasting two kinds of righteousness, that which comes "from God" (*tēn tou theou dikaiosynēn*), to which the Jews did not submit, and "their own" (*tēn idian*), that is, the righteousness that the Jews "seek to establish" through the Law. In the verses that immediately follow, Paul contrasts the righteousness that comes "from the law" (*ek [tou] nomou*) with that which comes "from faith" (*ek pisteōs*). Christ has brought the Law to an end with the result that righteousness comes to those who believe. A few verses later Paul turns the words of Moses on their head when he applies them to the gospel rather than to the commandment. Thus what Moses said was "near you, on your lips and in your heart" (Deut 30:14) is taken to refer to confessing Jesus as Lord and believing the resurrection in one's heart. This too involves anti-Judaism.

A final passage that indicates Paul's personal break with the Law, 1 Cor 9:19–23, is also particularly helpful in understanding the complexity of his perspective. Here he frankly admits a pragmatism that enables him to "become all things to all people." This meant, as he says, that "to the Jews I became as a Jew, in order to win Jews." Very specifically he adds, "To those under the law [*hypo nomon*] I became as one under the law (though I myself am not under the law) so that I might win those under the law." In certain contexts, then, Paul observed the Law for the sake of allowing the gospel to be heard by Jews. But he did not regard himself as principally obligated to such observance. In this respect he had made a break with the Judaism from which he had come. (On 2 Cor 3:6–11, which could also be considered here, see below.)

Another statement in this passage is especially revealing. When he indicates his practice among Gentiles, he writes, "To those outside the law [*tois anomois*] I became as one outside the law" (1 Cor 9:20–21). He inserts parenthetically "though I am not free from God's law [*anomos theou*] but am under Christ's law [*ennomos Christou*]." Although he has just asserted quite clearly that he is not under the Law—that is, he is free from the Law—in the very next sentence he states that he is not free from the law of God! The key, of course, is that in being subject to the law of Christ (i.e., the teachings of Jesus known to him through the oral tradition), he is at the same time obeying the law of God (i.e., the correct interpretation of the Mosaic Law). The pattern of righteousness taught by Jesus amounts in essence to an exposition of the Law of Moses.

Paradoxically the Law is abolished only in order to be newly established, albeit by a metamorphosis, in the ethical tradition of the church that stems from Jesus. Paul is thus an antinomian only formally; in practice he can fairly be described, like Jesus, as one who finally upheld the Law. Granted, it is the Law as filtered primarily through the love commandment (see Rom 13:8-10), but it is nonetheless the Law, and recognizably so. This is very probably how we are to explain Paul's positive statements about the Law, some of which have been mentioned above. Although the gospel meant the end of the Law, there was a sense in which the Law was not overthrown by the gospel. Righteous living and not merely justification—the righteousness reckoned by faith—remains after all a vitally important goal of the Christian (see Rom 8:4, referring to "the just requirement of the law").

There is a sense, then, in which Paul remains faithful to the Law, and a sense in which, despite his language about the end of the Law, he cannot properly be called an antinomian. We face here in the question of Paul's view of the Law the same problematic complexity as in the question of Paul and Judaism. That is, just as Paul regarded his faith as the true Judaism, he regarded his stance toward the Law as ultimately one of faithfulness. What he turned his back on was a distortion of Judaism and an inappropriate understanding of the Law. Paul's "anti-Judaism," so far as the Law is concerned, amounts in fact to nothing other than a new adaptation of the Jewish Law appropriate to the newly dawned age of eschatological fulfillment.

PAUL'S VIEW OF ISRAEL

We turn now to look at a few other pertinent passages under the rubric of the closely related question of Paul's view of Israel. Here too we encounter various statements that not only involve aspects of discontinuity but that also imply the displacement of Israel and that have therefore again given rise to the charge of anti-Semitism.

Paul illustrates his theological argument concerning the Law in Galatians with the so-called allegory of Sarah and Hagar (Gal 4:21-31). Hagar, the slave woman, bore Abraham a son described as "according to the flesh [*kata sarka*]"; Sarah, the free woman, bore him a son "through the promise [*di' epangelias*]." Paul proceeds to liken the women to two "covenants [*diathēkai*]": Hagar to Mount Sinai, "bearing children for slavery [*eis douleian*]" and corresponding to "the present Jerusalem"; Sarah to "the Jerusalem above [*anō*]" that is "free [*eleuthera*]" and that is further described as "our mother," that is, the mother of the "children of the promise [*epangelias tekna*]." Paul adds that as the son of the slave persecuted the son born "according to the Spirit [*kata pneuma*]," "Spirit" now being substituted for "promise"!), "so it is now also [*houtos kai nyn*]." Then in answer to his question "What does the scripture say?" he quotes Gen 21:10, "Drive out the slave and her son; for the son of the slave will not share the inheritance with the son of the free woman," to which he adds: "So, brethren, we are not children of the slave but of the free woman."

Although Paul has in mind primarily the Judaizers, it is very difficult to conclude that this passage does not also involve an indictment of Judaism itself.[50] Consonant with what we have seen him argue concerning the Law, Paul describes "the present Jerusalem" (i.e., contemporary Judaism) as "being in slavery" to the Law. The Jews, who thought of themselves as descended from Abraham and thus the children of the promise, are surprisingly categorized as the descendants of Hagar and as children born "for slavery."[51] The point is that they are "under the law [*hypo nomon*]," from which Christians have been "redeemed" (Gal 4:5) and to

---

50. Yet G. Brouwer can conclude after studying the passage, "One cannot accuse Paul of anti-Judaism on the basis of this passage, Gal 4:21-31 . . . He does not make the Jews the sons of Hagar. The two women are symbols of two types of existence, which are not typical of Judaism on the one side or of Christianity on the other, but which are found in both religions" ("Die Hagar- und Sara-Perikope [Gal 4, 21-31]: Exemplarische Interpretation zum Schriftbeweis bei Paulus," *ANRW* II.25.4:31-52). See, too, Gaston, *Paul and the Torah*; Gager, *Origins*, 241-43. To the contrary, see, e.g., Hübner, *Law in Paul's Thought*, 34; Ruether, *Faith and Fratricide*, 102ff., 134. See H. J. Schoeps, *Paul: The Theology of the Apostle in the Light of Jewish Religious History*, trans. H. Knight (Philadelphia: Westminster, 1961): "The conclusion of this passage is again that the Christian community is the Israel of God whereas the old Israel has been rejected of God" (234). See H. D. Betz, *Galatians* (Hermeneia; Philadelphia: Fortress, 1979) 245.

51. According to C. K. Barrett, Paul here uses a text of his Judaizing opponents, but draws opposite conclusions from it ("The Allegory of Abraham, Sarah, and Hagar in the Argument of Galatians," in *Essays on Paul* [Philadelphia: Westminster, 1982] 154-70).

which they are no longer to be enslaved (Gal 5:1). The contrast is drawn, furthermore, explicitly in terms of "two covenants [*dyo diathēkai*]," understood as the Mosaic covenant and the new covenant established by Christ. (Although the expression "new covenant" is not actually used here, it was a part of Paul's vocabulary; see 1 Cor 11:25 and especially 2 Cor 3:6.) This criticism of the old covenant involves something more fundamental than merely that the Jews put such emphasis on the elements of their national distinctiveness,[52] or boundary markers, and that they thereby excluded Gentiles from salvation.[53]

A second passage, closely related to the preceding, is found in 2 Cor 3:6-17. Here Paul uses the language "old covenant [*palaia diathēkē*]" and "new covenant [*kainē diathēkē*]." He contrasts the two covenants by referring to the old as "the letter [*gramma*]" that "kills," a "ministry of death/condemnation," and to the new as characterized by "the Spirit," a ministry of the Spirit/righteousness (*dikaiosynē*; but NRSV: "justification"). The former reflects Moses and the Law, the latter the new covenant inaugurated in Christ. The glory of the two dispensations is also set in strong contrast: "For if what was set aside [*to katargoumenon*] came through glory, much more has the permanent [*to menon*] come in glory." To be sure, Paul says, the old covenant had its glory. But that glory is now far exceeded by the glory of the new covenant, wherein we are granted "the light of the knowledge of the glory of God in the face of Jesus Christ" (2 Cor 4:6).

In this passage not only is the Mosaic Law spoken of as abolished by the establishment of the new covenant. The people of Israel, now as in the day of Moses, have hardened their minds so that when they read Moses, "a veil lies over their minds." That veil, which prevents them from a correct understanding of the old covenant, is taken away only by believing the gospel: "since only in Christ is it set aside." And a few lines later he adds that "if our gospel is veiled, it is veiled to those who are perishing"

---

52. G. Lüdemann correctly concludes: "For the Paul of Galatians, just as in 1 Thessalonians, unbelieving Judaism has no theological dignity (any longer)" (*Paulus und das Judentum*, 30). If in Gal 6:16 the church is referred to as *ton Israēl tou theou*, the point is underlined.

53. See Dunn, who in this way tries to minimize the differences between Paul and Judaism ("The Theology of Galatians," in *Jesus, Paul, and the Law*, 242-64). Gaston's attempt to deny that Gal 4:21-31 involves a polemic against Judaism seems to go against a natural reading of the passage (*Paul and the Torah*, 82-91).

(2 Cor 4:3). Again, despite the disclaimers of a few,[54] we are confronted with an anti-Judaism in Paul that can hardly be evaded.[55]

We look finally at several passages in Romans 9–11, where Paul addresses the question of Israel at the peak of his theological maturity. First, in Rom 9:30–33 after Paul has stated that the Gentiles have arrived at righteousness-through-faith, he continues with these words:

> But Israel, who did strive for the righteousness that is based on law, did not succeed in fulfilling that law [*eis nomon ouk ephthasen*]. Why not? Because they did not strive for it on the basis of faith [*ek pisteōs*], but as if it were based on works. They have stumbled over the stumbling stone [*tō lithō tou proskommatos*], as it is written, See, I am laying in Zion a stone that will make people stumble, a rock that will make them fall [*petran skandalou*], and whoever believes in him will not be put to shame" [Isa 28:16; see 8:14].

Here Paul simply articulates the problem that gives rise to these chapters: the failure of Israel to believe in the gospel (see 9:1ff.). He begins his answer with what might be called "remnant theology," asserting that "not all Israelites truly belong to Israel, and not all of Abraham's children are his true descendants" (9:6–7). He had already distinguished

---

54. Gaston employs a "hermeneutic of experimentation" to arrive at the conclusion that Paul in 2 Corinthians 3 argues not against Israel, but against his opponents in Corinth (*Paul and the Torah*, 151–68). This conclusion had earlier been argued by H. Ulonska, "Die Doxa des Moses," *EvT* 26 (1966) 378–88. See Gager: "Paul's language is meant to contrast not Israel and Christianity but the old and the new for Gentiles!" (*Origins*, 216). For another attempt at construing the passage positively, see T. E. Provence, "Who Is Sufficient for These Things? An Exegesis of 2 Corinthians ii:15–iii:18," *NovT* 24 (1982) 54–61.

55. Beck concludes that apart from Romans, 2 Corinthians is "our most important source of information about Paul's attitude toward the Jews who did not accept Jesus as the Messiah." He continues with these words: "Paul claimed in this epistle a new ministry, which to him was superior to the ministry of his ancestors and of his own earlier experiences. It was a ministry that in his opinion superseded the ministry revealed by God through Moses" (*Mature Christianity*, 59). See C. H. Talbert, "Paul on the Covenant," 304: "Paul thought the new covenant not only surpassed the old but also replaced it." See too M. J. Cook, "The Ties That Blind: An Exposition of II Corinthians 3:12–4:6 and Romans 11:7–10" (125–39), and G. W. Buchanan, "Paul and the Jews (II Corinthians 3:4–4:6 and Romans 11:7–10)" (141–62), both in J. J. Petuchowski, ed., *When Jews and Christians Meet* (Albany: State University of New York Press, 1988). Although Buchanan finds Paul's views objectionable, he does not try to make Paul say something other than he does. "However arrogant and offensive Paul's judgments seem to twentieth-century Jews and Christians, apparently it did not seem out of order to Jewish Christians of Paul's day" (158).

a true Jew from a physical Jew (3:28-29) and identified the descendants of Abraham as those who share the faith of Abraham, the faith that was "reckoned to him as righteousness" (4:16, 22-25).

Although Paul appeals to God's inscrutable purpose in election and the reality of a believing remnant, it remains a fact that Israel as a whole has not believed. Rather, it has taken the wrong path and has stumbled and fallen (see 9:27-29). In turning from the general election of Israel and allowing that only the remnant of Jews who believed in the gospel were to be saved, Paul adopts a position that must again be described as anti-Judaic.

At the end of chap. 10 Paul cites Isaiah's bitter criticism of Israel: "All day long I have held out my hands to a disobedient and contrary people" (Rom 10:21, citing Isa 65:2, according to the LXX). After referring to the elect remnant (11:5) who have received the gospel, he again relies upon Scripture to describe those who remain hardened. Thus in Rom 11:8-10 we encounter some of the harshest language used in the New Testament to depict unbelieving Jews. First Paul cites what appears to be a combination of Deut 29:3 (LXX 29:4) and Isa 29:10: "God gave them a sluggish spirit, eyes that would not see and ears that would not hear, down to this very day." This is followed by the citation of Ps 69:22-23, but according to the LXX (68:22-23): "Let their table become a snare and a trap, a stumbling block and a retribution [*antapodoma*] for them; let their eyes be darkened so that they cannot see, and keep their backs forever [*dia pantos*] bent." In Paul's use of this passage the personal enemies of the psalmist have become the enemies of the gospel (see Rom 11:28).[56]

It is worth emphasizing that in these verses we have the language of the Old Testament and not that of Paul. Again, as in 1 Thess 2:14-16, the language exemplifies the conventional, heightened rhetoric used in polemical utterances. The point, nevertheless, is that Paul chooses to apply this language to the Jews who have not believed in the gospel. They are regarded as blind and unreceptive in both passages. Again we confront what must be called anti-Judaism. The second quotation is particularly vitriolic, with its wish for retribution and that their backs be bent forever. The last sentiment, employing the word "forever," recalls the statement in

---

56. There is no need to translate Rom 11:28 as "enemies of God," as does the RSV (and NRSV). In the Greek text, where there is no mention of God, "enemies [*echthroi*]" is modified by the preceding phrase, "as regards the gospel [*kata men to euangelion*]." They are enemies so far as the gospel is concerned.

1 Thess 2:16, which we considered above. Here we have material indeed that comes close to rivaling that passage for its anti-Judaism.

An element in these citations, especially in the first, that gives them a special character is the sovereignty of God that lies behind Israel's unbelief. Paul seizes upon this motif in order finally to resolve the problem with which he began. God has planned it this way, according to God's mysterious will, so that the gospel might go to the Gentiles (11:11–12, 15, 25, 28, 30). At the same time, Paul does not use this as a way to excuse Israel's unbelief. They are still held accountable for not receiving the gospel (see 10:21; 11:20). Now, however, their unbelief is clearly spelled out as temporary, as but the shadow side of the Gentiles' opportunity and the prelude to a turning from that unbelief. Here Paul breaks new ground that brings a quite new dimension to our subject.

THE SALVATION OF ISRAEL

After the devastating passage just considered, Paul returns to his initial question,[57] which now has more edge than ever: "So I ask, have they stumbled so as to fall?" He answers the question with a very strong negation: "By no means!" (11:11). Before he indicates specifically what he means by this response, he anticipates his answer in several places. In 11:12, in contrast to Israel's "trespass" and "failure," he refers to "their full inclusion [*to plērōma autōn*]"; in 11:15, in contrast to Israel's "rejection," he mentions "their acceptance [*hē proslēmpsis*]." In the olive tree metaphor he states that the Jews, "if they do not persist in unbelief [*tē apistia*], will be grafted in, for God has the power to graft them in again" (11:23), and then he adds "how much more will these natural branches be grafted back into their own olive tree" (11:24).

But it is only in Rom 11:25–26 that he finally comes to the "mystery" that he has been hinting at in these passages: "A hardening has come upon part of Israel, until the full number of the Gentiles has come in. And so all Israel will be saved [*pas Israēl sōthēsetai*]." All of Paul's earlier statements about Israel in Romans and his other letters are relativized by this final assessment concerning Israel's future. In the final analysis,

---

57. The problem that dominates chaps. 9–11 is posed from the beginning of chap. 9. The question occurs in its most pointed form in 11:1, "I ask, then, has God rejected his people?" There too the answer is "By no means!"

then, Paul turns out to be decidedly pro-Israel, despite all of the instances where he appears to reflect an anti-Judaism.[58]

It deserves to be pointed out that this is not a conclusion to which Paul was forced out of theological necessity in order to preserve the faithfulness of God to his promises. The question of God's faithfulness to his promises has already been answered in the existence of a remnant of Jews that has believed in the gospel,[59] Paul himself being concrete evidence of that faithfulness (see 11:1-6). The salvation of all Israel is instead a part of the extravagance of God, an example of grace that continually surprises. Paul is nevertheless happy to indicate how this abundant grace underlines election and the fact that "the gifts and the calling of God are irrevocable" (11:28-29). Israel thus retains a special place in the purpose of God that will work itself out in history.

It remains a much-debated question as to how Israel is to be saved, not to mention the nature of the salvation in view. The question is an important one for our subject. For some, only if this salvation of Israel is independent of the necessity of faith in Christ, and therefore separate from the church, can Paul finally escape the charge of anti-Judaism (and anti-Semitism).[60] For them Paul must be the advocate of a two-covenant theory wherein the old covenant is for Israel, and retains full validity in itself, while the new covenant is for only the Gentiles, of whom alone is faith in Christ required. Only the acceptance of the continuing legitimacy of Judaism can make Paul acceptable.

These issues cannot be examined in detail here.[61] I can only indicate that in my opinion "the Deliverer" of Israel (11:26) can for Paul be

58. See U. Luz, "Zur Erneuerung des Verhältnisses von Christen und Juden," *Judaica* 37 (1981) 206-7. With Rom 11:25-26 in mind, he writes: "Paul is the only New Testament theologian who has not finally condemned unbelieving Israel" (206).

59. This point is neglected by J. C. Beker, "The Faithfulness of God and the Priority of Israel in Paul's Letter to the Romans," in G. W. E. Nickelsburg and G. W. MacRae, eds., *Christianity among Jews and Gentiles* (Philadelphia: Fortress, 1986) 10-16.

60. J. T. Pawlikowski, who admits that in Romans 9–11 Paul envisions the salvation of Israel through faith in Christ, is both fair to Paul and refreshingly frank: "This section of the epistle ends on a conversionalist note that I personally find unacceptable in light of what we have come to know about Judaism and by virtue of the Jewish experience of the Nazi Holocaust." See his useful survey, "New Testament Antisemitism: Fact or Fable?" in M. Curtis, ed., *Antisemitism in the Contemporary World* (Boulder, CO: Westview, 1986) 123.

61. The bibliography is enormous. A good place to begin is with that provided in H. Räisänen's overview, "Römer 9–11: Analyse eines geistigen Ringens," in *ANRW* II.25.4: 2891-939. This article in abbreviated form can be found in English in "Paul, God, and Israel: Romans 9–11 in Recent Research," in J. Neusner et al., eds., *The Social*

no other than Jesus Christ, and the way of salvation for both Jew and Gentile can only be one and the same.[62] The argument of the book of Romans throughout has been that Jew and Gentile are in effect on the same ground. The "advantage" of the Jew (3:1-2) is only of a preliminary or preparatory kind. In the last analysis it avails little: "What then? Are we any better off? No, not at all; for we have already charged that all, both Jews and Greeks, are under the power of sin" (3:9). The human plight is a universal one: "Now we know that whatever the law says, it speaks to those who are under the law, so that every mouth may be silenced, and the whole world may be held accountable to God. For 'no human being will be justified in his sight' by deeds of the law, for through the law comes the knowledge of sin" (3:19-20). It is for this reason that the salvation announced in the gospel must go "to the Jew first and also to the Greek" (1:16). If the problem is common to Jew and Greek, so also is the answer to the problem. Paul makes this quite clear: "For there is no distinction, since all have sinned and fall short of the glory of God; they

---

World of Formative Christianity and Judaism (Philadelphia: Fortress, 1988) 178-206. A few other items may be mentioned here: J. Munck, *Christ and Israel: An Interpretation of Romans 9-11*, trans. I. Nixon (Philadelphia: Fortress, 1967); P. Stuhlmacher, "Zur Interpretation von Römer 11, 25-32," in H. W. Wolff, ed., *Probleme biblischer Theologie* (Munich: Kaiser, 1971) 555-70; O. Betz, "Die heilsgeschichtliche Rolle Israels bei Paulus," *TBei* 9 (1978) 1-21; F. Hahn, "Zum Verständnis von Römer 11:26a: , . . . und so wird ganz Israel gerettet werden,'" in M. D. Hooker and S. G. Wilson, eds., *Paul and Paulinism: Essays in Honour of C. K. Barrett* (London: SPCK, 1982) 221-34; M. Barth, *The People of God* (Sheffield: JSOT Press, 1983); O. Hofius, "Das Evangelium und Israel: Erwägungen zu Römer 9-11," *ZTK* 83 (1986) 297-324; G. Wagner, "The Future of Israel: Reflections on Romans 9-11," in W. H. Gloer, ed., *Eschatology and the New Testament: Essays in Honor of G. R. Beasley-Murray* (Peabody, MA: Hendrickson, 1988) 77-112. Volume 4 of ExAuditu (1988) is devoted to the theme of "The Church and Israel (Romans 9-11)." See now too especially, J. D. G. Dunn, *Romans 9-16*, WBC (Waco: Word, 1988).

62. Pace Mussner: "He saves Israel by a 'special path' which apparently bypasses the gospel" (*Tractate on the Jews*, 146), and Gager: "When Paul thinks and speaks of Israel's imminent restoration he does not construe this to imply conversion to Christianity" (*Origins of Anti-Semitism*, 261). Räisänen does not exaggerate when he concludes: "It is quite incredible that Paul should have heeded the notion that Israel could be saved apart from Christ" ("Paul, God, and Israel," 191). Räisänen provides an effective refutation of the Gaston-Gager hypothesis on pp. 189-92. See O. Hofius, "Das Evangelium und Israel," 318-20; Munck, *Christ and Israel*, 141; Davies, "Paul and the People of Israel," 28; S. Hafemann, "The Salvation of Israel in Romans 11:25-32: A Response to Krister Stendahl," *Ex Auditu* 4 (1988) 38-58; Sanders, *Paul the Law, and the Jewish People*, 192-98; Dunn, *Romans*, 681, 691. An especially effective refutation can now be found in R. Hvalvik, "A 'Sonderweg' for Israel? A Critical Examination of a Current Interpretation of Romans 11.25-27," *JSNT* 38 (1990) 87-107.

are now justified by his grace as a gift, through the redemption that is in Christ Jesus" (3:22-24; see 3:29-30).

The same perspective is present in chaps. 9–11. The advantages of the Israelites are enumerated in 9:4-5, culminating in the reference to the Messiah coming from them.[63] Yet these advantages have not benefited them since they have not put their faith in that Messiah. Paul intensely desires and prays "that they may be saved" (10:1). He means here nothing different from the salvation about which he has been speaking previously in his letter. This is unmistakably clear when in the lines that follow he refers to salvation as dependent upon confessing Jesus as Lord and believing in his resurrection (10:9-10). The point is confirmed when Paul adds again: "For there is no distinction between Jew and Greek; the same Lord is Lord of all and is generous to all who call on him. For, 'Everyone who calls on the name of the Lord shall be saved'" (10:12-13). That name, according to the context (see 10:9), can be none other than Jesus. Then with their unbelief in mind, Paul struggles with questions concerning whether the Jews have "heard" the gospel and whether they have "understood" it (10:18-19). What is in view here is the kerygma that makes salvation possible, the kerygma that is absolutely essential to both Jew and Gentile. "Faith comes from what is heard, and what is heard comes through the word of Christ [*dia rhēmatos Christou*]" (10:17).

Even in chap. 11, therefore, we are to conclude that Israel is saved in the same way and on the same basis as the Gentiles. It is true that neither the name Jesus nor the name Christ occurs in this chapter.[64] But to take this to mean that another salvation is in view, one altogether apart from Christ, is to make an enormous leap in logic to explain what may be purely fortuitous and to contradict what Paul has earlier said quite clearly. There are, moreover, a couple of indirect indications in the chapter that point to a consistency in Paul's perspective. In v. 23 he writes of the branches that were broken off from the olive tree (i.e., the Jews who did not respond to the gospel) that can be grafted onto the tree again, but with the important stipulation, "if they do not persist in unbelief [*ean mē*

---

63. Referring to Rom 9:5, C. E. B. Cranfield notes that "the Jewishness of Jesus of Nazareth is the final and irrevocable condemnation of every form of anti-Semitism, whether it be blatant and brutal or subtle and even more or less unconscious, and the unbroken bond between believing Christian and unbelieving Jew" ("Light from St. Paul on Christian-Jewish Relations," in *The Bible and the Christian Life* [Edinburgh: T. & T. Clark, 1985] 40).

64. Much is made of this by, e.g., K. Stendahl, *Paul among Jews and Gentiles* (Philadelphia: Fortress, 1976) 4; Beck, *Mature Christianity*, 66.

epimenōsin tē apistia]." It is extremely difficult to imagine that this can refer to anything other than faith in Jesus Christ.

In the scriptural citation used to support the statement concerning all Israel being saved, there is an allusion to Isa 27:9 in the words "when I take away their sins." But this is precisely what Paul has earlier described as the work of Jesus Christ for Jew and Gentile alike (see esp. 3:21-26). It is hardly possible to dissociate the taking away of Israel's sins from faith in Christ's atoning death.

Finally, when Paul speaks of the future salvation of Israel, he draws his contrast in these words: "So they have now been disobedient in order that, by the mercy shown to you [*tō hymeterō eleei*], they too may now receive mercy" (11:31). If this translation is allowed (see the RSV, NRSV, NIV, NJB), that is, if the Greek phrase indicated is to be taken as part of the *hina* clause (which it precedes), then a further indication is provided that the mercy to be shown to the Jews is the same as that mercy shown to the Gentiles. Since, however, it may be more natural to take the phrase as belonging to what precedes (i.e., "so they have now been disobedient for the mercy shown to you, in order that they too may now receive mercy"), the point cannot be pressed.[65]

The fact that Paul insisted upon the necessity of Jews being saved in the same way as Gentiles, through faith in Christ, should not be allowed to detract from the true significance of his statement that a time is coming when all Israel will be saved. It is furthermore clear that Paul rejoiced in the prospect of this salvation and the sense in which it so beautifully rounded out God's initial work with the patriarchs, and substantiated even beyond the remnant the covenant faithfulness of God to his people. Paul is by nature pro-Israel and exults in the eventual fruition of Israel's faith in their arrival at the true fulfillment of Judaism. Ironically, Paul's "anti-Judaism" is for the sake not only of Gentiles, but also for the Jews,[66] and as it ultimately turns out, for the sake of all Israel.

---

65. See Cranfield for arguments in favor of the reading of the main translations (*Epistle to the Romans*, 2.582-85). For an answer to Cranfield, see Dunn, *Romans 9-16*, 688.

66. Paul has reversed a Jewish expectation that after Israel's salvation, the Gentiles would also experience the grace of God. Now it is the salvation of the Gentiles that will lead to Israel's salvation, and thus Paul, as the apostle sent to the Gentiles, has a supremely important role to play in the eventual salvation of his own people. See J. Munck, *Paul and the Salvation of Mankind*, trans. F. Clarke (London: SCM, 1959); Sanders, *Paul, the Law, and the Jewish People*, 179-90; see, too, C. K. Barrett, "The Gentile Mission as an Eschatological Phenomenon," in Gloer, ed., *Eschatology and the New Testament*, 65-75. In J. Jervell's words, "Paul regards himself primarily and in the long

CONCLUSION

To summarize and conclude: Anti-Judaism is part and parcel of Paul's theological position.[67] Indeed, it is intrinsic to his Christianity.[68] We see it in his polemical outbursts against those who oppose and hinder his mission, conditioned as they are by the conventions of the day. We see it in his rejection of the Law as central to human salvation, and his insistence upon the necessity of faith in Jesus Christ. It is also evident in his view of contemporary Israel as being in slavery, blindness, and disobedience.

Yet this break with Judaism, this so-called anti-Judaism, must in no sense be taken to mean that Paul had turned against his people or against his Jewish heritage. The Jewish scholar Hans Joachim Schoeps was exactly correct when he wrote: "Paul is in fact convinced that he has never seceded from Judaism, since the Christian confession means for him the completion of the Jewish faith."[69] Paul is the true Jew; his gospel the message that goes back to Abraham; his Lord the One promised in the Scriptures. Beyond these facts is the supreme affirmation of Israel in Paul's resounding statement in Romans 11 that all Israel will be saved. There is no way, with all of this in mind, that Paul can fairly be regarded as disloyal to his people.

---

term as a missionary to the Jews, sent to Israel in order to proclaim salvation for the people. As apostle to the Gentiles he has the salvation of Israel in mind" (*The Unknown Paul* [Minneapolis: Augsburg, 1984] 59).

67. Ruether is right when she concludes, "Paul's position was unquestionably that of antiJudaism . . . The polemic against 'the Jews' in Paul, as in the New Testament generally, is a rejection of Judaism, i.e., 'the Jews' as a religious community" (*Faith and Fratricide*, 104). See Sandmel: "Paul's criticism, if we may use that word, is directed not so much toward Jews as it is toward Judaism . . . It is thus essentially Judaism that Paul denigrates" (*Anti-Semitism in the New Testament?* 16). So, too, J. D. Levenson concludes that Paul "is not anti-Semitic, but he is profoundly antiJudaic" ("Is There a Counterpart in the Hebrew Bible to New Testament Antisemitism?" *JES* 22/2 [1985] 244). Attempts to deny this are not persuasive. Thus, for example, Gager's argument that the only objection Paul had with the Jews was "their refusal to recognize that God had now done for the Gentiles what he had already done for Israel" (*Origins of Anti-Semitism*, 264) is hardly adequate to account for the opposition and hostility Paul experienced from the Jews. If this alone was really Paul's concern, he could have stated it more clearly and thereby avoided the wrath of the Jews. First-century Judaism, after all, had room for the salvation of Gentiles, even apart from their becoming full proselytes.

68. Cf. G. Lüdemann: "In the present, the church stands in an indissoluble theological conflict with Judaism" (*Paulus und das Judentum*, 42–43). He adds to this a positive point: "The gentile church must remain in connection with its Jewish roots."

69. Schoeps, *Paul*, 237. W. D. Davies: "Paul did not think in terms of moving into a new religion but of having found the final expression and intent of the Jewish tradition within which he himself had been born" ("Paul and the People of Israel," 20).

If this is true, it is all the more inappropriate to connect Paul with antiSemitism of any kind. It is possible to love those with whom we may disagree, even if we disagree on supremely important issues. Indeed, to do so is to practice the ethic of Jesus. Speaking of the Jews who had not accepted the gospel, Paul writes: "I have great sorrow and unceasing anguish in my heart. For I could wish that I myself were accursed and cut off from Christ for the sake of my own people, my kindred according to the flesh" (Rom 9:2-3). Paul's sentiment here is motivated by love for his people. Anyone who is tempted to misuse Pauline texts for anti-Semitic purposes ought to remember this *cri de coeur*. As much as the unbelief of his people frustrated him, Paul never stopped loving them.

If anti-Judaism is essential to the Pauline gospel, as I have argued, then those who would follow Paul must make every effort to distinguish it sharply from anti-Semitism. To understand Paul is to know how far anti-Semitism was from his thinking. Paul emphasized the importance of Israel as the servant of the Lord whereby the good news of salvation came to the Gentiles (see Rom 9:5, "from them, according to the flesh, comes the Messiah"; see also 11:18; 15:8-12).[70] The salvation of the world comes through the Jews. Israel can receive its rightful honor and anti-Semitism can be avoided without distorting Paul's theology. Any who wish to identify themselves with Pauline Christianity will he most faithful to Paul when they see to it that the connecting nerve between anti-Judaism and anti-Semitism is cut, and never allowed to grow again. Nothing would honor the memory of Paul more and nothing could be fairer to his theology.

---

70. On this, see especially O. Betz, "Die heilsgeschichtliche Rolle Israels bei Paulus," *TBei* 9 (1978) 1-21.

10

Paul and Judaism: Testing the "New Perspective"

NEARLY HALF A CENTURY ago, E. P. Sanders published his book *Paul and Palestinian Judaism* (Philadelphia: Fortress, 1977) and began what could well be called a Copernican revolution in Pauline studies.[1] One of the leading advocates of the newer knowledge has dubbed it "The New Perspective on Paul."[2] The revolution, however, is far from complete. Some of us, moreover, continue to believe that the evidence still points to a geocentric universe — at least so far as Paul's theology is concerned. In this essay I can hardly do justice to the subject, but I propose briefly to

---

1. This was followed by a second important book on the subject before us, *Paul, the Law and the Jewish People* (Philadelphia: Fortress, 1983).

2. This was the title of J. D. G. Dunn's Manson Memorial Lecture given at the University of Manchester in November of 1982, published originally in *BJRL* 65 (1983) 95-122, and reprinted together with an "Additional Note" in Dunn's collected essays, *Jesus, Paul and the Law. Studies in Mark and Galatians* (Louisville: Westminster John Knox, 1990) 183-214. See too his chapter "Paul and 'Covenantal Nomism,'" *The Partings of the Ways Between Christianity and Judaism and their Significance for the Character of Christianity* (London: SCM, 1991) 117-39; his Henton Davies Lecture, given at Regents Park College, Oxford, "The Justice of God: A Renewed Perspective on Justification by Faith," *JTS* 43 (1992) 1-22; "In Search of Common Ground" in *Paul and the Mosaic Law*, ed. J. D. G. Dunn (Tübingen: Mohr Siebeck, 1996) 309-34; "Paul and Justification by Faith," in *The Road from Damascus. The Impact of Paul's Conversion on His Life, Thought, and Ministry*, ed. R. N. Longenecker (Grand Rapids: Eerdmans, 1997) 85-101; and now, his *The Theology of Paul the Apostle* (Grand Rapids: Eerdmans, 1998) 334-89. On the pertinent passages in Romans and Galatians, see respectively Dunn's Word Biblical Commentary (2 vols., 1988) and Black's New Testament Commentary (1993).

analyze the new perspective on Paul and Judaism and also at the same time to offer some critique of it.

1. The fundamental point of the new perspective on Paul has to do not with Paul himself, but with the nature of first-century Judaism: contrary to the widespread view held even in leading reference works, *Judaism was not and is not a religion where acceptance with God is earned through the merit of righteousness based on works.* In the same way that Copernicus had his predecessors, this main insight of the new perspective on Paul was adumbrated long before Sanders' book (as he himself readily admits). Moises Silva expresses his surprise—and I share it—at the flurry caused by Sanders' book, since its primary thrust "had been demonstrated in not a few books and was readily accessible in standard works of reference."[3] Silva mentions George Foot Moore's three volume *Judaism in the First Centuries of the Christian Era* (1927–30).[4] To that we may add Moore's earlier and well-known article entitled "Christian Writers on Judaism," where like Sanders he criticizes the work of Ferdinand Weber, as well as Schürer and Bousset, lamenting that legalism "for the last fifty years has become the very definition and the all-sufficient condemnation of Judaism."[5] Further to be mentioned is the work of such scholars as Solomon Schechter,[6] R. Travers Herford,[7] A. Marmorstein,[8] and especially C. G. Montefiore.[9]

To my mind what explains the impact of Sanders' book is that it was the first lengthy and strongly articulated statement of the case in the post-holocaust era. Thanks to the work of many Jewish writers—and non-Jewish too—people have become sensitized concerning the role

---

3. "The Law and Christianity: Dunn's New Synthesis," *WTJ* 53 (1991) 339–53, here 348.

4. The book bears the subtitle *The Age of the Tannaim* and was published in Cambridge, by Harvard University Press. Silva calls attention to the following passages: 1:110–21, 520–45.

5. *HTR* 14 (1921) 197–254, here 252.

6. *Aspects of Rabbinic Theology* (Macmillan, 1909; reprinted New York: Schocken, 1961).

7. See especially *Judaism in the New Testament Period* (London: Lindsey, 1928); "The Fundamentals of Religion as Interpreted by Christianity and Rabbinic Judaism," *HJ* 21(1922–23) 314–26.

8. *The Doctrine of Merits in Old Rabbinical Literature* (1920; reprint New York: Ktav, 1968).

9. See, e.g., "On Some Misconceptions of Judaism and Christianity by Each Other," *JQR* 8 (1896) 193–216; "Jewish Scholarship and Christian Silence," *HJ* 1 (1902–3) 335–46; *Rabbinic Literature and Gospel Teaching* (1930; reprint New York: Ktav, 1970).

of anti-Judaism in nourishing the evil of anti-Semitism. It was a point whose time had come.

2. A second and nearly as important point in the new perspective on Paul is again one that had been made much earlier: contrary to the Reformation understanding of Paul, *justification by faith is not the center of Paul's theology but instead represents a pragmatic tactic to facilitate the Gentile mission*. It will be easily seen how well this works together with the preceding point. If Judaism is not a religion of works-righteousness, then it hardly needs to hear the message of justification by faith, whereas that message makes perfect sense if it was directed solely to the Gentiles.

Although this point is not very important in Sanders' book, he does review the arguments of Albert Schweitzer concerning the relatively small importance of justification by faith in Paul's theology, concluding that "they have never been effectively countered."[10] Schweitzer put his conclusion in a typically vivid metaphor: "The doctrine of righteousness by faith is therefore a subsidiary crater, which has formed within the rim of the main crater — the mystical doctrine of redemption through the being-in-Christ."[11] The conclusion concerning the subordinate importance of the doctrine was not even original with Schweitzer. having already been argued at least as early as 1853 by Lipsius, and also Sabatier, Lüdemann, Weizsäcker, and Wrede.[12] The new perspective on Paul has given new life to this argument.[13]

3. These two main foundations of the new perspective on Paul thus raise again two fundamental questions: What was the nature of first-century Judaism? and What is at the heart of Paul's Christianity? Or, to put the question differently, What was the difference between Saul the Pharisee and Paul the Christian? The answers to these interrelated questions have produced a number of corollary conclusions, and to these we now turn.

3.1. The new perspective on Paul maintains that *Paul's theology has been misunderstood because it has been read through the lens of Luther*

---

10. *Paul and Palestinian Judaism*, 440.

11. *The Mysticism of Paul the Apostle*, trans. W. Montgomery (New York: Seabury, 1931) 225.

12. See the informative article by R. Y.-K. Fung, "The Status of Justification by Faith in Paul's Thought: A Brief Survey of a Modern Debate," *Themelios* 6 (1981) 4–11. See too the Appendix in Sanders' *Paul and Palestinian Judaism* by M. Brauch, "Perspectives on 'God's Righteousness' in Recent German Discussion," 523–42.

13. Cf. K. Stendahl, *Paul Among Jews and Gentiles* (Philadelphia: Fortress, 1976) 1–2.

and the Reformation. Luther's rediscovery of the gospel was preceded by an agonizing personal struggle with the problem of sin and of attempted self-justification. Such was not the case with Paul, as Phil 3:6, referring to Paul's background as a Pharisee, indicates: "As to righteousness under the law I was blameless." Since Judaism was not a religion of works-righteousness, Paul did not have to move from legalism to grace, as in the typical protestant schema.

Proponents of the new perspective on Paul have made much of K. Stendahl's 1963 article, "The Apostle Paul and the Introspective Conscience of the West."[14] It was indeed a pathbreaking article in some ways, anticipating much of the new perspective, yet even its main point had been articulated much earlier. T. W. Manson had already in 1938 written that "The Faith and Works controversy has obtained an undue emphasis through our reading of Paul in the light of the soul-strivings of Luther."[15] For Stendahl, the former Lutheran bishop, Luther has now come into disfavor — at least so far as being a guide to the interpretation of Paul's gospel is concerned.[16]

3.2. A further, related corollary in the new perspective argues that *Paul experienced not conversion to a new faith, not a change of religion, but a call and commission to bring the gospel to the Gentiles*. Paul remained a fully faithful Jew throughout his life.[17] This again is not a particularly new claim. Jewish scholars have for some time been engaged in reclaiming Paul for Judaism, arguing not only his enduring Jewishness but also that his task was in effect that of bringing Judaism to the Gentiles.[18]

---

14. First published in *HTR* 56 (1963) 199-215; now available in Stendahl's collected essays, *Paul Among Jews and Gentiles*, 78-96.

15. "Jesus, Paul and the Law," *Judaism and Christianity*, vol. III, *Law and Religion*, ed. E. I. J. Rosenthal (1938; reprint, New York: Ktav, 1969) 125-41, here 132.

16. See the especially strong attack on Luther and the "protestant" understanding of the question in Francis Watson, *Paul, Judaism and the Gentiles: A Sociological Approach*, SNTSMS 56 (Cambridge: Cambridge University Press, 1986) 1-22.

17. See especially Stendahl's "Call Rather than Conversion," *Paul Among Jews and Gentiles*, 7-23. Cf. Dunn, "'A Light to the Gentiles', or 'The End of the Law?' The Significance of the Damascus Road Christophany for Paul," in *The Glory of Christ in the New Testament: Studies in Christology in Memory of George Bradford Caird*, eds. L. D. Hurst and N. T. Wright (Oxford: Clarendon, 1987) 251-66, available now with an "Additional Note" in *Jesus, Paul and the Law*, 89-107; see too Dunn, *The Partings of the Ways*, 122, and P. J. Tomson, *Paul and the Jewish Law: Halakha in the Letters of the Apostle to the Gentiles*, CRINT 3/1 (Minneapolis: Fortress, 1990).

18. For a full account of Jewish scholarship on Paul, see S. Meißner, *Die Heimholung des Ketzers: Studien zur jüdischen Auseinandersetzung mit Paulus*, WUNT 2/87 (Tübingen: Mohr Siebeck, 1996); cf. D. A. Hagner, "Paul in Modern Jewish Thought,"

3.3. Closely related to the preceding is the conclusion that *Paul's main concern was the Jewish/Gentile problem, specifically the conversion of the Gentiles, rather than any universal human problem.* That is, Paul's theological thinking is dominated by the need to defend the right of the Gentiles to become full members of the people of God, without the need first to become Jews. Stendahl again puts it very clearly when he writes that the "doctrine of justification by faith was hammered out by Paul for the very specific and limited purpose of defending the rights of Gentile converts to be full and genuine heirs to the promises of God to Israel."[19] This is of course also closely related to the claim made in §2 above, since it further relativizes the doctrine of justification by faith.

3.4. A conclusion drawn from a number of the preceding points is that *Paul had no quarrel with the law (and hence Judaism) per se.* This has become one of the central tenets of the new perspective on Paul. If Judaism was a "covenantal nomism," to use Sanders' nomenclature — i.e., a law-centeredness in the context of prior experience of grace — then Paul could hardly have been unhappy with it, even as a Christian. His apparently negative statements concerning the law are therefore dictated solely by the exigencies of the Gentile mission. Paul's "new understanding of the law" is the result of his call to evangelize the Gentiles.[20] Sanders explains Paul's rejection of his earlier faith with these words: "In short, *this is what Paul finds wrong in Judaism: it is not Christianity.*"[21]

3.5. Since he had no quarrel with the law, according to the new perspective, *Paul's arguments against "works of the law" do not concern the issue of righteousness by obedience to the law, but simply Jewish badges of identity that separated Jews from the Gentiles.* Dunn in particular has stressed that "works of the law" refers to "national righteousness."[22] Ac-

---

in *Pauline Studies: Essays Presented to Professor F. F. Bruce on His 70th Birthday*, eds. D. A. Hagner and M. J. Harris (Grand Rapids: Eerdmans, 1980) 143-65.

19. Stendahl, *Paul Among Jews and Gentiles*, 2.

20. Stendahl, *Paul Among Jews and Gentiles*, 9.

21. Sanders, *Paul and Palestinian Judaism*, 552.

22. This phrase (and insight?) is borrowed from Tom Wright's 1980 Oxford dissertation, "The Messiah and the People of God: A Study in Pauline Theology with Particular Reference to the Argument of the Epistle to the Romans." So far as I can see, Dunn nowhere refers to Wright's 1978 Tyndale NT Lecture titled "The Paul of History and the Apostle of Faith," which already articulates key aspects of the new perspective on Paul. The lecture was published in *Tyndale Bulletin* 29 (1978) 61-88. C. Bryan, in an article without a single mention of Dunn, concludes that the issue in Rom 9:30–10:4 is "that concern with personal and corporate holiness which had characterized the Judaism in which he [Paul] grew up" ("Law and Grace in Paul: Thoughts on E. P. Sanders," *Saint*

cording to him, the "boasting" of the Jews which Paul repeatedly criticizes refers not to self-confidence, but to "Jewish" confidence.[23]

Dunn has labored hard to defend the interpretation of "works of the law" as the marks of Jewish privilege,[24] tackling first Gal 2:16 in his new perspective article, then turning to Gal 3:10-14,[25] and of course the Romans passages in his commentary. Recent monographs on Galatians by John Barclay and Walter Hansen join in the conclusion that the issue in Galatians is not Jewish legalism but national righteousness or the law in terms of badges of Jewish identity.[26] Francis Watson and Donald Garlington (who did his research under Dunn) examine Romans from this perspective and come to similar conclusions.[27]

3.6. It is not far from these conclusions to a final deduction–one not drawn, however, by all advocates of the new understanding of Paul. If Judaism is a religion of grace, and there is nothing wrong with its nomism in Paul's view, and if Paul's message therefore concerns the Gentiles rather than the Jews, a natural conclusion is that *the covenantal nomism of the OT is God's way of salvation for Israel, while the law-free gospel is God's way of salvation for the Gentiles.* The pressure towards the so-called two covenant theory of salvation continues to be a constant factor in Jewish-Christian dialogue today.[28] Four advocates of the new view of

Luke's Journal of Theology 34 [1991] 33-52, here 50).

23. "The Justice of God," 11.

24. For the similar view of Sanders, see *Paul, the Law, and the Jewish People*, 160.

25. "Works of the Law and the Curse of the Law (Gal 3:10-14)," *Jesus, Paul and the Law*, 215-41. See too, "Yet Once More-'The Works of the Law': A Response," *JSNT* 46 (1992) 99-117.

26. John Barclay, *Obeying the Truth: A Study of Paul's Ethics in Galatians* (Edinburgh: T. & T. Clark, 1988) 235-42; Walter Hansen, *Abraham in Galatians: Epistolary and Rhetorical Contexts*, JSNTSS 29 (Sheffield: JSOT, 1989) 161-62.

27. Francis Watson, *Paul, Judaism and the Gentiles*, 88-176; D. B. Garlington, "The Obedience of Faith": A Pauline Phrase in Historical Context, WUNT 2/38 (Tübingen: Mohr Siebeck, 1991). Similar in many ways are N. Elliott, *The Rhetoric of Romans: Argumentative Constraint and Strategy and Paul's Dialogue with Judaism*, JSNTSup 45 (Sheffield: JSOT, 1990); and C. T. Rhyne, *Faith Establishes the Law*, SBLDS 55 (Chico, CA: Scholars, 1981).

28. For shrewd observation of a number of ironies in aspects of the new perspective on Paul, see R. B. Matlock, "Almost Cultural Studies? Reflections on the 'New Perspective' on Paul," *Biblical/Cultural Studies: The Third Sheffield Colloquium*, eds. J. Cheryl Exum and Stephen D. Moore JSOTSup 266 (Sheffield: Sheffield Academic, 1998) 433-59. For a merciless deconstruction of the new perspective, see Matlock's "Sins of the Flesh and Suspicious Minds: Dunn's New Theology of Paul," *JSNT* 72 (1998) 67-90. Dunn responds to the latter in "Whatever Happened to Exegesis? In Response to the Reviews by R. B. Matlock and D. A. Campbell," *JSNT* 72 (1998) 113-20.

Paul who have also accepted the two covenant approach are Stendahl,[29] Markus Barth,[30] G. Gager,[31] and Lloyd Gaston.[32] Others, such as Sanders and Dunn,[33] have resisted this conclusion. It is not difficult to see how the various elements of the new perspective on Paul can lead to this appealing, but in my view unbiblical, conclusion.

4. Naturally in this brief review we have not done justice to the strength of the arguments that have been put forward by the advocates of the new perspective on Paul. Our purpose has merely been to note the major assertions in the discussion of Paul and Judaism that blend together to produce that new perspective. It will of course be impossible to respond adequately to these arguments in the confines of this essay. But I do want to comment briefly on each of them.

There have been a number of responses to various aspects of the new perspective, as we shall see. Among the more substantial treatments of the whole subject, we may note Stephen Westerholm's *Israel's Law and the Church's Faith: Paul and his Recent Interpreters*,[34] Colin Kruse's *Paul, the Law and Justification*,[35] and Mark A. Seifrid's *Christ, Our Righteousness: the Justification of the Ungodly as the Theology of Paul*.[36]

---

29. For Stendahl, Paul's gospel was only for the Gentiles. See *Paul Among Jews and Gentiles*, 2.

30. See Barth's collection of essays titled *The People of God*, JSNTSup 5 (Sheffield: JSOT Press, 1983), where a two-covenant theory is at least implied.

31. *The Origins of Anti-Semitism* (Oxford: Oxford University Press, 1983).

32. See Gaston's collected essays in *Paul and the Torah* (Vancouver: University of British Columbia Press, 1987).

33. Explicitly in *The Partings of the Ways*, 250: "Jewish/Christian dialogue in this area has tended to pose the issue in terms of one covenant or two; and clearly I lean to the 'one covenant' side." Yet his position is very nuanced and it is not always clear how his conclusions are compatible with a one covenant position. Perhaps this explains the word "lean."

34. Grand Rapids: Eerdmans, 1988. See too his "Paul and the Law in Romans 9–11," in *Paul and the Mosaic Law*, ed. J. D. G. Dunn (Tübingen: Mohr Siebeck, 1996) 215-37; and "Sinai as Viewed from Damascus: Paul's Reevaluation of the Mosaic Law," in *The Road from Damascus. The Impact of Paul's Conversion on His Life, Thought, and Ministry*, ed. R. N. Longenecker (Grand Rapids: Eerdmans, 1997) 147-65.

35. Leicester, UK: Apollos, 1996.

36. Downers Grove, IL: IVP Academic, 2001. Adapted from this book is Seifrid's "The 'New Perspective on Paul' and Its Problems," *Themelios* 25 (2000) 4-18. Also worthy of mention is the brief but insightful excursus on Rom 3:20 ("Paul, 'Works of the Law,' and First-Century Judaism") in Douglas Moo's commentary on Romans. *The Epistle to the Romans*, NICNT (Grand Rapids: Eerdmans, 1996) 211-217. Much of Moo's helpful and insightful review article, "Paul and the Law In the Last Ten Years" (*SJT* 40 [1987] 287-307) is also relevant to the subject of the present article. See too,

We turn first then to the two main points considered above in §§1 and 2.

4.1. Few if any will want to deny that what is found in the OT, namely the religion of Israel, is indeed a religion of grace rather than works-righteousness. To say this, however, is not enough. In the postexilic period, beginning with the prototypical scribe Ezra, there was understandably a turning to the law with a new intensity of commitment. The exile was widely perceived as the result of Israel's failure to keep the law. In this new development, which constitutes the beginning of Judaism, it is hardly surprising that the law assumed central importance. Judaism is of course in continuity with the OT and grace was not necessarily occluded by the heightened emphasis on the law. But that it was overshadowed by the new emphasis on the law seems highly probable to me.

Heikki Räisänen, it should be noted, has adamantly continued to argue against Sanders and Dunn that Paul *does* portray Judaism as legalistic. Then, however, he asserts that Judaism could not have been legalistic (an a priori conclusion dependent on Sanders) and that therefore Paul is responsible for a distortion of first-century Judaism, being concerned only to defend and promote the Gentile mission.[37]

It is a good question to what extent the rabbis or proto-rabbis of the first century assumed and articulated the grace that was foundational to the religion of their OT forebears. Apart from the notorious problem of what in the rabbinic literature can be taken as going back to or reflecting the situation of the first century, one must note not only the lack of systematic thinking but the presence of (and delight in!) contradictory opinions. It is furthermore the case that there *are* plenty of legalistic-sounding statements in the rabbinic literature. Klyne Snodgrass gently points this out when he writes, "There is an emphasis on weighing good deeds against bad in some writings and on the keeping of ledger books in others, and this cannot be dismissed as easily as Sanders would like."[38]

R. B. Matlock, "A Future for Paul?," in *Auguries: The Jubilee Volume of the Sheffield Department of Biblical Studies*, JSOTSup 269, eds. D. J. A. Clines and S. D. Moore (Sheffield: Sheffield Academic, 1998) 144-83.

37. *Paul and the Law*, xxvi-xxix.

38. "Justification by Grace—to the Doers: An Analysis of the Place of Romans 2 in the Theology of Paul," *NTS* 32 (1986) 72-93, here 78. Cf. R. H. Gundry: "If we weigh their emphases—quite a different impression may be gained, an impression of Palestinian Judaism as centered on works-righteousness and Paul's theology as centered on grace ("Grace, Works, and Staying Saved in Paul," *Bib* 66 [1985] 1-38, here 6). Although Jacob Neusner agrees with Sanders' portrayal of Judaism, a comment he makes

Such statements collected, for example, in Billerbeck and Kittel do exist; the just criticism is that these works cite only these texts and not others that point in a different direction.

In a thorough survey of the pertinent materials, Friedrich Avemarie has demonstrated that the rabbinic soteriology contains two different— indeed, contrary—models, one based on the election of Israel, the other on the deeds of the individual. In different places, one or the other can come to expression in apparently absolute terms, and it is impossible finally to give priority to either.[39] It is thus not a matter of *either* grace *or* merit, but the two together in an unresolved tension.

Earlier Jewish scholars were ready to allow the very strong emphasis on works among the rabbis. Schechter cites the famous paradox attributed to R. Akiba (Abot 3:20): "The world is judged by grace, and yet all is according to the amount of work."[40] Israel Abrahams refers to the Jewish doctrine as "something like the *synergism* of Erasmus which, as his opponents saw, was radically opposed to the Pauline theory of grace." After citing the same logion of Akiba, he adds that "the antinomy [of grace and works] is the ultimate doctrine of Pharisaism."[41] Even if we allow that the

---

in his review of Sanders' book points in the same direction: "An apology for Rabbinic Judaism bypassing the whole of the *halakhic* corpus which constitutes its earliest stratum is cosmically irrelevant to the interpretation of Rabbinic Judaism, therefore to the comparison of that system to others in its own culture" ("Comparing Judaisms," *History of Religions* 18 [1978-79]) 177-91, here 187, n. 14). This article is taken up in slightly altered form within "The Use of the Later Rabbinic Evidence for the Study of Paul," in *Approaches to Ancient Judaism*, vol. 2, ed. W. S. Green (Chico, CA: Scholars, 1980) 43-63, where the above quotation has been moved from the footnote to the text. Sanders responds to Neusner and to the similar criticisms of A. J. Saldarini (in his review of Sanders' book [*JBL* 98 (1979) 299-303]) in an article that follows Neusner's "Puzzling Out Rabbinic Judaism," 65-79.

39. "Erwählung und Vergeltung: Zur optionalen Struktur rabbinischer Soteriologie," *NTS* 45 (1999) 108-26; *Torah und Leben: Untersuchungen zur Heilsbedeutung der Torah in der frühen rabbinischen Literatur* (Tübingen: Mohr Siebeck, 1996); "Bund als Gabe und Recht," in *Bund und Tora: Zur theologischen Begriffsgeschichte in alt-testamentlicher, frühjüdischer und urchristlicher Tradition*, ed. F. Avemarie and H. Lichtenberger (Tübingen: Mohr Siebeck, 1996) 163-216.

40. *Aspects of Rabbinic Theology*, 15. Schechter calls attention to the variant reading, "and *not* according to the amount of work," and the interesting fact that the difference was of no real concern to the commentators.

41. *Studies in Pharisaism and the Gospels* (First Series, 1917; reprint, New York: Ktav, 1967) 146. For a fascinating and illuminating discussion of the subject from a Jewish point of view, see C. G. Montefiore's long comment on Matt 7:24-27 in *Rabbinic Literature and Gospel Teachings* (1930; reprint, New York: Ktav, 1970) 154-201. For the explanation of Judaism as a *synergistic* nomism, see Timo Eskola, "Paul, Predestination and 'Covenantal Nomism'—Re-assessing Paul and Palestinian Judaism," *JSJ* 28 (1997)

emphasis on works has to do with "staying in" rather than "getting in," as Sanders maintains, we may still be confronted with a decided preoccupation with works, a preoccupation which by its very nature makes for human insecurity and thus prepares a promising ground for the nurture of legalistic tendencies. The line between getting in and staying in can furthermore become a thin one that tends to disappear.[42]

Since the rabbis can also speak of grace and since a religion should always be judged by its best representatives, is it not fair to admit that Judaism is a religion of grace and not one where God's favor is earned through righteous works? This seems true, at least at the theoretical level. In its best theology, Judaism *is* a religion of grace. Often, however, its gracious foundations are tacitly assumed[43] and often the law takes a place of overwhelming priority. It is not surprising if a religion whose heart lies in praxis rather than theory (theology), a religion dominated by nomism, where the covenant is more presupposed than articulated, inadvertently produces followers who fall into a legalistic mode of existence. This may explain the "exception" of 4 Ezra (cf. 2 Baruch) with its clear legalism, which Sanders does not deny.[44] Thus, it is not hard to believe that during the time of Jesus and Paul there were many who—against the best understanding of their faith—had fallen into legalism, against which both Jesus and Paul had therefore to contend.[45] A covenantal nomism will only re-

---

390-41; see too his monograph, *Theodicy and Predestination in Pauline Soteriology*, WUNT 2/100 (Tübingen: Mohr Siebeck, 1998); and "*Avodat Israel* and the 'Works of the Law' in Paul," in *From the Ancient Sites of Israel: Essays on Archaeology, History and Theology in Memory of Aapeli Saarisalo*, eds. T. Eskola and E. Junkkaala (Helsinki: Theological Institute of Finland, 1998) 175-97.

42. C. F. D. Moule points this out in the following words: "maintenance of it [the covenantal relation] in Judaism by 'works' . . . does seem to me not far off from the 'legalism' . . . which Dr Sanders holds that Paul is not attacking . . . I am asking whether 'covenantal nomism' itself is so far from implicit 'legalism.'" "Jesus, Judaism, and Paul" in *Tradition and Interpretation in the New Testament*, FS E. E. Ellis, ed. G. F. Hawthorne and O. Betz (Grand Rapids: Eerdmans, 1987) 43-52, here 48.

43. T. F. Best has called attention to this problem in the following words: "His [Sanders'] insistence that the covenant-concept is central in the rabbinic literature, though virtually unmentioned, depends on the ability to demonstrate that it was in fact in the background of the documents as the inescapable presupposition of their discussion on matters of ritual purification, means of atonement, and the definition of 'work.' But in other areas he uses the argument from silence to cut the other way: Since a treasury of merits is not mentioned in the literature, such a concept was not a part of Judaism in this period." See "The Apostle Paul and E. P. Sanders: The Significance of Paul and Palestinian Judaism," *RestQ* 25 (1982) 65-74, here 73.

44. *Paul and Palestinian Judaism*, 421-22.

45. So too, Silva, "The Law and Christianity," 349: "Sanders is insensitive to the

main "covenantal" where very deliberate and explicit measures are taken to guard it as such; there will otherwise be a natural human tendency toward legalism. There have been many instances where the experience of Christian congregations substantiates this. The situation of the Jews in the post-exilic period, suffering under Roman rule, naturally heightened the emphasis on the performance of the law.

It is therefore not at all evident, in my opinion, that there were no Jews around in the time of Paul who corresponded to the legalists attacked by him in the traditional understanding of works-righteousness. I am reminded of the wry remark of C. K. Barrett: "He is a bold man who supposes that he understands first-century Judaism better than Paul did."[46]

4.2. It is of course debatable whether justification by faith is the "center" of Paul's theology. What is more important for our purposes is whether justification by faith is *important* for Paul, indeed, to the extent that it is more than a ploy merely to advance the Gentile mission, but a doctrine indispensable even for the salvation of the Jews. I am persuaded by those who have argued that the most fundamentally important element in Paul's theology is that the work of Christ inaugurates an eschatological turning point in history.[47] Within that overarching *Heilsgeschichte* framework (which to my mind provides continuity between Jesus and Paul), justification assumes an especially important place.[48] This is seen

---

fact that both in [Christian theologians of] medieval times and in Judaism many lay people may indeed have perceived salvation along those [legalistic] lines." Among other scholars who argue that first-century Judaism was legalistic, cf. H. Hübner, "Pauli Theologiae Proprium," *NTS* 26 (1979-80) 445-73; and T. R. Schreiner, "'Works of Law' in Paul," *NovT* 33 (1991) 217-44. Schreiner continues to hold to the so-called Reformation understanding of Paul: "What he [Paul] opposes is the delusion of those who think they can earn merit before God by their obedience to the law, even though they fail to obey it" (244). See his *The Law and Its Fulfillment: A Pauline Theology of Law* (Grand Rapids: Baker, 1993).

46. *Paul. An Introduction to his Thought* (Louisville: Westminster John Knox, 1994) 78.

47. To my mind Neusner is entirely correct when he points to this as constituting the real difference between Paul and the perspective of the Pharisees: the Christian view presupposes "an ontology quite distinct from that of the cult, an ontology which centers, as I just said, on a profoundly disruptive historical event, one which has shattered all that has been regular and orderly. So far as history stands at the center of being, so that the messiah and the conclusion of history form the focus of interest, the ontological conception of Christianity scarcely intersects with that of Pharisaism" ("The Use of the Later Rabbinic Evidence for the Study of First-Century Pharisaism," in *Approaches to Ancient Judaism: Theory and Practice*, ed. W. S. Green [Missoula, MT: Scholars, 1978] 215-28, here 225).

48. See E. Käsemann, "Justification and Salvation History in the Epistle to the Romans," in *Perspectives on Paul*, trans. M. Kohl (London: SCM, 1971) 60-78. In

especially, of course, in the closely argued soteriological sections of Galatians and Romans, but it is also found in the Corinthian letters,[49] as well as in Philippians and, were we allowed to appeal to it, Ephesians too.[50]

J. G. Machen's response to Wrede on this very point is worth quoting in full: "The real reason why Paul was devoted to the doctrine of justification by faith was not that it made possible the Gentile mission, but rather that it was true. Paul was not devoted to the doctrine of justification by faith because of the Gentile mission; he was devoted to the Gentile mission because of the doctrine of justification by faith."[51]

Without question, the doctrine of justification by faith in and through the finished work of Christ made the Gentile mission a possibility. But from Paul's perspective it also made possible the salvation of the Jews. Justification by faith is addressed to both Jew and Gentile because it addresses a universal human need.[52]

5. We press on now to respond albeit briefly to the corollaries mentioned above in §3.

5.1. Although justification by faith is often criticized for being concerned only with the salvation of the individual, as in the crisis of

---

Käsemann's view, "It has rightly been repeatedly noticed that the apostle's message of justification is a fighting doctrine, directed against Judaism" (70). Cf. R. Bultmann: "still more would he [a Jew] contradict the proposition that *justification by works of the Law and justification by divine grace appropriated in man's faith exclude each other*. But that is the decisive thesis of Paul: 'for Christ is the end of the law, that every one who has faith may be justified' (Rom. 10:4); i.e. 'Christ means the end of the Law; he leads to righteousness everyone who has faith'" (*Theology of the New Testament*, trans. K. Grobel [London: SCM, 1952] 1.263).

49. See R. Y.-K. Fung, "Justification by Faith in 1 & 2 Corinthians," *Pauline Studies*, 246-61.

50. For an excellent discussion of the subject, see John Reumann, *"Righteousness" in the New Testament: "Justification" in the United States Lutheran-Roman Catholic Dialogue*, with responses by J. A. Fitzmyer and J. D. Quinn (Philadelphia: Fortress, 1982). Reumann notes his continuing conviction concerning "the soundness of the Reformation choice in this perspective" and that "while righteousness/justification is by no means the only way to express Paul's message, the case for regarding it as the central one remains a persuasive one" (108).

51. *The Origin of Paul's Religion* (London: Hodder & Stoughton, 1921) 278-79. I owe this quotation to R. Y.-K. Fung, "The Status of Justification by Faith in Paul's Thought," 8.

52. For an excellent discussion of this whole question, see K. T. Cooper, "Paul and Rabbinic Soterlology: A Review Article," *WTJ* 44 (1982) 123-39, esp. 136ff. As Cooper says, "Paul's soteriology forms a much more specific and pointed contrast to covenantal nomism than Sanders has observed" (136). On the whole matter, we may look forward with anticipation to a two-volume work entitled *Justification and Variegated Judaism*, edited by D. A. Carson, forthcoming from Mohr-Siebeck in Tübingen.

an individual over the problem of sin—on the model of Luther—properly understood, it has corporate and cosmic aspects too.[53] Leaving that point aside, however, and coming to the personal level, I want to make the following observations. In my opinion we read too much into Paul's statement in Phil 3:6, "as to righteousness under the law [I was] blameless (*amemptos*)," when we conclude from it that Paul was fully pleased with both the law and his performance of it. He indicates here only that by the standards of practicing Pharisees he had an exceptionally good performance record (cf. Gal 1:13–14).[54] It is certainly not anything in the end that he as a Jew felt he could rely upon. Quite the contrary, all his credentials and efforts amounted to worthless rubbish, as he goes on to say, putting himself in complete dependence upon Christ, "not having a righteousness of my own that comes from the law, but one that comes through faith in Christ" (Phil 3:8–9).

Timo Laato has shown how Paul is critical of Jewish soteriology on anthropological grounds.[55] Laato indicates how, unlike the more optimistic Jewish view, Paul views human nature as dominated by sin and the flesh. Laato notes that Robert Gundry had already come to a similar conclusion about the importance of human weakness for Paul's understanding of salvation.[56] The result is that Paul abandoned the synergism of Jewish soteriology for the monergism of total dependence upon the grace of God in Christ. Laato concludes, rightly in my opinion, that Paul

---

53. Cf. Reumann, *Righteousness in the New Testament*, 73–74: "Righteousness/justification in Paul has a cosmic side, relating God's faithfulness and saving righteousness to all creation, within a new covenant setting. This emphasis is utterly necessary alongside the individual emphasis." See esp. E. Käsemann, "Justification and Salvation History in the Epistle to the Romans," *Perspectives on Paul* (Philadelphia: Fortress, 1971) 32–59; and P. Stuhlmacher, *Reconciliation, Law, and Righteousness: Essays in Biblical Theology* (Philadelphia: Fortress, 1986) 68–93.

54. For some thought-provoking reasons to reconsider Stendahl's conclusions, see J. M. Espy, "Paul's 'Robust Conscience' Re-Examined," NTS 31 (1985) 161–88. See too, C. K. Barrett, "Paul and the Introspective Conscience" in *The Bible, the Reformation and the Church*, FS James Atkinson, ed. W. P. Stephens (Sheffield: Academic, 1995) 36–48.

55. *Paul and Judaism: An Anthropological Approach*, South Florida Studies in the History of Judaism 115, trans. T. McElwain (Atlanta: Scholars, 1995). Laato takes his point of departure from a suggestion of Hugh Odeberg, who was Professor of NT at Lund in the middle of this century. See his *Pharisaism and Christianity*, (trans. J. M. Moe; St. Louis: Concordia, 1964), which in a number of ways anticipated much of the recent discussion.

56. "Grace, Works, and Staying Saved in Paul," Bib 66 (1985) 1–38. Laato quotes these words of Gundry: "It appears that the twin pillars of human weakness and salvation-history, not just salvation-history, uphold justification by faith alone" (209).

thus repudiates the Jewish understanding of righteousness and the Jewish soteriology. We may compare these conclusions with those of Stephen Westerholm, who also argues that in Paul's view "human sin has rendered the righteousness of the law inoperable as a means to life," and who also points out Paul's pessimism, compared to Judaism, in holding the impossibility of human beings ever satisfying the divine requirements.[57]

The question remains concerning when Paul came to this more negative assessment of the human condition.[58] In my view there is some truth in Sanders' argument that Paul moved from solution to problem. I am not convinced that Paul was problem-free before the Damascus Road experience, but I am confident that as Paul began to make sense of the reality of the crucified Messiah as the single *hilasterion* for the forgiveness of sin that his sense of the enormity of the human problem increased dramatically. Although I cannot prove it, I suspect that his experience as a Pharisee had already shown him something of the problem. The law after all can be experienced as both a blessing and a burden at the same time (as I take Acts 15:10 to indicate). And it is impossible to believe that Saul the Pharisee did not know from his own experience what it was like to struggle against the *yetzer ha-ra* (the evil inclination) which is described by Montefiore as "a sore burden and a heavy trial."[59]

It may well be then that Paul is not so far from Luther as some have recently argued. Instead, Luther may indeed have been quite a good exegete of Paul and his theology truly Pauline. Westerholm's tongue-in-cheek comment at the end of his chapter on justification is apropos: "Students who want to understand Paul but feel they have nothing to learn from a Martin Luther should consider a career in metallurgy."[60]

5.2. In my opinion, conversion is the right word to use for Paul's rejection of Judaism and turning to the faith of the Christian community he had been persecuting. But I do *not* think that it is correct to say that he converted to a new religion, or that Paul himself would ever have thought so. Christianity, for Paul, is nothing other than the faith of his ancestors come to an eschatological phase of fulfillment before the final consummation. The Christian community is the true Israel, if not the new Israel.

---

57. *Israel's Law and the Church's Faith*, 142.

58. In Gundry's view, this question is of no significance since it does not affect the position Paul takes in his writings; "Grace, Works," 21.

59. *Rabbinic Literature and Gospel Teachings*, 180. It is quite probable that Romans 7, if it is autobiographical, reflects something of this agonizing struggle under the law.

60. *Israel's Law and the Church's Faith*, 173.

The church has for the time being taken the place of Israel, but not altogether, since Paul foresees a future for physical Israel in Romans 11. That future, I hasten to add, involves Israel's response of faith to Jesus Christ. Paul, in my opinion, knows of no salvation — not even for Israel — apart from the cross of Jesus. The church and believing Israel compose one entity, the people of God, who together experience the eschatological goal towards which God's work from Abraham onwards was aimed.[61]

Along with his conversion, Paul of course received a call and commission to evangelize the Gentiles. But again, Paul did not think of a second religion for the Gentiles. He was calling them to his fulfilled Judaism, nothing other than the faith of Israel beginning with Abraham. For Paul, becoming a Christian did not mean becoming a Gentile; it would be truer to say that the Gentiles became fulfilled Jews, the children of Abraham by faith, grafted onto the olive tree of Israel.

5.3. Paul's gospel addresses not merely the plight of the Gentiles, strangers to the covenants, but that too of the Jews. He addresses a human condition. This I think can be shown by a careful exegetical analysis of Rom 1:18—3:20. The very way Paul has constructed the argument indicates that he means to indict all humanity, both Gentiles and Jews (and the latter despite all their advantages), under the curse of sin (see especially 3:9, 19-20; and further in Rom 5:18-19). We cannot stop here to look at these and other relevant passages that could be mentioned.

Paul was of course concerned especially with the problem of the salvation of the Gentiles, for whom he had been given special responsibility. At the same time, however, he believed his gospel to be universally relevant. In a poignant passage he reveals his concern for the evangelization of the Jews as well as the Gentiles: "For though I am free with respect to all, I have made myself a slave to all, so that I might win more of them. To the Jews I became as a Jew, in order to win Jews. To those under the law I became as one under the law (though I myself am not under the law) so that I might win those under the law" (1 Cor 9:19-20). Indeed, the gospel was *first* for the Jews and only subsequently for the Gentiles (Rom 1:16).

This means that Paul had modified the "standard" view of the unconditional election of all Israel, namely its secure place within the covenant promises without qualification. In a recent, thorough examination of the Judaism of the Pseudepigrapha and the Dead Sea Scrolls, Mark Adam Elliott has shown that in at least one major strand of Judaism the

---

61. See Scott Hafemann, "The Salvation of Israel in Romans 11:25-32. A Response to Krister Stendahl," *Ex Auditu* 4 (1988) 38-58.

expectation was that only a remnant of Israel would experience salvation and that judgment would come upon the nation as a whole. Thus a number of NT motifs questioned in the recent emphasis on covenantal nomism and the new perspective on Paul are found to have a background within Judaism itself:

> including that Israel, God's chosen people, is in danger of judgment and in this regard has been placed on a par with Gentiles; that the historical covenants are not unqualifiedly valid for all who consider themselves participants in them; that the normal rites of maintaining the covenant have become ineffective; that an individual soteriology *apart from* previous divine acts of deliverance on behalf of Israel has now become necessary.[62]

5.4. The subject of Paul and the law has received much attention lately. It would be impossible to review the discussion here.[63] What we can do is to respond briefly to the claim that Paul has no quarrel with the

---

62. Mark Adam Elliott, *The Survivors of Israel: A Reconsideration of the Theology of Pre-Christian Judaism* (Grand Rapids: Eerdmans, 2000) 664.

63. At least the following significant monographs may be listed: H. Hübner, *Law in Paul's Thought*, trans. J. C. G. Greig (Edinburgh: T. & T. Clark, 1984); H. Räisänen, *Paul and the Law* (Tübingen: Mohr Siebeck, 1983; 2d ed., 1987); E. P. Sanders, *Paul, the Law, and the Jewish People* (Philadelphia: Fortress, 1983); B. L. Martin, *Christ and the Law in Paul* (NovTSup 62; Leiden: Brill, 1989); F. Thielman, *From Plight to Solution: A Jewish Framework for Understanding Paul's View of the Law in Galatians and Romans*, NovTSup 61 (Leiden: Brill, 1989); P. J. Tomson, *Paul and the Jewish Law: Halakha in the Letters of the Apostle to the Gentiles* (Minneapolis: Fortress, 1990); J. D. G. Dunn's collected essays, *Jesus, Paul and the Law: Studies in Mark and Galatians* (Louisville: Westminster John Knox, 1990); Michael Winger, *By What Law? The Meaning of Nomos in the Letters of Paul* (SBLDS 128; Atlanta: Scholars, 1992); Thomas R. Schreiner, *The Law and its Fulfillment. A Pauline Theology of Law* (Grand Rapids: Baker, 1993); Frank Thielman, *Paul and the Law. A Contextual Approach* (Downers Grove, IL: InterVarsity, 1994); Colin G. Kruse, *Paul, the Law and Justification* (Leicester, UK: Apollos, 1996); and especially the essays from the third Durham-Tübingen Symposium on Earliest Christianity and Judaism edited by J. D. G. Dunn, *Paul and the Mosaic Law* (Tübingen: Mohr Siebeck, 1996). For useful and contrasting reviews of scholarship in this area, see D. Moo, "Paul and the Law in the Last Ten Years," *SJT* 40 (1987) 287-307; A. J. M. Wedderburn, "Paul and the Law," *SJT* 38 (1985) 613-22; J. M. G. Barclay, "Paul and the Law: Observations on Some Recent Debates," *Themelios* 12 (1986) 5-15; F. F. Bruce, "Paul and the Law in Recent Research," *Law and Religion: Essays on the Place of the Law in Israel and Early Christianity*, ed. B. Lindars (Cambridge: James Clarke, 1988) 115-25; and A. J. Bandstra, "Paul and the Law: Some Recent Developments and an Extraordinary Book," *CTJ* 25 (1990) 249-61. Also worth mentioning is the "Postscript to the Second Edition," in S. Kim, *The Origin of Paul's Gospel* (Tübingen: Mohr Siebeck, 1984), where Räisänen and, to a lesser extent, Sanders are sharply criticized (345-58).

law.[64] Some preliminary comments will lead us quickly to the question of "works of the law," which will require a little more detailed treatment.

Recent discussion of the subject shows how difficult and complex it is. My conviction is that on this subject, as on not a few others too, we must learn to tolerate the paradoxical both/and. That is, Paul both does away with and upholds the law—in different senses, of course, unless we are to accept Räisänen's desperate conclusion that Paul was simply very confused.[65] But is Paul's dialectic on this subject really so hard to understand? The assertion that the law has come to an end (e.g., Rom 7:4-6; Gal 3:23-25; 4:4-5) is fundamentally important for Paul's soteriology (note the first person pronoun in Gal 2:4; cf. 2:15-16), this in the first instance in response to what *de facto* legalism may have existed, but also in response even to an authentic covenantal nomism. Paradoxically, however, those free from the law who follow the teaching of their Lord fulfill the righteousness of the law apart from the law—that is, they fulfill the moral law, especially as summarized in the love commandment (Rom 13:9-10; cf. Matt 22:37-40). Thus it can be said that the gospel does not overthrow the law in the sense that righteousness is abandoned; rather, the gospel upholds the ultimate intention of the law (Rom 3:31).[66] As I see it, the *telos* of Rom 10:4 may itself thus bear both the nuance of "end" and "goal." Both are surely true from the Pauline viewpoint.

If Paul in this sense still upholds the law, may it not be said that his Christianity amounts simply to a variant form of "covenantal nomism"? Is it not a following of the law in the context of experienced grace? Several scholars have noted the duality of covenant grace and meritorious works in Judaism, and have found a similar synergism in Paul. Mikael Winninge can speak of justification in Paul as a "continual participation, where God and the Christian 'cooperate' in a progressive dialectic," in

---

64. For full treatment of the question, see D. A. Hagner, "Paul's Quarrel with Judaism," in *Anti-Semitism and Early Christianity. Issues of Polemic and Faith*, C. A. Evans and D. A. Hagner, eds. (Minneapolis: Fortress, 1993) 128-50.

65. *Paul and the Law*, e.g., 264: "He [Paul] is torn into [sic] two directions, and he is incapable of resolving the tension in terms of theological thought." There have been many responses to Räisänen's book. He responds to these (up to 1987) in the preface to the second edition of his book. See further now G. Klein, "Ein Sturmzentrum der Paulusforschung," *Verkündigung und Forschung* 33 (1988) 40-56; and C. E. B. Cranfield, "Giving a Dog a Bad Name: A Note on H. Räisänen's *Paul and the Law*," *JSNT* 38 (1990) 77-85.

66. For a somewhat similar perspective, see P. Stuhlmacher, "Paul's Understanding of the Law in the Letter to the Romans," *SEÅ* 50 (1985) 87-104; and also his *Reconciliation, Law, and Righteousness*, 134-54.

which God by grace confers righteous status (cf. Israel's election) and the Christian produces the necessary works that determine reward or punishment.[67] Very similar is Kent Yinger's conclusion that as in Judaism, so in Pauline Christianity, despite differences, "the fundamental structure of grace and works, election and obedience, salvation and judgment, remains the same."[68] Hendrikus Boers takes almost exactly the same line, stressing that Paul the Christian remained Jewish in his valuation of the law and the necessity of works of the law, and that "in many ways he can be understood better as a Jewish sectarian (in the sense of Acts 24:14) than as a Christian."[69]

While there is indeed some overt similarity between the soteriology of Paul and that of Judaism, the very basis of Paul's soteriology is different. We can do no better than quote Morna Hooker here:

> Clearly we cannot speak of "covenantal nomism" in Paul's case, since that would run counter to Paul's basic quarrel with the Law. But the point is that for Paul, the Law has been replaced by Christ — or rather, since the Law was an interim measure, it has been shown in its true character as a stand-in, now that the reality has arrived. The questions, "Who belongs to the covenant?," and "How does one respond to the covenant?, are answered by Paul in terms of Christ, by Judaism in terms of the Law.[70]

In short, while Judaism is nomocentric, Paul is christocentric. And as serious as Paul is about righteous conduct, he cannot be fairly

---

67. *Sinners and the Righteous: A Comparative Study of the Psalms of Solomon and Paul's Letters*, ConBNT 26 (Stockholm: Almqvist & Wiksell, 1995) 334. Winninge denies that his view involves a legalism or Pelagianism since righteous status is a divine gift.

68. *Paul, Judaism, and Judgment According to Deeds*, SNTSMS 105 (Cambridge: Cambridge University Press, 1999. Yinger says that for Paul the Jew there was no theological tension between judgment according to works and justification by faith. But if Paul saw no problem with works-righteousness, why did he repeatedly argue so strongly against it?

69. "Judaism and the church in Paul's thought," *Neotestamentica* 32 (1998) 249-66. Boers differs markedly from Yinger, however, in detecting not merely tensions in Paul's theology, but contradictions, à la Räisänen: "These contradictions constitute one of the most fundamental problems in the interpretation of Paul. The question can no longer be *whether* Paul makes contradictory statements, but *how it was possible* for him to do so" (256).

70. "Paul and 'Covenantal Nomism,'" in *Paul and Paulinism*, Festschrift C. K. Barrett, eds. M. D. Hooker and S. G. Wilson (London: SPCK, 1982) 47-56, here 52. Hooker has more than once been quoted as though she equated Paul's Christianity with a covenantal nomism.

characterized as a nomist (cf. Gal 3:1-5). He has in a fundamental way broken with the law,[71] and hence with Judaism.[72]

5.5. That brings us finally to the vexed question of the meaning of "works of the law" in Paul. The attempt to avoid a negation of the law on Paul's part makes necessary a re-understanding of this phrase as referring to something other than the performance of the law itself. Already in 1975 Daniel P. Fuller, in pursuit of the unity of the testaments, argued that "works of the law" referred to a legalistic distortion of the law on the part of the Judaizers.[73] The recent attempts of a number of scholars to understand the phrase as referring to "boundary markers" or the specific indicators of Jewish distinctiveness has essentially the same motivation. This is indeed a key element in the new perspective on Paul as defended particularly by Dunn.

This understanding of "works of the law" has not been without its share of critics. In the informative "Additional Notes" to the relevant chapters (8 and 9), Dunn responds in turn to the criticisms of Räisänen, Hübner, Stuhlmacher, Sanders, Bruce, Schreiner, Fung, and Westerholm.[74] More recently, in a separate article, he responds to the criticisms of C. E. B. Cranfield.[75] It is impossible here to review these discussions in any detail, and we shall content ourselves with noting a couple of common motifs in the objections and a few additional observations.

It is a frequent, and to my mind justifiable, objection among these writers that in Paul's soteriological arguments works of the law and gospel are antithetical and that one aspect of the good news of the gospel is that it involves a break with the law, and hence that Paul's Christianity includes a break with Judaism. This of course amounts to a denial of the

---

71. So rightly Räisänen, who notes that "The real difference between Dunn and me (and Sanders) is not the assessment of the social function of the law but the question of whether or not Paul criticized the *law as such and as a whole* or just the law as viewed from a limited perspective" (*Paul and the* Law, xxx). For a particularly strong statement concerning Paul's rejection of the law, see R. G. Hamerton-Kelly, "Sacred Violence and 'Works of Law': Is Christ Then an Agent of Sin?'" (Galatians 2:17)," *CBQ* 52 (1990) 55-75. See now too, his *Sacred Violence: Paul's Hermeneutic of the Cross* (Minneapolis: Fortress, 1992).

72. See especially Räisänen, "Galatians 2.16 and Paul's Break with Judaism," *NTS* 31 (1985) 543-53.

73. "Paul and 'The Works of the Law,'" *WTJ* 38 (1975-76) 28-42.

74. See *Jesus, Paul and the Law*, 206-14; 237-41.

75. Cranfield, "'The Works of the Law' in the Epistle to the Romans," *JSNT* 43 (1991) 89-101; Dunn, "Yet Once More—'The Works of the Law': A Response," *JSNT* 46 (1992) 99-117.

new perspective at its very center. A further point is that Paul's argument is not simply against the so-called boundary markers, but refers to the entirety of the law (a point admitted by Dunn). Dunn consistently faults his critics for failing to appreciate the social function of the law, by which he appears to mean failing to explain "works of the law" solely in terms of social boundary markers.

Now it can hardly be denied that Dunn's fundamental point is true. The law does play a socially determinative role in its boundary markers separating Jew from Gentile, and Paul would have used all resources at his disposal to argue against wrong soteriological inferences from this.[76] But the fact that there was such a social aspect involving such boundary markers does not warrant reducing the entirety of Paul's polemic against the law to this one single point. Precisely because the law was what distinguished the Jew from the Gentile, the boasting which Paul attacks can be explained as boasting in national privileges. That, however, is not a necessary explanation of the relevant Pauline texts; it remains possible that Paul attacks a legalistic boasting. Gundry's conclusion is correct: "The use of the law to establish one's own righteousness is what Paul finds wrong in Palestinian Judaism, including his past life."[77] For all its undeniable truth, one may wonder whether the view of works of the law as badges of national identity really provides the best explanation of all the data.[78]

---

76. I do not see that a full admission of this point can help bring the two sides together (the old and new perspectives on Paul) into some kind of blend, as the irenically-minded Bruce Longenecker would have it, nor do I understand why Longenecker describes himself as an advocate of the new perspective when he seems to accept the essentials of the so-called Lutheran understanding of Paul and the law. See his *The Triumph of Abraham's God: The Transformation of Identity in Galatians* (Edinburgh: T. & T. Clark, 1998) 76-77, 179-83; and "Lifelines: Perspectives on Paul and the Law," *Anvil* 1 (1999) 125-30. Note especially his statement that there are Pauline passages (e.g., Rom 4:4-5; 9:32; 11:5-6) "where Paul does seem to suggest that nomistic observance can be a form of legalism." "Contours of Covenant Theology in the Post-Conversion Paul," in *The Road from Damascus. The Impact of Paul's Conversion on His Life, Thought, and Ministry*, ed. Richard N. Longenecker (Grand Rapids: Eerdmans, 1997) 125-46, here 140.

77. "Grace, Works, and Staying Saved," 16. At the end of his article, Gundry states that it was "because of a conviction that works-righteousness lay at the heart of Judaism and Judaistic Christianity" that Paul rejected them (37-38).

78. In addition to the literature mentioned above in note 63, among the ever-burgeoning literature on the subject the following may also be noted: E. P. Sanders, "On the Question of Fulfilling the Law in Paul and Rabbinic Judaism," in *Donum Gentilicium*, Festschrift D. Daube, eds. E. Bammel et al. (Oxford: Clarendon, 1978) 103-26; (R. Smend) and U. Luz, *Gesetz* (Stuttgart: Kohlhammer, 1981) 45-144; the following three articles in the same volume: W. D. Davies, "Paul and the Law: Reflections

on Pitfalls in Interpretation" (4-16); U. Wilckens, "Statements on the Development of Paul's View of the Law" (17-26); and F. F. Bruce, "The Curse of the Law" (27-36), in *Paul and Paulinism*, Festschrift C. K. Barrett, ed. M. D. Hooker and S. G. Wilson (London: SPCK, 1982); D. Moo, "'Law,' 'Works of the Law,' and Legalism in Paul," *WTJ* 45 (1983) 73-100; N. M. Watson, "Justified by Faith, Judged by Works—An Antinomy?" *NTS* 29 (1983) 209-21; T. R. Schreiner, "Is Perfect Obedience to the Law Possible? A Re-Examination of Galatlans 3:10," *JETS* 27 (1984) 151-60; T. R. Schreiner, "Paul and Perfect Obedience to the Law: An Evaluation of the View of E. P. Sanders," *WTJ* 47 (1985) 245-78; B. Reicke, "Paulus über das Gesetz," *ThZ* 41 (1985) 237-57; P. Stuhlmacher, "Paul's Understanding of the Law in the Letter to the Romans," *SEÅ* 50 (1985) 87-104; H. Hübner, "Was heißt bei Paulus 'Werke des Gesetzes'?" in *Glaube und Eschatologie*, Festschrift W. C. Kummel, eds. E. Gräßer and O. Merk (Tübingen: Mohr Siebeck, 1985) 123-33; H. Räisäinen, *The Torah and Christ: Essays in German and English on the Problem of the Law in Early Christianity* (Helsinki: Finnish Exegetical Society, 1986); T. L. Donaldson, "The 'Curse of the Law' and the Inclusion of the Gentiles: Galatians 3.13-14," *NTS* 32 (1986) 94-112; J. Lambrecht, "Gesetzesverständnis bei Paulus," in *Das Gesetz im Neuen Testament*, ed. K. Kertelge (Freiburg: Herder, 1986) 88-127; K. R. Snodgrass, "Justification by Grace—to the Doers: An Analysis of the Place of Romans 2 in the Theology of Paul," *NTS* 32 (1986) 72-93; C. H. Cosgrove, "Justification in Paul: A Linguistic and Theological Reflection," *JBL* 106 (1987) 653-70; T. D. Gordon, "The Problem at Galatia," *Int* 41(1987) 32-43; K. R. Snodgrass, "Spheres of Influence: A Possible Solution to the Problem of Paul and the Law," *JSNT* 32 (1988) 93-113; B. L. Martin, *Christ and the Law in Paul*, NovTSup 62 (Leiden: Brill, 1989); F. Thielman, *From Plight to Solution: A Jewish Framework for Understanding Paul's View of the Law in Galatians and Romans*, NovTSup 61 (Leiden: Brill, 1989); T. L. Donaldson, "Zealot and Convert: The Origin of Paul's Christ-Torah Antithesis," *CBQ* 51(1989) 655-82; T. R. Schreiner, "The Abolition and Fulfillment of the Law in Paul," *JSNT* 35 (1989) 47—74; R. G. Hamerton-Kelly, "Sacred Violence and 'Works of Law.' 'Is Christ Then an Agent of Sin?' (Galatians 2:17)," *CBQ* 52 (1990) 55-75; C. D. Stanley, "'Under a Curse': A Fresh Reading of Galatians 3.10-14," *NTS* 36 (1990) 481-511; J. A. D. Weima, "The Function of the Law in Relation to Sin: An Evaluation of the View of H. Räisänen," *NovT* 32 (1990) 219-35; P. Richardson, S. Westerhoim et al., *Law in Religious Communities in the Roman Period: The Debate Over Torah and Nomos in Post-Biblical Judaism and Early Christianity*, Studies in Christianity and Judaism 4 (Waterloo, ON: Wilfrid Laurier University Press, 1991); D. B. Garlington, *"The Obedience of Faith": A Pauline Phrase in Historical Context*, WUNT 2/38 (Tübingen: Mohr Siebeck, 1991); D. B. Garlington, "The Obedience of Faith in the Letter to the Romans," *WTJ* 52 (1990) 201-24; 53 (1991) 47-52; J. P. Braswell, "'The Blessing of Abraham' Versus 'The Curse of the Law': Another Look at Gal 3:10-13," *WTJ* 53 (1991) 73-91; T. R. Schreiner, "'Works of Law' in Paul," *NovT* 33 (1991) 217-44; R. B. Sloan, "Paul and the Law: Why the Law Cannot Save," *NovT* 33 (1991) 35-60; Hermann Lichtenberger, "Paulus und das Gesetz," in *Paulus und das antike Judentum*, WUNT 58 (Tübingen: Mohr Siebeck, 1991) 361-78; J. D. G. Dunn, "What Was the Issue Between Paul and 'Those of the Circumcision'?," in the preceding volume, 295-318; N. T. Wright, *The Climax of the Covenant: Christ and the Law in Pauline Theology* (Minneapolis: Fortress, 1992); H. Boers, "'We Who Are by Inheritance Jews; Not From the Gentiles, Sinners,'" *JBL* 111 (1992) 273-81; F. Thielman, "The Coherence of Paul's View of the Law," *NTS* 38 (1992) 235-53; J. M. Scott, "'For as Many as are of Works of the Law Are under a Curse' (Galatians 3.10)," in *Paul and the Scriptures of Israel*, ed. C. A. Evans and J. A. Sanders, SSEJC 1 (Sheffield: Academic, 1993) 187-221; *Paul and the Mosaic Law*, ed. J.

5.6. This is not the place to argue against the two-covenant theory concerning the salvation of the Jews and the Gentiles.[79] As we have noted earlier, not all advocates of the newer approach to Paul hold to this view. Here I refer only to a significant article by Sanders in which, critiquing the views of Stendahl, he argues that according to Paul Torah obedience is not "the necessary or sufficient condition of salvation" for Israel, and that when Paul envisages the salvation of Israel, he has no other way in mind than "the requirement of faith in Christ."[80] Sanders himself dissents from this viewpoint, but he is fair enough to indicate what Paul's view was. For Paul, Christ was not merely one event in a series of salvation-historical events.[81] Those who agree with Paul here, I hasten to add, must oppose anti-Semitism with all the strength available to them.

6. The ultimate test of the new perspective on Paul is how well it can explain all the pertinent texts. Proponents of the new perspective, like those of the old perspective (if we may call it that), must not only occupy themselves with texts that seem to support their views, but also explain those that seem to go against them.[82] Those who are unconvinced by the new perspective, must be able to handle such texts as Rom 2:6-10, 13-16; 3:31; and 8:3-4. Supporters of the new perspective have to explain such texts as Rom 3:20, 28; 4:4-6; 5:20;11:6; and Gal 2:16; 3:10-14, and convince us that "works of the law" in every case refers only to boundary markers and the social function of the law. Dunn has of course addressed these texts in his various articles, his Romans and Galatians commentaries,

---

D. G. Dunn (Tübingen: Mohr Siebeck, 1996; reprint, Grand Rapids: Eerdmans, 2000).

79. See Kai Kjær-Hansen, "The Problem of the Two-Covenant Theology," *Mishkan* 21 (1994) 52-81.

80. "Paul's Attitude Toward the Jewish People," *USQR* 33 (1978) 175-87, here 184. The article is followed by "A Response" from Krister Stendahl, 189-91. See especially the excellent articles of R. Hvalvik, "A 'Sonderweg' for Israel: A Critical Examination of a Current Interpretation of Romans 11, 25-27," *JSNT* 38 (1990) 87-107; and Scott Hafemann, "The Salvation of Israel in Romans 11:25-32: A Response to Krister Stendahl," *Ex Auditu* 4 (1988) 38-58.

81. Cf. D. C. Allison Jr.: "The NT nowhere holds that salvation is to be found apart from Jesus, the Messiah and Son of God. Although this may ride roughshod over our modern sensibilities, it remains no less true. The NT does not know two ways of salvation — one in Jesus, one apart from him" ("Jesus and the Covenant: A Response to E. P. Sanders," *JSNT* 29 [1987] 57-78, here 74). See too Räisänen, *Paul and the Law*, xxiv.

82. Silva calls for a closer examination of a number of texts by Dunn, adding that "no explanation of Paul's theology can prove ultimately persuasive if it does not arise from the very heart of Paul's explicit affirmations and denials" ("The Law and Christianity," 353).

and in the exchange with Cranfield referred to above.[83] It will naturally be a matter of opinion as to which view in the end does the best justice to the texts. The discussion seems destined to go on for yet some time.

7. The new perspective on Paul has been effectively argued by its most able proponent, J. D. G. Dunn. Taking the groundwork laid by Sanders and giving full due to the social situation of the early church, Dunn has been able to provide a remarkably cohesive explanation of the texts in which Paul addresses the issue of the law. It cannot reasonably be in question that Paul disapproved of viewing the law as a boundary marker of Jewish righteousness over against the Gentiles. Paul *does* do away with Jewish privileges and the Jewish/Gentile distinction so far as salvation is concerned. This was clearly of supreme importance to the success of the Gentile mission to which he had been called. It is precisely because this is important in the Pauline texts that Dunn's case can be as strong as it is. Many of us continue to wonder, however, whether this is *all* Paul fights against in his polemic against the law and whether the improper "boasting" he opposes does not involve something else equally serious, if not more so. In some of us there lingers the feeling that in a number of instances Paul seems to have picked a strange way of arguing—a way that must be regarded as indirect and misleading—if he is concerned *solely* about the national distinctives and privileges of Israel, and nothing more.

To be fair to Dunn, he does state unequivocally that his main contention concerning boundary markers does not cancel out the importance of the Protestant doctrine of justification by faith.[84] My impression, however, is that the emphasis on boundary markers or national righteousness

---

83. Dunn summarizes his differences with Cranfield as centering on two key issues: (1) "Did Paul accuse his fellow Jews of seeking to earn salvation by works of the law, or of seeking to preserve their covenantal privileges as God's righteous ones (over against Gentile sinners) by works of the law?" and (2) "Did Paul think the law could not be obeyed and that Israel's fault was in assuming that it could? Or did he think that Israel was going about obeying the law in the wrong way, by treating the realm of righteousness as exclusively Jewish territory (marked out by works of the law), and thereby failing to recognize the seriousness of their sin and that they (as much as any Gentile) fell under the law's curse?" In both instances, Cranfield opts for the first alternative, Dunn for the second (cf. "Yet Once More—'The Works of the Law,'" 116).

84. See, e.g., "The Justice of God," 2, 21. I do not understand Dunn's praise of the Reformation doctrine of justification by faith as "a restatement of central biblical insights of incalculable influence and priceless value" (2), when his approach explains the pertinent passages in a quite different way. I also find it difficult to understand J. Ziesler's claim that justification by faith can be preserved in the new perspective as an analogy. See "Justification by Faith in the Light of the 'New Perspective' on Paul," *Theology* 94 (1991) 188-94.

in fact pushes justification by faith very much to the periphery, making it pertinent only to the Gentiles. The problem is a bigger one than simply holding the two emphases in balance. Despite Dunn's claim, I do not see how his approach can do anything but take all vitality out of the doctrine.

That some valid insights have emerged in the new perspective on Paul I do not wish to deny. I find myself doubtful, however, that the new perspective itself constitutes a major breakthrough to a truer estimate of Paul and Judaism. This Copernican revolution is taking us down the wrong path.

11

Paul's Christology and Jewish Monotheism

THE APOSTLE PAUL DESCRIBES himself as possessing the fullest Jewish pedigree (Phil 3:4-6; cf. Acts 22:3) and regards his gospel as nothing less than the fulfillment of the hope of Israel as contained in the Old Testament Scriptures (cf. Rom 15:8). At the same time, as is well known, he was a diaspora Jew, deeply Hellenized, and a Roman citizen who was equally well at home in the Greco-Roman world of his day. Pauline scholarship has continued to debate whether Paul's theology is to be understood primarily in light of his Jewish or his Greek background.[1] Although it cannot be denied that both backgrounds are important and helpful in understanding Paul, to my mind Paul's Jewish background is by far the more determinative for his theology.[2]

Many Jewish scholars as well as radical-critical Christian scholars regard Paul as the virtual creator of Christianity. To the degree that his theology is thought to be incompatible with or disloyal to Judaism, these scholars appeal to the influence of pagan Greek ideas upon his thought.[3]

---

1. The alternative is clearly posed by Leander E. Keck in *Paul and His Letters*, 2nd ed. (Philadelphia: Fortress, 1988). Scripture citations in this essay are translated directly from the Greek text.

2. This is a conclusion I cannot defend here. I find convincing the arguments of W. D. Davies, *Paul and Rabbinic Judaism*, 4th ed. (Philadelphia: Fortress, 1980), and more recently, J. C. Beker, *Paul the Apostle* (Philadelphia: Fortress, 1980).

3. There is, however, a modern trend among Jewish scholars to reclaim even Paul for Judaism. I have documented this in "Paul in Modern Jewish Study" in *Pauline Studies: Essays Presented to F. F. Bruce*, ed. Donald A. Hagner and Murray J. Harris (Grand

This is especially the case with regard to Paul's "high" Christology. Is not that very Christology an insuperable argument against the fundamental Jewishness of Paul's theology? How can a Jew, particularly one who allegedly remained faithful to his Jewish convictions, have held the view of Jesus that he did? Is not Paul's Christology incompatible with the monotheism of his forefathers?

To answer these questions it will be necessary to look in turn at the content of Paul's Christology, at Jewish monotheism, and at Paul's monotheistic texts, and finally to make some comments on the nature and complexity of Paul's Christology. The focus will be on what Paul himself has to say, with the goal of arriving at a better understanding of his Christology and thus of his theology as a whole. Because the problem in view is not Paul's alone, the discussion will broaden toward the end of the essay to include the Christology of the New Testament writers generally.

I.

That Paul's theology is Christocentric becomes readily apparent from the sheer mass of material that may be designated Christological.[4] It is of course impossible to give a complete survey of that material in an article of this length. Instead, we present a review of elements of Paul's Christology that are of key importance to the subject under discussion.

The elements of Paul's Christology, like that of the New Testament itself, can be analyzed as constituting a continuum. That continuum moves from, on the one hand, the view of Jesus as one sent by God though even here he is never one among others whom God has sent, but a unique one who can be described as the supreme Agent of God—to one who, on the other hand, is to be put with God over against all else that exists, one who is somehow the very manifestation of God himself. Indeed, it is perhaps just because of the things that can be said of Jesus as God's Agent that the continuum extends as far as it does to include Jesus as God. Thus, although the two categories are hardly distinct and inevitably overlap, we will look first at Jesus as God's Agent and then at Jesus as God.

Rapids: Eerdmans, 1980) 143-65.

4. It is also true that there are distinctly theocentric aspects to Paul's thought. This merely serves to highlight the problem before us.

Jesus as God's Agent

For some scholars all of Paul's Christology can be categorized under this rubric.[5] It cannot be denied that most of Paul's Christology fits this classification, nor is the richness of this material to be doubted.

At the outset it is also worth emphasizing that the real and full humanity of Jesus was for Paul a given. It was a man who had been crucified and who had risen from the dead (cf. Rom 5:15-19; 1 Cor 15:21, 47; Phil 2:7). This fact has its inevitable effect on Paul's Christological thinking and language. We begin with the observation that Paul can at times use adoptionist sounding language. Thus, in the well-known passage Rom 1:3-4, he refers to Jesus as "descended from David according to the flesh and designated Son of God in power according to the Spirit of holiness by his resurrection from the dead." The implied, simple, two-stage Christology would seem ideal for Jewish-Christians, including Paul, and it may well represent the most primitive Christology of the early Jerusalem church (cf. Acts 2:36; 3:22-26; cf. also the use of Ps 2:7 in Acts 13:33). Paul's language in this passage, however, probably does not reflect a strict two-stage adoptionist Christology. The beginning of v. 3 indicates that it is God's Son who was born of the seed of David. Thus the passage could represent only the second and third parts of what may in reality be a three-stage Christology. The three-stage Christology of the hymn in Phil 2:5-11 can also sound adoptionist (see v. 9).[6]

Paul refers to Jesus as one *sent by God*. The two main passages here are Gal 4:4 and Rom 8:3, where in both instances it is God's Son who is sent forth. The sending language alone does not guarantee the preexistence of the Son.[7] Despite Dunn's arguments to the contrary,[8] however, both passages probably assume a three-stage Christology. This is clearer in the Romans passage than it is in the Galatians passage, despite the words in the latter, "when the time had fully come." When Paul writes, "sending his own Son in the likeness of sinful flesh (*en homoiōmati sarkos*

---

5. James D. G. Dunn, for example, argues that Paul does not teach the preexistence, incarnation, or deity (at least in the traditional sense) of Jesus. *Christology in the Making* (Philadelphia: Westminster, 1980) 211-12

6. Dunn denies a three-stage Christology (i.e., including preexistence) in the Phil 2 hymn, but his arguments have not persuaded many. What is interesting is that the argument can be made so effectively at all. *Christology in the Making*, 114-21.

7. See Dunn, who refers to two groups sent forth by God: heavenly beings and human messengers. *Christology in the Making*, 38-39.

8. Dunn, *Christology in the Making*, 38-46.

harmartias)," he probably reflects the perspective of a three-stage Christology, such as is contained in the hymn of Philippians 2 (cf. Phil 2:7, "being born in the likeness of men" [*en homoiōmati anthrōpōn genomenos*]).

One of the most striking of Paul's Christological passages, and one that clearly points to Christ as God's Agent, is that of 2 Cor 5:19, "in Christ God was reconciling the world to himself." The reconciliation that is the message of the Gospel is the work of God accomplished "in Christ (*en Christō*)" or "through Christ (*dia Christou*)," as it is also put in v. 18. The first of these prepositional phrases occurs often in the Pauline letters in describing God's accomplishment of his saving purposes through the agency of Christ. By way of example, note "in Christ" in passages such as Rom 3:24–25; 6:23; 1 Cor 15:22; 2 Cor 2:14; [Eph 4:32],[9] where God acts in Christ to accomplish something. The more obvious "through Christ" (or with the pronoun, "through him"), with God as the assumed acting subject, occurs (in addition to 2 Cor 5:18) in Rom 2:16; 5:21; 1 Cor 8:6; 15:57; Col 1:16, 20; and 1 Thess 4:14 ("through Jesus"). The ubiquitous occurrence in the Pauline letters of "through Christ" in reference to what Christians are enabled to do or get is in reality only the obverse of this. That is, Christ is the means and thus used by God—whereby humanity can appropriate the benefits of God's salvific work.

So indispensable is the agency of Christ in the accomplishment of God's work that the name of Jesus Christ becomes regularly and naturally associated with God. In the salutations of the letters we encounter regularly the formula, "Grace to you and peace from God our Father and the Lord Jesus Christ" (Rom 1:7; 1 Cor 1:3; 2 Cor 1:2; Gal 1:3; [Eph 1:2]; Phil 1:2; 2 Thess 1:2; Phlm 3). Even where the formula is lacking, the association can be present (2 Cor 13:14; [Eph 6:23]), or there is simply reference to the grace of Jesus Christ (e.g., 1 Cor 16:23; Gal 6:18; Phil 4:23; 1 Thess 5:28). There are places, moreover, where the names are closely associated in the body of the letters, beyond the constant reference involved specifically in agency (e.g., 1 Thess 3:11; 2 Thess 2:16).

The titles "Messiah" and "Son of God" occur most often in contexts where the unique agency of Jesus is in view. For Paul, of course, "Christ" is used almost exclusively as a proper name rather than as a title (for a probable exception, see Rom 9:5), although there are times when the titular aspect of the name may also be in Paul's mind (e.g., 1 Cor 1:23–24).[10]

---

9. Because some question the Pauline authorship of Ephesians, references to Ephesians in this essay are placed in brackets.

10. Oscar Cullmann notes that the titular aspect may also be in Paul's mind when

Paul's reference to Jesus as "the Son of God" is much less frequent and has primarily in view agency rather than the ontology of Jesus' person (Rom 5:10; 8:32; and the sending passages noted above, Rom 8:3 and Gal 4:4).[11]

In his role as the unique Agent of God, it is clear that Jesus functions on behalf of God, i.e., in God's place. We may conveniently summarize this under the words *creation* (1 Cor 8:6; Col 1:16), *redemption-salvation* (Rom 3:24; 5:9-10, 18; 1 Cor 1:30; Col 1:14; 1Thess 5:9; cf. Phil 3:20, *judgment* (1 Co 4:5; 11:32; 2 Cor 5:10; [Eph 6:8]), and *eschatological restoration* (1Th 1:10; 4:15-17; 1Co 15:22; Col. 3:4). All of these items are also associated directly with God, and such references are of course more abundant. But one who is said to function as God in these and other ways, one who is thus like no other Agent ever used by God, one who is uniquely associated with God, can begin to be thought of as one who somehow manifests the very presence of God.

The "gospel of God" (Rom 1:1; 15:16; 1 Thess 2:2, 8-9) can at the same time be called the "gospel of Christ" (Rom 15:19; 1 Cor 9:12; Gal 1:7; Phil 1:27; 1 Thess 3:2; 2 Thess 1:8). The "love of God" (Rom 5:5; 2 Cor 13:13) is also the "love of Christ" (Rom 8:35; 2 Cor 5:14; [Eph 3:19]). The "grace of God" (Rom 5:15; 1 Cor 3:10; 2 Cor 1:12; 6:1; 8:1; et al.) becomes also "the grace of our Lord Jesus Christ" (2 Cor 8:9, and often in the concluding benedictions in Paul's letters). There is of course more of this type of material than can be tabulated here.[12] The point to be made, however, is the ready application of the same language to God and to Jesus.

A further and important element in Paul's Christology is what C. F. D. Moule has called the "understanding and experience of Christ as corporate."[13] In view here are the remarkable ways Paul (and the Fourth

---

he reverses the usual order of the names and writes "Christ Jesus." *Christology of the New Testament*, trans. S. C. Guthrie and C. A. M. Hall (Philadelphia: Westminster, 1963) 134. See also Martin Hengel, "'Christos' in Paul," in his collection of essays *Between Jesus and Paul* (Philadelphia: Fortress, 1983) 65-77.

11. Hengel, however, concludes that for Paul the "Son of God" title indicates that Christ "is identical with a divine being, before all time, mediator between God and his creatures." *The Son of God* (Philadelphia: Fortress, 1976) 15.

12. R. T. France points out similar correspondences between "the kingdom of God" (Col 4:11) and the "kingdom of his son" (Col 1:13), "the Spirit of God" and "the Spirit of Jesus Christ" (both in Rom 8:9), and "the churches of God" (1 Cor 11:16; 1 Thess 2:14) and "the churches of Christ" (Rom 16:16) ("The Worship of Jesus: A Neglected Factor in Christological Debate?" in *Christ the Lord: Studies in Christology Presented to Donald Guthrie*, Harold Hamlyn Rowdon, ed. [Leicester, UK: Intervarsity, 1982], 31-32).

13. *The Origin of Christology* (Cambridge: Cambridge University Press, 1977) 47.

Gospel) can speak of the believer's relation to Christ, particularly being "in Christ" (a favorite Pauline idiom), Christ's indwelling of believers, and the metaphor of the church as "the body of Christ." The Adam Christology of Rom 5:12-21 and 1 Cor 15:21-22, 45-49, with its corporate basis, also comes into view here.[14] That these things can be said with respect to an individual person who had recently appeared in history is astonishing. As Moule puts it, "A person who had recently been crucified, but is found to be alive, with 'absolute' life, the life of the age to come, and is found, moreover, to be an inclusive, all-embracing presence—such a person is beginning to be described in terms appropriate to nothing less than God."[15]

We turn now to Paul's belief in the preexistence of Christ,[16] which is discussed still under the heading of the Agent of God because preexistence need not entail the conclusion that Jesus was actually God.[17] The rabbis spoke of several things as preexisting the world, that is, created before the world.[18] Far more significant for the Christology of Paul and that of other New Testament writers is the background of preexistent Wisdom. New Testament scholars increasingly appeal to Wisdom as one of the important factors, if not the most important, that enabled New Testament Christology to become what it is. What is said of Wisdom in such passages as Prov 8:22-31, Sir 24, and Wis 6-9 is very similar to what Paul says about Christ. Although the conclusion has recently been

---

14. Herman N. Ridderbos puts very great emphasis on the determinative importance of this view of Christ as the Second Adam for the formation of Paul's Christology. *Paul: An Outline of His Theology* (Grand Rapids: Eerdmans, 1975) esp. 77-78.

15. *The Origin of Christology*, 53. We are driven, writes Moule, to ask, "Who is this, who can be understood in much the same terms as a theist understands God himself— as personal, indeed, but more than individual?," 87.

16. See Robert G. Hamerton-Kelly, *Pre-Existence, Wisdom, and the Son of Man*, SNTSMS 21 (Cambridge: Cambridge University Press, 1973) 103-96; Adolf von Harnack's appendix "On the Conception of Pre-Existence," in *History of Dogma*, trans. N. Buchanan, 7 vols. (New York: Dover, 1961) 1:318-31; Reginald H. Fuller, "Pre-Existence Christology: Can We Dispense With It?" *Word & World* 2 (1982) 29-33.

17. A. E. Harvey makes this point emphatically (*Jesus and the Constraints of History* [Philadelphia: Westminster, 1982] 177-78).

18. "Seven things were created before the world was created, these they are: the Torah, repentance, the Garden of Eden, Gehenna, the Throne of Glory, the Temple and the name of the Messiah." Babylonian Talmud Pesahim 54a. As Alan Segal points out, "the corner toward pre-existence of the messiah was turned by suggesting that God knew the messiah's name from creation" ("Pre-Existence and Incarnation: A Response to Dunn and Holladay," in *Christology and Exegesis: New Approaches*, ed. Robert Jewett *Semeia* 30 [1985] 93).

challenged,[19] Paul almost certainly held a three-stage Christology—that is, one that included the preexistence of Christ. This seems clearest in the Christ-hymn of Phil 2:5-11, in which v. 6a is most naturally read as referring to Christ's existence prior to his "being born in the likeness of men" (v. 7c).[20] Christ's role in the Creation, according to Paul, also points to his preexistence (Col 1:16; 1 Cor 8:6). As supportive of these clearer passages, we may mention Paul's statement concerning Christ, that unlike the first Adam, "the second man is from heaven" (1 Cor 15:47; further possibilities to be considered are 1 Cor 10:4; Rom 8:3; and Gal 4:4).[21]

The material surveyed thus far has its focus in Jesus as one who functions on behalf of God. But such is the uniqueness of this incomparably supreme Agent in the accomplishment of God's will and especially his saving purposes, that it is no exaggeration to say that he functions as God. It is well known that most of the Christology of Paul, like that of the New Testament generally, is functional rather than ontological in character.[22] But function, especially the over-loaded kind in this instance, cannot help but imply ontology. What can be, what must be, said of an agent such as this? Does Paul's functional Christology ineluctably move to ontological assertions about the deity of Jesus?

Jesus as God

We may begin with a look at one of the most frequent titles Paul uses in referring to Jesus, one we have not yet mentioned. Whatever *kyrios* may be taken to mean at different points in the Gospels, as used by Paul it means "Lord," that is, it connotes deity. To confess Jesus as Lord (cf. Rom 10:9; 1 Cor 12:3) is to put him together with God as one who is

---

19. Dunn, *Christology in the Making*, 255.

20. Cf. Ralph P. Martin's treatment of v. 6a under the heading, "The Pre-Existent Being," in *Carmen Christi* (Grand Rapids: Eerdmans, 1983 ed. of 1967 original) 99-133.

21. Vincent Taylor, commenting on 1 Cor 15:47, writes: "Christ is not the Last Adam because He is divine: He is the Last Adam and therefore divine. Divinity is the inevitable attribute of His person and work" (*The Names of Jesus* [London: Macmillan, 1954] 155).

22. In his masterly survey, Cullmann concluded that the New Testament generally contains only functional Christology. *Christology of the New Testament*, 326. Strictly speaking this may be correct. But it is wrong to overlook the ontological implications of this functional Christology. Although Paul, for example, may not have been concerned with ontology per se, he may still have made statements or used terminology having ontological significance.

sovereign and transcendent, to make him practically equal to God.²³ For Paul, Jesus is one no less than "the Lord of glory" (1 Cor 2:8), the one who can be described as "Lord both of the dead and of the living" (Rom 14:9), "a life-giving spirit" (1 Cor 15:45; cf. Rom 4:17) This exaltation of Jesus is not original with Paul, but marks the faith of the church from the beginning (cf. Acts 2:36). Paul's encounter with the risen Christ on the road to Damascus confirmed to Paul beyond any shadow of doubt that Jesus was the *kyrios*.

What is particularly revealing about the term *kyrios* is the fact that the Septuagint, the Greek translation of the Old Testament made by Jews and completed before the Christian era, used it to translate the tetragrammaton *YHWH*, Yahweh—the name of God introduced to Moses in Exod 3:13ff. This opened the door for the early church to identify Jesus with Yahweh where appropriate, and the writers of the New Testament were not slow to enter that door. Thus Paul can at the end of the Christhymn, which he probably borrowed from his predecessors in Christ, include the words: "Therefore God has highly exalted him and bestowed on him the name which is above every name, that at the name of Jesus every knee should bow, in heaven and on earth and under the earth, and every tongue confess that Jesus Christ is Lord, to the glory of God the Father" (Phil 2:9-11). But in Isa 45:23, the passage alluded to here, it is Yahweh who is the speaker, who identifies himself as God (Isa 45:22), and to whom every knee shall bow and every tongue confess. Similarly, the Old Testament quotations in Rom 10:11 (Isa 28:16) and 10:13 (Joel 2:32) are applied to Jesus, whereas in fact they speak of Yahweh (in the first instance of Adonai Yahweh, which the RSV translates "Lord God").²⁴

Further to be considered for their ontological implications are Paul's descriptions of Jesus using such language as the following: "He is the image [*eikōn*], of the invisible God" (Col 1:15), and "in him all the fullness of God was pleased to dwell" (Col 1:19), or even more strikingly, "in him all the whole fullness of deity [*pan to plērōma tēs theotētos*] dwells bodily [*sōmatikōs*]" (Col 2:9). As we have already noted, in the Christ-hymn Paul speaks of Christ as being "in the form [*morphē*] of God" (Phil 2:6).

---

23. With regard to the confession of Jesus as Lord, Taylor concludes: "Invocation is next door to prayer and confession to worship. Implicit in the recognition of the lordship of Jesus is the acknowledgment of His essential divinity" (*The Names of Jesus*, 51).

24. R. de Lacey also calls attention to 2 Thess 1:8-10 (cf. also 2 Thess 2:8), where the Lord of v. 9 is Jesus, but the Old Testament texts alluded to refer to God: see his "'One Lord' in Pauline Christology," in *Christ the Lord*, Harold H. Rowdon, ed., 197-98. Cf. Denys E. H. Whiteley, *The Theology of St. Paul* (Philadelphia: Fortress, 1964) 106ff.

In the same passage he indicates that Christ possessed "equality with God [*isa theō*]." Elsewhere, Paul can speak of Christ as "the likeness [*eikōn*] of God" (2 Cor 4:4)[25] and refer to "the light of the knowledge of the glory of God in the face of Christ" (2 Cor 4:6). He speaks too of Christ as "the Lord of glory" (I Cor 2:8) and "Christ the power [*dynamin*] of God and the wisdom [*sophian*] of God" (1 Cor 1:24).

Also significant for our discussion is the fact that Paul can pray to Jesus (cf. 1 Cor 16:22; 1 Thess 3:11; 2 Thess 2:16; 2 Cor 12:8). Passages such as Phil 4:4, "Rejoice in the Lord always," and Col 3:15-17, as well as the Christological benedictions at the end of the letters (noted above) and the centrality of the Lord's Supper in the worship of the early church, together with the singing of Christological hymns (such as Phil 2:6-11; Col 1:15-20; and others like them, of which we have abundant evidence in the New Testament besides in the Pauline letters), point to the place of Jesus in the worship of the Pauline churches. R. T. France concludes his discussion of the subject by noting that there is "convincing evidence that the attitude to Jesus which Paul and his churches shared could fairly be called 'worship.'"[26] In a recent and particularly helpful discussion of our subject, Larry W. Hurtado finds in the "religious devotion" of Christians to Christ the fundamental factor in determining the Christology of the early church in its distinctiveness over against Jewish monotheism.[27]

But granted all this, does Paul in fact ever refer to Jesus explicitly as God? In light of what has been said above, it may seem surprising that this possibility emerges in only a very few instances, and even those are subject to differing interpretations.[28] The most important of these is Rom 9:5, where, to simplify the options, depending on how one punctuates, the doxological utterance refers to Christ as the one "who is God over all, blessed for ever," or begins a new sentence: "God who is over all

---

25. According to Taylor, in referring to Jesus as the image of God, Paul "was attempting to say who Christ is; and his conviction is that he is not merely a reflection of God, but that in Him, so to speak, God comes to light and is expressed" (*The Names of Jesus*, 127).

26. "The Worship of Jesus," 32.

27. He mentions six factors in that early Christian devotion: "(1) hymnic practices, (2) prayer and related practices, (3) use of the name of Christ, (4) the Lord's Supper, (5) confession of faith in Jesus, and (6) prophetic pronouncements of the risen Christ" (*One God, One Lord: Early Christian Devotion and Ancient Jewish Monotheism* [Philadelphia: Fortress, 1988], 100).

28. See Raymond E. Brown, *Jesus, God and Man: Modern Biblical Reflections* (New York: Macmillan, 1967) 1-38; and A. E. Harvey, *Jesus and the Constraints of History*, 176ff.

be blessed for ever." Although the most natural rendering of the Greek favors the former translation,[29] it still remains true that the other is a possibility, and thus the conclusion cannot be beyond question.[30] The only other Pauline text that offers a possible reference to Jesus as God is even less likely. In a formulaic utterance in 2 Thess 1:12 the phrase, "our God and Lord Jesus Christ" is governed in the Greek by one definite article. Ordinarily this would indicate that one person is in view, but in this instance it is possible, and perhaps probable, that two (closely associated) individuals are in view; a third passage, Titus 2:13, is far less ambiguous, where Jesus Christ is referred to as "our great God and Savior."[31] This was probably not written by Paul himself, but as the work of a Pauline disciple it may be taken as fairly representative of Pauline thought.

Far from discouraging us in our quest, the meagerness of these direct references to Jesus as God is just what we might expect under the circumstances. That is, granted the strength of Paul's monotheism (see below) and the uniqueness of what Paul encountered in the person of Christ, it is not at all unusual that he should be slow in being able to refer to Christ as explicitly "God." The fact, however, that such an abundance of material exists that implicitly points to Christ as the unique manifestation of God, makes it possible, perhaps even probable, that Paul could have thought of Jesus as God, without yet being able comfortably to formulate the thought into the corresponding language. The further fact that the possible references that do occur are found in liturgical or formulaic contexts—just as much of the high Christological material considered above is found in hymns—suggests that the Christology of the early church was most naturally expressed in its worship and with a focus on the function of Jesus Christ as God's Agent rather than on questions of ontology. Yet this emphasis inevitably implied certain ontological conclusions. But we must now turn to Paul's monotheism and the tenacity with which he continued to hold to it despite his very high Christology.

---

29. See especially Bruce M. Metzger, "The Punctuation of Rom. 9:5," in *Christ and Spirit in the New Testament, Studies in Honour of C. F. D. Moule*, ed. Barnabas Lindars and Stephen S. Smalley (Cambridge: Cambridge University Press, 1973) 95–112.

30. Among recent commentators who argue against the conclusion that Christ is referred to as God here are Kasemann, Robinson, Wikkens, Harrisville, and Dunn.

31. See Murray J. Harris, "Titus 2:13 and the Deity of Christ," in *Pauline Studies*, 262–77.

II

Paul, or Saul, as he was then called, was brought up as a strict monotheist. Through all of his adult life he said the *Shema* twice daily in accordance with Jewish practice. The fundamental text of the Shema was Deut 6:4-5, which begins, "Hear, O Israel: The LORD our God is one LORD." It would be hard to imagine a more fundamentally important Jewish text than this.[32] The pious Jew hoped to be able at the moment of death to utter this as a creedal statement of his loyalty to the God of Israel. For it was this belief especially that marked off the Jew from the surrounding pagan and idolatrous polytheism.[33]

The uncompromising monotheism of the Jews also characterized the early Jewish Christians[34] and had its predictable effect in the slowness and guardedness with which they articulated their Christology.[35] Despite his high Christology, Paul shows that same concern to protect monotheism. Several passages must be noted here, and as will be seen, they stand in some tension with Paul's Christology as outlined above.

The most striking of Paul's monotheistic texts is found in 1 Cor 8:4-6.[36] After an explicit citation of the beginning of the *Shema* in v. 4, perhaps reflecting the statement of the Corinthians themselves, he writes in v. 6, contrasting the popular belief in many "gods" and "lords": "Yet for us there is one God, the Father, from whom are all things and for whom we exist, and one Lord, Jesus Christ, through whom are all things and through whom we exist" (cf. the related passage in 1 Cor 12:4-6). Here the words "God" and "Father,"[37] as well as the preposition *ek*, "from," in

---

32. See the ninth excursus, on "the Shema," in Hermann L. Strack and Paul Billerbeck, *Kommentar zum Neuen Testament aus Talmud und Midrasch*, 6 vols. (Munich: Beck, 1922-61) 4.1:189-207.

33. Arthur Marmorstein's essay on "The Unity of God in Rabbinic Literature" in his posthumous volume, *Studies in Jewish Theology* (London: Oxford University Press, 1950) 72-105.

34. In the New Testament, in addition to the Pauline passages about to be examined, the Shema' shows its influence in, among other passages, especially Mark 12:29, 32 and Jas 2:19.

35. The primitive character of the Christology reflected in the early chapters of Acts underlines this point. For discussion, see S. S. Smalley, 'The Christology of Acts Again," in *Christ and Spirit in the New Testament*, 79-93.

36. These texts are carefully discussed by Charles H. Giblin in his article, "Three Monotheistic Texts in Paul," *CBQ* 37 (1975) 527-47.

37. The title "Father" is of course always reserved for God himself. The vast majority of Pauline references to God as Father occur in connection with mention of Jesus Christ, who by implication is indicated as the Son, with an implied economical

the sense of source, are reserved for the one God of the *Shema* (the allusion back to v. 4 is unmistakable). Paul refers to Jesus Christ, on the other hand, as "the one Lord," and employs the preposition *dia*, "through," in the sense of agency. The viewpoint is consonant with the agency of Christ in creation according to Col 1:16, which uses both *en autō*, "in (or by) him," as well as *dia*. In the latter passage, however, everything is said to be created *eis auton*, "unto him," a statement our passage makes of the Father rather than of Christ.

Paul leaves unclear what we are to make of the statement that there is one God and one Lord. Although, to be sure, as Giblin rightly points out, Paul is not concerned here with ontological questions,[38] for us his language cannot fail to raise the question of the relation between the two, especially since according to the *Shema*, God is the one Lord. It seems to me that the deity of Christ is an unavoidable conclusion from this passage and yet at the same time that this affirmation is to be maintained within the boundaries of monotheism.[39] If God is the Father (and by implication Jesus is the Son; cf. 1 Cor 1:9), and Jesus Christ is the Agent of God (as the preposition *dia* indicates), then clearly a subordination of economy is assumed—a point that will become clear in 1 Cor 15:28.

A second text where Paul refers to God as "one" is Gal 3:20, where Paul is pointing out the inferiority of the reception of the Law at Sinai "by the hand of a mediator" (Moses) compared with the fulfillment that has come in Jesus Christ. Although we cannot go into the considerable exegetical difficulties presented by this verse, the point seems to be that by contrast with Sinai, in Christ the encounter with God is direct rather than indirect. The effect of the verse is paradoxically to heighten the implied Christology by viewing Christ as directly representing deity. In view, according to Giblin, is "oneness in the sense of a unique, divinely personal *immediacy* of action entailing what may be called the '*im*mediatorship' of Christ."[40] A high agency Christology is entailed—one that in-

---

subordination (as also in the present passage). This is obviously one important way in which Paul distinguishes between God and Jesus.

38. Giblin shows that when seen in the larger context of 1 Cor 8, "Paul's monotheism is personalistic rather than ontological, functional rather than notionally abstract" ("Three Monotheistic Texts," 537).

39. De Lacey comes to the same conclusion in his discussion of 1 Cor 8:6: "From within the security of Jewish monotheism, therefore, Paul was able to see a duality within the Godhead well expressed in the phrase 'one God . . . and one Lord'" ("'One Lord' in Pauline Christology," 202).

40. "Three Monotheistic Texts," 538.

volves unavoidable ontological implications, which, however, Paul does not spell out. Again the emphasis is on function.

A third passage where Paul speaks of the oneness of God is Rom 3:30.[41] Here the affirmation is made in connection with God's salvific work on behalf of both Jew and Gentile. God, the only God, is the God of both Jew and Gentile (cf. v. 29). By implication, there are no other gods. Paul assumes, but does not mention, that Jesus Christ is the unique Agent in the accomplishment of the justification by faith of both Jew and Gentile that is in view here (cf. vv. 22, 24-25, 26).

Yet a fourth passage, which if it is a post-Pauline addition to the text at least represents Pauline tradition, refers to the oneness of God: "to the only wise God be glory for evermore through Jesus Christ" (Rom 16:27). In this instance the adjective *monos*—rather than *heis*—is used, and thus it is unlikely that we have here an allusion to the *Shema*, as in the previous instances. Again, however, where the uniqueness of God is in view, so also Jesus Christ is closely associated with God, and the uniqueness of his agency is stressed. Two references in the deutero-Pauline 1 Timothy also employ *monos* in describing God.[42]

Related to these monotheistic texts are those passages that refer to the subordination of Christ to God. First Corinthians 15:28 is perhaps the most specific of these: "When all things are subjected to him, then the Son himself will also be subjected to him who put all things under him, that God may be everything to every one." This motif is already anticipated earlier in 1 Corinthians, when Paul says that "Christ is God's" (1 Cor 3:23) and that "the head of Christ is God" (1 Co 11:3). It should be noted that these statements refer to the risen and exalted Christ and not simply to the earthly Jesus.

There can be little doubt but that the Pauline material just surveyed results from the continuing strong commitment of Paul to a monotheistic perspective. But how are we to put this together with the very high Christology we have previously found in the Pauline letters? Failure to face the full range of the content of Paul's Christology and to maintain the tension within certain of its elements can lead to Arianism on the

---

41. See Nils A. Dahl, "The One God of Jews and Gentiles (Romans 3:29-30)" in his collected essays, *Studies in Paul: Theology for the Early Christian Mission* (Minneapolis: Augsburg, 1977) 178-91.

42. 1 Tim 1:17 contains a doxology to "the King of the ages, immortal, invisible, the only God." A further doxology in 1 Tim 6:15-16 refers to "the blessed and only Sovereign, the King of kings and Lord of lords, who alone has immortality and dwells in unapproachable light, whom no man has ever seen or can see."

one hand or ditheism on the other. Quite clearly the Christology of Paul involves a complexity that does not lend itself to easy formulas. What finally may we say in analysis of this situation? What explains Paul's insistence upon what seem to us to be apparently contradictory elements in his Christology?

III

Before we attempt to say something in answer to the preceding questions, it is worth pointing out that the problems confronted in Paul's Christology are hardly unique in the New Testament. They are also found particularly in the Fourth Gospel, which, it is widely admitted, contains the highest Christology of the New Testament. Here we may see that our analysis of the Pauline data in all their complexity—and in particular that we have not created an artificial problem by overestimating the Pauline view of Christ—receives a degree of confirmation. There can be no question but that, in addition to the high Christology throughout the Gospel, the Evangelist can refer to Jesus as God quite explicitly (cf. John 1:1, 18 [reading *monogenēs theos*, "the unique God"]; 20:28). At the same time, however, the Evangelist affirms a monotheistic viewpoint (cf. 5:44; 17:3; to which may be added 1:18, "no one has ever seen God," and 8:41, despite the fact that it is spoken by the Jewish opponents of Jesus). As in Paul, Jesus is the supreme Agent of God, but with far more emphasis on his being "sent" by the Father (e.g., 5:23-24, 37; 6:38-39; 12:45, 49; 20:21). Despite the unique relationship between the Father and the Son, which involves an unparalleled oneness of Jesus with God (e.g., 5:18; 10:30),[43] there are also distinct subordinationist notes, in addition to the distinction between the Father and the Son: the Son does only what the Father does (5:36; 10:37; 14:10); the Son speaks only what the Father speaks to him (7:16; 8:28); he came not to do his will, but only that of the One who sent him (6:38); and most strikingly, the statement of 14:28 that "the Father is greater than I." Here we encounter the same complex

---

43. In John 10:33ff. the Evangelist comes close to addressing the problem before us. The Jews were about to stone Jesus "for blasphemy; because you, being a man, make yourself God." Jesus answers with the words, "Is it not written in your law, 'I said, you are gods'?" If the people of Israel can be called "gods" (*elohim*, LXX: *theoi*)—"sons of the Most High," as Ps 82:6 continues—it is not wrong that Jesus be called "the Son of God." The divine claim, however, is hardly thereby turned away. The unique Son of God is also nothing less than God. Thus an apparent consciousness of the problem does not lead to any attempt at its solution.

of elements we encountered in Paul's Christology, with perhaps an even more sharply posed problem. What is particularly interesting is the fact that a Christology that does not shy away from the explicit affirmation of the deity of Christ is at the same time able to put the greatest emphasis on the agency accomplished by the Son on behalf of the Father and to accept the clear subordination of the Son to the Father.

In Paul's Christology, as in that of the Fourth Gospel, we are left with the quandary of an estimate of Jesus Christ that amounts to an affirmation of his deity, but yet with an unflinching commitment to Jewish monotheism that involves the subordination of Christ to God. It remains for us now to make some concluding remarks about this complexity of the Pauline Christology.

1. To begin with, the origin of Paul's Christology, like that of his predecessors in the Christian faith, is to be found in *the uniqueness of this Agent, Jesus the Christ*. Jesus Christ is the Agent of God, quite unlike all other agents of God in the history of salvation. He is, of course, on the one hand, quite like the rest of God's agents (angels excepted) in his full humanity (the confirmation—indeed, the purpose—of which is to be found in his death). Yet as they knew him during his ministry, he was more than a man. No one had spoken as he spoke; no one had done the deeds he did. And in particular, no one had proclaimed with such conviction and reality the dawning of the kingdom of God. Preeminently, however, it was his resurrection as the climactic sign of the establishment of a new order that served as the catalyst for Christological thinking. It was Paul's encounter with the risen Christ on the Damascus road that fundamentally altered his estimate of Jesus[44] and transformed him into the Apostle to the Gentiles. The uniqueness of Jesus Christ in God's salvific activity was unmistakable.

2. In the earliest Christology as also in the Christology of Paul (and indeed most of the New Testament), *the emphasis is on function rather than ontology*. Jesus is the incomparable Agent of God who is so closely associated with God that he acts as only God can act. By articulating the way Christ functions, Paul like his predecessors is virtually driven to affirm the deity of this person. That is, function implies an ontology, even if the ontological implications are not spelled out in so many words.[45] The

---

44. For the extent to which Paul's Christology is dependent on his experience of the risen Christ, see especially Seyoon Kim, *The Origin of Paul's Gospel* (Tübingen: Mohr Siebeck, 1981) 100-268.

45. Whiteley's comment is helpful: "It might be said that he [Paul] came as near

ontological aspect is an inevitability, given the affirmations Paul makes concerning the work of Jesus, past, present, and future. Who is this concerning whom such astonishing statements are made? It is impossible to avoid putting him with God over against all else that exists.

3. A centrally important fact that accounts for the unresolved complexity we have encountered in Paul's Christology is to be found in *the constraint of monotheism*.[46] The natural slowness and reluctance of Paul (and other New Testament writers) to refer to Jesus as God is surely the result of this constraint.[47] It is this, too, that prevents Paul from drawing ontological conclusions otherwise implied by his high Christology. In appealing to the force of this constraint, however, A. E. Harvey goes so far as to deny that the Christology of the New Testament (including that of the Fourth Gospel) can actually have contained the belief that Jesus Christ was "divine."[48] He accordingly attempts to press all the New Testament data into the category of Jesus as Agent. Harvey can show that practically all the Christological language of the New Testament is explainable in this way and need not be taken as indicating the actual deity of Christ.[49] It is tempting to take Harvey's solution to the complexity we have noted above, that is, to reduce all the language of high Christology to the category of unique Agent—especially since, as we have seen, this is the main way in which the New Testament writers conceived of Jesus. But given the full scope of the data of the New Testament, which we have only cursorily reviewed above, such a reductionism does not seem adequate.[50]

---

to asserting a metaphysical equality of community of natures as his non-metaphysical framework of thought permitted him to do" (*The Theology of St. Paul*, 123).

46. A. E. Harvey devotes a chapter to the discussion of this constraint in his stimulating book *Jesus and the Constraints of History*, 140-41.

47. Cf. Richard N. Longenecker, *The Christology of Early Jewish Christianity* (London: SCM, 1970) 140-41.

48. *Jesus and the Constraints of History*, 167.

49. Harvey focuses on the Son of God title, concluding: "To call Jesus Son of God was therefore to accept the claim implied in his words and actions that he was totally obedient to the divine will, that he could give authoritative teaching about God, and that he was empowered to act as God's authorised representative and agent" (ibid., 164).

50. Harvey essentially restricts his discussion to the Son of God title. If he had expanded his field of study to other Christological data, the problem would have emerged more sharply. An indication of this is already apparent when he attempts to apply his thesis to the confession of Thomas in John 20:28, "My Lord and my God!" Harvey at one point can write of the confession that "the presence of Jesus is acknowledged to amount to the presence of God himself" (ibid., 166), but then later he adds an "as if," which to my mind hardly does justice to the intent of the Evangelist: "[Thomas] is portrayed as acknowledging Jesus to be the fully accredited divine agent, to speak to

The nagging question that remains after reading Harvey's discussion is whether the New Testament writers really adhered so closely to the sort of rigid monotheism he is so intent for them to preserve. And if so, why were they not more meticulous in their choice of language? To put the question in another way: if in Jesus Christ they had encountered the Agent of God whose uniqueness was of the staggering character we read of in the New Testament, was it impossible that they could have spoken as they did, i.e., to let function imply ontology, yet without compromising their basic monotheism?

It cannot be denied that the constraint of monotheism is a particularly important factor in accounting for the slowness of the earliest Christians in drawing out the ontological implications of their Christology. When one remembers the full humanity of Jesus—that he represents not a theophany, but an incarnation—the significance of this constraint becomes all the more apparent.

4. A key question in the whole discussion concerns *the nature of monotheism*. It is important to emphasize that no New Testament writer, however high his Christology, would want to be thought of as having given up monotheism. A number of scholars have thought it appropriate, however, to speak of a Christian modification of monotheism,[51] or as L. Hurtado puts it, a "mutation" of Jewish monotheism.[52] Certainly it is the case that monotheism has been defined by Judaism, and indeed from very early in the Christian era,[53] so as to exclude the Christology of Christianity. The result is that our monotheisms today are different. But

---

whom was as if to speak to God himself" (ibid., 172).

51. See especially the essay by Gösta Lindeskog, with a focus on Jewish scholars: "Jüdischer und christlicher Monotheismus—ein dialogisches Problem," in *Der Herr Ist Einer, unser gemeinsames Erbe*, Karl-Johan Illman and Jukka Thuren, eds. (Åbo, Finland: Åbo Akademi, 1979) 66–80. Lindeskog himself concludes, "Der Gottesbegriff des jüdischen Monotheismus is ein anderer als der des Christentums" (ibid., 79). Hans J. Schoeps has put the Jewish objection in the strongest language: "Pauline Christology and soteriology is a dogmatic impossibility from the standpoint of strict Jewish transcendent monotheism." He attributes Paul's views to the "acute Hellenization of Christianity" (*Paul: The Theology of the Apostle in the Light of Jewish Religious History*, trans. H. Knight [Philadelphia: Westminster, 1961] 166–67).

52. *One God, One Lord*, 95–124.

53. A famous example from *Exod. R.* 39.5: "R. Abbahu said: An earthly king has a father, a brother or a son. With God it is not so. Because God says: I am the first, because I have no father. I am the last, because I have no brother, and there is no God besides me, because I have no son.'" For other references, see Marmorstein, *Studies in Jewish Theology*, 100ff.

was Christian monotheism really a *modification* of first-century Jewish monotheism?

Two important points support a negative answer to this question. First, the concept of oneness reflected in the *echad* ("one") of the *Shema*, rather than referring to a strict monism,[54] allowed a degree of self-expression or self-manifestation that made possible the Christology of the New Testament writers. As the Jewish scholar Pinchas Lapide has put it, "The Oneness of God, which could be called Israel's only 'dogma,' is neither a mathematical nor a quantitative oneness in the sense of a rigid uniformity, but rather a living, dynamic Oneness out of whose inner essence the becoming-one of humanity in the reconciliation of the all-embracing Shalom comes forth."[55] Christian scholars have often pointed out that the Old Testament doctrine of God, rather than being a hindrance to the advance of Christology, provided a rich background against which the New Testament could move in the direction of trinitarianism.[56] There were, of course, still problems for the early Christians in coping with the uniqueness of Christ, but they were not insuperable.[57] The monotheism of the Old Testament was amenable to the data with which Paul and the apostles had been confronted. According to Reginald H. Fuller, a "modification of Jewish monotheism without its abandonment" had already occurred in Hellenistic Judaism by the New Testament period, wherein

---

54. As articulated, for example, in the second (on the unity of God) of Maimonides' thirteen Articles of Faith (in his commentary on the Mishnah, introducing his discussion of Sanhedrin 10). Giblin correctly notes that, "Within the limited horizons of Paul's functional theology, the oneness of God remains at odds with a barren arithmetical soleness as well as with pagan pluralism" ("Three Monotheistic Texts," 546–47).

55. Pinchas Lapide and Jürgen Moltmann, *Jewish Monotheism and Christian Trinitarian Doctrine*, trans. L. Swidler (Philadelphia: Fortress, 1981) 29. Moltmann makes a similar point in his contribution to the dialogue, 45–50.

56. On plurality within the unity of God, see, among others, George A. F. Knight, *A Biblical Approach to the Doctrine of the Trinity* (Edinburgh: Oliver & Boyd, 1953); A. R. Johnson, *The One and the Many in the Israelite Conception of God*, 2nd ed. (Cardiff: University of Wales Press, 1961); and Arthur W. Wainwright, *The Trinity in the New Testament* (London: SPCK, 1962).

57. Wainwright calls attention to the main one in these words: "The extension of the divine personality was not the main problem for the interpreters of the Christian doctrine of God. The doctrines of Wisdom and the Spirit were generally acceptable to Jews. Rigid monotheists did not find in them an insuperable obstacle to their faith. The problem which was presented by the Christian belief in Christ was of a different order. For Christ was no emanation from the Godhead. He was not a personified concept, an invisible idea which thought like a man or felt like a man. Christ did not resemble a man. He was a man" (ibid., 38). Cf. James D. G. Dunn, "Was Christianity a Monotheistic Faith from the Beginning?" *Scottish Journal of Theology* 35 (1982) 330.

there was a movement from functional to ontological thinking and towards making "a distinction within the deity, between God as he is in himself and God going out of himself in revelatory and salvific activity."[58] Paul and his contemporary Christians were able to say the stupendous things about Jesus Christ they did without believing that they had infringed on the monotheism of the faith they now believed had found its fulfillment in that very person.

Second, in the context of our discussion it has been seldom appreciated enough that the purpose of monotheism was to protect against false gods. In Deut 6:14 the point of the *Shema* is underlined with the command, "You shall not go after other gods, of the gods of the peoples who are round about you." Now the thought furthest from Paul and from his contemporary Jewish Christians would have been that Jesus was a false god, a god somehow in competition with the true God.[59] Any debate about whether monotheism in this sense might be impugned by their high Christology could only have been met by scorn. It is thoroughly a feature of their Christology that Jesus is the Son who has come in obedience to the will of the Father. As we have seen above, the Son is constantly identified with the Father. Jesus is not a second god, nor does he himself in any sense exhaust what God is; he is rather the self-expression and Agent of the one true God. Jesus thus represents exactly the opposite of the threat monotheism is designed to counteract. If, furthermore, we look at the places in the Old Testament where the *Shema* is alluded to, we can see how the New Testament writers could have believed that their proclamation of Jesus was consonant with the intent of the *Shema*. The apocalyptic emphasis in Zech 14:9, "And the LORD will become king over all the earth; on that day the LORD will be one and his name one," would have been regarded as finding its fulfillment in Christ. The universalist perspective of Mal 2:10, "Have we not all one father? Has not one God created us?" also finds its fullest realization in the gospel of Christ (Paul indeed alludes to this very text in 1 Cor 8:6, see above; cf. Rom 3:29-30).[60]

---

58. "The Theology of Jesus or Christology? An Evaluation of the Recent Discussion," *Semeia* 30 (1985) 109.

59. In a discussion of the problem of "Monotheism and High Christology in the Gospel of Matthew," B. Gerhardsson makes this point ("Monoteism och högkristologi i Matteusevangeliet," *Svensk Exegetisk Årsbok* 37-38 (1972-73) 125-44). For Gerhardsson, Matthew's high Christology involves an enrichment of monotheism, not its betrayal.

60. Cf. the stimulating essay of U. Mauser, "*Heis Theos* und *Monos Theos* in Biblischer Theologie," in *Einheit und Vielfält Biblischer Theologie*, Jahrbuch für Biblische Theologie 1 (Neukirchen-Vluyn: Neukirchener, 1986) 71-87.

That the highest Christology of the New Testament is no threat to monotheism is clear particularly from the subordination passages. Although the New Testament writers could not express themselves in these words, it remains true that their economical subordination of Christ to the Father allows the possibility of the affirmation of his full deity without at the same time necessitating a backing away from monotheism.

5. A final point to be emphasized again is that the Christology of the New Testament writers, including Paul, is not stated in abstract, theoretical, or discursive prose. It is articulated almost exclusively in hymnic or liturgical fragments, borrowed from the worshiping church. Paul's most revealing Christological passages appear to be borrowed in this way from those "in Christ" before him. This material is not any the less true because of not appearing in expository prose. Indeed, it may be the truer just because it reflects the living experience and witness of the first-century church.[61] Perhaps it was easier for the earliest church to speak of its Christ in this way; its view of Jesus Christ could thus be left implicit.[62]

Paul and the other New Testament writers with him are confronted in Jesus Christ with a mystery that they are ill-equipped to understand and express. The difficulty is caused by their experience of one who was supremely the Agent of God, one who far exceeded all others God had sent and used, one who clearly belonged with God against all else, yet one who was fully human and who was put to death by the Romans as a criminal. They were, in short, confronted with a Christ *sui generis*; all parallels were only superficial.[63] It is not surprising that they were unable

---

61. Hurtado has recently called attention to this importance of early Christian experience for the development of Christology: 'This innovation was first manifested in the devotional life of early Christian groups, in which the risen Christ came to share in some of the devotion and cultic attention normally reserved for God: the early Christian mutation in Jewish monotheism was a religious devotion with a certain binitarian shape. The earliest and key innovation in Christianity was not the use of certain honorific titles or other christological rhetoric. Rather, it was the nature of the religious praxis of early and influential groups" (*One God, One Lord*, 124). Cf. Wilhelm Bousset's comment that the early Christian community's faith "unconsciously has that mystery [of the deity of Christ] already in cult and praxis" (*Kyrios Christos*, trans. John E. Steely [Nashville: Abingdon, 1970] 210).

62. In his valuable article on "Hymns and Christology," Hengel has expressed the point well: 'The Spirit urged them on beyond the content of preaching, the exegesis of scripture and indeed the content of confessional formulae expressed in prose to express new, bolder, greater things in 'the new song' of the hymn to Christ, because earthbound language could not do justice to God." *Between Jesus and Paul*, 95.

63. On the failure of *religionsgeschichtliche* parallels to explain New Testament Christology, see esp. Dunn, *Christology in the Making*. Cf. Frances Young, "Two Roots

finally to resolve the inherent tensions between what they were forced to conclude about Jesus and the monotheism that was their second nature. If they lived with these tensions—how uncomfortably we do not know—a time was to come when the church would be forced to articulate its doctrine of Christ in a high degree of explicitness. The Christological councils of the fourth and fifth centuries attempted to do justice to the data of the New Testament. Faced with those data, they could—rightly, in my opinion, do nothing other than affirm the deity of Jesus Christ, while yet at the same time insisting that there is only one God.[64] If we today find their language less than ideal and if we therefore find it necessary to reexpress the central mystery of our faith, we cannot sacrifice the truth they affirmed and also be faithful to the New Testament.

---

or a Tangled Mess?" in *The Myth of God Incarnate*, ed. John Hick (Philadelphia: Westminster, 1977) 119.

64. Dunn's conclusion is apposite: "The testimony of the first Christians and of the NT writers left them no choice. Because the man Jesus was from the first at the centre of Christianity, Christianity had to redefine its monotheism. But because it was the one God of Jewish faith whom those first Christians recognized in and through this Jesus it was a redefinition and not an abandoning of that monotheism. It is thus a fundamental insight and assertion of Christianity that the Christian doctrine of the Trinity is but a restatement of Jewish monotheism" ("Was Christianity a Monotheistic Faith from the Beginning?" 335-36).

12

The Apostle Paul's Christianity as an Expression of His Jewish Faith

FOR THE TWO MILLENNIA between his time and the present, the Apostle Paul has frequently been regarded as an apostate from Judaism, a convert from one religion to another, and even as the virtual creator of Christianity. These and similar conclusions rest upon what appear to be fundamental and irreconcilable differences between "Judaism" and "Christianity" as commonly known. With the dawn of the modern period,[1] the familiar polarities began to soften, and in the post-Holocaust period much energy has been devoted to ecumenical dialog between synagogue and church that has produced better understanding of both faiths.[2] Eventually, through careful historical study, the interconnection and interrelated nature of matters previously thought irreconcilable began to emerge.[3] Understandably, at first it was the Jesus of the Gospels who came under scrutiny. The new openness of Jewish scholars enabled them to see Jesus with fresh eyes and led to what is called "the Jewish reclamation of

---

1. In the emancipation of the Jews and the birth of the *Haskala* ("Enlightenment") movement in the 1 second half of the eighteenth century.

2. A particularly helpful example from the Christian side is the statement of the Pontifical Biblical Commission on *The Jewish People and their Sacred Scriptures in the Christian Bible* (Vatican City: Libreria Editrice Vaticana, 2002).

3. Two books may serve as worthy examples: *Christianity in Jewish Terms*, Tikva Frymer-Kensky et al. eds. (Boulder, CO: Westview, 2000); and *Irreconcilable Differences? A Learning Resource for Jews and Christians*, ed. David F. Sandmel et al. (Boulder, CO: Westview, 2001).

Jesus."[4] Jesus was increasingly seen as thoroughly Jewish. In a kind of "homecoming," Jesus was now regarded as belonging more properly to Judaism than to the church which, it was claimed, grievously misunderstood and thus distorted him.[5]

The more Jesus was seen to be in line with Jewish theology, the more attention naturally turned to Paul as possibly the real founder of Christianity. Paul has long fascinated Jewish scholars. The NT provides more information concerning Paul, direct and indirect, than it does for Jesus. And, most interesting, this information provides us with insight into the before and after of being a Jew and becoming a Christian. The new openness of the modern period enabled Jewish scholars to explore Paul's Jewishness. Especially intriguing to Jewish scholars is the challenge of accounting for the fully Jewish Paul producing a theology that is, or appears to be, so discordant with much of Judaism. This challenge was much greater than explaining Jesus, and a Jewish reclamation of Paul, analagous to the Jewish reclamation of Jesus, was much less successful, at least until more recent times.[6]

F. F. Bruce summarizes the situation:

> Although [Paul] was rabbinically trained, his reappraisal of the whole spirit and content of his earlier training was so radical that many Jewish scholars have had difficulty in recognizing him as the product of a rabbinical education. They have found it easier to appreciate the Prophet of Nazareth (who, indeed was not rabbinically trained) than the apostle to the Gentiles. Paul presents an enigma with which they cannot readily come to terms.[7]

---

4. See D. A. Hagner, *The Jewish Reclamation of Jesus: An Analysis and Critique of the Modern Jewish Study of Jesus* (Grand Rapids: Zondervan, 1984; reprint, Eugene, OR: Wipf & Stock, 1997).

5. This trend continues down to the present in such books as: among several of Geza Vermes, e.g., *The Religion of Jesus the Jew* (Minneapolis: Fortress, 1993); *The Authentic Gospel of Jesus* (London: Penguin, 2004); Amy-Jill Levine, *The Misunderstood Jew: The Church and the Scandal of the Jewish Jesus* (San Francisco: HarperSanFrancisco, 2006); Daniel Boyarin, *The Jewish Gospels: The Story of the Jewish Christ* (New York: New Press, 2012).

6. See the account given by Stefan Meissner, *Die Heimholung des Ketzers: Studien zur jüdischen Auseinandersetzung mit Paulus*, WUNT 2/87 (Tübingen: Mohr Siebeck, 1996).

7. *Paul: Apostle of the Free Spirit* (Grand Rapids: Eerdmans, 1977) 462. The Eerdmans' subtitle was changed to *Apostle of the Heart Set Free*, it being felt that "free spirit" had undesirable connotations for American readers!

PART TWO | PAUL

I.

1. From the beginning, Paul's eccentric views were regarded as caused by his unusual background. Paul, as a diaspora Jew, would have been under the heavy influence of Hellenistic Judaism, long regarded as very different from the Palestinian Judaism of the rabbis. Further diaspora influence would have been available in the mystery religions and Gnosticism.

Practically all Jewish writers on Paul in the initial phase of modern scholarship conclude that Paul is to be explained by *Hellenistic* Judaism.[8] Kaufmann Kohler[9] appealed to Gnosticism and the mystery religions, but concluded that Paul nevertheless remained recognizably Jewish. Claude Goldsmid Montefiore[10] made much of the difference between rabbinic Judaism and the Hellenistic Judaism of the diaspora that Paul imbibed, the latter being particularly "cheap and poor" by comparison. According to Joseph Klausner,[11] Paul was torn between Palestinian Pharisaism, Jewish Hellenism, and pagan Hellenism. Paul's dependence on Hellenism ironically resulted in an "anti-Judaism," completely foreign to Palestinian Jews. Martin Buber[12] concludes that through the influence of Hellenism Paul transformed the Jewish concept of faith into an individualistic conversion experience. Paul also borrowed from Gnosticism and the mystery religions, ultimately producing a theology quite unlike that of Jesus. Samuel Sandmel[13] stresses Paul's Hellenistic background and finds the most convincing parallel to Paul in the Hellenistic Jew Philo. He denies that Paul had any contact with Palestinian Judaism. Paul the Jew is most like a Hebrew prophet. He was not the founder of Christianity, but he "recreated" it.

2. One of the first Jewish scholars to affirm and emphasize Paul's background as essentially Jewish was Leo Baeck.[14] Paul's Christianity was rooted in Judaism. The determinative point for Baeck was not that

---

8. For a more detailed overview of the mainly twentieth-century Jewish scholars mentioned here, see D. A. Hagner, "Paul in Modern Jewish Thought," in *Pauline Studies: Essays Presented to Professor F. F. Bruce on His 70th Birthday*, ed. Donald A. Hagner and Murray J. Harris (Grand Rapids: Eerdmans, 1980) 143–65.

9. "Saul of Tarsus," in *Jewish Encyclopedia* 11:79–87.

10. *Judaism and St. Paul: Two Essays* (London: Goschen, 1914).

11. *From Jesus to Paul*, trans. W. F. Stinespring (New York: Macmillan, 1943).

12. *Two Types of Faith*, trans. N. P. Goldhawk (London: Routledge, 1951).

13. *The Genius of Paul: A Study in History* (New York: Farrar, Straus & Cudahy, 1958).

14. *Paulus, die Pharisäer und das Neue Testament* (Frankfurt: Ner-Tamid, 1961).

there were no Hellenistic ideas in Paul's theology, but rather that much of Hellenism was already at home in Palestinian Judaism. The conclusion that there was no absolute dichotomy between the Hellenistic perspective of diaspora Judaism and Palestinian Judaism[15] has become increasingly influential in explaining Paul. And accordingly, nowadays the appeal to a distinctive Hellenistic Judaism in contrast to Palestinian Judaism as the explanation of Paul's theology is seldom made.

The best of the earlier books by Jewish scholars, and one of the first to anticipate the trend of later Jewish scholarship on Paul was that of the anti-Zionist Hans Joachim Schoeps.[16] Going against the description of Paul as an aberrant Hellenistic Jew, Schoeps sketches a view of Paul as consistent at many points with the rabbinic Judaism of Palestine and stresses Paul's religion as a "radicalized Pharisaism." Here is a Paul nearly in reach of reclamation as a Palestinian Jew.

The same may be said of Schalom ben-Chorin's description of Paul as one who was and remained a Pharisee.[17] Paul was a *Talmid-Chacham*, a Yeshiva student, during his time at the feet of Rabbi Gamaliel. Despite the clear influence of Hellenism on Paul, Ben-Chorin affirms his continuing deep and thorough Jewishness. Paul, in short, was a Hellenistic Jew, very similar in his makeup to Philo, from whom he is said to have learned much. His success was due largely to his ability to be "a Jew to the Jews and a Greek to the Greeks" (1 Cor 9:20).

Richard Rubenstein's unusual book, *My Brother Paul*,[18] although mainly concerned to show how Paul anticipates the ideas of Sigmund Freud, makes numerous observations that are pertinent to our subject. Rubenstein recognizes the evidence of Greek influence upon Paul, but regards Paul as far more Jewish than Greek. Paul's preoccupation with the Gentile mission grew out of his conviction that eschatological fulfilment

---

15. Established convincingly by Martin Hengel in *Judaism and Hellenism: Studies in their Encounter in Palestine during the Early Hellenistic Period*, trans. J. Bowden (London: SCM, 1974). See too his *Jew, Greeks and Barbarians: Aspects of the Hellenization of Judaism in the Pre-Christian Period*, trans. J. Bowden (London: SCM, 1980).

16. *Paul: The Theology of the Apostle in the Light of Jewish Religious History*, trans. Harold Knight (Philadelphia: Westminster, 1961).

17. *Paulus* (Munich: List, 1970). While the book is sympathetic to Paul, Ben-Chorin does not go so far as to refer to Paul as his brother in its title. Cf. the title of his book on Jesus, *Bruder Jesus*.

18. (New York: Harper & Row, 1972). The brotherhood Rubenstein has in mind, however, is one of a common existential humanness rather than specifically religious in nature.

had begun, and this was therefore "prototypically Jewish." Remarkably, Rubenstein goes against the practically universal conclusion of Jewish scholars when he writes "In reality it was not Paul but Jesus who instituted the irreparable breach with established Judaism."[19]

In a highly acclaimed book,[20] Alan F. Segal has argued that Paul is thoroughly Jewish, being in particular deeply dependent upon Jewish apocalyptic and merkebah mysticism. This is evident from the language he uses to describe his conversion experience and his description of his mystical experiences referred to in 2 Cor 12:1-7. Segal is one of the few Jewish scholars who accept the appropriateness of the word "conversion" in referring to Paul's Damascus Road experience. Segal, however, also regards Paul's experience as a "call," analogous to the prophetic callings of the OT. Paul was transformed by that experience and by his encounter with the risen Christ, the promised Messiah, which indicated to him the beginning of the promised eschatological age.

Daniel Boyarin is another Talmudic scholar who has written an engaging book on Paul,[21] which has as a goal "to reclaim Paul as an important Jewish thinker." Boyarin finds similarities between the Jewish Hellenism of Paul and Philo. Paul's liberal Hellenism gave him a desire for universal salvation, and this constituted a pre-conversion struggle that turned his mind to the universality of Jewish apocalyptic. He regarded the risen Jesus as the expected Messiah and as such the beginning of the fulfilment of the apocalyptic hope for the renewal of all things.

3. Mark D. Nanos, one of the leading lights of the current "Paul within Judaism" movement, joined up with Magnus Zetterholm to edit an important book on our subject, published in 2015.[22] Especially useful are the Introduction by Nanos (pp. 1–30),[23] Zetterholm's essay "Paul within Judaism: The State of the Questions" (pp. 31–52),[24] and Anders Runes-

---

19. Ibid., 121.

20. Alan F. Segal, *Paul the Convert: the Apostolate and Apostasy of Saul the Pharisee* (New Haven: Yale University Press, 1961).

21. *A Radical Jew: Paul and the Politics of Identity* (Berkeley: University of California Press, 1994).

22. *Paul within Judaism: Restoring the First-Century Context to the Apostle* (Minneapolis: Fortress, 2015).

23. Cf. his essay, "Paul and Judaism: Why Not Paul's Judaism," in *Paul Unbound: Other Perspectives on the Apostle*, Mark D. Given, ed. (Peabody, MA: Hendrickson, 2010) 117–60.

24. See too Zetterholm's textbook, *Approaches to Paul: A Student's Guide to Recent Scholarship* (Minneapolis: Fortress, 2009), especially chapter five, "Beyond the New

son's essay "The Question of Terminology: The Architecture of Contemporary Discussions on Paul" (pp. 79–104). The volume concludes with a response from Terence L. Donaldson, "Paul within Judaism: A Critical Evaluation from a 'New Perspective' Perspective" (pp. 277–301).

Further evidence of the vitality of the newer emphasis in the study of the Jewish roots of the NT, including Paul, can be seen in the establishment in 2014 of a new journal titled *Journal of the Jesus Movement in Its Jewish Setting from the First to the Seventh Century*.[25] Thus far, it is issue number 5 (2018) that is perhaps of most interest to the question of Paul's Judaism. The issue collects papers presented at the 2017 SBL celebration of the fortieth anniversary of the publication of E. P. Sanders's classic *Paul and Palestinian Judaism*. The second part of the issue specifically concerns the "Paul within Judaism" movement, focusing on two important recent volumes, namely John Gager's *Who Made Early Christianity? The Jewish Lives of the Apostle Paul* (New York: Columbia University Press, 2015)[26] and Paula Fredriksen's *Paul: the Pagans' Apostle* (New Haven: Yale University Press, 2017). The important discussion includes the following articles: Gregory Tatum, "Did Paul Find Anything Wrong with Judaism?"; James Crossley, "Paul Within Judaism? A Response to Paula Fredriksen and John Gager"; Margaret M. Mitchell, "Paul and Judaism Now, Quo vadimus?"; Matthew V. Novenson, "Whither the Paul within Judaism *Schule*?"; and Paula Fredriksen, "Putting Paul in His (Historical) Place: A Response to James Crossley, Margaret Mitchell, and Matthew Novenson."

4. Several surveys of the more recent Jewish scholarship may be mentioned here. Gabriele Boccaccini and Carlos A. Segovia have edited a book of essays that deal with various aspects of the location of Paul in his Jewish context.[27] Boccaccini announces that the goal of the volume is the affirmation of the "Radical New Perspective," not as the conclusion but as the starting point for the understanding of Paul. At the heart of this starting point is Paul's affirmation of Jesus as the culmination of a Jewish messianic movement.

Perspective."

25. The members of the editorial committee are listed as: Torleif Elgvin, Paula Fredriksen, Anders Runesson, and Alexei Sivertsev.

26. Gager, of course, was a pioneer in the revisionist understanding of Paul, along with such scholars as K. Stendahl, L. Gaston, and S. Stowers.

27. *Paul the Jew: Rereading the Apostle as a Figure of Second Temple Judaism* (Minneapolis: Fortress, 2016).

Especially noteworthy is the survey by Michael F. Bird and Preston M. Sprinkle, "Jewish Interpretation of Paul in the Last Thirty Years."[28] The authors rightly call attention to the diversity of the Jewish viewpoint on Paul. A clear positive contribution has been the correction of the all too common misrepresentation of Judaism. Bird and Sprinkle further note the increasing affirmation of the authentic Jewishness of Paul. Yet they end up saying that "there will never be a Jewish 'reclamation' of Paul." This conclusion may be a little premature. Certainly Jewish scholars are a lot closer to reclaiming Paul than was the case just a few decades ago.[29]

Daniel R. Langton has produced a very informative and insightful survey of Jewish writers on Paul, published in two parts in the *Journal for the Study of the New Testament*. In the first of these, Langton deals with the subject in terms of the religious agenda of Jewish Christian dialogue.[30] By the "myth of the traditional view" he indicates that only relatively recently has it been possible to speak of a unified, widely-held "Jewish view of Paul." In the second article, Langton focuses on the Jewish study of Paul as an "in-house debate about the nature of Judaism and Jewish identity."

A very helpful collection of essays is contained in *Paul and Judaism: Crosscurrents in Pauline Exegesis and the Study of Jewish-Christian Relations*, Reimund Bieringer and Didier Pollefeyt, eds.[31] The editors provide an interesting and helpful prologue entitled "Wrestling with the Jewish Paul," in which they make use of a twofold grid: the historical dimension, concerned with continuity and discontinuity between Christianity and Judaism, and the soteriological dimension concerned with the issue of

---

28. *Currents in Biblical Research* 6 (2008) 355–76. Michael Bird has also written an excellent book on our subject: *An Anomalous Jew: Paul among Jews, Greeks, and Romans* (Grand Rapids: Eerdmans, 2016); see too, Thomas G. Casey and Justin Taylor, eds. *Paul's Jewish Matrix* (Rome: Gregorian & Biblical Press, 2011); also useful are: S. E. Porter, "Was Paul a Good Jew? Fundamental Issues in a Current Debate," in *Christian-Jewish Relations Through the Centuries*, ed. Brook W. R. Pearson and Stanley E. Porter JSNTSup 192 (Sheffield: Sheffield Academic, 2000) 148–174, and "New Understandings of Paul and His Jewish Heritage: A Select Bibliography Compiled by David Bolton and Emmanuel Nathan." *Studies in Christian-Jewish Relations* 3 (2008) Bibliography, 1–7.

29. "Jewish Interpretation of Paul in the Last Thirty Years," 372.

30. "The Myth of the 'Traditional View of Paul' and the Role of the Apostle in Modern Jewish-Christian Polemics," *JSNT* 28 (2005) 69–10; and "Modern Jewish Identity and the Apostle Paul: Pauline Studies as an Intra-Jewish Ideological Battleground," *JSNT* 28 (2005) 217–58. See too Langton's *The Apostle Paul in the Jewish Imagination: A Study in Modern Jewish-Christian Relations* (New York: Cambridge University Press, 2010).

31. LNTS 463 (London: T. & T. Clark, 2012).

exclusivism, inclusivism, and pluralism. The essays themselves exhibit a great variety of opinion on these questions. James D. G. Dunn provides a constructive "epilogue."

5. The literature we have looked at so far, although indicating a better (i.e., more positive) understanding of the variety of first-century Palestinian Judaism, has opened up more possibilities for explaining Paul's unique views as being within the realm of authentic Judaism, rather than a Hellenistic import. Still this is not quite enough to be named a "Jewish reclamation of Paul."

There still are, for example, differences in understanding Paul, including even some polar extremes. In one, it is argued that Paul was *not a Jew*, while in another that Paul was *not a Christian*!

In 1986, Talmudic scholar Hyam Maccoby published what can only be described as an eccentric book on Paul, entitled *The Myth-maker: Paul and the Invention of Christianity*.[32] Maccoby transcends the question of Paul's Judaism by denying altogether that he was a Jew. Confronted by the strangeness of Paul from a Jewish perspective, Maccoby goes so far as to conclude that Paul was in fact a Gentile, albeit a proselyte to Judaism (incidentally a view held by the Ebionites), who deeply desired to be a Pharisee. As a Greek boy, Paul would have been exposed to Gnosticism and the mystery religions, which were eventually so important to the formation of the new religion's doctrine, as for example in his creation of the Eucharist and the story of the descent of the divine savior, as well as the story of the dying and rising god. Maccoby relies heavily on late traditions of the Ebionites, against the evidence of the NT. He depends also on the questionable hypothesis of the old Tübingen school concerning the differences between Petrine and Pauline Christianity.[33]

On the other extreme, Jewish NT scholar Pamela Eisenbaum has written a book titled *Paul was Not a Christian: The Original Message of a Misunderstood Apostle*.[34] Eisenbaum presents a robust defence of Paul's Jewishness, with which there is little to disagree. Unfortunately, she falls into the logical fallacy of concluding that since the word "Christianity"

---

32. (San Francisco: Harper & Row). This was followed up by Maccoby's *Paul and Hellenism* (London: SCM, 1991). For a critique, see D. A. Hagner, "The Making of a Myth: Hyam Maccoby's View of Paul" in *Jesus, Early Judaism and Early Christianity*.

33. For a full review, see D. A. Hagner, "The Making of a Myth: Hyam Maccoby's View of Paul," in *The Cradle of Christianity: Judaism, Jesus, and the New Testament*. Essays in Honor of Craig A. Evans. Thomas R. Hatina and Stanley E. Porter, eds. (Leiden/Boston: Brill, 2024) 236–257.

34. (New York: HarperOne, 2009).

does not occur in the NT, there cannot have been any Christians in the first century (pp. 6, 135, 144). But because a word is not found in the NT is no proof that the word did not exist at that time. Furthermore, and more seriously, the reality can exist before vocabulary is invented to describe it. Eisenbaum argues that Paul "does not use the designation 'Jew' of himself as a label of his religious past" (p. 6). But what about his reference to "my earlier life in Judaism" (Gal 1:13f.) or to the "gains" he had as a Jew, which he now counts as "loss because of Christ" (Phil 3:4-8)? Like other Jewish authors, Eisenbaum attempts to solve the difficult question of Paul and the Law by arbitrarily assigning all of Paul's letters to a Gentile readership (p. 61). This supposedly explains passages that argue freedom from the Law; Jews, on the other hand, remain under the Law. Paul's polemic against the Law applies only to Gentiles. Eisenbaum's Jewish Paul does not allow him to be a Christian, and his theology is virtually split in half because he cannot address Jews and Gentiles at the same time. Each group has its own distinctive story: the Jews have election and Torah, and have no need of Jesus; the Gentiles have the atoning death of Jesus.

Both Maccoby and Eisenbaum dismiss the idea that Paul could have been a Jew and a Christian at the same time. He must be one or the other; he cannot be both. But are the two mutually exclusive? Paul would have thought such a conclusion as nothing short of preposterous. For him his Jewishness was basic to his life and thought, and it found its fullest expression in his Christian faith.

II.

Both Acts and Paul's letters provide clear evidence of Paul's Jewishness. In his defence after his arrest in the temple he addresses the crowd "in the Hebrew language," refers to his listeners as "brothers and fathers," and then states unequivocally "I am a Jew, born in Tarsus in Cilicia" (Acts 22:3; note the present tense here and in the identical statement to the tribune in 21:39). Luke informs us that Paul had been given the Jewish name Saul (*Saulos*; Heb. *Sha'ul*; first occurrences in Acts 7:58; 8:1; cf. 13:9), after the name of the Benjaminite who became Israel's first king. Saul is the name used by the risen Jesus to address Paul on the Damascus Road.[35]

---

35. Nowhere in his letters does Paul make use of the name Saul.

Paul's Jewishness, however, was not merely a matter of birth. He was "brought up[36] in this city at the feet of Gamaliel, educated strictly according to our ancestral law, being zealous for God, just as all of you are this day" (Acts 22:3). This information from the evangelist Luke is confirmed by Paul's repeated eagerness in his letters to stress his Jewish identity. "You have heard, no doubt, of my earlier life in Judaism. I was violently persecuting the church of God and was trying to destroy it. I advanced in Judaism beyond many among my people of the same age, for I was far more zealous for the traditions of my ancestors" (Gal 1:13–14). Later in Galatians he states: "We ourselves are Jews by birth and not Gentile sinners" (2:15). He is most explicit in Phil 3:4-6, "I, too, have reason for confidence in the flesh. If anyone else has reason to be confident in the flesh, I have more: circumcised on the eighth day, a member of the people of Israel, of the tribe of Benjamin, a Hebrew born of Hebrews; as to the law, a Pharisee, as to zeal, a persecutor of the church; as to righteousness under the law, blameless." He makes a similar statement in Rom 11:1-2 "I ask, then, has God rejected his people? By no means! I myself am an Israelite, a descendant of Abraham, a member of he tribe of Benjamin. God has not rejected his people whom he foreknew." Cf. Rom 9:3, "For I could wish that I myself were accursed and cut off from Christ for the sake of my own people, my kindred according to the flesh." And we may add the brief reference in 2 Cor 11:22, "Are they Hebrews? So am I. Are they Israelites? So am I. Are they descendants of Abraham? So am I."

Clearly this information is of fundamental importance to Paul's identity and calling. This has to be the orientation point for any adequate understanding of Paul. At the same time, of course, Paul was a complex man. He was notably a Roman citizen (Acts 16:37-38; 22:25-27) and a Diaspora Jew with a Hellenistic education. With one foot in the Jewish world and one in the Greek world, Paul was remarkably well-equipped for the mission God called him to. But it was above all his Jewish faith that determines the framework of his understanding of what eventually was to become "Christianity."[37]

---

36. *anatethrammenos* probably refers to Paul's early childhood being spent in Jerusalem. See W. C. van Unnik, *Tarsus or Jerusalem: The City of Paul's Youth* (London: Epworth, 1962).

37. "Paul's special achievement was bringing the Christian message to Gentiles. Christianity was originally a Judaism." (S. Sandmel, *Judaism and Christian Beginnings* (New York: Oxford University Press, 1978) 310.

III.

As we have seen, the question that has puzzled many Jewish scholars is how to account for Paul's peculiar theological views. What accounts for the differences in the views of the pre- and post-Damascus Road Paul? This question, of course, is but a part of the larger question of the OT and the NT, and indeed of Judaism and Christianity.

The key here is *newness*, its nature and extent, its causes and consequences. Despite the attempts of the current "Paul Within Judaism" movement to minimize or explain it away, newness pervades the NT—indeed it is even of central importance.[38] It is no coincidence that the writings of the earliest Christians were collected under the title "the New Covenant." The two issues that are determinative and decisive for the NT, and also for Paul, are christology and eschatology.

The stunning *novum* that constitutes the origin of Christianity is *the presence of the promised Messiah*. As the narratives inform us, it was while on the road to Damascus that Saul, the Pharisee, encountered the risen Jesus, known immediately by Paul to be "the Lord [*kyrios*]." It was, as Paul later describes it, a christophany, i.e. an appearance of the risen Messiah (Gal 1:12: "a revelation of Jesus Christ"), "God's Son" (Gal 1:16). "For it is the God who said, 'Let light shine out of darkness,' who has shone in our hearts to give the light of the knowledge of the glory of God in he face of Jesus Christ" (2 Cor 4:6). Paul's gospel is described as "the light of the gospel of the glory of Christ, who is the image [*eikōn*] of God" (2 Cor 4:4)[39] Since Paul's commitment to the risen Jesus as Israel's Messiah and his Lord was absolute, "then all other matters on his agenda as a Christian, while of importance individually, must be seen as being dependent on that central conviction."[40]

---

38. See my *How New is the New Testament?—First-Century Judaism and the Emergence of Christianity* (Grand Rapids: Baker Academic, 2018); and "Paul as a Jewish Believer—According to His Letters," in *Jewish Believers in Jesus: The Early Centuries*, Oskar Skarsaune and Reidar Hvalvik, eds. (Peabody, MA: Hendrickson, 2007) 96–120. See too the fine essay of John M. G. Barclay, ""Paul, Judaism, and the Jewish People," in *The Blackwell Companion to Paul*, Stephen Westerholm, ed. (Oxford: Wiley Blackwell, 2011) 188–201, at 199.

39. See Seyoon Kim, *The Origin of Paul's Gospel*, WUNT 2/4 (Tübingen: Mohr Siebeck, 1981) 55–56, 137.

40. Richard N. Longenecker, "A Realized Hope, a New Commitment, and a Developed Proclamation: Paul and Jesus," in *The Road from Damascus: The Impact of Paul's Conversion on His Life, Thought and Ministry*, R. N. Longenecker, ed. (Grand Rapids: Eerdmans, 1997) 18.

For Paul, God's Son has appeared in history. This overwhelming fact has brought us to the *eschatological timeframe* where the fulfilment of God's promises to Israel is to be expected. It is above all the resurrection of Jesus that is the sign of dawning eschatology. God's promises centered on the transformation of the present age (cf. "the present evil age," Gal 1:4) into an age of perfection, where evil would cease to exist. Such a thing as radical as the "age to come" could only come through direct divine intervention—through a "revelation" of God's power. This radical eschatology is therefore called "apocalyptic." The OT prophets, especially Isaiah (see, e.g., Isa 2:2-4; 25:6-9; 35:1-10; 42:9-10; 65:17-25), speak of the new creation that God will bring about with the full arrival of the new age. This perspective becomes increasingly important in the interpretation of the gospel in the Pauline letters and other NT writings. And the book of Isaiah accordingly becomes among the most quoted. The amount of apocalyptic literature increases dramatically in the Second Temple period. With the coming of the Messiah, the new had clearly begun, but—and here was the great surprise—without bringing the old to its expected end. The early church, and indeed the church down to the present, has had to cope with what has been called an "overlap of the ages,"[41] i.e., the delay of the *parousia*.

This is of great importance especially in understanding one of the more difficult questions concerning Paul's Jewishness, namely the mission to the Gentiles, and with that the complicated question of the role of the Mosaic law. For Paul, this calling was in accord with apocalyptic expectation concerning the salvation of the nations. This is most clear in his remarkable statement in Rom 15:8-9: "For I tell you that Christ has become a servant of the circumcised on behalf of the truth of God in order that he might confirm the promises given to the patriarchs, and in order that the Gentiles might glorify God for his mercy." These words are followed in Rom 15:9-12 by quotations from the Psalms, Deuteronomy and Isaiah, reenforcing the place of the Gentiles alongside the Jews in the will of God and that the Gentiles find their salvation in the God of Israel.[42]

---

41. See I. Howard Marshall, "A New Understanding of the Present and the Future: Paul and Eschatology," in *The Road from Damascus: The Impact of Paul's Conversion on His Life, Thought and Ministry*, ed. Richard N. Longenecker (Grand Rapids: Eerdmans, 1997) 43–61.

42. "Paul sees the sending of the Son of God into the world as the fulfilment of the messianic promises to Israel and the nations." Peter Stuhlmaher, *Biblical Theology of the New Testament*, trans. Daniel P. Bailey (Grand Rapids: Eerdmans, 2018) 325. Cf.

IV.

These insights into Paul and his mission are increasingly affirmed by various Jewish writers who conclude that Paul was faithful to his Jewish heritage and Jewish hopes. One of the best of these, in my opinion, is by Paula Fredriksen: *Paul: The Pagans' Apostle* (New Haven: Yale University Press, 2017). She portrays Paul as fully Jewish and describes his context in these appropriate words: "a Jewish world incandescent with apocalyptic hopes: that God verged on realising his ancient promises to Israel; that the messiah had come, and would soon come again; that the dead were about to be raised and, together with the living, shortly turn to worship the god of Israel."[43] "Apocalyptic eschatology" she writes, "filled a gap perceived between lived experience and the promises, covenants, and hopes that shaped Jewish scriptures."[44] In this context Fredriksen describes Paul, like Jesus, as a proclaimer of the coming of the Kingdom of God. Unlike most Jewish scholars, who draw a sharp line between the message of Jesus and Paul, Fredriksen writes: "The origins of Paul's gospel trace not only to the mission and message of Jesus of Nazareth (27–30 C.E.?), but even more dramatically and specifically, to traditions about his resurrection."[45] In short, Paul, like Jesus, was an apocalyptic preacher.

This understanding of Paul stands in sharp contrast to that of the veteran scholar, John Gager: "My proposal is that we strip away the apocalyptic framework of Paul's thought in a different way. If we remove the apocalyptic mystery altogether, that is, the notion that in the final days of this era God causes Israel's momentary stumble in order to redeem the Gentiles, we are left with two basic affirmations: one, God's unshakeable commitment to Israel and to the holiness of the law (=Judaism); and, two, the redemption of the Gentiles through Jesus Christ (=Christianity)."[46]

Gager's perspective raises a difficult question concerning the relation between Jews and Gentiles in early Christianity. In effect it puts a dividing wall between Jews and Gentiles. The bifurcation of the people

---

G. K. Beale's description of the church as "the transformed and restored eschatological Israel." *A New Testament Biblical Theology: The Unfolding of the Old Testament in the New* (Grand Rapids: Baker Academic, 2011) 651–749.

43. *Paul: the Pagans' Apostle*, xii.

44. Ibid., 9. See Martinus C. de Boer, "Apocalyptic Eschatology as the Expectation of God's Definitive Intervention," in *Paul and the Apocalyptic Imagination*, Ben C. Blackwell et al. eds. (Minneapolis: Fortress, 2016) 45–63.

45. *Paul: the Pagans' Apostle*, 3.

46. *Reinventing Paul* (Oxford: Oxford University Press, 2000) 151–52.

of God comes to a particular focus in soteriology and the place of the law. Many scholars, both Jewish and Gentile, have found a two-covenant solution appealing. The old covenant is the story of Israel's election and the giving of the law to Israel, which stand as the basis for Israel's relationship to God. That is understood to be Israel's distinct advantage over all nations. The new covenant, on the other hand, depends on the work of Jesus Christ, and is exclusively applicable to the Gentiles. There are, in short, not only two distinct peoples but also two distinct ways of relationship with God. Jews and Gentiles are thus kept quite separate.

The major difficulty with such a conclusion is that it cannot be squared with the NT data. In order to defend their views, most recent Jewish scholars argue that Paul's letters were written exclusively to Gentiles.[47] In this way, for example, these scholars can explain Paul's statements about Christians as no longer (=not) being under the law. But Paul neither states, nor gives reason to believe, that he conceives of the body of Christ as consisting of two separate groups of people, or that the atoning death of the Messiah is applicable only to the Gentiles. Paul is keen to point out that there is one salvation for Jews and Gentiles. He writes to the Roman Christians that the gospel "is the power of God for salvation to everyone who has faith, to the Jew first and also to the Greek" (Rom 1:16). It is furthermore not unusual for Paul to speak of issues for both Gentile and Jewish Christians in the same letter. Indeed, this is his most common practice.

Gentiles do not need to become Jews to become one with God's people. Pagans "enter into God's Kingdom as 'eschatological gentiles,' ex-pagan pagans, their inclusion now linked to Christ's return and to the impending redemption of Israel."[48]

V.

Regardless of one's final assessment of the significance of the Apostle Paul for the beginnings of Christianity, his importance remains indisputable. All the more remarkable, therefore, is the disagreement about exactly how Paul himself is to be explained. How did he understand himself and

---

47. Fredriksen who, in my opinion, otherwise has so many things about Paul right, opts for this conclusion, 122.

48. Fredriksen, *Paul: the Pagans' Apostle*, 94.

his life work? And how shall we understand him with the insight that time and history now allow?

Paul's thorough Jewishness has become clearer in recent years, and is increasingly recognized by Pauline scholars. The work of recent Jewish scholars has provided us with a better understanding of Judaism and the variety within it, as well as a better understanding of Paul. This work has put us much further down the road to the Jewish reclamation of Paul, than was the case forty years ago.

What has helped in particular is the increasing appreciation of the newness of early Christianity and the extent to which it informs Paul's theological perspective. As we have seen, that newness is most evident in christology and eschatology, which can be called "quintessential pivots of the NT."[49] It is important to note that the newness involves distinctly Jewish matters, namely the beginning of eschatological time and the fulfilment of the apocalyptic expectation.

The newness of the Pauline gospel does not involve the importation of Hellenistic or pagan ideas as many argued, especially in the nineteenth century. Martin Hengel stresses this point: "Christianity grew *entirely* out of Jewish soil . . . early Christianity is completely a child of Judaism"; "whatever pagan influences have been suspected in the origins of Christianity were mediated without exception by Judaism."[50]

Klausner's conclusion was similar: "Intensive 49 research over many years has brought the writer of the present book to a deep conviction that there is nothing in the teaching of Paul—not even the most mystical elements in it—that did not come to him from authentic Judaism." Although there was no direct borrowing from Hellenism, "it *is* a fact that most of the elements in his teaching which came from Judaism received unconsciously at his hands a *non Jewish colouring* from influence of the Hellenistic-Jewish and pagan atmosphere with which Paul of Tarsus was surrounded during nearly all of his life, except for the few years which he spent in Jerusalem."[51]

According to Samuel Sandmel, "Jews such as Paul could absorb aspects of hellenism without any sense of the loss of personal loyalty to Judaism. Paul, of course, understood the difference between his inherited

---

49. See Hagner, *How New is the New Testament?* 174f.; see too Hagner, "Paul as a Jewish Believer—According to His Letters" in *Jewish Believers in Jesus*, 118-20.

50. *Conflicts and Challenges in Early Christianity*, ed. D. A. Hagner (Harrisburg, PA: Trinity, 1999) 1, 2-3.

51. *From Jesus to Paul*, trans. W. F. Stinespring (London: Macmillan, 1943) 466.

Judaism and his new convictions. He considered the latter, though, to be the true and sure version of Judaism."[52]

Unquestionably there are new things in Paul's gospel. Klausner points out the paradox: "Paul's new religion was 'Judaism and non-Judaism at the same time."[53] N. T. Wright, a strong advocate for continuity between Judaism and Christianity, can write: "Being a 'Jew' was no longer Paul's basic identity."[54] Wright's descriptive phrase for Paul's gospel is "eschatological messianism."[55] "For Paul something radically new had happened, something which was at the same time the radical fulfilment of Israel's ancient hopes."[56] "By working to turn pagans from their gods to his god, Paul worked as well, beneath a canopy of biblical promises, for the redemption of his own people."[57] The emerging consensus among recent Pauline scholars is that Paul the Christian apostle was preserving and fulfilling the Jewish apocalyptic hopes. "Paul would not have recognised his message in these rigid polarities [i.e., Law or gospel; works or grace; Judaism or Christianity]. He conceived of his mission to pagans as entirely consistent with God's promises to his own people, Israel."[58]

Paul was unique and held to undeniably new views, yet he never would have accepted the idea that he was in any sense disloyal to the God of Israel.

Paul was actively playing out his role in fulfilling the promise/call of Isaiah 49: "I will give you as a light to the nations, that my salvation may reach to the end of the earth" (Isa 49:6; 42:6–9). He is called to fulfil a priestly service: "to be a minister of Christ Jesus to the Gentiles in the priestly service of the gospel of God, so that the offering of the Gentiles may be acceptable, sanctified by the Holy Spirit" (Rom 15:16). If not Paul himself, then a disciple of Paul, writes in Ephesians 3:6 about "the mystery of Christ," namely that "the Gentiles have become fellow heirs, members of the same body, and sharers in the promise in Christ Jesus through the gospel." Wright puts it this way: "Every single thing we know about Paul, particularly from his own writings, makes the sense it

---

52. *Judaism and Christian Beginnings* (New York: Oxford University Press, 1978) 336.

53. *From Jesus to Paul*, 465.

54. *Paul and the Faithfulness of God* (Minneapolis: Fortress, 2013) 1436.

55. Ibid., 1440.

56. Ibid., 1443.

57. Fredriksen, *Paul: the Pagans' Apostle*, 166.

58. Fredriksen, *Paul: the Pagans' Apostle*, 173.

makes on the basic jewish assumption that when the Messiah appeared he would bring about the fulfilment of God's ancient promises to Israel."[59]

We deal here not with two different religions, not with two different world views. Rather, the issue concerns discerning the times. Paul is convinced that the end of the ages has come. We have moved from the era of promise to the era of fulfillment. "See, now is the acceptable time; see, now is the day of salvation!" (2 Cor 6:2). Adolf von Harnack could therefore hardly have been further from the truth when he made the claim that Paul "delivered the Christian religion from Judaism."[60] In actuality, Paul's gospel brought Judaism to its culmination and consummation in an expected transformation of the creation that would fulfil Israel's apocalyptic hopes. Paul's Christianity is an expression of his Jewish faith. At the end of his brief but helpful essay on "Paul's Jewishness," E. P. Sanders provides a concise summary that would serve well as a summary of the present essay:

> To summarize: Paul lived and worked in the Greek-speaking world. Whatever his knowledge of that environment, his education and upbringing were Jewish; the main categories of his thought were Jewish; his mission was set in the framework of Jewish eschatology; the final outcome for which he longed was a universal form of Jewish hope. Temporarily, he thought, he was creating a third group, distinguishable from both Judaism and paganism, as part of the new creation that would fully arise when the God of Israel, who was the only true God, brought ordinary history to its conclusion."[61]

---

59. *Paul and the Faithfulness of God*, 1409.
60. A. von Harnack, *What Is Christianity?* (New York: Harper & Row, 1957) 176.
61. E. P. Sanders, *Comparing Judaism and Christianity: Common Judaism, Paul, and the Inner and the Outer in Ancient Religion* (Minneapolis: Fortress, 2016) 285.

13

The Newness of Paul's Gospel

CHRISTIANITY, BY ITS NATURE, is very Jewish. And it was certainly more Jewish in its early years than it became as the centuries passed. But do these facts justify the current trend among some scholars to regard early Christianity as a sect *within* Judaism? In particular, is Paul to be understood as in full continuity with Judaism—indeed, as remaining *within* Judaism?[1]

I am fully aware that the words "Judaism" and "Christianity" are anachronistic. It is of course clearly wrong to read the content of the fully developed Judaism and Christianity of later centuries into our first-century sources. It is also clear that there was much more variety within each of the two groups at the beginning than was the case in later centuries. At the same time, however, it seems impossible, given the evidence we have, to deny that there was an identifiable Judaism and an identifiable Christianity already in the first century. It is obvious from the NT that there were specific things believed by the Jews who followed Jesus and those who did not. Virtually all Jews held to a set of core beliefs such as monotheism, the election of Israel, the covenant and Torah, the Temple and the promise of the land. And, on the other hand, from the NT itself it is clear that the earliest believers in Jesus already in the first century shared core Christian beliefs; e.g., confession of Christ as Lord, his atoning death, belief in his resurrection from the dead, belief in the present dawning of a new age, and salvation by faith in Christ. That there

---

1. This essay is based largely on material from my book *How New Is the New Testament?* (Grand Rapids: Baker, 2018), used here with the permission of the publisher.

was also some variety in the beliefs of the two groups is hardly to be denied. But at the same time, it is not difficult to see considerable stability in both groups, easily sufficient enough to establish the identity of one over against the other. It therefore seems more appropriate to speak of varieties of, or within, Judaism than of "Judaisms" in the plural. So too of varieties of Christianity rather than "Christianities." There is enough of a common core within the actual varieties to justify speaking of singular entities within which some (limited) variety existed.

The frequently heard red herring that one cannot meaningfully speak of "Christianity" until the second century at the earliest because the actual word is not found until Ignatius is clearly a non sequitur. In addition to the obvious fact that *our* knowledge of the first use of a word is hardly proof that the word was not used earlier, it is perfectly possible for the reality to exist before the minting of the word. Already in the NT we have the word "Christian" (Acts 11:26; 26:28; 1 Pet 4:16) and the Pauline designation of being "in Christ" also functions as a clear identity marker. Therefore I do not think it is necessary, with the qualifications just noted, to avoid speaking of "Judaism" and "Christianity" in the first century.

Through most of the history of the church the emphasis has been on the discontinuity between Judaism and Christianity. But with the coming of the Enlightenment and the Emancipation of the Jews, beginning in the late 18th century, the climate began to change. Here we encounter the beginnings of a *gradual movement from stress on discontinuity to stress on continuity*. For the first time it became possible for a more positive Jewish approach to Jesus. This new, open attitude, exhibited almost exclusively among Reform Jews, not among Orthodox Jews, gave rise in the twentieth-century to what would become known as "the Jewish reclamation of Jesus."[2]

Exactly because Jesus was so Jewish, it is not such a great surprise that Jews would be able to think of him as belonging within the fold. With "the homecoming of Jesus," it was thought no longer possible to understand Jesus as the founder of Christianity. It was Paul who now became regarded as mainly responsible for Christianity as we know it. All the more surprising then is the rise of a parallel movement: namely, the Jewish reclamation of Paul. The rediscovery of the Jewishness of Jesus has progressed to the rediscovery of the Jewishness of Paul. Here again,

---

2. See my discussion in *The Jewish Reclamation of Jesus: An Analysis and Critique of Modern Jewish Study of Jesus* (Grand Rapids: Zondervan, 1984; reprint, Eugene, OR: Wipf & Stock, 1997).

and startlingly, the pendulum has shifted from discontinuity to continuity. Given the hitherto common, seemingly self-evident, understanding of Paul as having in some sense broken with the law and Judaism—a view prevalent from Luther until recent times—the emphasis had always been on the discontinuity between Judaism and Paul's Christianity.[3]

These developments stressing the full continuity of early Christianity and Judaism are consonant with the emerging view that Christianity from the beginning was and remained a sect within Judaism and that consequently there never was a parting of the ways between synagogue and church.[4] This extreme view is not shared by many, but an increasing number of scholars would place the parting no earlier than the fourth century.[5] In summary, it is clear that, nowadays, for many the pendulum is swinging completely to the side of *full continuity between Judaism and Christianity*, on the part of both Jewish and Christian scholars. This development accords not only with the relativistic spirit of our age, but especially with the concerns of post-Holocaust Jewish Christian dialog.[6]

It is the thorough Jewishness of the NT, and of Paul too, that makes it possible to think of early Christianity as simply another sect of Judaism. Nevertheless, given the dominant reading of Paul vis-à-vis Judaism,

---

3. See D. A. Hagner, "Paul's Quarrel with Judaism," in *Anti-Semitism and Early Christianity: Issues of Polemic and Faith*, 128-50. Hagner, "Paul as a Jewish Believer in Jesus—According to His Letters," in *Jewish Believers in Jesus: The Early Centuries*, ed. O. Skarsaune and R. Hvalvik (Peabody, MA: Hendrickson, 2007) 1:96-120. See too Hagner, "Paul in Modern Jewish Thought," in *Pauline Studies. Essays Presented to Professor F. F. Bruce on his 70th Birthday*, ed. D. A. Hagner and M. J. Harris (Grand Rapids: Eerdmans, 1980) 143-65.

4. See A. H. Becker and A. Y. Reed, eds., *The Ways That Never Parted: Jews and Christians in Late Antiquity and the Early Middle Ages* (Tübingen: Mohr Siebeck, 2003; reprint, Minneapolis: Fortress, 2007). For a defense of a gradual parting of the ways, underway almost from the beginning, see D. A. Hagner, "Another Look at the 'Parting of the Ways'" in *Earliest Christian History: History, Literature and Theology. Essays from the Tyndale Fellowship in Honor of Martin Hengel*, ed. M. F. Bird and Jason Maston, WUNT 2/320 (Tübingen: Mohr Siebeck, 2012) 381-427.

5. Much depends on how one defines the "parting(s)." If one thinks merely of the cessation of contact and discussion between Jews and Christians, then of course there may never have been a parting of the ways. But if one thinks of irreconcilable differences that made it impossible for a person to belong to both camps at the same time, then we must conceive of partings that began very early and continued at different speeds in different areas.

6. The impact of Jewish-Christian dialog on the conclusions of NT scholarship is worth pondering. It has become increasingly difficult for Christian scholars to say anything negative about Judaism for fear of being labelled anti-Semitic.

it was rather surprising when the Jewish reclamation of Paul began.[7] There is currently a lively trend underway among a growing number of scholars to place Paul comfortably *"within Judaism."*[8] It is not only Jewish scholars who have begun to read the NT in this way. Indeed, encouraged to an extent by Jewish-Christian dialogue, there are some for whom the goal seems to be the Jewish reclamation of the NT and early Christianity itself. This approach puts all stress on continuity and ignores or avoids speaking of discontinuities or newness; at least it empties them of any significance. These scholars have invented new vocabulary to describe what they believe they encounter in the NT, such as "NT Judaism," "Apostolic Judaism," and and even "Christian Judaism." For them the NT represents a form of Judaism. The separation of Christians and Jews, the "parting of the ways," as we have noted, is now put as late as the fourth century, and denied by some as happening at all.

The traditional reading of Paul has regularly put him in considerable tension with, sometimes even in opposition to, Judaism. So it is no surprise that these revisionist scholars have focused their efforts on Paul, in pursuing an understanding of him they describe as being "beyond the new perspective," or as "a radical new perspective."[9] Essential to this new perspective or new paradigm is the denial of any "dichotomy" between Paul and Judaism.

A substantial recent treatment of the subject is to be found in Pamela Eisenbaum's book *Paul Was Not a Christian: The Original Message*

---

7. See already Markus Barth, "St. Paul—A Good Jew," *HBT* 1 (1979) 7–45, who mentions before him the Jewish scholars Joseph Klausner, Martin Buber, Leo Baeck, Hans-Joachim Schoeps, Michael Wyschogrod, and Schalom Ben-Chorin.

8. The title of a recent representative volume is *Paul within Judaism: Restoring the First-Century Context to the Apostle*, ed. Mark D. Nanos and Magnus Zetterholm (Minneapolis: Fortress, 2015); cf. the earlier essay by Nanos, "Paul and Judaism: Why Not Paul's Judaism?" in *Paul Unbound: Other Perspectives on the Apostle*, ed. Mark D. Given (Peabody, MA: Hendrickson, 2010) 117–60. See too, K. Stendahl, *Paul Among Jews and Gentiles and Other Essays* (Philadelphia: Fortress, 1976); W. S. Campbell, *Paul and the Creation of Christian Identity*, LNTS 322 (London: T. & T. Clark, 2006); Mark D. Nanos, *The Mystery of Romans: The Jewish Context of Paul's Letter* (Minneapolis: Fortress, 1996); Nanos, *The Irony of Galatians: Paul's Letter in First-Century Context* (Minneapolis: Fortress, 2002); M. Zetterholm, *Approaches to Paul: A Student's Guide to Recent Scholarship* (Minneapolis: Fortress, 2009) 95–164; Kimberly Ambrose, *Jew Among Jews: Rehabilitating Paul* (Eugene, OR: Wipf & Stock, 2015); Gabriele Boccaccini and Carlos A. Segovia, eds., *Paul the Jew: Rereading the Apostle as a Figure of Second Temple Judaism* (Minneapolis: Fortress, 2016).

9. They project an image of themselves as interested only in "scientific historiography," not "faith commitments." See *Paul Within Judaism*, 4; and Magnus Zetterholm, *Approaches to Paul: A Student's Guide to Recent Scholarship* (Minneapolis: Fortress, 2009).

of a Misunderstood Apostle.[10] Here we find practically all of the emphases made by the "Paul-within-Judaism" movement: there was no "Christianity" when the NT was written; believers in Jesus constituted a sect within Judaism; Paul continued to obey Torah; Paul did not preach justification by faith; an important key to understanding Paul's letters is that he wrote them not to Jews but to Gentiles; Paul's negative statements about the law therefore apply only to Gentiles; Paul was called rather than converted; and he rejected none of the fundamental tenets of Judaism.

These conclusions flow from the a priori starting point that Paul is to be understood as within Judaism, indeed as a good representative of Judaism. This exegesis of the Pauline texts is no less dominated by an a priori than is that of the "traditional" understanding of Paul within Christianity and as a representative of Christianity. Furthermore, as Magnus Zetterholm frankly admits, "the radical new perspective" is "neither neutral nor objective" and is affected by "ideological factors" such as "involvement in Jewish-Christian dialogue" and "a general consciousness about the connection between the traditional anti-Jewish theology of the church and the Holocaust, in some cases leading to a wish to contribute to the development of theological alternatives."[11]

The so-called "historical" readings of the Paul-within-Judaism scholars can often make sense of the Pauline texts only by means of a tortuous exegesis.[12] Quite remarkable is the fair-minded comment of Zetterholm: "It is, of course, fully possible that the theological interpretation of Paul that has developed over the centuries represents an accurate reconstruction of the historical Paul's thought world."[13] To my mind, the

---

10. New York: HarperOne, 2009. The title reminds one of the title of Amy-Jill Levine's book about Jesus: *The Misunderstood Jew: The Church and the Scandal of the Jewish Jesus* (San Francisco: HarperSanFrancisco, 2006). Cf. too, the books by Daniel Boyarin, *A Radical Jew: Paul and the Politics of Identity* (Berkeley: University of California, 1994); and Boyarin, *The Jewish Gospels: The Story of the Jewish Christ* (New York: New Press, 2012).

11. *Approaches to Paul*, 232-33.

12. Eisenbaum frankly admits there are "a few stubborn passages," and that the meaning of some texts is debatable owing to exaggeration and rhetoric. *Paul Was Not a Christian*, 251.

13. *Paul Within Judaism*, 42. The comment, however, simply reflects Zetterholm's post-modern hermeneutical conviction that there is no way of knowing Paul's intentions in the texts (see Zetterholm, *Approaches to Paul*, 237). Unfortunately, Zetterholm thinks that "the fundamental assumption" in the traditional understanding of Paul is "the vile character of ancient Judaism," and thus he finds it unacceptable. The traditional view of Paul, however, in no way requires such hostility towards Judaism.

traditional understanding of Paul is indeed highly probable and makes by far the best sense of Paul. The understanding of Paul-within-Judaism can hardly account for the vast amount of *newness* in the Pauline letters.

The discussion of this subject has been seriously hindered by the frequent use of simplistic dichotomies on the part of those arguing for Paul-within-Judaism. Thus Paul affirmed Judaism *or* Paul opposed Judaism; Paul was a Jew *or* Paul was a Christian; Paul affirmed Torah *or* he rejected Torah; Paul's views involve absolute continuity *or* discontinuity with Judaism and the OT. Historical reality, however, is usually more complicated, especially within a period of gradual transitions.

The challenge is to make coherent sense of not just some of the Pauline texts—but *all* of them together, unless we are content with the conclusion that Paul was hopelessly confused and made numerous irreconcilable statements about important matters. The advocates of the Paul-within-Judaism perspective give insufficient consideration to the complexity of reality. They confront their readers with a kind of rigid either/or mentality that fails to allow tensions, nuances, and subtleties in Paul's affirmations. There is often a sense in which both sides of an either/or can be true and when it is necessary to conclude both/and. This is especially so in the present case, where we are dealing with the genealogical relationship of promise and fulfillment, the new flower growing out of the old seed.

It is of course occasionally possible to understand the same texts in different ways, which is one reason why starting assumptions are so important. Starting with the a priori convictions of the Paul-within-Judaism movement, certain texts can be taken as supporting their viewpoint. The question is: given the totality of the Pauline texts, which interpretations are the most plausible? The preponderance of relatively clear texts favors the traditional understanding of Paul and, indeed, makes the Paul-within-Judaism reading of the NT far less than convincing. So too the understanding of Christianity as a sect within Judaism.[14]

The new appreciation of Judaism as a religion of grace, and not a legalism wherein salvation is earned by works of righteousness,[15] is thought by some to support the idea of Christianity as a sect within Judaism.

---

14. See further Donald A. Hagner, "Matthew: Apostate, Reformer, Revolutionary?" *NTS* 49 (2003) 193-209.

15. The key work here is E. P. Sanders' *Paul and Palestinian Judaism* (Philadelphia: Fortress, 1977). This book was followed by his *Paul, the Law, and the Jewish People* (Philadelphia: Fortress, 1983). See now his *Paul: The Apostle's Life, Letters and Thought*

Contrary to the Lutheran reading of Paul where the law is problematic, to say the least, serving primarily as a propaedeutic to the gospel (a *paidagōgos*, lit. "child-guide," a role of the law stressed by Paul in Gal 3:24), in the new perspective[16] the law retains a positive function of enabling the achievement of righteousness. What then does Paul polemicize against when he speaks negatively of the law and works of the law, as he so often does? "Works of the law" are understood by Dunn and others not as general observance of the law, but very specifically as referring to "Jewish badges of identity" (or "national righteousness") that mark out Jews from the Gentiles, namely circumcision, sabbath observance, and *kashrut* (the dietary restrictions). Since Paul was called to preach the gospel to the Gentiles it is fully understandable that he would have been very much against "works of the law" in this sense, distinguishing the Jews, as the people of God, from the Gentiles. Given the understanding of Judaism as a "covenantal nomism," where, from the start, grace is an experienced reality, N. T. Wright's quip is appropriate: the issue for Paul is not grace but race.[17]

But an examination of the Pauline texts shows that Paul has a more fundamental problem with the law, one that applies equally to Jews and Gentiles.[18] It is well known that Paul makes both negative and positive statements about the law. Negatively he can write: "Now it is evident that no one is justified before God by the law" (Gal 3:11). "For if a law had been given that could make alive, then righteousness would indeed come through the law" (Gal 3:21); "For 'no human being will be justified in his sight' by deeds prescribed by the law, for through the law comes the knowledge of sin" (Rom 3:20); "For we hold that a person is justified by

---

(Minneapolis: Fortress, 2015).

16. For definitive essays on the subject, see J. D. G. Dunn, *The New Perspective on Paul*, WUNT 185 (Tübingen: Mohr Siebeck, 2005). For a full critique of the new perspective, see S. Westerholm, *Perspectives Old and New on Paul: The "Lutheran" Paul and His Critics* (Grand Rapids: Eerdmans, 2004); and S. Kim, *Paul and the New Perspective: Second Thoughts on the Origin of Paul's Gospel* (Grand Rapids: Eerdmans, 2001). See too D. A. Hagner, "Paul and Judaism: Testing the New Perspective," in *Revisiting Paul's Doctrine of Justification*, ed. Peter Stuhlmacher (Downers Grove, IL: IVP Academic, 2001) 75–105.

17. *The Climax of the Covenant: Christ and the Law in Pauline Theology* (Minneapolis: Fortress, 1991) 168.

18. For helpful discussion, see Thomas R. Schreiner, *The Law and Its Fulfillment: A Pauline Theology of Law* (Grand Rapids: Baker, 1993); and Schreiner, *40 Questions about Christians and Biblical Law*, 35–152. See too Hagner, "Paul's Quarrel with Judaism," in *Anti-Semitism and Early Christianity: Issues of Polemic and Faith*, ed. Craig A. Evans and Donald A. Hagner (Minneapolis: Fortress, 1993) 128–50.

faith apart from works prescribed by the law" (Rom 3:28). "For Christ is the end[19] of the law so that there may be righteousness for everyone who believes" (Rom 10:4). "You are not under law but under grace" (Rom 6:14-15); "But now we are discharged from the law, dead to that which held us captive, so that we are slaves not under the old written code but in the new life of the Spirit" (Rom 7:6); "before faith came, we were imprisoned and guarded under the law until faith would be revealed. Therefore the law was our disciplinarian until Christ came, so that we might be justified by faith. But now that faith has come, we are no longer subject to a disciplinarian" (Gal 3:23-25).

It is evident that the issue here is not merely a sociological one, but also a soteriological one, and thus one of universal significance, i.e., for both Jews and Gentiles. The law had only a temporary role to play in the pursuit of righteousness, and that role has come to an end with the coming of Christ. As in so much of what the NT has to say, a key turning point has now been reached in the history of salvation. We are in a new situation. Righteousness clearly remains the goal of God's people (e.g., Rom 8:4), who are God's people by grace, and *in that sense* Paul's gospel upholds the law. The radical difference in the new situation is the dynamic by which righteous living is now possible, namely the empowering of the Holy Spirit, which so characterizes the remarkable newness that arrives with the coming of the Christ. The Holy Spirit thus accomplishes what the law could not.

This situation is true for both Jews and Gentiles. The conclusion of some that Paul's view of the law applies only to Gentile converts, not to the Jews, is unjustifiable. Neither the language nor the logic of these passages supports any such idea. Although Paul allows the specialness of Israel because of election, his argument (especially in Romans) applies to all of humanity, including the Jews. Therefore it is necessary that the gospel be preached to Israel—indeed, first to them—as well as to the Gentiles.

But were there really any Jews in the first century, like those Paul seems to criticise, who were attempting to earn God's acceptance by their righteousness? It is admitted by more and more scholars that Sanders overstated his conclusion that the Jews universally recognized the foundation of their salvation as resting on covenant grace. There is a fair amount of evidence that some, even many, Jews thought of their salvation as being dependent upon their obedience to the law. Even Sanders had to take

---

19. The word "end" (NRSV), *telos*, can also be translated "goal," but it is difficult here to rule out the notion of the law coming to an end.

note of 4 Ezra, with its emphasis on works of the law, as an exception to the pattern of religion he presented from the literature of Second Temple Judaism.[20] The situation in the rabbinic sources is anything but clear and consistent. So, it is not difficult to find legalistic-sounding passages in the rabbinic literature. The argument of Sanders and others is that the grace of the covenant is the underlying assumption of such passages. What we appear to have in first-century Judaism is a classic instance of synergism, where grace and merit were held together in tension. In this paradoxical situation, we have an antinomy, famously articulated by Rabbi Akiba: "The world is judged by grace, and yet all is according to the amount of work" (Abot 3:20).[21]

The balance between covenant grace and works of the law was lost in post-exilic Israel. The experience of the exile understandably drove the Jews to observance of the law with a renewed dedication and energy. The result appears to have been a legalism that became dominant and all but obscured the reality of covenant grace. Under these circumstances, it should not be surprising to discover that many or even most Jews of Paul's day were *de facto* legalists, in contradiction of a proper understanding of covenant grace. Paul is not necessarily arguing against a straw man, as many scholars claim.

Although the contexts were decidedly different, Paul's argument against works-righteousness is similar to Luther's, who after all is dependent on Paul. Both writers are concerned with salvation, i.e. how sinners can stand justified before God. For Paul, and Luther, all of humanity, both Gentiles and Jews, are under judgment as sinners. The law, Paul argues, followed by Luther, has no answer to this universal problem, neither for the Jews nor the Gentiles. The solution to humanity's common plight is found in one way only: by faith in Christ's atoning sacrifice on the cross.

The recent, remarkable stress on continuity between Judaism and Christianity raises the question of whether and to what degree the NT is to be regarded as new at all,[22] and to what extent, if any, this newness creates an appreciable discontinuity.

---

20. "In IV Ezra, in short, we see an instance in which covenantal nomism has collapsed. All that is left is legalistic perfectionism." *Paul and Palestinian Judaism*, 409; 2 Baruch, probably dependent on 4 Ezra, contains a similar perspective.

21. After citing this text, Israel Abrahams adds, "the antinomy is the ultimate doctrine of Pharisaism." *Studies in Pharisaism and the Gospels*, First Series (Cambridge: Cambridge University Press, 1917; reprint, New York: Ktav, 1967) 146.

22. I must here mention the recent book by my Fuller Seminary colleague, OT scholar John Goldingay, entitled *Do we need the New Testament? Letting the Old Testament*

It is important to insist from the start that there is no doubt about the extensive and substantial continuity between Christianity and Judaism. This is not at all in question. There is hardly much need to document or review the vast discussion that supports this conclusion. I accept it as a given. Both Jesus and Paul are of course intensely Jewish, as indeed is the entire NT, and so too the earliest church and its theology. A church that is truly biblical, therefore, cannot affirm Marcionism. For the Christian the OT and the NT belong together. What happens in Jesus and the coming of the kingdom of God through him is part of the one great metanarrative of the Bible: the history of salvation.[23] Christianity is the goal and culmination of the story of Israel. In and through the church the story of Israel continues. So thought all the writers of the NT. Herein lies the *continuity*. The extensive discontinuity we encounter in the NT itself presupposes this continuity.

We have therefore to deal with *both* old and new. This point is famously made by Jesus according to Matthew: "Therefore every scribe who has been trained for the kingdom of heaven is like the master of a household who brings out of his treasure what is new and what is old" [*kaina kai palaia*, lit. "new things and old things"]. The unexpected order of new things mentioned before old things places an extra emphasis on the new. For this reason, the biblical word *fulfillment* is the perfect word to describe what we encounter in the NT. The concept of fulfillment reaches both ways, back to the promises of the past and forward to future (and present) realization of the promises. The word "fulfillment" captures *the unity of the realization together with its promise*, and it is thus no surprise that it becomes such an important word in the vocabulary and conceptuality, not only of Matthew, but of all the NT writers.

Christianity is not *other* than Judaism; it is the *fulfillment of Judaism*. The early church was at first entirely Jewish, and although it remained a sect within Judaism for a very short time, Christianity is to be

---

Speak for Itself (Downers Grove, IL: InterVarsity, 2015). While I appreciate Goldingay's opposition to Marcionism and his desire to value the OT on its own terms, I think he underestimates the extent and importance of the newness of the NT. His answer to the question posed in his title would seem to be something like: Yes, but just barely. Goldingay emphasizes continuity and downplays discontinuity between the testaments. There are some good things and some important correctives to gain from reading Goldingay's book, but the idea of the NT as little more than an extension of the teaching of the OT fails to appreciate the radical newness that so captivated the authors of the NT.

23. See Tom Schreiner's masterful book *The King in His Beauty: A Biblical Theology of the Old and New Testaments* (Grand Rapids: Baker Academic, 2013).

understood as a *fulfilled Judaism,* and could be described as a Judaism coming to its divinely intended goal in the full inclusion of the Gentiles in the people of God.

While all this is true, at the same time the extent of newness in the Gospels—and indeed the whole of the NT—is such that an unavoidable *discontinuity* with Judaism is caused. Fulfillment includes forward movement and thus inevitably involves discontinuity. It is the eschatological/apocalyptic character of what the Gospels announce in the coming of Jesus[24] that marks the pivotal turning point in salvation history. Roy Harrisville's conclusion remains valid:

> That which is concealed and only intimated here [in Matt 13:52] is that the new which Jesus embodies is not merely the chronologically new, but above all, the *eschatologically new*. The element of continuity between new and old is indeed present, but it is a continuity which must not be allowed to deprive the new of its uniqueness (its contrast with the old), its finality, and its dynamic, i.e., its eschatological character.[25]

The nature and extent of this newness makes it impossible to describe Christianity as merely a sect or a reform movement within Judaism.[26] As C. F. D. Moule said: "It is the positive note of fulfilment that, ironically, constitutes the real offence—the *skandalon*. Christianity is undoubtedly new wine."[27]

---

24. "Paradoxically, therefore, the greatest discontinuity is in the coming of Jesus. From one perspective he fulfilled the promises and hopes of the Old Testament, and yet from another he surpassed all expectations so that his coming inaugurated a new and final stage in the history of salvation." David L. Baker, *Two Testaments, One Bible: The Theological Relationship Between the Old and New Testaments*, 3rd ed. (Downers Grove, IL: InterVarsity, 2010) 223–24.

25. *The Concept of Newness in the New Testament*, 28, my italics. The concept of newness "with its attendant aspects of continuity, contrast, finality and the dynamic is central to the New Testament literature as a whole." Ibid., 108.

26. Thus rightly, M. D. Hooker, *Continuity and Discontinuity: Early Christianity in its Jewish Setting* (London: Epworth, 1986) 23.

27. He adds "What, in the light of the facts, are we really saying about those wineskins?" This quotation is from Moule's "Introductory Essay" to the Festschrift written in honor of Morna Hooker, which is entirely dedicated to our subject, viz., "continuity and discontinuity between early Christianity and its Jewish parent." *Early Christian Thought in Its Jewish Context*, ed. John Barclay and John Sweet (Cambridge: Cambridge University Press, 1996) 6.

PART THREE

Judaism and Christianity

14

Another Look at "The Parting of the Ways"

ALTHOUGH MARTIN HENGEL WROTE so extensively on both Judaism and Christianity, only seldom did he directly address the subject of this essay.[1] His views on the subject would have to be described as "traditional," but that hardly means he has nothing to offer. He is often in his own way "radical," or perhaps better, "original," mainly because of his incessant returning to the primary materials.

Over the past decade or two scholars have been actively promoting what may be called a new paradigm of Christian origins. In what seems to be an increasingly popular pattern of understanding, the NT and early Christianity are perceived in as fully Jewish terms as possible.[2] Thus Jesus

---

1. E.g., "Das früheste Christentum als eine jüdische messianische und unveralistische Bewegung," in *Judaica, Hellenistica et Christiana. Kleine Schriften II*, WUNT 109 (Tübingen: Mohr Siebeck, 1999) 200-218. An English translation of an earlier, somewhat briefer version of this essay, but also with much new material, can be found in "Early Christianity as a Jewish-Messianic, Universalist Movement," in *Conflicts and Challenges in Early Christianity*, ed. D. A. Hagner (Harrisburg, PA: Trinity, 1999) 1-41; cf. especially the new section on "The Final Separation," 31-40. See too the discussion of Paul as a persecutor of the church, in "Der vorchristliche Paulus," in collaboration with R. Deines, *Paulus und Jakobus. Kleine Schriften III*, WUNT 141 (Tübingen: Mohr Siebeck, 2002) 68-192, originally published in *Paulus und das antike Judentum. Tübingen-Durham-Symposium im Gedenken an den 50. Todestag Adolf Schlatters (†19. Mai 1938)*, ed. M. Hengel and U. Heckel, WUNT 58 (Tübingen: Mohr Siebeck, 1991) 177-293. Available in English translation, *The Pre-Christian Paul*, trans. J. Bowden (London: SCM, 1991) especially 79-86.

2. See the R. Scroggs summary, "The Judaizing of the New Testament," *Chicago Theological Seminary Register* 75 (1986) 36-45.

is understood as a Jewish charismatic healer-teacher, who fits comfortably among other such figures in first-century Palestine. Even Paul is an unexceptional Jew, with no disagreement with Judaism or the law, but for his desire to include the Gentiles as also the subjects of God's grace.[3] The Gospel of Matthew is to be understood as representing a Christian sect of *Judaism* rather than a Jewish Christianity.[4] Many now think that it is improper to speak of "Christianity" at all until, at the earliest, the middle of the second century, or indeed as late as the fourth century. Hence, in the first century—and thus through the whole of the NT period—it is thought improper to speak of "Jewish Christians," but only of "Jewish believers in Jesus." Indeed, it is even improper to speak of Gentiles as "Christians." What we have traditionally called "Christianity" in the first century, and even later, is now regarded as simply a "sect" of Judaism, like other sects, such as the Essenes or the Pharisees.[5]

There is much that is good and helpful about this new realization of the Jewish character of the Christian faith. Martin Hengel turned his face against the syncretism of the Religionsgeschichtliche Schule when he asserted "without qualification that Christianity grew *entirely* out of Jewish soil."[6] Of course, it is true that the whole of Christianity is and remains in a sense Jewish. But the insight that the NT is so thoroughly Jewish can also cause distortion, if it neglects or underestimates the dramatic newness that is intrinsic to Jesus and the faith of his followers—something Hengel was never guilty of. A correct understanding of that faith comes only through an appreciation of both the old *and the new*. The Evangelist

---

3. E.g., J. G. Gager, *Reinventing Paul* (Oxford: Oxford University Press, 2000).

4. E.g., A. J. Saldarini, *Matthew's Christian-Jewish Community* (Chicago: University of Chicago Press, 1994); D. Sim, *The Gospel of Matthew and Christian Judaism: The History and Social Setting of the Matthean Community* (Edinburgh: T. & T. Clark, 1998). In disagreement with this view, see D. A. Hagner, "Matthew: Apostate, Reformer, Revolutionary?" *NTS* 49 (2003) 193–209.

5. Thus, e.g., J. D. Crossan, *The Birth of Christianity*, XXXIII. Cf. J. G. Gager: "prior to the book of Acts (which I am inclined to date rather late, well into the second century) we are dealing with something that we cannot reasonably label as Christianity. Just to make myself perfectly clear in the Gospels of Mark, Matthew, and John; in the letters of Paul; in the book of Revelation; and in the letter of James (just to name the most obvious cases) we encounter forms of literature, practice, community and belief that are best designated as streams within Judaism of the first two centuries of the common era . . . there is no hint or trace of anti-Judaism in any of these texts and no sense of a departure from or a rejecting of Judaism." "Where Does Luke's Anti-Judaism Come From?" in *Heresy and Identity in Late Antiquity*, ed. E. Iricinschi and H. M. Zellentin, TSAJ 119 (Tübingen: Mohr Siebeck, 2008) 207-8.

6. "Early Christianity as a Jewish-Messianic, Universalistic Movement," 1 (italics his).

Matthew records Jesus as making the point in these words: "Therefore every scribe who has been trained for the kingdom of heaven is like a householder who brings out of the treasure box what is new [*kaina*] and what is old [*palaia*]" (Matt 13:52), even placing priority upon the new by mentioning it before the old.[7] But the revisionist readings of the NT that have become fashionable in recent years are so fascinated with Christianity's roots in the old that they pay little or no attention to the new. There is far more newness in the gospel and early Christianity than can be contained within a sect of Judaism;[8] the old wineskins cannot contain the new wine.

Given the nature of the subject, it is hardly surprising that the "parting of the ways," i.e., the parting of the church from the synagogue, the separation of Christians from the Jews, in the early centuries of our era, is seen differently by different people. From the outset, it must be stressed that it is not possible to do justice to the full complexity of reality. No one has the unlimited time or the energy or indeed, the actual capability, of dealing exhaustively with a single event, much less a process, that has occurred in history.[9] The possibility of knowledge always depends therefore on the ability to select and to simplify. And thus any claim that deals with a decades-long process can easily be criticized and deconstructed.[10] We leave aside for the present moment, the further complicating factor of the unavoidable bias that affects every interpreter, even those who would maintain a supposed "neutrality."

The concept of "the parting of the ways" is of necessity a gross simplification. It cannot tell the whole story. It is meant to refer to the early differences between Judaism and Christianity that eventuated, with the passing of time, in two separate, but undeniably related, religions.[11] The

---

7. See D. A. Hagner, "New Things from the Scribe's Treasure Box (Mt 13:52)," *ExpT* 109 (1998) 329-34.

8. David Flusser makes the point in these words: "It would be unreasonable to underestimate the newness of the message of the Church and the difference between the main structure of the Jewish faith and the Christocentricity of the Church." "The Jewish-Christian Schism (Part I)," 36.

9. Along the same lines, see the comments of Luomanen, "Ebionites and Nazarenes," 116: "Categorization is one of the most elementary functions of human cognition. Since our brains are incapable of processing millions of unrelated details simultaneously, we are bound to categorize, to form simplified pictures of ourselves and of the reality to which we are related."

10. Cynically put, you can always outdo the scholarship of another by showing the subject to be more complex than he/she had taken account of.

11. For a judicious survey of approaches to the problem of the parting of the ways,

challenge of identifying the differences is complicated by the fact that first-century Judaism was hardly monolithic, and itself undergoing a process of development, while nascent Christianity was in a process of self-discovery and increasing articulation of its theology. How can anything meaningful be said about realities so volatile?

THE CHALLENGE

These days a growing number of scholars maintain that there never was a "parting of the ways."[12] There is no doubt that these scholars intend to be radical. The editors of a recent volume on the subject have no hesitation in saying that the purpose of the essays is "to dismantle traditional models and trenchant biases in scholarship on Judaism and Christianity."[13] Looked at more closely, at least for the editors and some of the contributors, it is not denied that there was a parting,[14] but rather that it occurred in a "single, early, decisive" act that involved an absolute split, excluding all further contact between Jews and Christians. But it seems to me that such a simplistic idea of the parting of the ways is a straw man, easy to knock down. Most who use the expression are well aware of the fact that the parting is a process that took place over decades, with differing rapidity in different places, and never to the point that future contact, mutual interest and influence between Jews and Christians ceased altogether. One may of course at the same time point to a moment of key significance, such as the fall of Jerusalem in 70 or the Bar Kokhba revolt in 132–35, but these simply mark major turning points in what was a long and ongoing process.

The first problem the question of the parting of the ways presents to us is that neither Judaism nor Christianity were settled, clearly bounded realities in the first century. Daniel Boyarin denies that Judaism is the

---

see T. A. Robinson, *Ignatius of Antioch and the Parting of the Ways*, chapter 6, "Boundaries, Identity, and Labels," 203–41. Robinson makes the excellent point that "Instead of dismissing boundary-marking terms as mere rhetoric and as misrepresentations of reality we should try to see rhetoric as providing as essential tool for mapping and describing new territory. Indeed, the rhetoric of group boundaries corresponds to the reality much as a political map corresponds to the physical world," 228.

12. See A. H. Becker and A. Y. Reed, eds., *The Ways That Never Parted: Jews and Christians in Late Antiquity and the Early Middles Ages*. Along similar lines, A. K. Petersen, "At the End of the Road."

13. Ibid., xiii.

14. The title of P. Fredriksen's article implies otherwise, however: "What 'Parting of the Ways?'"

parent religion to Christianity, and denies that we can "speak of a religion, Judaism, at all in the sense of a bounded institution existing before the Christian era (and even fairly deep into that era), of which it could be said that it was hostile to any one thing."[15] He sees no "absolute point" of difference, where the two groups are "fully formed, bounded, and separate entities and identities."[16] He notes approvingly the trend of referring to the "fourth century as the first century of Judaism and Christianity."[17] It has therefore become fashionable for scholars to speak of first-century Judaisms, in the plural.[18]

While it would be foolish to deny that there was variety within the Judaism of the Second Temple period, Judaism cannot be everything. If Judaism, like a wax nose, can be anything, then obviously Christianity too can be considered a manifestation of Judaism.[19] Despite the real diversity that may be demonstrated, there are at the same time some distinctives that mark out Judaism(s) over against non-Judaism(s). There are core elements that are common to, and unite, all manifestations of Judaism—serving as a *sine qua non*.

The earlier language of "normative Judaism,"[20] which was used to refer to the Judaism of the Second Temple period as uniformly that of

---

15. "Semantic Differences; or 'Judaism'/'Christianity,'" 65. The two groups represent "existent realities but not defined nor clearly distinguished ones, that is, a stiuation of hybridity." Ibid., 67. See too, along the same lines, A. D. Crown, "Judaism and Christianity: The Parting of the Ways."

16. *Border Lines*, 7. "Until the end of the fourth century, if we consider all of their varieties and not just the nascent "orthodox" ones—Judaism and Christianity were phenomenologically indistinguishable as entities." Ibid., 89.

17. The quoted words are from J. Neusner, *The Three Stages in the Formation of Rabbinic Judaism*, 77. This viewpoint was already espoused by R. Ruether in 1972. See her "Judaism and Christianity: Two Fourth-Century Religions."

18. "There is no Judaism but, in today's world as well as in the past, only Judaisms—a set of parallel systems in competition. The fundamental characteristic of Judaism is its fragmentary nature, that is, the constant co-existence of a plurality of groups, movements, and traditions of thought." Boccaccini, *Roots of Rabbinic Judaism*, 14. Cf. Neusner, "The issue, how to define Judaism, is now settled: we do not. We define Judaisms." *The Judaism the Rabbis Take for Granted*, 12. See too, R. A. Kraft, "The Weighing of the Parts"; J. Neusner et al., eds., *Judaisms and Their Messiahs at the Turn of the Christian Era* (Cambridge: Cambridge University Press, 1987).

19. Precisely the conclusion of Chilton and Neusner, *Judaism in the New Testament*. See too, G. Boccaccini, *Middle Judaism*, 15–18. Yet (paradoxically?) Neusner writes that "Judaism and Christianity are completely different religions, not different versions of one religion" . . . they "respectively stand for different people talking about different things to different people" "Judaism and Christianity in the First Century," 258.

20. Classically represented in G. F. Moore's comprehensive *Judaism*. According to R.

post-70 rabbinic Judaism, has rightly been rejected by scholars. Now stressed is the plurality of viewpoint that characterized the period before 70. Nevertheless, underlying that diversity is a common basis shared by Judaism through the Second Temple period. The essence of Judaism, "common Judaism," has been found in such things as "covenantal nomism" (Sanders, famously) or the history/experience of the Jewish people. More helpful, it seems to me, is to list a cluster of ideas, such as, e.g., one God, one Torah, and one Temple.[21] J. D. G. Dunn suggests that Second Temple Judaism has at its core four pillars: monotheism, election, covenant focused in Torah, and land focused in Temple.[22] All forms of Second Temple Judaism adhered in principle to these fundamental realities (even Qumran, where it was not the Jerusalem Temple that was rejected but rather its leadership). As Dunn goes on to show,[23] and we will explore below, Christianity in one way or another eventually questioned and modified each of them.[24] The point to emphasize here, however, in response to Boyarin's claim, is that there were some things that were vital to Judaism and its ongoing existence, things that Judaism of whatever variety was bound to protect. Any challenge to any one of the pillars of Judaism would put a dissident group in considerable difficulty. Jews were bound to become hostile towards those who denied or in significant ways modified matters that were at the heart of their faith.

In a rather intriguingly parallel way, ever since the time of Walter Bauer's influential book,[25] scholars have argued that early Christianity

---

Deines, Pharisaic Judaism qualifies to be considered as normative Judaism. *Die Pharisäer*, 534-55; see too his "The Pharisees Between 'Judaisms' and 'Common Judaism.'"

21. Thus S. Schwartz, *Imperialism and Jewish Society, 200 B.C.E. to 640 C.E.* See the overview in Boccaccini, *Roots of Rabbinic Judaism*, 8-14.

22. *The Partings of the Ways*, 18-36. Cf. Douglas Hare, *The Theme of Jewish Persecution of Christians in the Gospel according to St Matthew*, 3-18.

23. In a new introduction to the 2nd edition of his *Partings of the Ways*, Dunn says that in the intervening 15 years he has come to regard the subject as more complex than he had realized. He denies now his earlier conclusion that a final parting took place at 135 or at least by the end of the second century, and now concludes with Daniel Boyarin and others that "throughout the first three to four centuries what we might call 'ordinary Christians' did *not* see Christianity and Judaism as two separate far less opposed religions."

24. Cf. A. F. Segal's statement that "The decisive theoretical issues dividing Christianity from Judaism were the interpretation of Torah and the concept of God's unity." *Rebecca's Children*, 174. Segal holds that "After the first and second Jewish wars against Rome, the paths of Judaism and Christianity parted more rapidly" (173).

25. *Orthodoxy and Heresy in Earliest Christianity*. The enormous influence of Bauer's book, along with the fact that its thesis is rarely challenged, may be due to the

was no less in flux than contemporary Judaism. At the beginning there was a variety of Christianities,[26] with the concern for orthodoxy emerging only in later centuries. Such a conclusion, however, is hard to reconcile with the evidence of the NT itself, as Howard Marshall showed us more than 30 years ago.[27] Marshall points out that there is a strong concern for orthodoxy not only in the Pastoral Epistles and the Catholic Epistles, but also in Paul's letters as well. Paul regularly opposed false teaching and did not tolerate the preaching of another Jesus, another gospel, or another Spirit. There was of course a *limited* degree of variety in the teaching of the early church, as Marshall also admits. But the important point here is that there was enough of a consensus to be able to define Christianity, from the beginning. A. M. Hunter found the unity of NT to consist in one Lord, one church and one salvation.[28] Dunn argues for "the unity between the historical Jesus and the exalted Christ," which he expands to include several additional elements.[29] One might refer very generally to the gospel or the elements of the basic kerygma of the early church. Hengel says the following primarily about the four Gospels, but would no doubt speak similarly of the whole NT:

> Looking back on the history of the church which is now almost two thousand years old we must say that, thank God, the real unity of the churches does not lie in our different, indeed controversial human convictions and efforts, but in the one Lord, the "head," i.e. "God incarnate," the judge who himself took judgment upon himself, who, "obedient to death on the cross," became the redeemer of all; whose body is the church, despite all the failure, selfishness and self-righteousness of its members, because he alone can pronounce us "godless" righteous. By the

---

consonance of its conclusions with the contemporary *Zeitgeist*. Holmberg's criticism is worth noting: "A question seldom broached or answered is how and when a movement with a one-person origin and indubitable continuity from this origin to a known group of Galileans exploded into a plethora of wildly divergent Christ-believing groups that it took some two centuries to connect to each other in a semblance of unity." *Exploring Early Christianity*, 12-13. See T. A. Robinson, *The Bauer Thesis Examined*; for some helpful correctives, F. Wisse, "Heterodidaskalia: Accounting for Diversity in Early Christian Texts"; cf. L. Goppelt, "The Plurality of New Testament Theologies and the Unity of the Gospel as an Ecumenical Problem."

26. For a typical example of emphasis on this, see K. L. King, "Which Early Christianity?"

27. "Orthodoxy and Heresy in Earlier Christianity."

28. *The Unity of the New Testament*.

29. See *Unity and Diversity in the New Testament*, 369; cf. 371.

will of God we have the one—unique—"good news," the one Gospel which stands at the beginning of the church, in sometimes very different and human forms. Yet all four Gospels proclaim solely the one Lord of the church and the one salvation brought about by him.[30]

Only if by "orthodoxy" one means the fully developed manifestation of an established church and its elaborated ecumenical statements must we wait until the fourth century.[31] That there were sometimes fuzzy boundaries and a variety of expressions should not be doubted. But as witnessed by the NT itself there is enough definition at the beginning to be able to lay some boundary markers.[32] To refer to Judaism and Christianity in these terms does not involve anachronisms that make it impossible to speak of a parting of the ways.[33] As Carleton Paget says, moving away from the abstract, in the final analysis, "there were people who called themselves Jews and people who called themselves Christians and these people did not regard themselves as a single group."[34]

---

30. *The Four Gospels and the One Gospel of Jesus Christ*, 167f.

31. Cf. B. Holmberg: "The use of such general terms [Judaism and Christianity] does not necessitate the importing of, say, fourth-century Judaism or Christianity into the term when used about first-century phenomena. Words are not receptacles that *have* to contain every meaning that anybody ever put into them." "The Life in the Diaspora Synagogues," 228.

32. Boundaries can exist even apart from terminology. T. A. Robinson rightly notes that "The crucial issue is whether there was a distinctive Christian self-understanding, not whether the group in question had a particular label, for a community need not have a distinctive *term* for itself in order to have a clear *sense* of its separate and distinctive identity." *Ignatius and the Parting of the Ways*, 205–6.

33. See the balanced, insightful work of G. Jossa, *Jews or Christians?* A. Runesson, rather oddly, allows the use of the words "Judaism" (and "Jew," "Jewish") in reference to the first century, but not "Christianity" or "Christian," which he allows only beginning in the fourth century. "Inventing Christian Identity," 71. M. Zetterholm similarly rejects the term "Christianity" for the first century. "A Covenant for Gentiles," 170–71. B. Holmberg responds with the following appropriate remark: "Now, if "Christian" is a term used about a specific group of people and their specific faith and ethos by others and themselves *already in the first century*, it is hard to understand why modern anxieties about how the term might be misunderstood should prevent its use in historical investigation of this very phenomenon." "The Life in the Diaspora Synagogues," 228. For a defense of the use of the word in referring to the first century, see T. Hegedus, "Naming Christians in Antiquity," SR 33 (2004) 173–90.

34. *Jews, Christians and Jewish-Christians in Antiquity*, 9.

ANOTHER LOOK AT "THE PARTING OF THE WAYS"

ON THE DEFINITION OF KEY WORDS

If ever the definitions of words was of importance to a subject, it is here. We have just seen this in the words Judaism and Christianity. If one means by them static entities, like forms of set concrete, we shall find them only later. If, on the other hand, one means emerging systems undergoing active development, yet with enough focus and fixity to make them essentially definable, then we can speak of them in the first century.

If, for the sake of the argument, we are granted the permission to speak of essential Judaism and Christianity in the first century, we are, as also noted above, still left with the need to define whatever may be meant by the phrase "the parting of the ways." Is the "parting" to be understood as the separation of Jewish Christians from the Gentile church, or their separation from Judaism?[35] Even more problematic is the idea of a "final" parting of the ways. If the parting of the ways involves an absolute break that occurred at a single point of time and altered forever the relationship between Jews and Christians, that is one thing, and we shall be inclined to find it only late, if at all. If, however, we define it as the process of division that occurred as the result of Jews (initially) affirming and proclaiming things "unacceptable" to Judaism, then perhaps it is to be found remarkably early. By "unacceptable," we mean not merely things different or unpleasing, but things intolerable because of their tension with basic components of common Judaism. Samuel Sandmel once defined the parting of the ways in the words of a question: After mentioning the Pharisees' and Sadducees' awareness of their differences, he asks "When and how did the Christians' comparable awareness of difference *within* Judaism lead to their awareness of a difference *from* Judaism?"[36] I would add a difference that could not be tolerated and had to be deliberately opposed.

There are many other tricky words, for example, "new," "old," "telos" ["goal" or "end"], and "fulfillment." One sometimes has the feeling that the issue comes down to semantics, i.e., the selection of the right words, understood with the "right" meaning. Even the word "Jew" can be ambiguous. One must ask, Is it being used to refer to ethnicity or religion? If the latter, can the Gentile Christian also be called a "Jew,"—a descendant

---

35. M. Heemstra argues that "the fundamental break happened between Jewish Christians and mainstream Judaism." *The Fiscus Judaicus and the Parting of the Ways*, 209. Yet, as we will see below, Jewish Christianity hardly thought of itself as involving a break with Judaism.

36. *The First Christian Century in Judaism and Christianity*, 158-59.

of Abraham, the true circumcision, a member of the Israel of God? It is possible to think of fully developed Christianity as a new manifestation of Judaism for the Gentiles.

To my mind, the word "fulfillment" is the most useful and important because it captures in itself both the continuity with the old and the discontinuity involved in the new. More than renewal or reform, fulfillment refers to the arrival at a novel stage of the realization of the promises to Israel. But everything new can be traced back to the promises to Israel—which were always intended as ultimately universal.

It is not unusual to hear the options expressed antithetically: either, on the one hand Christianity is radically discontinuous with Judaism; or, on the other hand, Christianity is fully in continuity with Judaism, as the true, fulfilled Judaism. There are enough substantial continuities to argue that Christianity is a species of Judaism. But at the same time the discontinuities are so extensive and significant, there is enough newness that Christianity is necessarily separate from, and other than, Judaism. Such is the complexity of fulfillment. Just as a glass may be described as half full or half empty, depending on what perspective one chooses—and both statements are true at the same time—so one may describe Christianity in terms either of continuity or discontinuity. Fulfillment, pulling together past and present, describes a situation where *both are true at the same time*.

C. F. D. Moule once wrote "But it is the positive note of fulfilment that ironically, constitutes the real offence—the *skandalon*. Christianity is undoubtedly new wine."[37] What is fulfillment to one often sounds like supersessionism to another.[38] But fulfillment need not entail supersession—at least it did not for Paul (Rom 9–11).

THE MARKS OF NEWNESS

The NT is so full of new things—new things of such great significance—that one may wonder how anyone could justly describe it as representing merely another strain of Judaism. The marks of newness we shall now briefly review (one can hardly do more in this essay than point to them)

---

37. In the "Introductory Essay" to *Early Christian Thought in Its Jewish Context*, J. Barclay and J. Sweet, eds., 6.

38. Once after presenting a lecture in which I argued for this notion of fulfillment, a questioner accused me of being a supersessionist, although I am not. The lecture can be found in "A Positive Theology of Judaism from the New Testament," *Svensk Exegetisk Årsbok* 69 (2004) 7–28.

are revolutionary and unacceptable—indeed, intolerable—to Judaism, Second Temple and otherwise. They are therefore the immediate causes of the parting of the ways, and it is their cumulative effect that causes the process to gain momentum as time passes.[39]

1. *Jesus according to the Gospels.* Already with the appearance of Jesus we encounter dramatically new things that anticipate the process of the parting of the ways. The seeds of the eventual separation are already planted in the ministry of Jesus. He came not, like an OT prophet, to reform Judaism. Not even, to use the increasingly popular phrase, did he come "to restore Judaism." He was about something new—vitally related to the old, yes—but as its fulfillment: i.e., the dawning of the Kingdom and the fulfilling of the promises. It is this that explains the radical things Jesus says and does, together with his own unique personal identity. In what follows we deliberately ignore the extent to which Jesus and his message are also thoroughly Jewish, and the extent to which in his own way he can be seen as positive towards the pillars of Judaism. We choose instead to focus on elements of discontinuity.

It is clear that Jesus came to bring fulfillment *to Israel as God's chosen people*. This is particularly clear in the Gospel of Matthew, where Jesus restricts both his and his disciples' ministry to Israel. To the Canaanite woman he says "I was sent only to the lost sheep of the house of Israel" (15:24); to his disciples he says "Go nowhere among the Gentiles, and enter no town of the Samaritans, but go rather to the lost sheep of the house of Israel" (10:5-6). The reason that Matthew, alone among the Gospels, records this restriction is to underline the priority of the God's covenant faithfulness to his people. At the same time, however, the evangelist knows well that the ultimate goal of the gospel is a universal one.[40] In Matthew's eschatological discourse, Jesus says "this gospel of

---

39. D. G. Horrell concludes his survey of the NT data with the following: "This early period of Christian origins is clearly the crucial period for the development of a distinctively 'Christian' identity... This new group identity 'In Christ'... establishes a new boundary between insider and outsider." "Becoming Christian," 331-32.

40. G. N. Stanton finds in Matthew a reflection of the parting of the ways: "Many of the gospel's most distinctive features are related to the 'parting of the ways': the strengthening of anti-jewish polemic; the greater prominence given to apocalyptic themes; the evangelist's claim that the church is the true heir and interpreter of Scripture; the care with which a Gentile mission is defended." He further mentions that "cohesion is necessitated both by the perceived threat from Judaism and by the new communities' need for self-definition and legitimation." Stanton finds Matthew's Christology to be similar to that of the Fourth Gospel, namely "shaped (in part) by the experiences and self-understanding of minority 'sectarian' communities at odds with

the kingdom will be preached throughout the whole world, as a testimony to all nations" (24:14) and at the end of the Gospel, Jesus presents the famous commission to "make disciples of all nations" (27:19). And throughout the Gospel there have been hints of that universalism, e.g., in the reference to Jesus as not only the son of David, but also the son of Abraham (alluding to the universalism of the Abrahamic covenant), the coming of the magi to worship the King; in John the Baptist's belittling of Abrahamic descent and the remark that God can raise up raise up children to Abraham from the stones; in the contrasting of the Roman centurion's faith with the unbelief of Israel, together with Jesus' statement that "many will come from east and west and sit at table with Abraham, Isaac, and Jacob in the kingdom of heaven, while the sons of the kingdom will be thrown into the outer darkness" (8:10–12); in the praise of the Canaanite woman's faith and the healing of her daughter (15:28); in the statement that "the kingdom of God will be taken away from you and given to a nation producing the fruit of it (21:44); and in the parable of the wedding feast, where those invited refuse to come, and the servants are told to go "to the thoroughfares" and to "invite to the marriage feast as many as you find" (22:9). The election of Israel is not quite done away with here, but it is being pushed to the margins.

Jesus' radical attitude to *the Temple* is well known and many think that it was the main catalyst leading to the death of Jesus.[41] To attack the Temple was to attack the center of Jewish worship and piety, the cult itself, and the very notion of ritual purity. The prophetic symbolism of Jesus' cleansing of the Temple (Mark:11:15–19 parr; cf. Zech 14:21b) points to its destruction, which he seems also to have prophesied (Mark 13:1–4 parr; cf. 14:58; 15:29). The implications of Jesus' stance toward

---

their Jewish neighbors." (191) "Christology and the Parting of the Ways," 169 and 191. Stanton concludes rightly, in my opinion, that "the communities for which Matthew wrote have recently parted company painfully with local synagogues. 'Church' and 'synagogue' are at odds with one another . . . Matthew's increased use of apocalyptic motifs, his strong call for a 'greater righteousness.' and his insistence on 'high community boundaries' are all related to this social setting." *A Gospel of a New People*, 280. Stanton regards the parting of the ways as a gradual process, "not precipitated by any one historical event," nor "a formal decision taken by either group. It was the eventual result of mutual incomprehension and suspicion" (ibid.).

41. "The gun may already have been cocked, but it was the temple demonstration which pulled the trigger." Thus E. P. Sanders, *Jesus and Judaism*, 305. Cf. J. D. G. Dunn: "*the most probable historical reconstruction of the death of Jesus is that on the Jewish side the principal movers were the high-priestly faction. In which case once again we see that the primary issue would have been the Temple and Jesus' perceived challenge to it.*" *The Partings of the Ways*, 53 (italics his).

the Temple were enormous, but at this point they remained implications, whose real significance was hardly evident.

Jesus' attitude toward *the Torah* is also remarkably ambiguous. His fundamental loyalty to the Law is hardly questionable. At the same time, however, Jesus interprets the law like no other, with a shocking sovereignty, and in ways that can be said to violate the letter of the law. Hengel began his little book on following Jesus with a study of the remarkable logion in Matt 8:21-22, where Jesus instructs a would-be disciple to ignore burying his father: "Let the dead bury their dead." According to Hengel, "there is hardly one logion of Jesus which more sharply runs counter to law, piety and custom."[42] Jesus' leniency concerning the sabbath commandment,[43] his absolute prohibition of divorce, his lack of concern for the dietary laws, together reveal a radical position that was unacceptable to the religious authorities. So when they perceived the teaching of Jesus as being incompatible with Torah, one of the pillars of the Jewish faith, they began to think of taking action against him (cf. Mark 3:6 parr; 14:2 parr).

Hengel's remark is again on target: "Jesus' attitude towards the Torah and the temple possesses, over against that of all other Jewish groups, an unmistakable, original stamp. He thereby brings something really *new*, and he continues this new thing in the Church made up of his disciples. Both Jesus and the Church fall outside the framework provided by the idea .. of a harmonious 'common Judaism.'"[44]

Finally we must at least mention the remarkable personal claims of Jesus, according to the gospel tradition. Jesus not only tacitly accepts the messianic acclamation of the crowds in his entry into Jerusalem (Mark 11:1-10 parr), and Peter's confession (Matt 16:16) but, according to Mark, affirms that he is the Messiah, "the Son of the Blessed," in his answer to the High Priest (Mark 14:62). He also indicates that he is the unique Son of God (Mark 12:6-8; 13:32; cf. Matt 27:43) and especially in Matt 11:27=Luke 10:22 (cf. too the demons' knowledge in Mark 3:11; 5:7). To this material we must add the direct association of his announcement of

---

42. *The Charismatic Leader and His Followers*, 14. Cf. E. P. Sanders, "Jesus, Paul and Judaism," 413-15.

43. For full discussion of Jesus and the sabbath, see D. A. Hagner, "Jesus and the Synoptic Sabbath Controversies," *BBR* 19 (2009) 215-48. The same essay appears in *Key Events in the Life of the Historical Jesus: A Collaborative Exploration of Context and Coherence*, ed. D. L. Bock and R. L. Webb, WUNT 247 (Tübingen: Mohr Siebeck, 2009) 251-92

44. M. Hengel and R. Deines, "E. P. Sanders' 'Common Judaism,' Jesus and the Pharisees," 15.

the arriving of the kingdom of God with his own person (Luke 17:21), his unparalleled authority (Mark 1:22; 11:28; Mt 7:28ff.), the call to follow him rather than God or Torah (Mark 8:34-38; Matt 10:37-39 par),[45] and his eventual return as judge (Mark 13:26 par; Matt 24:50-51; 25:31-46).[46]

Jesus, fully the Jew, at the same time repeatedly exhibits a shocking newness in his acts and deeds. In Jesus we have only the adumbrations of what is to come. But in retrospect they are unmistakable enough and they are ultimately inseparable from his personal identity. It is little surprise that the Jewish authorities perceived him as a threat to the central, fixed elements at the heart of Judaism.[47] "Early Christianity's relatively quick break with Sanders' 'common Judaism,' despite the fact that it rested entirely on Jewish roots, is a phenomenon which we believe *ultimately* goes back historically and theologically to Jesus' words and deeds, in combination with his claim to have been sent from God. This development is without analogy in Palestinian Judaism."[48]

2. *The Earliest Church.* If ever one is justified in referring to the church as a sect within Judaism it would be in the case of the first few years of its existence. In retrospect, of course, we may well regard the earliest believers in Jesus as Christians. They themselves could have had no such notion. They would have thought of themselves as Jews who had begun to experience the fulfillment of their Jewish hopes and expected the eschaton in the immediate future (Acts 1:6). They lived in a period of rapid transition as they began to explore the meaning of the strange and spectacular events they had so recently seen and experienced.

---

45. See M. Hengel, *The Charismatic Leader and His Followers*. To summarize the conclusions of his study, Hengel quotes the words of E. Fuchs: "that Jesus 'dared to act in God's place.'"

46. Hengel has called our attention to "the concrete offence which Jesus, through his words and deeds, caused his opponents, who were well-versed in, and zealous for, the law—offence in view of the Sabbath purity regulations, acceptance of sinners without a return to the Torah, and indeed Jesus' whole preaching of the dawning, present reign of God without any reference to the prevailing traditional understanding of the Torah." M. Hengel and R. Deines, "E. P. Sanders' 'Common Judaism,' Jesus and the Pharisees," 14. Cf. D. A. Hagner, "Jesus' Self-Understanding," in *Encyclopedia of the Historical Jesus*, ed. C A. Evans (London: Routledge, 2008) 324-33.

47. At the end of his discussion of Jesus and Judaism, Sanders concludes: "We further see why, after his death and the resurrection appearances, there emerged a community which was distinct from the rest of Judaism in a way that permitted its persecution." "Jesus, Paul and Judaism," 429.

48. M. Hengel and R. Deines, "E. P. Sanders' 'Common Judaism,' Jesus and the Pharisees," 16. On Jesus and Judaism see G. Jossa, *Jews or Christians?*, 45-63.

But already from the beginning they experienced new things, pre-eminently the experience of the outpoured Holy Spirit, which served both as a mark of their new identity and a sign of the beginning of the eschatological age. Nevertheless, they are described as "day by day, attending the temple together," and as "having favor with all the people" (Acts 2:46-47; cf. 3:1, 3). But when Peter and John heal a lame man "in the name of Jesus Christ" (3:6, 16) and preach concerning the resurrection of Christ, they were arrested by the temple authorities. They are arrested a second time for the same reason (5:18), and after more preaching they are arrested a third time (5:27). This time they so offend the council by their words that "they were enraged and wanted to kill them" (5:33). What was the cause of this new level of hostility toward the disciples of Jesus? Possibly it was the charge that they had killed Jesus (cf. 5:28: "you intend to bring this man's blood upon us"), but more probably it was what was being said about the crucified man, Jesus—namely that "God exalted him at his right hand as Leader [*archēgon*] and Savior, to give repentance to Israel and forgiveness of sins" (5:31). Forgiveness of sins was the prerogative of those responsible for the temple cult, not of a man who was cursed by hanging on a tree. It was blasphemous to say that he had been exalted to God's right hand as Leader and Savior. This implied, if it was not actually, an intolerable rejection of the temple, based on intolerable claims made concerning Jesus. The disciples continue to go to the temple, but it appears that their main reason was to preach Jesus as the Christ (5:42). The early Christians would immediately have had to cope with the stumbling block of a crucified Christ.[49] It cannot have taken long for them to explain the death of the Messiah in terms of the finally efficacious sacrifice for sin (cf. Mark 10:45; 14:24), and then to draw the conclusion concerning the obsolescence of the temple cultus.

The transition and the parting of the ways take a leap forward with the new faith's first martyr. Stephen, a Hellenistic Jewish believer in Jesus, was a powerful debater for the gospel (6:10). Although we have next to nothing concerning what Stephen said, there is every reason to believe, despite that the witnesses against him are called "false witnesses [*martyras pseudeis*],"[50] that he did say things about Torah and temple that could be

---

49. Craig Evans finds in the crucified Messiah and the failure of the kingdom to come, i.e., in the overthrow of the Roman domination, the fundamental divisive point between the Christians and the Jews. "Root Causes of the Jewish-Christian Rift."

50. F. F. Bruce notes that "Anyone who bears witness against a spokesman of God is *ipso facto* a *false* witness, like those who bore witness against Jesus at his trial (Mk

used against him (6:13). Hengel understands the episode to mean that the Hellenists "called for the eschatological abolition of Temple worship and the revision of the law of Moses in the light of the true will of God." They thus "put forward the offensive claim that the significance of Jesus as the Messiah of Israel essentially superseded that of Moses in the history of salvation."[51] The Jesus tradition, after all, contained controversial material on both temple and law.[52] Unfortunately, what is presented by Luke as Stephen's response to the accusations against him is not so much a defense as it is an indictment of the unbelief of the Jews, culminating in their rejection of Jesus (7:2-53). Whatever it was that Stephen said about the law and the temple, it remains clear that it was regarded as something that had to be opposed by those who were zealous for Judaism.[53]

Acts 8:1 speaks of "a great persecution" that arose against the Jerusalem church, scattering the believers into Judea and Samaria. The believers in Jesus seem identifiable enough, and are unable to avoid persecution by any claim to be an acceptable variant of, or sect within, the Jewish faith. Immediately we read of the persecution of the church by Saul. Why did Saul feel compelled to "ravage" the church? It was because he perceived the believers in Jesus as constituting a threat to "what was most holy in Israel."[54]

Fulfilling the commission of Acts 1:8, the gospel is preached to the Samaritans (8:5-6) and then to Gentile God-fearers (8:26-39) first by Philip, one of the Seven Hellenists (8:5-6), then by Peter (10:1-48), and finally to pagan Gentiles by some of those who had been scattered because of the persecution (11:20). These developments caused controversy among the conservative believers in Jerusalem. The status of the Gentile

---

14:55-59)." *The Acts of the Apostles*, 3rd ed. (Grand Rapids: Eerdmans, 1990) 188.

51. *Acts and the History of Earliest Christianity*, 72-73. Cf. J. T. Sanders: "a consistent, albeit not universal aspect of early Christian theology was opposition to the temple and to Mosaic tradition, and that such opposition struck at Jewish identity sufficiently to bring almost certain reaction from the enforcers of that identity." *Schismatics, Sectarians, Dissidents, Deviants*, 230. A quite different reading of Stephen and the Hellenists is offered by C. C. Hill, *Hellenists and Hebrews: Reappraising Division within the Earliest Church*.

52 In his discussion of the Stephen episode, Hengel mentions that some scholars act as though Jesus had been rapidly forgotten. *The Pre-Christian Paul*, 82.

53. See G. Jossa, *Jews or Christians?*, 76-89.

54. *The Pre-Christian Paul*, 80; pace J. Taylor, who finds the reason in the Jewish Christians' lack of support for the national struggle against Rome. "Why Did Paul Persecute the Church?" 112. Cf. S. Kim, *The Origin of Paul's Gospel*, 44-50; A. J. Hultgren, "Paul's Pre-Christian Persecutions of the church: Their Purpose, Locale, and Nature."

believers in particular was debated, eventually making necessary the formal discussion recorded in Acts 15. When at the council circumcision was *not* required of the Gentile believers, and thus they were *not* required to become proselytes to the Jewish faith, another pillar of Judaism, the unique election of Israel, was seriously challenged. In Antioch the disciples of Jesus were given the name "Christians," and with it an identity that distinguished them from the Jews (11:26; cf. 26:28).

No reason is given why Herod Agrippa put the Apostle James to death (12:2), but it is significant that "it pleased the Jews" (12:3; cf. 12:11c). This contrasts strongly with the Jewish approval of the believers in the early chapters of Acts. Clearly it did not take long for the hostility to develop. Already it was evident that this new movement represented something other than a mere sect of Judaism — indeed, something that was perceived as a threat to Judaism.

It is often said that self-definition is possible only when a group experiences opposition.[55] If that is true, then the self-definition of the Jewish believers in Jesus and differentiation from the other Jews must have begun early. Larry Hurtado has shown the great importance of the christology of the earliest Christians, which necessitated a 'mutation' in Jewish monotheism.

> Within the first years, however, Christian believers (still mainly Christian Jews) put Christ with God at the centre of their devotional life, including their worship practices, and this would have made their 'binitarian' devotion seem not merely offensive but dangerous for the wider religious integrity of Judaism. In these cases, charges of 'blasphemy' connoted an infringement of the uniqueness of God, the most important teaching of Torah among devout Jews of the Roman period.[56]

3. *Paul.* As soon as he began his missionary journeys, Paul the persecutor became Paul the persecuted. In a repeated pattern, Paul preaches in the synagogue, only to encounter opposition to his message (13:45, 50; 14:5, 19; 16:20-24; 17:5-7; 18:6, 12-13; 19:9).[57] Probably it was the stress

---

55. E.g., J. Lieu: 'It is in opposition that Christianity gains its true identity, so all identity becomes articulated, perhaps for the first time, in the face of "the other," as well as in face of attempts by the "other" to deny its existence' "'I am a Christian'": Martyrdom and the Beginning of "Christian Identity," in *Neither Jew Nor Greek?*, 215-16.

56. "Pre-70 CE Jewish Opposition to Christ-Devotion," *JTS* 50 (1999) 58.

57. One may note the prophecy of Jesus according to Matt 10:17: "Beware of men; for they will deliver you up to councils, and flog you in their synagogues."

on a crucified Messiah who rose from the dead and was now proclaimed as Lord that produced the hostility of the Jews. Knowing the danger that awaited him, Paul determined nevertheless to go to Jerusalem: "For I am ready not only to be imprisoned but even to die at Jerusalem for the name of the Lord Jesus" (21:13). The Asian Jews stir up opposition to Paul in Jerusalem with these words: "This is the man who is teaching men everywhere against the people and the law and this place; moreover, he also brought Greeks into the temple, and he has defiled this holy place" (21:28). Here, as in the case of Stephen, we again see three pillars of Judaism perceived as under threat: election, the law, and the temple. So hostile to Paul are the Jews that they plot to kill him (23:12-15).

In their presentation to Felix of the case against Paul, he is referred to as "a ringleader of the sect [*hairesis*] of the Nazarenes" (24:5). Paul's own words in his defense are of interest: "But this I admit to you, that according to the Way [*tēn hodon*], which they call a sect, I worship the God of our fathers, believing everything laid down by the law or written in the prophets" (24:14).[58] And again, to Festus Paul says, "Neither against the law of the Jews, nor against the temple, nor against Caesar have I offended at all" (25:8). In Jewish contexts Paul had always observed the law (1 Cor 9:20), and he had not brought Gentiles into the temple. Explaining the case to Agrippa, Festus gives us an idea of the real concerns of the Jews: "they had certain points of dispute with him about their own superstition and about one Jesus, who was dead, but whom Paul asserted to be alive" (25:19). Paul presents the kerygma to Agrippa (26:23), who responds "In a short time you think to make me a Christian!" (26:28). Finally, Paul in Rome presents his gospel, "the hope of Israel" (28:20), to the Jews: "testifying to the kingdom of God and trying to convince them about Jesus both from the law of Moses and from the prophets" (28:23).

Two main points are obvious from Acts: (1) the believers in Jesus are clearly recognized as distinct from the Jews and identifiable as a "sect," whether as Christians, people of the Way, or the Nazarenes; (2) the believers in Jesus were perceived as a threat to the essentials of Jewish faith and were therefore not acceptable to the Jews and thus experienced persecution at their hand. The Jews were unable to see Paul as representing any kind of acceptable variant of Judaism.

---

58. A few lines later it is noted that Felix had acquired "a rather accurate knowledge of the Way" (24:22).

Although we cannot go into any detail here, we must give some attention to Paul's attitude toward Judaism.[59] His harshest statement against the Jews is found in one of his earliest letters, 1 Thess 2:14-16, where he writes: "For you, brethren, became imitators of the churches of God in Christ which are in Judea; for you suffered the same things from your own countrymen as they did from the Jews, who killed both the Lord Jesus and the prophets, and drove us out, and displease God and oppose all men by hindering us from speaking to the Gentiles that they may be saved—so as always to fill up the measure of their sins. But God's wrath has come upon them at last [*eis telos*]!" Although some argue that the passage is not from Paul,[60] most scholars accept its authenticity, attributing its harshness to Paul's frustration over the Jewish opposition to his mission work.

Paul's letter to the Galatians contains a strong polemic concerning the law (3:15—4:7), describes the Jews as "children of slavery" (4:21-31), and Paul speaks explicitly of his "former life in Judaism" (1:13-14) as a thing of the past (cf. Phil 3:4-9).[61] The special status of Israel is negated: in Christ "there is neither Jew nor Greek" (3:28). Very possibly he refers to the church as "the Israel of God" (6:16). Hans Dieter Betz justly concludes that "In Galatians, Christianity is distinguished from the Jewish religion."[62]

In 1 Corinthians Paul reveals his essential indifference to the law. For pragmatic reasons he would become "as one under the law—though not being myself under the law" (9:20). But he could also become "as one outside the law," though under the "law of Christ" (9:21). In 10:32 he distinguishes "the church of God" from both Jews and Greeks, which would lead to the later designation of the church as a "third race."

The famous passage in 2 Cor 3:6-17 describes the old covenant in very negative terms as a "ministry of death/condemnation" that "kills," in contrast to the new covenant which is a "ministry of righteousness" that through the Spirit "gives life." In a midrashic treatment of Exod 34:29-35,

---

59. See D. A. Hagner, "Paul's Quarrel with Judaism"; Hagner, "Paul as a Jewish Believer in Jesus—According to His Letters."

60. E.g. B. A. Pearson, "1 Thessalonians 2:13-16: A Deutero-Pauline Interpretation," *HTR* 64 (1971) 79-91.

61. These verses contain the two occurrences of the word *Ioudaïsmos* in the NT. The earliest known occurrence of the word is in 2 Macc 2:21; 8:1; 14:38.

62. "Christianity as Religion," 317. Boyarin's statement (*Border Lines*, 2) that the idea of "orthodoxy" comes only in the second century is hardly correct. Already with Paul the beliefs and practices of the Judaizers (for the word, see Gal 2:14) were declared "out of bounds."

Paul points to the inability of the Jews to read the scriptures with understanding, thus pointing to the hermeneutical chasm that separated the Jews and the Christians. Paul the Christian had learned to read his Bible very differently from Saul the Pharisee: "when a person turns to the Lord, the veil is removed" (3:16).

In Romans, Paul addresses all the issues that are central to Judaism. The election of Israel is brought into question by the fact that the Jews are in the same need of salvation as the Gentiles (2:1—3:20). Being a "Jew" is redefined so that uncircumcised Gentiles may qualify (2:28-29). But whereas salvation has come to, and been accepted by the Gentiles (11:11-14), only a remnant of Jews has believed (11:5). The unbelief of Israel, stumbling over the stumbling stone of Christ (Isa 28:16), comes clearly into focus in 9:30-33, in 10:21 (quoting Isa 65:2: "a disobedient and contrary people"), and in the harsh statement concerning Israel's blindness in 11:8-10 (quoting Isa 29:10 and Ps 69:22-23). This unbelief, however, cannot overthrow the election of Israel; the branches broken off can be restored if the Jews do not persist in their unbelief (11:23). "For the gifts and the call of God are irrevocable" (11:29). Paradoxically, then, Paul finally speaks of the salvation of "all Israel" (11:26). There is a sense in which Israel remains special and unique.[63]

Romans seems ambiguous concerning the Torah, famously so in Rom 10:4 "For Christ is the end of the law, that everyone who has faith may be justified," where the word *telos* makes very good sense in both meanings, i.e., "end" and "goal," and not a few have argued for the double entendre here. The ambiguity is found in the earlier chapters of the book: the law has been brought to an end (3:20, 28; 4:14; 6:14-15; 7:6) and the law is also "upheld" (3:31; 2:13, 25; 7:12). Paul seems to envisage *arriving at the righteousness of the law by a different means* than the commandments themselves, i.e., other than by being "under the law."[64] The new conception and underlying dynamic involve a break with the Jewish perspective.

The description of the atoning death of Christ in the language of the temple cultus, points to its demise: "they are justified by his grace as a gift, through the redemption which is in Christ Jesus, whom God put forward as a *hilastērion* ["propitiation" KJV; "expiation" RSV; "a sacrifice of atonement" NRSV] by his blood, to be received by faith" (3:24-25; cf. 4:25).

---

63. See B. Longenecker, "On Israel's God and God's Israel: Assessing Supersessionism in Paul," *JTS* 58 (2007) 26-44.

64. For elaboration of this point, see Hagner, "Paul as a Jewish Believer in Jesus—According to His Letters," 111-12.

Monotheism seems preserved by the direct statements in 3:29–30, "Or is God the God of Jews only? Is he not the God of the Gentiles also? Yes, of Gentiles also, since God is one." At the same time, it may be that Paul refers to Jesus as God in 9:5, but even apart from that, the christology of Romans is impressive: Lord, Son of God, the second Adam, the one raised to the right hand of God (cf. 1 Cor 8:6).[65]

In Paul we have abundant evidence for a Christianity vitally related to Judaism,[66] but also readily identifiable and distinguishable from Judaism.[67] It is difficult to deny the critique of Judaism that runs through the Pauline letters. E. P. Sanders' assessment is that Paul "denies two pillars common to all forms of Judaism: the election of Israel and faithfulness to the Mosaic law."[68] R. Ruether's conclusion, although overstated, is basically correct: "What Paul taught . . . is unmistakably negative: the religion of Israel is now superseded, the Torah abrogated, the promises fulfilled in the Christian Church, the Jews struck with blindness, and whatever remains of the election to Israel rests as a burden upon them in the present age."[69] According to Betz, Christianity is not the continuation of Judaism: "any attempt to conceive of Christian religion as reform, reorganization, or reconceptualization of pre-christian religion would amount to merely symbolic cures of symptoms."[70]

E. P. Sanders is one of the few Pauline scholars who resist the currently popular trend that sees no difference between Paul and Judaism. He writes,

---

65. See G. Jossa, *Jews or Christians?*, 63–76; 93–94. See too Hagner, "Jewish Monotheism and Paul's Christology."

66. See J. Frey, "Paul's Jewish Identity." Frey supplies abundant evidence of Paul's continuing Jewishness, but cannot finally avoid the aporia caused by Paul's "radical 'reconfiguration' of the criteria of salvation" (321).

67. Dunn concludes that although Paul remained a Jew, he did not remain "in Judaism:" "the term had become too much identified with ethnicity and separation from other nations; and Paul's self-understanding on just these points had been too radically transformed by his conversion, his personal encounter with the risen Christ and his apostolic commission from the risen Christ, for 'Judaism,' to continue to define and identify himself or his apostolic work." Dunn goes on, however, oddly to deny that Paul "had left behind (Second Temple) Judaism." "Who Did Paul Think He Was? A Study of Jewish-Christian Identity," 192. Cf. G. Theissen, "Judentum und Christentum bei Paulus."

68. *Paul, the Law, and the Jewish People*, 208.

69. *Faith and Fratricide*, 6. Cf. S. Sandmel: "Paul's criticism, if we may use that word, is directed not so much toward Jews as it is toward Judaism. . . .It is essentially Judaism that Paul denigrates." *Anti-Semitism in the New Testament?*, 16.

70. "Christianity as Religion," 329. Betz finds the roots of Christianity in the faith of Abraham rather than in the Sinai covenant. He goes too far, however, when he says that "present Judaism is, in Paul's view, hardly different from corrupt paganism," 326.

"Taken together, Paul's positions on the law and on the Jewish people mean that he explicitly denied the saving efficacy of the covenant between God and Israel, confidence in which was the heart of the covenantal nomism which we described as basic to the Judaism of the period."[71]

Francis Watson is another Pauline scholar who observes crucial differences between Paul and Judaism. In his recently revised and expanded *Paul, Judaism, and the Gentiles*, he approaches the subject from a sociological perspective, and concludes that in Paul we reach a stage of development that he describes as "the transformation of a reform movement into a sect."[72] He argues further that "the gospel required the formation of a distinct Christian identity over against Judaism," and necessitated "an ideology legitimating its state of separation."[73] "This separation is not a mere parting of the ways within a pluralistic environment, resulting perhaps in mutual indifference. On the contrary, this is separation in the form of an ongoing argument about scriptural interpretation, an attempt to show that the true sense of scripture—the one that attests the truth of the gospel—belongs to 'us' rather than 'them.'"[74]

4. *The remainder of the NT.* Although aspects of our subject are evident in most of the writings of the NT, we limit ourselves here to three further NT writings, Hebrews, 1 Peter, and the Gospel of John.

Although the date of Hebrews is debated, it is surely to be put well within the first century. It provides exceptionally rich content embodying both continuity and discontinuity, and is highly relevant to our interests.

Hebrews presupposes a clear distinction between the church and the Jews; indeed, the author's purpose is to keep his readers from lapsing back into their previous Judaism. So strong are the contrasts in Hebrews that it is widely regarded as supersessionist in perspective.[75] If it is supersessionist, as many have concluded,[76] it is not so in the simple sense of one thing being superseded by something unrelated.[77] The author would never, for example, have thought of one religion taking the place of

---

71. "Jesus, Paul and Judaism," 434.

72. *Paul, Judaism, and the Gentiles*, 51.

73. Ibid., 52, 54.

74. Ibid., 21-22. See too G. Jossa, *Jews or Christians?*, 89-102.

75. Richard Hays tells amusingly of his change of mind on this issue. "'Here We Have No Lasting City': New Covenantalism in Hebrews," 151-52.

76. E.g., Wilson, who discusses it together with Barnabas, *Related Strangers*, 110-42.

77. For an insightful study, see L. Kim, *Polemic in the Book of Hebrews: Anti-Judaism, Anti-Semitisim, Supersessionism?*

another religion. For him, as for all NT writers, the faith of the Christian believers is vitally related to the promises of Israel's scriptures. What has come is the fulfillment of what had been promised, the fulfillment of Jewish hopes intended for Jews. Fulfillment, however, involves both continuity and discontinuity.

Our author unhesitatingly affirms the discontinuities. Most notable is the fact that the new covenant has replaced the Mosaic covenant, as Jeremiah had promised (the whole of Jer 31:31-34 is quoted in Heb 8:8-12). "Christ has obtained a ministry which is as much more excellent than the old as the covenant he mediates is better, since it is enacted on better promises" (8:6). The author adds to his quotation from Jeremiah the concluding statement: "In speaking of a new covenant he treats the first as obsolete and growing old... ready to vanish away" (8:13; cf. 7:18).

The Levitical priesthood and sacrifices have been made obsolete by the one, sufficient sacrifice of the high priest, Christ (9:11-28; 10:1-4). In this sense both Torah and temple are regarded as outmoded and invalid. So too the christology of Hebrews requires an adjustment of monotheism. Whether one describes it as a matter of "inclusive monotheism"[78] or "christological monotheism,"[79] the affirmation of the divine identity of Christ in Hebrews is striking.[80]

The differences between the old and new in Hebrews make it difficult to deny Christianity and Judaism are identifiable entities that disagree on fundamental points and thus that Hebrews exhibits a stage in the process of the parting of the ways. It seems hardly adequate to conclude with Richard Hays that Hebrews represents a Jewish sectarianism which he names "New Covenantalism."[81] Jimmy Dunn is more correct when he

---

78. W. Horbury, "Jewish and Christian Monotheism in the Herodian Age," in *Early Jewish and Christian Monotheism*.

79 R. Bauckham, *God Crucified: Monotheism and Christology in the New Testament*.

80. Hebrews 1," in *Early Jewish and Christian Monotheism* (eds. L. T. Stuckenbruck and W. E. S. North, JSNTSup 263; London: T & T Clark, 2004). 167-85, idem, "The Divinity of Jesus Chrust in the Epistle to the Hebrews," in *The Epistle to the Hebrews and Christian Theology* (eds. R. Bauckham et al.; Grand Rapids: Eerdmans, 2009) 15-36. See too Hagner, "The Son of God as Unique High Priest: The Christology of the Epistle to the Hebrews" in *Contours of Christology* (ed. R. N. Longeneccker: Grand Rapids Eerdmans, 2005), 247-67. See R. Bauckham, "Monotheism and Christology in Hebrews 1"; "The Divinity of Jesus Christ in the Epistle to the Hebrews." See too Hagner, "The Son of God as Unique High Priest: The Christology of the Epistle to the Hebrews."

81. *"Here We Have No Lasting City,"* 155. Hays then goes on to say, however, that Jesus brings a "major plot twist" wherein as the mediator of a new covenant he "*transforms* Israel's identity" (his italics). But the transformation of Israel's identity is

concludes "*For Hebrews and a Judaism still focussed on the Temple and its cult the ways had parted.*"[82]

The letter known as 1 Peter also provides indications of a parting of the ways. Already in the address of the letter Gentile Christians are referred to as "exiles of the Dispersion" (1:1). They are further designated as part of a "spiritual house" and "a holy priesthood" (2:5). In contrast to the Jews, who stumble on the stone that is Christ—"as they were destined to do" (2:8)—the church is referred to as "a chosen race, a royal priesthood, a holy nation, God's own people" (2:9), very familiar language that in the OT is carefully restricted to Israel. Once these Gentiles "were no people," but now they "are God's people," people who once had not received mercy, but who now have (2:10). 1 Peter, moreover, is the only NT writing besides Acts to use the word "Christian" in reference to a distinct group (4:16; cf. Acts 11:26; 26:28).[83] This new application of the language cancels the uniqueness typical of the doctrine of election. The priesthood language applied to the Christians together with the definitive atonement accomplished by Christ (1:18f.; 2:24), on the other hand, involves a fundamental challenge to the importance of the temple.

Toward the end of the first century, the Gospel of John reflects a significant separation of Christian believers from Jewish non-believers.[84] Most conspicuous is the occurrence of the term *aposynagōgos* (9:22; 12:42; 16:2) which refers to Jews who believe in Jesus being forced out of the synagogue, undoubtedly for their witness to Jesus. Although apparently anachronistic for the time of Jesus, these references reflect the

---

something so radical that it no longer qualifies as a sect within Judaism. In response to Hays, M. D. Nanos rightly remarks that if the readers "are being told to abandon [the sacrificial system] as bankrupt because there is now a new and better way that makes that covenantal behavior obsolete or counter-faithful, then it would seem to represent a new religious movement or if a Judaism still, then one that denies to all other Jewish practitioners the viability of their claims; that is, it represents supersessionism and replacement theology if not of Jews by Gentiles, then of all other Jews by Christ-believing Jews." "*New or Renewed Covenantalism?*" 185.

82. *The Partings of the Ways*, 91 (italics his).

83. Holmberg rightly comments: "If the label was felt to fit already by first-century Christ-followers, it is hard to understand why modern anxieties about how the term can or might be misunderstood should prevent its use in historical investigation of this very phenomenon." *Exploring Early Christian Identity*, 5. One may also point to the use of "Christian" in the early second-century Graeco-Roman writers Tacitus, Suetonious and the younger Pliny.

84. See J. L. Martyn, *History and Theology in the Fourth Gospel*; J. McHugh, "'In Him Was Life': John's Gospel and the Parting of the Ways," in *Jews and Chrisfians: The Parting of the Ways A.D. 70 to 135*, 123-58.

rejection of Jewish believers in Jesus that came into effect with the so-called *birkath ha-minim*, the "blessing" of the heretics (very probably meaning Jewish Christians). This was an addition to the synagogue liturgy, as the twelfth of the "eighteen benedictions," added probably ca. 90, although this is much debated.[85] The "blessing" was in fact a curse that made it impossible for Christians to participate.

There is much in the Gospel of John itself that points to a high level of hostility between the Jews and the Christians. Already in the beginning of the first chapter, we read that "his own people" did not accept Christ whereas "all who received him were given "power to become children of God" (1:11-12). The contrast of 1:17 is revealing: "for the law was given through Moses; grace and truth came through Jesus Christ." The slander of 8:44 is well-known: in his exchange with the Jews, Jesus says "You are of your father the devil, and your will is to do your father's desires."

In John, all four of the pillars of Judaism are called into question. So far as the *law* is concerned, several times Jesus is accused of violating the sabbath and said to be the reason for the Jews' hostility toward him (5:16, 18; 7:23; 9:16). The *temple* receives an implied criticism in 4:21 (cf. 2:19-21). Throughout the Fourth Gospel the *election* of the Jews is obviated by the their unbelief. The purpose of the coming of Jesus is to save the world, including the Gentiles (3:16-17, 36; and especially 10:16; cf. 12:20-24). Perhaps most remarkable in John is the adjustment to *monotheism* necessitated by the clear affirmation and emphasis put upon the deity of Christ.[86] This is evident most remarkably in the *logos* passage (1:1, 14, 18), but elsewhere in the Gospel too. Thus, John records that "the Jews sought all the more to kill him, because he not only broke the sabbath but also called God his own Father, making himself equal with God" (5:18). When Jesus says "Truly, truly, I say to you, before Abraham was, I am," the Jews "took up stones to throw at him" (8:58). After his statement that "I and the Father are one," the Jews again want to stone him (10:30-31). "It is not for a good work that we stone you but for blasphemy; because you, being a man, make yourself God" (10:33). At end of the Gospel is the climactic statement of Thomas: "My Lord and my God"

---

85. The best discussion is W. Horbury, "The Benediction of the *Minim* and Early Jewish-Christian Controversy," *JTS* 33 (1982): 19-61. See too J. Marcus, "Birkat ha-minim Revisited," *NTS* 55 (2009): 523-51.

86. See R. Bauckham, "Monotheism and Christology in the Gospel of John," in *Contours of Christology in the New Testament*. "The Fourth Gospel . . . redefines Jewish monotheism as christological monotheism . . . in which the relationship of Jesus the Son to his Father is integral to the definition of who the one true God is" (165).

(20:28). Adele Reinhartz concludes that the Gospel of John "clearly testifies to a painful separation between a group of people who believe Christ to be the Messiah and a Jewish group that does not," and that "the groups themselves are presented as mutually exclusive."[87]

A strong indication of division and hostility at the end of the first century is found in the opening chapters of the Apocalypse, where we have the repeated reference to "those who say that they are Jews and are not, but are a synagogue of Satan" (2:9; cf. 3:9). Here a Jewish Christian goes so far as not only to deny authentic Jewish identity to the Jews who stand opposed to the church, but to castigate them as belonging to Satan.[88]

5. *The Second Century.* If there is abundant evidence in the NT for the ongoing separation of Jews and Christians in the first century,[89] even more exists for the second century. Since the NT, apart from the synoptic

---

87. "A Fork on the Road or a Multi-Lane Highway? New Perspectives on the 'Parting of the Ways' Between Judaism and Christianity," in *The Changing Face of Judaism, Christianity and Other Greco-Roman Religions in Antiquity* (Gütersloh, 2006), 281, 291. Reinhartz accepts that "the ways have parted," yet at the same time she denies that this is to be thought of as "*the* definitive split," 292.

88. Looking at three strands of NT material, the Gospel of John, letters of Paul, and the Gospel of Matthew, W. A. Meeks ("Breaking Away: Three New Testament Pictures of Christianity's Separation from the Jewish Communities," in *To See Ourselves as Others See Us: Christians, Jews, "Others" in Late Antiquity*, 94) concludes "that each of them gives some reason for affirming that Christianity indeed *had* been a sect of Judaism, but we shall find that each looks back at that connection from a point just *after* a decisive break has occurred" (italics his).

89. We have not mentioned the Roman perception of Jews and Christians. A study of the subject by E. A. Judge concludes that the Romans did not regard Christianity as a part of Judaism. "A socially clear-cut separation from an early stage must be assumed if we are to explain the fact that Romans seem to have been unaware of the links between Jews and Christians." "Judaism and the Rise of Christianity: A Roman Perspective," TynB 45 (1994) 366. See M. Tellbe, "The Temple Tax as a Pre-70 CE Identity Marker," in *The Formation of the Early Church*, WUNT 183 (Tübingen: Mohr, 2005) 19-44. Cf. Jossa, who dates the Roman differentiation of the two groups to the time of Nero (*Jews or Christians?*) 131-38. Jossa also indicates as a mark of the distinction the fact that Christians did not have to pay the *fiscus Judaicus*, the temple tax required of the Jews after 70. Cf. Hengel, "Early Christianity as a Jewish-Messianic, Universalist Movement," 37; and J. Carleton Paget, *Jews, Christians and Jewish Christians in Antiquity*, 9-10. M. Heemstra calls attention to the significance of the *fiscus Judaicus* for dating the parting of the ways: "the decisive separation between Judaism as we know it today and Christianity as we know it today, took place at the end of the first century, as the combined result of a decision by representatives of mainstream Judaism (exclusion of Jewish Christians, who were members of mixed Christian communities from the 'congregation of Israelites') and the Roman redefinition of the taxpayers to the *fiscus Judaicus*, excluding these same Jewish Christians" (*The* Fiscus Judaicus *and the Parting of the Ways*, 189).

prophecies, does not refer explicitly to the fall of Jerusalem, we have paid no attention to it.[90] Many, however, have found in the destruction of Jerusalem in 70 a decisive turning point in the relation between the Jews and the Christians,[91] caused especially by the unwillingness of the Christians to stand with the Jews in their revolt against the Romans. The destruction of the temple would have provided a strong argument for the Christians concerning the correctness of their separation from the Jews. The events of 132-35, and the messianic claims of Bar Kokhba, provided a similar pattern that would have further alienated Jews and Christians.[92]

It is hardly surprising, then, to encounter a greater polarization between the two groups in the second century.[93] How early the Didache may be is disputed, but it makes a clear differentiation between Christian and Jewish days for fasting (8.2) and worship (14.2). Ignatius in the earlier part of the century (ca. 110 or 115) provides us with material reflecting the increasing division.[94] Ignatius speaks of two clearly bounded entities, "Judaism" and "Christianity." "For if we have lived according to Judaism [*Ioudaïsmos*] until now, we admit that we have not received God's gracious gift" (*Magnesians* 8.1).[95] "Let us learn to live according to Christianity [*Christianismos*]. For whoever is called by a name other than this does not belong to God. So lay aside the bad yeast, which has

---

90. Gundry's observation is worth quoting: "By the time Jerusalem was destroyed, the church had long since become a counterpart to the synagogue." *Matthew: A Commentary on His Literary and Theological Art* (Grand Rapids: Eerdmans, 1982) 601.

91. Cf. Hengel, "Early Christianity as a Jewish-Messianic, Universalistic Movement," 32-33.

92. Note the conclusion of P. Tomson, "All indications are that as from the Bar Kokhbar war, there was a steep development towards a general separation of Judaism and Christianity. More precisely, over against self-contained rabbinic Judaism, there now developed a rather homogeneous Gentile Christianity. It identified itself on the one hand by identifying with the tradition of the apostles and their Scriptures as against Gnostics and Marcionites, and on the other, by setting itself off against Judaism and Judeo-Christianity." "The Wars against Rome, the rise of Rabbinic Judaism and of Apostolic Gentile Christianity, and the Judaeo-Christians: elements for a synthesis" in *The Image of the Judeo-Christians in Ancient Jewish and Christian Literature*. WUNT 158 (Tübingen: Mohr Siebeck, 2003) 22. Tomson, however, sees no reasons for separation before 70.

93. On the writings considered here, see G. N. Stanton, "Other Early Christian Writings: 'Didache', Ignatius, 'Barnabas', Justin Martyr" in *Early Christian Thought in its Jewish Context* (Cambridge: Cambridge University Press, 1996), 174-90; C. K. Barrett, "Jews and Judaizers in the Epistles of Ignatius," in *Essays on John*, 133-58.

94. See especially T. Robinson, *Ignatius of Antioch and the Parting of the Ways*.

95. Translations from the Apostolic Fathers are those of Bart D. Ehrman in the Loeb Classical Library (2003).

grown old and sour, and thru to the new yeast, which is Jesus Christ ... It is outlandish to proclaim Jesus Christ and practice Judaism. For Christianity did not believe in Judaism, but Judaism in Christianity—in which every tongue that believes in God has been gathered together" (*Magnesians* 10.1–3). That Judaism is viewed so negatively here points to the separation of the two groups.

In *Philadelphians* 6.1, Ignatius writes "But if anyone should interpret Judaism to you, do not hear him. For it is better to hear Christianity from a man who is circumcised than Judaism from one who is uncircumcised. But if neither one speaks about Jesus Christ, they both appear to me as monuments and tombs of the dead, on which are written merely human names." Here Ignatius polemicizes against Judaizers, i.e., Gentiles who were attracting Christians to Jewish practices.

We again encounter evidence of a distinct identity in *Romans* 3.2–3: "that I not only be called a Christian but also be found one. For if I be found a Christian, I can also be called one and then be faithful ... For our God Jesus Christ, since he is in the Father, is all the more visible ... but Christianity is a matter of greatness, when it is hated by the world." For Ignatius "Christian" means not "Jew" and "Christianity" means not "Judaism." In *Smyrneans* 8.2 Ignatius also speaks of the defined entity of the church: "wherever Jesus Christ is, there also is the universal [*katholikē*] church."

The Epistle of Barnabas is well-known for its anti-Judaism.[96] Probably the most striking point made by Barnabas is that because of disobedience the Jews did not receive the covenant, but the Christians did. Barnabas accordingly does not speak of an old covenant once possessed by the Jews, replaced by a new covenant enjoyed by the Christians, but of only one covenant. "Watch yourselves now and do not become like some people by piling up your sins, saying that the covenant is both theirs and ours. For it is ours. But they permanently lost it ... when Moses had just received it" (4.6–7). The same point is made again in chapter 14.

God gave the covenant to Israel, "but they were not worthy to receive it" (14.1). He continues, "Now learn how we have received it. Moses received it as a servant, but the Lord himself gave it to us, as a people of the inheritance, by enduring suffering for us. He was made manifest so

---

96. See especially, R. Hvalvik, *The Struggle for Scripture and Covenant: The Purpose of the Epistle of Barnabas and Jewish-Christian Competition in the Second Century*, , WUNT 2.82 (Tübingen: Mohr Siebeck, 1996) and J. Carleton Paget, *The Epistle of Barnabas: Outlook and Background*, WUNT 2.64 (Tübingen: Mohr Siebeck, 1994).

that those people might be completely filled with sins, and that we might receive the covenant through the Lord Jesus" (14.4).

The bulk of Barnabas is given over to a critique of various Jewish observances, re-understanding them in Christian terms. "But how could they know or understand these things? We, however, speak as those who know the commandments in an upright way, as the Lord wished. For this reason he circumcised our hearing and our hearts, that we may understand these things" (10.12). It seems clear that Barnabas is anxious to keep Christians separate from Jews and from interest and participation in Jewish observances. "And so he revealed all things to us in advance, that we not be dashed against their law as newcomers [or: *proselytes*]" (3:6).[97]

Another indication of the identifiability of Christianity as a group distinct from Judaism can be seen in the middle of the second century, in the account of Polycarp's martyrdom, where Polycarp says to the proconsul: "listen closely: I am a Christian. But if you wish to learn an account of Christianity, appoint a day and listen" (*Martyrdom of Polycarp* 10.1).

The last of the second-century writers to be considered here is Justin Martyr, whose *Dialogue with Trypho* was probably written just after the middle of the second century. The *Dialogue* provides evidence for a well-defined Christianity over against a Judaism whose viewpoint is rejected.[98] Justin makes the point repeatedly that it is the Christians who constitute the people of God, not the Jews.

"As Christ is called Israel and Jacob, so we, hewn out of the side of Christ, are the true people of Israel" (135.3).[99] "God promised Abraham a religious and righteous nation of like faith and a delight to the Father; but it is not you, in whom there is no faith" (119.6). "We have been led to God through this crucified Christ, and we are the true spiritual Israel, and the descendants of Judah, Jacob, Isaac, and Abraham, who, though uncircumcised, was approved and blessed by God because of his faith,

---

97. On Barnabas and Justin, see W. Horbury, "Jewish-Christian Relations in Barnabas and Justin Martyr," in *Jews and Christians: The Parting of the Ways A.D. 70-135*, WUNT 66, 315-45, reprinted in *Jews and Christians in Contact and Controversy*, 127-61. Horbury begins his essay with the words: "The ways have parted already for the writers considered here," 315.

98 "The text of the *Dialogue* itself confirms that in the middle of the second century there was keen rivalry between Jews and Christians." Stanton, "Other Early Christian Writings," 184.

99. Translations are those of T. B. Falls, *St. Justin Martyr: Dialogue with Trypho*, revised with new introduction by T. P. Halton, edited by M. Slusser (Washington, DC: Catholic University Press, 2003).

and was called the father of many nations" (11.5). Trypho cannot believe what he hears. Thus, he asks: "Do you mean to say that you are Israel, and that God says all this about you?" to which he gets the following response: "Therefore, as your whole people was called after that one Jacob, surnamed Israel, so we who obey the precepts of Christ, are, through Christ who begot us to God, both called and in reality are, Jacob, and Israel and Judah and Joseph and David and true children of God" (123.7, 9).

One of Trypho's main arguments against Justin is that Christians do not obey the law. Early in the *Dialogue*, Justin responds in terms of strong discontinuity: "The law promulgated at Horeb is already obsolete, and was intended for you Jews only, whereas the law of which I speak is simply for all men. Now a later law in opposition to an older law abrogates the older; so, too, does a later covenant void an earlier one. An everlasting and final law, Christ himself, and a trustworthy covenant has been given to us, after which there shall be no law or commandment, or precept" (11.2).

It is clear that with these second-century writers' viewpoints have polarized, solidified, and intensified in comparison with what we find in the NT. Yet they are in continuity with, and the natural extension of, what already begins there. What we have seen in these writers is the result of an ongoing process with roots that go back to the beginning. We dealing with a developing trajectory.

C. K. Barrett puts it well: "Throughout the [second] century, indeed, from New Testament times, we can dimly trace the progressive formulation of a *regula fidei* or *regula veritatis*, which enshrined the essentials of Christian belief."[100]

JEWISH CHRISTIANITY

If it is true that at the beginning all the believers in Jesus were Jews, it is also true that there has always been a remnant of Jewish believers even when Christianity became overwhelmingly Gentile.[101] To the extent that they eventually formed a distinctive "Jewish Christianity"[102] they are the

---

100. *The Gospel According to John*, 2nd ed. (London: SPCK, 1978) 142; cf. Barrett, *Essays on John* (Philadelphia: Westminster, 1982) 122. See too the discussion in C. E. Hill, *The Johannine Corpus in the Early Church* (Oxford: Oxford University Press, 2004) 3–10.

101. On this subject see now the collection of essays titled *The Image of the Judaeo-Christians in Ancient Jewish and Christian Literature*, ed. P. J. Tomson and D. Lambers-Petry, WUNT 158 (Tübingen: Mohr Siebeck, 2003).

102. The definition of "Jewish Christianity" is difficult. See too J. Marcus, "Jewish

wild card in the question of the parting of the ways. They are Jewish *and* Christian. (In Jerome's view they succeeded in being neither.[103]) As James Carleton Paget puts it, "For Christians, Jewish Christians were intolerably Jewish, and for Jews they seemed intolerably Christian."[104] Obviously the Jewish Christians were inclined to see as much continuity with their former faith as possible, and perhaps also to downplay the discontinuity as much as possible. In their thinking *Christianity did not involve a parting of the ways, not a separation from their Jewish faith, but rather the movement toward the goal of their Jewish faith.*

I want to stress here that if there were any so-called "fuzzy boundaries" they were between Judaism and Jewish Christianity.[105] The boundaries between Judaism and (Gentile) Christianity, on the other hand, were increasingly clear and fixed. Moreover, by its nature, Jewish Christianity was subject to more variety depending on the pressures from the Christian or Jewish side. As the middle term it was much less fixed.[106] Moving from Jewish Christianity to Judaism or vice versa was accordingly not so difficult.

Christianity" in *The Cambridge HIstory of Christianity*, 1:87-102; J. Carlton Paget, "Jewish Christianity" in *The Cambridge History of Christianity*, 3:731-75; idem, "The Definition of the Terms *Jewish Christian* and *Jewish Christianity* in the History of Research," in *Jewish Believers in Jesus*, 22-52. In another place, Paget concludes that "possibly we should admit that the word 'Jewish Christian' remains the best, even if an inadequate, way" of referring to "some people in the ancient world who, while professing belief in Jesus, adopt a profile which looks distinctly Jewish, and description of whom is not well served by either declaring them Christian or Jewish." *Jews, Christians and Jewish Christians in Antiquity*, 32. O. Skarsaune employs only ethnicity in his definition, Cf. his "Jewish Believers in Jesus in Antiquity—Problems of Definition, Method, and Sources," in *Jewish Believers in Jesus*, 3-21. Here, I define it in terms of ethnicity, praxis (i.e. law-observance), and christology (i.e. worship of Jesus). That there was considerable diversity in Jewish Christianity should be stressed. For a helpful overview of the question, see M. Jackson-McCabe, "What's in a Name? The Problem of 'Jewish Christianity,'" in *Early Christianity and Judaism* 6:97-109. Cf. A. F. J. Klijn, "The Study of Jewish Christianity," NTS 20 (1973-74) 419-31.

103. *Ep.* 112.13

104. James Carleton Paget, "Jewish Christianity," 774.

105. Jewish Christianity "blurred the boundaries and retarded the final separation." P. S. Alexander. "'The Parting of the Ways' from the Perspective of Rabbinic Judaism," 3, in *Jews and Christians: The Parting of the Ways A. D. 70 to 135*, 3.

106. See especially R. E. Brown, "Not Jewish Christianity and Gentile Christianity but Types of Jewish/Gentile Christianity." Speaking of the early Jewish-Christian sects, M. Simon writes: "It is often quite difficult to decide just where to draw the line between Christianity and Judaism, to determine where the one stops and the other begins." *Verus Israel*, 95. Similarly, Boyarin: Jewish Christianity "needs to be understood as the third term that unsettles the opposition between the 'two religions.'" *Dying for God*, 17.

PART THREE | JUDAISM AND CHRISTIANITY

As long as one speaks of Jewish Christianity it is not difficult to think of Christianity as a sect of Judaism. This, as we have seen, was true at the beginning. With the passing of time, however, inevitably the extent of the newness entailed by fulfillment begins to become apparent, not only to the Jewish Christians themselves, but also to the non-Christian Jews who in turn become increasingly hostile to them.[107] In these circumstances the word "sect" becomes increasingly inappropriate. Joel Marcus refers to "the tension-filled existence of a Jewish-Christian church [of the Gospel of Matthew] that identified itself as the true Israel (cf. 21:43) while experiencing rejection and persecution from the leaders of the larger Jewish community in its locality."[108]

Earliest Christianity was Jewish Christianity. Were it not for the success of the Gentile mission, Jewish Christianity probably would have become "orthodox" Christianity. This is the reason that the decision of the Jerusalem conference (Acts 15) is of such very great importance. But with the growth of large numbers of Gentile converts, Jewish Christianity became minority, "heterodox" Christianity, especially in its later, variant forms. For Jewish Christians, as we have noted, there was no break or at least not much of a break with Judaism.[109] Obviously a key question was the extent of their loyalty to the four pillars of Judaism, which we now review in order of importance. (1) *Torah*. Jewish Christians would have had no problem in continuing to obey the law of Moses. The earliest Christians were faithful to Torah, and so too Jewish Christians onwards.[110] It is widely admitted that even Paul did not encourage Jewish believers in

---

107. Alexander catches something of their dilemma in these words: "Jewish Christianity found itself caught between Scylla and Charybdis: the closer it moved to the Gentile churches the less credible it would have become within the Jewish community; the more it emphasized its Jewishness the more difficult would have become its relations with the Gentile Churches." "'The Parting of the Ways' from the Perspective of Rabbinic Judaism," 24. In her survey of Jewish responses to Christians, C. J. Setzer concludes that "surely a world of difference separated Jews who believed in Jesus from Gentiles who did" *Jewish Responses to Early Christians*, 165.

108. "Jewish Christianity," 94. For persecution of Matthew's community and the Christian response to it, see D. R. A. Hare, *The Theme of Jewish Persecution of Christians in the Gospel according to St Matthew*, 130–66.

109. We may think of a sequence such as (1) within Judaism; (2) marginal to common Judaism, like the Qumran community; (3) separation from, yet relation to Judaism, like the Samaritans. Cf. R. Bauckham, "The Parting of the Ways: What Happened and Why," in *The Jewish World around the New Testament*, WUNT 233, 182.

110. But according to Ignatius, some Jewish Christians replaced the sabbath with the Lord's day (*Magnesians* 10.1).

Jesus to abandon living according to the law. He of course would not have allowed Jewish Judaizers to impose the law upon Gentile Christians.[111]

(2) *Monotheism.* Here we have a more complicated issue. The earliest Jewish Christians held a view of Jesus as not merely Messiah, but as *Kyrios*—as somehow a manifestation of deity. This involved the worship of Jesus and thus entailed what has been called a modified or christological monotheism. Peter sets the standard at the beginning: "Let all the house of Israel therefore know assuredly that God has made him both *kyrios* and *christos* this Jesus whom you crucified" (Acts 2:36). It is a good question whether the confession of Jesus as simply Messiah (i.e., an anointed person), as did the Ebionites for example, or Messiah-designate is sufficient to classify such persons as truly Christian. To believe someone to be the Messiah would have been no problem for the Jewish establishment[112] and certainly not grounds for persecution (although to proclaim a crucified and dead man as Messiah might well constitute a problem). The worship of this crucified man was another matter altogether,[113] and this started with the earliest Christians. "Within the first years, however, Christian believers (still mainly Christian Jews) put Christ with God at the centre of their devotional life, including their worship practices and this would have made their 'binitarian' devotion seem not merely offensive but dangerous for the wider religious integrity of Judaism."[114]

(3) *Election.* Jewish believers in Jesus, who saw their faith as the fulfillment of the promises of scripture, would have understood themselves

---

111. Cf. Justin, *Dialogue with Trypho* 47.

112. "There is no reason, a priori, for instance, why believing that Jesus as the Messiah would be considered as beyond the pale of rabbinic Judaism." Boyarin, *Dying for God,* 17. Boyarin's comment that "one could travel, metaphorically, from rabbinic Jew to Christian along a continuum where one hardly would know where one stopped and the other began," applies only to moving from Judaism to Jewish Christianity. Ibid., 9. Cf. D. Flusser, "The Jewish-Christian Schism (Part II)," *Immanuel* 17 (1983), 31.

113. Rightly David Flusser: "for the majority of Jews, even the Christology contained in the New Testament was clearly unacceptable, not only because such a belief was unusual, but also because the whole cosmic drama of Christ and the superhuman nature and task of Christ was in disharmony with the Jewish belief in the God who is One and whose Name is One." "The Jewish-Christian Schism (Part I)," 351.

114. L. W. Hurtado, "Pre-70 CE Jewish Oppostion to Christ-Devotion," 58. "In short, the most influential and momentous developments in devotion to Jesus took place in early circles of Judean believers. To their convictions and the fundamental pattern of their piety all subsequent forms of Christianty are debtors." L. W. Hurtado, *Lord Jesus Christ: Devotion to Jesus in Earliest Christianity,* 216. Cf. C. J. Setzer, "'You Invent a Christ!' Christological Claims as Points of Jewish-Christian Dispute," *USQR* 44 (1991) 315-28.

as hard evidence of the election of Israel. When Paul raises the question "Has God rejected his people" (Rom 11:1), he finds the answer in the existence of "a remnant, chosen by grace" (Rom 11:5), in which group he includes himself. God's faithfulness to Israel has never wavered. That covenant commitment remains in place despite what becomes the overwhelming Gentile makeup of the church. Israel's election was not for her own sake alone, but for the salvation of the world. The coming of the Gentiles into the family of faith is understood as the fulfillment of the commission given to Israel to become a light to the nations (Isa 42:6; 49:6; 60:3). And it is for these reasons that the notion of supersessionism is never ultimately justifiable (Rom 11:28–29). The church, even considered as the true Israel, never fully takes Israel's place; that place is secure, as represented by the Jewish remnant of believers in Jesus. When Paul looks forward to the day when all Israel is saved (Rom 11:26), it is through their faith in Christ (Rom 11:23) not via a *Sonderweg*.

(4) *Temple*. As inconsistent in retrospect as it seems, the early Jewish Christians continued to attend the temple and presumably to participate in the sacrifices.[115] It cannot have been long, however, before the death of the Messiah came to be understood as the fulfillment of the sacrificial ritual of the temple (as in the book of Hebrews).[116] The temple became identified as the Christian community (1 Cor 3:16f.; 6:19; 2 Cor 6:16), through the indwelling of the divine presence in the Holy Spirit. Bauckham focuses on the temple as a key element in the parting of the ways.[117] The destruction of the temple in 70 was no doubt seen as a divine confirmation that the sacrifice of Jesus had replaced the sacrifices of the temple.

Whatever modifications were necessary, Jewish believers in Jesus did not believe that their new faith had in fact fundamentally violated any of the four pillars. The discontinuities were a matter of fulfillment involving a more basic undergirding continuity. Depending on the ability or inability to accept the discontinuous elements of Christianity we must speak of orthodox and less-than-orthodox Jewish Christians. In the

---

115. It is intriguing, however, to note that there is no mention in Acts of Christians actually participating in the sacrifices. Rather it is said that they went there to pray, heal, and proclaim Jesus (e.g., Acts 2:46; 3:1; 4:20; 5:42; 21:26 would have involved sacrifices, but it is an exceptional case).

116. Dunn suggests that it occurred among the Hellenists of Acts 6, thus "within a year or two of the Easter event." "When Did the Understanding of Jesus' Death as an Atoning Sacrifice First Emerge?," in *Israel's God and Rebecca's Children: Christology and Community in Early Judaism and Christianity* (Waco: Baylor University Press, 2007), 181.

117. "The Parting of the Ways: What Happened and Why."

latter category we must place the sects of Jewish Christianity we know of from the early church fathers, namely the Ebionites, Nazoreans, Encratites, and possibly the Elkasaites, all or most of whom apparently held what by NT standards was a defective christology.[118]

Of course, as much as the scriptures can be said to be a uniting factor, their interpretation was a dividing factor. Jewish Christians would have read much of the OT differently than they did before their Christian faith. They made use of a christological hermeneutic which had as its premise the truth of the gospel. For Jewish Christians, and Gentile Christians too, the scriptures had prophesied all that had come to pass: a new covenant with the law written on the heart (Jer 31:31–34); a Son of Man to whom everlasting dominion is given (Dan 7:13–14); a suffering Servant who died for the transgressions of the people (Isa 53:5f.); a universalist hope that transcended the national-political dimension (Isa 42:6; 49:6; 66:22–23).

Jewish Christianity remained of great importance and influence throughout the NT period, and to a lesser extent in the immediately following centuries. Significant communities of Jewish Christians were found in Syria, Asia Minor, Rome and Alexandria. "The parting of the ways between Judaism and Christianity only takes on an air of finality with the triumph of Rabbinism within the Palestinian Jewish community and the virtual disappearance of Jewish Christianity."[119]

A final observation is necessary concerning the movement of Christians to Judaism in the early centuries. This should not be taken as evidence that there was thought to be no real difference between Christianity and Judaism. It is fully understandable that many Gentile Christians would have found Judaism attractive from the beginning. They knew that their faith came out of the same stream, and that in its Jewish origins there were important and good things. It is not that they necessarily wanted to give up their Christian faith, but more a matter of

---

118. M. Heemstra says "One could argue whether the term 'Christianity' is justified in this case, since these Jews were probably not regarded as Christians by the Romans and did not use this label for themselves." *The Fiscus Judaicus and the Parting of the Ways*, 210. See P. Luomanen, "Ebionites and Nazarenes"; O. Skarsaune, "The Ebionites"; W. Kinzig, "The Nazoraeans;" in *Jewish Believers in Jesus*; R. Bauckham, "The Origin of the Ebionites." in *The Image of the Judaeo-Christians in Ancient Jewish and Christian Literature*, WUNT 158, 162–81; J. Carleton Paget, "The Ebionites in Recent Research," in Paget, *Jews, Christians and Jewish Christians in Antiquity*, 325–79.

119. P. S. Alexander, "'The Parting of the Ways' from the Perspective of Rabbinic Judaism," 24.

wanting to know and affirm their roots: "Salvation is from the Jews" (Jn 4:22). This attraction to Judaism seems to be perennial. Even today not a few Gentile Christians have been attracted to "Messianic Judaism" for similar reasons. What is intriguing is the opposition to contemporary Messianic Judaism on the part of what we might call classic Judaism, on the one side, and classic Christianity, on the other.[120] It serves as the rather close parallel to Jewish Christianity of the early centuries, but in a more polarized situation at the end of a long history of separation.

CONCLUSION

Let us now review the points we have attempted to establish.

(1) It is clear that we have diversities of Judaism and Christianity in the first century. At the same time, however, there are core elements common to those diversities that remain constant and determinative.

(2) Thus there is plenty of evidence that the differences between Christianity and Judaism—both still in embryonic form—began to become clear in the earliest years of our era.[121] This evidence points to Christianity and Judaism as discrete, identifiable entities. Jewish persecution of Christians begins very early and indicates the perceived incompatibility of the Christian message and the pillars of Judaism. For persecution demands both identity and the perception of serious threat. The numerous texts we have looked at make the case a cumulative one.

(3) It is therefore not justifiable to speak of Christianity as a sect of Judaism, except perhaps for the first transitional year or two of its existence.[122]

---

120. See D. Cohn-Sherbok, "Modern Hebrew Christianity and Messianic Judaism" in *The Image of the Judaeo-Christians in Ancient Jewish and Christiqn Literature*, WUNT 158, 287–98; D. J. Rudolph, "Messianic Jews and Christian Theology," *Pro Ecclesia* 14 (2005) 58–84.

121. "When we read Christian sources from the apostolic and subapostolic age with open eyes, we find there almost all the later major anti-Jewish motifs, at least *in nuce*, which indicates that the later development was not only an unhappy deviation." D. Flusser, "The Jewish-Christian Schism (Part II)," 38.

122. "There were at first many ties, personal and customary; there were discussions and arguments; at first it looked as if the new, eschatological sect had only founded a new, synagogal assembly with some strange, but also many familiar customs. One read the old Scriptures, but with an entirely new, prophetic zeal; one prayed according to the trusted forms, but also in the name of Christ; one sang the same Psalter, but now along with christological hymns; one lived according to the same ethical commands of the Scriptures, but now with emphasis upon the commandment of love; one abhorred idolatry and pagan vices, and so forth. It is furthermore probable that some Jewish

(4) Although the parting of the ways began almost from the beginning, it was a process that took decades, proceeding at different speeds in different places. Gradually, it would seem, the lines hardened and the hostility escalated.[123]

All of this stands in contrast to the current, misleading trend of denying the correctness of speaking of Judaism or Christianity in the first century and of assigning the parting of the ways to the fourth century. Of course one *cannot* have the Christianity of the fourth-century councils until the fourth century; one *cannot* have Talmudic Judaism until centuries later than the first century. This, however, does not justify ignoring the data we have looked at, as though earlier all we had for the first few centuries was a great blur.

There will be no avoiding the criticism that the perspective expressed in this essay is theologically motivated rather than "objective" or disinterested history. Judith Lieu, a veteran scholar in the discussion of Christian and Jewish identity, and many others with her, never tire of warning against the bias that theology brings to the discussion. Lieu refers to "the parting of the ways" as "essentially a Christian model" that employs abstract conceptions, and "works best with a theological agenda."[124]

> The 'parting of the ways' may continue to be useful to explore theological development or to defend a theological interpretation; in trying to make sense of the uncertainties of the early history of Christianity it may prove to be theologically less satisfying but sociologically more persuasive to picture a criss-crossing of muddy tracks which only the expert tracer, or poacher can decipher."[125]

Christians continued to go to the synagogues, say, on great feast days while also going to the new, eschatological conventicles [*ekklēsiai*]." M. Hengel, "Early Christianity as a Jewish-Messianic, Universalistic Movement," 31.

123. "Thus, even after their separation, which becomes definitive in the first decades of the second century, the relationship between Jews and Christian remained special—one could even say unique." Hengel, "Early Christianity as a Jewish-Messianic, Universalistic Movement," 38. Cf. Stanton: "Long after Christian communities felt themselves to be quite distinct from Judaism, the direct and indirect criticisms of the synagogue 'across the street' continued to engage the attention of Christians." *A Gospel for a New People*, 233–34.

124. Lieu, "The Parting of the Ways," 18–19. Speaking of a parting of the ways "is a theological judgment," "but one perspective" among others (20).

125. Ibid., 29.

PART THREE | JUDAISM AND CHRISTIANITY

According to Lieu, "'Christian' scholarship" is burdened with "contemporary theological concerns which infuse their historical interests."[126] In her view, "the conceptual baggage these terms [Judaism and Christianity] carry belongs rather more to our contemporary agenda."[127] At the same time, however, she is quite open in expressing a viewpoint that seems to me to be an underlying motive of those who wish to deny the parting of the ways. She describes her conclusions as consonant with the "contemporary search for identity, where we are being urged to discover and to honour the value of difference and diversity, to give ear to the voices from the margins, to acknowledge the integrity of the 'other', and our need for them, and, only so, to affirm our own as well as their integrity."[128] A perspective such as this, admirable as it is, also affects perceptions, and of course does not lend itself to the drawing of lines. Philosophical issues also obviously come into play.[129]

According to Lieu, "'Christian' scholarship" is burdened with "contemporary theological concerns which infuse their historical interests."[130]

---

126. "History and Theology in Christian Views on Judaism," in *The Jews Among Pagans and Christians in the Roman Empire*, (eds. J. Lieu et al.; London: Routledge, 1992). See too Boccaccini, *Middle Judaism*, 7-13.

127. *Christian Identity in the Jewish and Graeco-Roman World* (Oxford: Oxford University Press, 2004), 306.

128. Another conspicuous example of how an agenda drives the argument, see K. L. King, "Which Christianity?" esp. 80f. Adele Reinhartz also points out that the currently popular viewpoint is "in tune with the current intellectual climate, and particularly the postmodern critique of the tendency to see the world and human history in terms of binary oppositions." "A Fork in the Road or a Multi-Lane Highway?" 281.

129. J. Carleton Paget perceptively remarks: "it is also important, I would suggest, to see aspects of this new approach to Jewish-Christian relations as emerging from an ever-growing influence of aspects of post-modern thought upon early Christian studies and Judaism." *Jews, Christians and Jewish-Christians in Antiquity*, 7.

130. See, e.g., Dunn, "Two Covenants or One? The Interdependence of Jewish and Christian Identity," in *Geschichte—Tradition—Reflexion* (eds. H. Cancik et al.; Tübingen: Mohr Siebeck, 1996) 3:119f.; D. Georgi, "The Early Church: Internal Jewish Migration or New Religion?" *HTR* 88 (1995) 35-68: There is wisdom in the comment of Daniel Stökl Ben Ezra (who dates the parting of the ways to the second century): "To me it seems not so much the sheer assumption of a 'parting of the ways' of Christianity from Judaism that might impede progress in the research of early Jewish-Christian relations but rather the unnecessary conjecture often going with it that non-violent interaction stagnated after such a parting." "On Trees, Waves, and Cytokinesis: Shifting Paradigms in Early (and Modern) Jewish-Christian Relations," in *Interaction between Judaism and Christianity in History, Religion, Art and Culture*, eds. M. Poorthis, et al. (Leiden: Brill, 2009) 137. A striking example of a priori agenda items can be seen in the opening remarks of P. S. Alexander's "'The Parting of the Ways' from the Perspective of Rabbinic Judaism," 1-2. See too, Boccaccini, *Middle Judaism*, 7-13.

When Lieu stresses "the conceptual baggage these terms [Judaism and Christianity] carry belongs rather more to our contemporary agenda,"[131] it should not be thought that she is neutral and has no agenda. On the contrary, she is quite open in expressing a viewpoint that seems to me to be an underlying motive of those who wish to deny the parting of the ways. She describes her conclusions as consonant with the "contemporary search for identity, where we are being urged to discover and to honour the value of difference and diversity, to give ear to the voices from the margins, to acknowledge the integrity of the 'other', and our need for them, and, only so, to affirm our own as well as their integrity."[132] A perspective such as this also affects perceptions, and of course does not lend itself to the drawing of lines. Ethical and philosophical issues are thus at stake.[133]

If it can be shown that for the first few centuries there was no significant difference between Judaism and Christianity, then that can serve as a model for today—as a corrective of anti-Semitism and a facilitation of Jewish-Christian dialogue. Another motive one often finds expressed is to arrive at a viewpoint that is more amenable to Jewish-Christian dialogue.[134] I do not dispute these as worthy motives, but merely want to indicate that they too constitute an "agenda" that may be imposed upon the data we

---

131. See Mikael Tellbe's criticism of J. Lieu in "The Prototypical Christ-Believer: Early Christian Identity Formation in Ephesus," in *Exploring Early Christian Identity* (ed. B. Holmberg, WUNT 226) 118–19.Cf. B. Holmberg, "Understanding the First Hundred Years of Christian Identity," 30.

132. Ibid., 316. Another conspicuous example of how an agenda drives the argument, see K. L. King, "Which Christianity?" esp. 80–81. Adele Reinhartz also points out that the currently popular viewpoint is "in tune with the current intellectual climate, and particularly the postmodern critique of the tendency to see the world and human history in terms of binary oppositions." "A Fork in the Road or a Multi-Lane Highway?," 281.

133. J. Carleton Paget perceptively remarks: "it is also important, I would suggest, to see aspects of this new approach to Jewish-Christian relations as emerging from an ever-growing influence of aspects of post-modern thought upon early Christian studies and Judaism." *Jews, Christians and Jewish-Christians in Antiquity*, 7.

134. See, e.g., Dunn, "Two Covenants or One?," 119–20; D. Georgi, "The Early Church: Internal Jewish Migration or New Religion?" There is wisdom in the comment of Daniel Stökl Ben Ezra (who dates the parting of the ways to the second century): "To me it seems not so much the sheer assumption of a 'parting of the ways' of Christianity from Judaism that might impede progress in the research of early Jewish-Christian relations but rather the unnecessary conjecture often going with it that non-violent interaction stagnated after such a parting." "On Trees, Waves, and Cytokinesis: Shifting Paradigms in Early (and Modern) Jewish-Christian Relations," 137. A striking example of a priori agenda items can be seen in the opening remarks of P. S. Alexander's "'The Parting of the Ways' from the Perspective of Rabbinic Judaism," 1–2.

work with. In fact, historical and sociological study may be no more objective, and perhaps sometimes less appropriate, than "theological" study.

The more I study this topic the more I become aware that we all wear our own glasses. Without yielding to a postmodern epistemological pessimism, we may admit that to a certain extent we see what we want to see, we are bound to see what our presuppositions and perspective allow. I am happy to grant that much, as long as it does not rule out the possibility of seeing and evaluating truth altogether. In my opinion, it remains possible to ascertain knowledge of historical reality that lies behind texts.[135]

The wise words of Martin Hengel are worth quoting:

> The goal of this mutual [Jewish and Christian] research of the sources should no longer be the apologetic definition and biased estimation of one's own position but the earnest understanding of classical texts of the other side, their authors and the events that they describe. At the same time, a better understanding is most possible when one does not fully shy away from one's own standpoint but expresses it in each case with the necessary clarity; for only when one strives to define one's own position can one understand and respect the different and consciously held position of others. For a person who thinks that everything should be true in the same way, truth has in effect ceased to be.[136]

For all the considerable Jewishness of Christianity, describing it as a sect within Judaism cannot do it justice. As Hengel remarks, "even an illegitimate daughter has decisive features in common with her mother."[137] To speak of the parting of the ways, as is sometimes wrongly assumed, necessitates neither anachronistic "essentialism" nor triumphalist supersessionism. For paradoxically, *the parting of the ways is itself the fulfillment of Israel's divine commission and thus the realization in part of Israel's hope.* When the old man Simeon referred to the salvation which God has prepared in the presence of all peoples, he described it poignantly as *"a light for revelation to the Gentiles, and for glory to thy people Israel"* (Luke 2:30-32).

---

135. See Mikael Tellbe's criticism of J. Lieu. "The Prototypical Christ-Believer: Early Christian Identity Formation in Ephesus," 118-19; cf. B. Holmberg, "Understanding the First Hundred Years of Christian Identity," 30.

136. "Early Christianity as a Jewish-Messianic, Universalistic Movement," 41.

137. "Early Christianity as a Jewish-Messianic, Universalistic Movement," 40. Although the two metaphors are usually understood as alternatives, Hengel finds both useful: "One might therefore express the relationship between Judaism and Christianity not only as one between mother and daughter but also as one between two siblings that have grown increasingly apart." Ibid., 34.

15

A Positive Theology of Judaism from the New Testament

NEW TESTAMENT SCHOLARS TODAY are more sensitive than ever before to the fact that interpreters unavoidably read texts from their own perspectives, their own backgrounds, and their own experience. No one comes to the text in a neutral mode or with a blank, unmarked page. Most often we are caught up with the disadvantages this imposes upon us in understanding the Bible. But in at least one important instance it can be a distinct advantage: it is good to read NT texts about the Jews with the memory of the holocaust in our minds. Not that we need to revise the whole of NT theology because of the holocaust, although not a few have called for this.[1] But rather so that we can prevent the misuse of NT texts about the Jews and avoid the resultant negative attitudes and behavior towards the Jews. Much has been written, and deservedly so, about the impact of the holocaust on NT interpretation.

There can be no question but that the grim reality of the holocaust calls for a rethinking of NT passages concerning the Jews and for a new emphasis on the continuing place of the Jews in God's mysterious purposes. It is thus exceptionally important for Christians to consider,

---

1. E.g., Rosemary Reuther, *Faith and Fratricide: The Theological Roots of Anti-Semitism* (New York: Seabury, 1974; reprint, Eugene, OR: Wipf & Stock, 1996). See recently, *Jesus, Judaism, and Christian Anti-Judaism: Reading the New Testament after the Holocaust*, ed. P. Fredriksen and A. Reinhartz (Louisville: Westminster John Knox, 2002).

and to espouse, a positive theology of Judaism.² In order to put matters into proper perspective, however, we cannot simply look at the positive material in the NT about the Jews. We must look at the full scope of the biblical data, negative as well as positive, painful though it be, and then make an attempt to make sense of the whole, if we are to come to an adequate understanding. In this essay I begin by posing the problem sharply in terms of two popular, contradictory, and, in my opinion, unsatisfactory proposals concerning the question of the place of the Jews in God's program of redemption. Then we will briefly look at the negative and positive material concerning the Jews in the NT. Finally, I will try to draw things together in a way that does justice to the complexity of the NT data, concluding with some remarks concerning the Jews and the church today.

1. POSING THE PROBLEM

Two major, contrasting views have dominated the question of the Jews in the NT. The first, held by the church as early as the second century, and by many down to the present, is commonly known as "supersessionism." The second, given renewed vitality because of the holocaust, is the so-called "two-covenant" theory.³ Although it is a gross simplification, it may be helpful for the sake of clarity if we characterize the first view as maintaining with respect to Israel, that everything has changed, and the second as maintaining that nothing has changed.

According to supersessionism, *everything has changed* for the Jews, in the sense that their earlier position of favor has been taken away from

---

2. Three recent books I recommend highly are R. Kendall Soulen, *The God of Israel and Christian Theology* (Minneapolis: Fortress, 1996); R. E. Diprose, *Israel in the Development of Christian Thought* (Rome: Istituto Biblico Evangelico Italiano, 2000); and C. E. Braaten and R. W. Jenson, eds., *Jews and Christians: People of God* (Grand Rapids: Eerdmans, 2003). See, too, the collection of essays edited by D. Pollefeyt, *Jews and Christians: Rivals or Partners for the Kingdom of God? In Search of an Alternative for the Theology of Substitution* (Leuven: Peeters, 1997); and the Pontifical Biblical Commission's *The Jewish People and Their Sacred Scriptures in the Christian Bible* (Vatican: Libreria Editrice Vaticana, 2002). Of special interest also is the statement of the Church of Sweden, *Guds vägar: Judendom och kristendom*. See the discussion in *STK* 79.3 (2003).

3. Key representatives of this viewpoint are K. Stendahl, *Paul Among Jews and Gentiles* (Philadelphia: Fortress, 1976); J. C. Gager, *The Origins of Anti-Semitism* (Oxford: Oxford University Press, 1983); and L. Gaston, *Paul and Torah* (Vancouver: University of British Columbia Press, 1983).

them, and has been given to the church. In this transference, the church thus displaces or supplants Israel. According to the two-covenant view, on the other hand, *nothing has changed* for the Jews: the original covenant made with them by God remains in force, being unaffected by the so-called new covenant, which in this view is understood as relevant only to the Gentiles. In my opinion, however, these stark, opposite alternatives are only partly true since each requires the neglect of important NT data. To return to the language of change, it seems evident from the NT that *some things have changed* for the Jews; but it also clear that *not everything has changed*. It should not surprise us, therefore, that in this matter we have to reckon with complexity. The rich mixture of continuity and discontinuity between the new covenant and the old covenant is a part of the very weave and texture of NT theology. Those who see in these materials only continuity (as, e.g., in a two-covenant framework) and equally those who see in these materials only discontinuity (as, e.g., in supersessionism) inevitably end up distorting the picture. With similar matters in view, the Jesus of the evangelist Matthew reminds us: "Therefore, every scribe who has been trained for the kingdom of heaven is like a householder who brings out of the treasure box new things and old (*kaina kai palaia*)" (Matt 13:52).[4] True insight and balance lie in giving rightful place both to new and old.

Before we assess the weaknesses of the two dominant proposals we have mentioned and attempt to articulate a more adequate understanding, we must briefly survey the NT evidence.

2. THE NEGATIVE PASSAGES (SEE APPENDIX 1)

So numerous and powerful are the negative passages that it is easy to understand why the supersession viewpoint has been so prevalent. As is well known, the material that indicates discontinuity and points to, or seems to point to, displacement of Israel is much more abundant than is the material pointing in the opposite direction. It is worth noting at the outset that the hostile tone of much of this material is the result of intramural differences. It reflects the polemic of Jews of one persuasion against Jews of another persuasion.

---

4. See D. A. Hagner, "Nytt från den skriftlärdes förråd (Matt 13:52)," in *Matteus och hans läsare—förr och nu*, given in the Matthew Symposium (Lund, 27-28 September, 1996) in honor of Birger Gerhardsson; ed. B. Olsson et al., *Religio* 48 (Lund: Teologiska Institutionen, 1997) 11-24.

In the first appendix I have gathered together some representative passages[5] under the following major headings that are critical of the very heart of Judaism: 1) Israel has no advantage over the Gentiles (election and covenant); 2) the role of the law has come to an end; 3) the temple is passé; and 4) the land is conspicuous by its (virtual?) absence from the NT. To summarize briefly the teaching under each of these headings, we may say the following.

1) The election of Israel as a special people, marking them off from all other nations, seems to become insignificant in much of the NT. All the more remarkable is the fact that it is just this election and separateness of Israel that is of crucial importance in Second Temple Judaism. In the new era of fulfillment brought by Christ, God is no longer partial to the Jews (Rom 2:11; 10:12; Acts 10:34f.). Further, the significance of circumcision, that crucial symbol marking out Jew from Gentile, is denied by Paul (Gal 6:15; Phil 3:3; Col 3:11). Again, it is a great shock to see Paul so unhesitatingly put the Jews with the Gentiles in the same predicament of being unavoidably trapped in sin and thus also in need of the salvation accomplished by Christ (especially Rom 1:18—3:20). Also striking is the ready application of the language of 1 Pet 2:9f., hitherto carefully reserved for Israel alone (Exod 19:4-6), now to the church. In Rom 9:25f., Paul quotes Hos 2:23-24, words used in Hosea to refer to the Jews, and applies them to the Gentiles: "Those who were not my people I will call 'my people,' and her who was not beloved I will call 'my beloved.'" And in the very place where it was said to them, 'You are not my people,' they will be called 'sons of the living God.'" Finally, both in Paul and in Hebrews we find the old covenant (with Israel) referred to as outmoded, inferior to, and replaced by the new covenant of Jer 31:31-34.

2) Although in the NT the righteousness about which the law speaks remains a goal, the role and function of the law *per se* has come to an end. This, of course, is a predominantly Pauline emphasis, but we see something of this also in Hebrews. The law turns out to function as a kind of parenthesis, having had a temporary role to perform, but not having the soteriological potential or significance attached to it by Judaism. Again

---

5. It is of course risky to deal with the NT as a whole. Certainly there were some differences of opinion among the different writers, and not all would have expressed themselves in the same manner. Nevertheless, there are remarkable similarities, if not coherence, in the list of passages I have drawn up. And there seems to be an advantage in at least attempting to deal with the whole of the NT.

we see here one of the pillars of Judaism, so terribly important in the Second Temple period, demoted in dramatic fashion.

3) The number of passages in the NT that point to the temple being no longer relevant is also remarkable. The atoning significance of the death of Christ was foreshadowed by the temple cultus, but now, with the definitive sacrifice of the cross, the sacrifices of the temple clearly no longer have any salvific significance. Language of the temple cultus is frequently spiritualized in the NT and applied to Christians and the Christian life.

4) Finally, as has often been noticed, the promise of the land, first made to Abraham, and a solid, ongoing expectation in Judaism, seems to play virtually no role in the NT.[6] That motif is transcended in favor of considerations involving universal apocalyptic restoration.

Now I am rather sure that some readers have been squirming all through this essay so far, eager to cry out "But these passages can be read in another way!" or "But there are many passages that contradict what you have been saying!" I must of course admit that *some* of these passages are ambiguous and can–and perhaps ought to be–read differently. I do not think, however, that all of them can be read against what appears to be their natural meaning, so that the strong discontinuity can be done away with altogether.[7]

In fact, it could well appear from these passages that the supersessionist argument is valid and convincing. And from the prevalence of passages such as these one can certainly see how the church so early and for so many centuries took up the supersessionist position. There is, however, another side to the question and passages that are much more positive in tone. To these we now turn our attention.

---

6. See especially W. D. Davies, *The Gospel and the Land: Early Christianity and Jewish Territorial Doctrine* (Berkeley: University of California Press, 1974); Davies, *The Territorial Dimension of Judaism* (Minneapolis: Fortress, 1991).

7. I note here the apparently increasing trend not only to see the full extent of the Jewishness of the NT, but now especially to see virtually everything in the NT as fully containable under the umbrella of Judaism. From Jesus to Paul, to the early church— now everything can be explained, it is maintained, as fully within the wide variety of first-century Judaism. And accordingly, some now insist that it is improper to speak of anything as "Christian" until we reach the second century at the earliest. This trend, in my opinion, is only partly true, and seriously underestimates the degree and character of the newness affirmed by the early Jewish believers in Jesus.

3. THE POSITIVE PASSAGES (SEE APPENDIX 2)

Although apparently not as numerous as the negative passages, there are many passages in the NT that stand in noticeable tension with passages examined above.

1) To begin with are those passages where the specialness of Israel continues. This motif is mainly in Paul and Matthew. The Gospel of Matthew, notably alone on this point, indicates that Jesus limited his ministry specifically to the Jews. It is "the lost sheep of the house of Israel" (Matt 10:6; 15:24) that are the focus of Jesus' ministry and even that of the disciples, at least in the time before the death and resurrection of Jesus, when the mission to the Gentiles is made an explicit reality. God's faithfulness to Israel is thus a prominent theme in the mission of Jesus. I judge Matthew to be historically correct here, and as having special interest in the theme because his readers were Jewish Christians. The specialness of the Jews is also seen in Jesus' prophecy of the eschatological time to come when the twelve disciples will sit upon twelve thrones judging over the twelve tribes of Israel. And even a special conversion of the Jews may possibly be in view at the *parousia* of the glorious Son of Man (Matt 23:38–39).

Chapters 9–11 of Paul's letter to the Romans are, of course, crucially important on the subject of the continuing election of Israel. Paul's view is notoriously complex. It is a paradox that the Jews have no advantage, on the one hand, but on the other hand, the Jews do have an advantage. That advantage does not consist in a so-to-say automatic salvation through the election of Israel. It is more a matter of their long-standing relationship with God. Jews who have not believed in the gospel are, of course, in a totally different category than the pagans. Paul recognizes their present zeal for God, although he regards it as sadly unenlightened.

In the argument of the first eight chapters of Romans one might be excused for thinking that Paul was himself a supersessionist (the number of passages from the Pauline letters in appendix 1 is impressive). Thus the conclusions of chapters 9–11 come as a distinct surprise. To the question of 11:1, "Has God rejected his people?, one might indeed expect a positive answer in light of Paul's previous argument in Romans. Instead, however, Paul strongly denies such a conclusion by appealing to the reality of the remnant of Jews who have accepted the gospel. This in itself Paul sees as a confirmation of God's faithfulness to Israel. An alert reader, however, will note that this does not yet speak to the issue of those

A POSITIVE THEOLOGY OF JUDAISM

Jews who have *not* accepted the gospel. In 11:11 Paul asks again: "Have they stumbled so as to fall?, here too emphatically denying the possibility. Then Paul provides us with a series of remarkable phrases that point to the ultimate salvation of the Jews: "full inclusion" (11:12); "their acceptance . . . life from the dead" (11:15); "how much more will these natural branches be grafted back into their own olive tree" (11:24); "they also may receive mercy" (11:31); "that he may have mercy upon all" (11:32). Three of these are especially noteworthy: "all Israel will be saved" (11:26); "as regards election they are beloved for the sake of their forefathers" (11:28); and "the gifts and the call of God are irrevocable" (11:29). *This section of Romans (11:11-32) by itself ought to rule out supersession as a biblical option.* Could Paul have made it any plainer that Israel retains its special status as his uniquely elected people and that this special status will be vindicated in the future?

As a further statement of the ongoing importance of Israel, Paul can write, "For I tell you that Christ became a servant to the circumcised to show God's truthfulness, in order to confirm the promises given to the patriarchs" (Rom 15:8).

We shall return to this material because of its importance.

2) Outside of the famous Matthean passage about the permanence of the law (Matt 5:17-20), the other significant material comes from the pen of Paul. Paul's view is again complex. We have already briefly seen his strong polemic against the law. It therefore comes as a surprise to hear Paul speak as positively about the law as he does: the law is upheld (Rom 3:31); "the law is holy, the commandment is holy and just and good" (Rom 7:12); and "the just requirement of the law" is to be fulfilled in the Christian (Rom 8:4). Unless we are to believe that Paul stupidly contradicts himself, we can only conclude that if there is *a sense in which* the law is done away with, there is *another sense* in which the law is also upheld. To cut through a hugely debated subject,[8] which we cannot enter into fully here, we may simply assert that the law as typically understood in Judaism is done away with, but that at the same time, the righteousness that is the ultimate goal of the law is upheld. In the NT, the dynamic

---

8. The debate about the law has increased in recent years because of the work of E. P. Sanders, and the development of the "new perspective" on Paul by J. D. G. Dunn. For analysis and critique, see D. A. Hagner, "Paul and Judaism: Testing the New Perspective," in P. Stuhlmacher ed., *Revisiting Paul's Doctrine of Justification: A Challenge to the New Perspective* (Downers Grove, IL: InterVarsity, 2001) 75-105; Seyoon Kim, *Paul and the New Perspective: Second Thoughts on the Origin of Paul's Gospel* (Grand Rapids: Eerdmans, 2001).

is entirely different, however, with the law being now written on the heart of the believer, not in terms of commandments but in terms of the life-giving Spirit (2 Cor 3:3, 6)–this itself being the eschatological fulfillment of Jer 31:31–34 and Ezek 36:26–27.

3) and 4) There is very little that can be brought forward as positive references to the temple or to the land in the NT. These elements have for practical purposes all but dropped out of consideration–or better, transposed into a new key–in the earliest church.

4. FINDING A MIDDLE WAY BETWEEN SUPERSESSIONISM AND TWO COVENANT THEOLOGY

A. The NT evidence that goes against supersessionism seems undeniable to me. It is true that the faithfulness of God to Israel can be substantiated by the mere existence of the remnant of Jewish believers in Jesus. Nothing more is needed to demonstrate that God's faithfulness is unshakable. The earliest church was, after all, made up exclusively of Jewish believers. Although, as we have seen, that is part of Paul's argument in Rom 11, Paul does not stop there. He goes on to speak in much more global terms. God is going to save all Israel, *because* of Israel's election, "for [*gar*] the gifts and the call of God are irrevocable" (11:29). With this one lapidary statement the whole structure of supersessionism collapses. God is not finished with Israel; the church has not taken her place *simpliciter*.

Nevertheless, we cannot ignore the data that *seems* (were it not for Paul's statements in Romans) to support the supersession perspective. It was the strength of this material that led the early church quickly and steadfastly to its assertion of supersessionism. The church portrayed in the NT in fact looks very much as though it has taken the place of Israel in the present time. This is why the statements of Paul in Rom 11 strike the reader as so surprising at first. As the redeemed people of God, the church is the center of God's purposes and saving activity. In the church most of the OT prophecies find their fulfillment. The special language used exclusively in reference to Israel in the OT is now freely applied to the church.[9]

---

9. E.g., Paul applies OT material to the Corinthian church in 2 Cor 6:16–18, with the words "since we have these promises"; 1 Pet 2:5, 9–10 provides a classic instance.

A POSITIVE THEOLOGY OF JUDAISM

The point I wish to make here is that all of this cannot mean that the Christian church is a new religion, or the replacement of Judaism. It is of the greatest importance to understand that theologically the church is the *fulfillment* of Judaism. On this point the Jewish remnant of believers in Jesus have always been rightly adamant. The church does not represent a non-Judaism; it is instead the *true Judaism*.

The word "fulfillment" is most useful in this regard, since it at once captures both the reality of continuity but also can allow the newness that necessarily brings with it a degree of discontinuity. The church is the fulfillment of what God had spoken about already in the Abrahamic Covenant, "in you shall all the nations of the earth be blessed" (Gen 12:3); in the death of Jesus on the cross, the sacrificial cultus of the temple finds its culmination; in the church the eternal kingdom promised to David's son finds its realization and the Davidic Covenant its fulfillment (2 Sam 7:16); Jesus presents himself as the final interpreter of the law of the Sinai Covenant and in his teaching that law finds its fulfillment (Matt 5:17-18).

Is the story of the Bible fundamentally about Israel or is it fundamentally about the church? The early Christians had not the slightest hesitation about their conviction that the Hebrew Bible is the book of the church, as much, or even more, than it is of Israel. Any notion that the church is an afterthought in God's purposes, or a parenthesis (as in classical dispensationalist thinking) or some kind of detour in God's plan is not satisfactory from the perspective of the NT.[10] The election of Israel was never merely for her own sake, but was for the sake of the nations. We see this wider interest already in the Abrahamic Covenant and we see it especially in the repeated emphasis in Second Isaiah upon the call of Israel to serve as a light to the nations: "I have given you as a covenant to the people, a light to the nations" (Isa 42:6); "I will give you as a light to the nations, that my salvation may reach to the end of the earth" (Isa 49:6).[11]

All that we have been saying is true, in my opinion, but none of it necessitates the conclusion of supersessionism. Although Israel was not elected for her own sake alone, but for the sake of the nations, it is important to insist that her election remains–a point we have seen Paul stress in Rom 11.[12]

---

10. *Pace* R. W. Jenson, in his essay "Toward a Christian Theology of Judaism," in *Jews and Christians* (n. 2 above) 7.

11. See too the implicit universalism anticipated in Isa 19:24-25; Jer 4:2.

12. David Novak writes: "Were the Jews no longer present in the world as a covenanted people, then one would have to conclude that God broke his promise to them.

B. Although the so-called two-covenant theory seems appealing at first glance, it too must be rejected as unsatisfactory because it is so incongruent with the teaching of the NT.[13] There is of course no problem with emphasizing God's faithfulness to the covenant promises made to Israel. As we have just noted, this is an important point for Paul, as it doubtless was for all Jewish Christians at the beginning. But to separate the old covenant from the new covenant and then argue that the former applies to Israel and the latter to the (Gentile) church is to depart entirely from the teaching of the NT in general and the teaching of Paul in particular.

Let us look at the main reasons that the two covenant theory is inconsistent with the NT, both historically and theologically:

(1) Historically the gospel was proclaimed by and exclusively to Jews. The early church was, in the early years of its existence, exclusively Jewish. In no way did these Christian Jews think of themselves as being disloyal to the faith of their scriptures and their forefathers. Quite the contrary. They saw themselves as participating in the *fulfillment* of Judaism and as therefore constituting *the true Israel* (even though that language is not used in the NT).[14] The new covenant that they had now begun to participate in was, in the first instance, as Jeremiah had prophesied, specifically about Jews. It is a covenant made with the house of Israel and the house of Judah (Jer 31:31).

According to the NT, the gospel is directed to the Jews–even with a priority—and then, only secondarily, to the Gentiles. Jesus came not to, or for, the Gentiles, but to the Jews (as Matthew makes very plain); Paul makes it explicit that the gospel is "to the Jew first and also to the Greek" (Rom 1:16). It could hardly be clearer that the gospel is intended for both Jew and Gentile. Paul speaks of the dynamic of the gospel in Rom 10:10, saying that one believes with the heart and so is justified, and confesses with the lips and so is saved; he adds: "For there is no distinction between Jew and Greek; the same Lord is Lord of all and bestows his riches upon all who call upon him. For 'everyone who calls upon the name of the

---

But, if God broke his original promise to Israel, which is precisely the hidden premise of supersessionism, then how could the church—as the branch grafted onto the tree-possibly believe God's ultimate promise to her?" "From Supersessionism to Parallelism in Jewish-Christian Dialogue," in *Jews and Christians* (n. 2 above) 99.

13. See D. E. Holwerda, *Jesus and Israel: One Covenant or Two?* (Grand Rapids: Eerdmans, 1995); Kai Kjaer-Hansen, "The Problem of the Two-Covenant Theology," *Mishkan* 21 (1994) 52–81.

14. This may, however, be the implication of the disputed phrase "the Israel of God" in Gal 6:16.

Lord will be saved'" (Rom 10:12-13, citing Joel 2:32 and equating Jesus with YHWH). As R. J. Neuhaus points out, "It is not Christian imperialism but fidelity to revealed truth that requires Christians to say that Christ is Lord of all or he is not Lord at all."[15]

There is thus not the slightest hint in the NT that the gospel of the new covenant was applicable only to the Gentiles. Everything points to the importance of the gospel to the Jews as well as the Gentiles.

(2) The NT knows only one way of salvation, one soteriology, namely *by faith in Jesus Christ*. Paul, especially, could never have tolerated the notion that salvation was possible for anyone, including the Jews, apart from the cross of Christ. This is crystal clear from the argument of Rom 1:18—3:20. All of humanity, Jews as well as Gentiles, stand united under the same curse of sin. And to that universal predicament there is only one answer: the redemption that is in Christ (Rom 3:23-24). Thus even though the Jews are the elect, covenant people of God, they must still come to faith in Jesus.

There seems to be a surprising amount of confusion on this point. Some reputable scholars seem to think that the salvation of Israel to which Paul refers in Rom 11 is something that refers to the Jews' acceptance on the basis of their elect status, quite apart from faith in Christ. This can hardly be the case, however. Jews who do not believe in the gospel are referred to by Paul as branches that were broken off from the olive tree (Rom 11:17-24). Paul makes the reason for the breaking off of these branches very plain: "They were broken off because of unbelief" (Rom 11:20)-that is, unbelief in the gospel (cf. Rom 9:1-5). These broken-off natural branches will be restored to the tree, says Paul, "if they do not persist in their unbelief" (Rom 11:23). Again, it can only be the gospel that is in view. Paul's hope for the salvation of his own people thus rests upon the same basis as the salvation of the Gentiles.

5. A POSITIVE THEOLOGY OF JUDAISM

There is hardly any need to review all that the church and Judaism have in common. This is well known. Simply by virtue of sharing the same scriptures, despite significant differences in interpretation, Judaism and Christianity share the same basic theological perspective: the same God, who is Creator of all; the same God, who enters into covenant relationship

---

15. "Salvation is from the Jews," in *Jews and Christians* (n2 above) 68.

and is faithful to his covenant promises; the same God, who stands ready always to forgive repentant sinners and restore the wayward. Paul, at the beginning of Romans 9, can thus point to the great theological advantage of the Jews: "To them belong the sonship, the glory, the covenants, the giving of the law, the worship, and the promises."

But now, Gentile Christians have become partakers of all this richness, enjoyed exclusively by the Jews for two millennia. The Gentiles *were not a part of this story* from the beginning, although it is important to remember that they *were in view* from the beginning. The Gentiles are brought into the story only relatively late, after a long history of God's dealing with Israel. They are described by Paul as the "wild" olive branches, who have been incorporated into an already existing olive tree to which they did not belong (Rom 11:24). Or, to switch to the analogy of Ephesians, the Gentiles were once "alienated from the commonwealth of Israel, and strangers to the covenants of promise, having no hope and without God in the world" (Eph 2:12).

There is a complicating factor that cannot be ignored, however. The Judaism we have been talking about is Second Temple Judaism, that of the time of Jesus and Paul. We can call it the religion of Israel to distinguish it from the rabbinic Judaism that began to emerge after AD 70. Christianity can perhaps be thought of as the daughter of the earlier Judaism, but not of the later Judaism. Indeed, it has often been pointed out that Christianity and rabbinic Judaism are two offsprings of Second Temple Judaism. Christianity shares less with rabbinic Judaism, as reflected in the Mishnah and Talmud, than it does with the more diverse, earlier, pre-70, forms of Judaism.

The point I wish to make here, however, is that the Jewishness of Christianity is unquestioned and increasingly appreciated. And that in itself is a considerable affirmation of Judaism. There are some who, rightly perceiving the thoroughly Jewish character of Christianity, go so far as to argue that the first-century Jewish believers in Jesus should be regarded as a sect within Judaism. One can see how this argument can be made since it builds on the great overlap of belief between the new community of faith and that of Israel. In my view, nevertheless, this conclusion seriously underestimates the extent of the newness encountered by the earliest Jewish believers in Jesus.[16] From the beginning Jesus

---

16. On giving sufficient recognition to the newness of Christianity, see D. A. Hagner, *How New is the New Testament? First-Century Judaism and the Emergence of Christianity* (Grand Rapids: Baker Academic, 2018).

takes the central place previously held by Torah. All now revolves around him.[17] Jesus the crucified Messiah becomes supremely the sign of God's covenant faithfulness to Israel.

Christianity is thoroughly Jewish in its theology, its worldview, and its fundamental moral commitments. Though it is not strictly correct, Christianity has with good reason been called a kind of Judaism for Gentiles. It would be better, as we have seen, to say that Christianity is the fulfillment of the universal dimensions inherent in Judaism's beginnings. The church is the climax of God's purposes for Israel, yet without that being the end of the story. The common Jewish expectation in the Second Temple period, probably shared by Saul the Pharisee, was that after Israel experienced eschatological salvation, then the righteous Gentiles would in turn find their place in eschatological blessing. But with the way things turned out historically, Paul the Apostle had to learn that the process was actually going to be the reverse. The Gentiles would first find their place in the eschatological kingdom, by faith in Jesus the Messiah, and only then would Israel enter into the promised eschatological salvation. As some have suggested, this means that Paul may have understood his mission to the Gentiles as having as its goal the eventual salvation of Israel. Paul, the Apostle to the Gentiles, would thus in the last analysis be serving his own people. "I want you to understand this mystery, brethren: a hardening has come upon part of Israel, until the full number of the Gentiles come in, and so all Israel will be saved" (Rom 11:25f.). After the conversion of the Gentiles, the Jews too would turn in faith to Jesus as Messiah, thus rounding out the great narrative of salvation history with an underlining of God's faithfulness to Israel.[18]

---

17. Cf the Jewish scholar, David Flusser: "It would be unreasonable to underestimate the newness of the message of the Church and the difference between the main structure of the Jewish faith and the Christocentricity of the Church." "The Jewish-Christian Schism," *Immanuel* 16 (1983) 36. See too, D. A. Hagner, "Matthew: Apostate, Reformer, Revolutionary?," *NTS* 49 (2003) 193-209.

18. I am painfully aware that a positive theology of Judaism that nevertheless insists on speaking of the salvation of the Jews through the atoning death of Jesus Christ will be unacceptable to Jewish readers. The comment of R. J. Neuhaus expresses well the tension I feel: "The end of supersessionism, however, cannot and must not mean the end of the argument between Christians and Jews. We cannot settle into the comfortable interreligious politesse of mutual respect for positions deemed to be equally true. Christ and his church do not supersede Judaism, but they do continue and fulfill the story of which we are both part-or so Christians must contend." "Salvation is from the Jews," in *Jews and Christians* (n. 2 above) 72.

6. THE CHURCH AND THE JEWS TODAY

We turn finally to some important implications that can be drawn from our presentation. Our main contention has been that although the NT brings us to a new frame of salvation history, wherein the church is seen as the fulfillment of Judaism, and the church becomes *de facto* a new Israel, yet God does not revoke his covenant promises to Israel. This state of affairs, as we have seen, causes a complexity that invalidates both supersessionist and two-covenant theology explanations of the data. But we may emphasize that despite the dramatic changes that have taken place, there naturally remains a great amount of overlap between the theologies of Judaism and Christianity.

I draw together the implications of this under two headings: (1) the salvation the church enjoys is from the Jews and for the Jews; (2) the Jews are a people special to the church.

1. The Salvation the Church Enjoys Is from the Jews and for the Jews

The statement that salvation is *from* the Jews alludes, of course, to the words of Jesus to the woman of Samaria in John 4:22: "You worship what you do not know; we worship what we know, for salvation [*hē sōtēria*] is from the Jews." The olive tree of Israel precedes the church; and the church represents the further growth of that olive tree. As we have seen, the church is the fulfillment of Judaism. The book of Acts ends in a striking way. Luke there records that Paul quoted the bitter words of Isaiah 6 about the blindness of Israel (Acts 28:26–27), applying it to the Jews of his day, and then added, "Let it be known to you then that this salvation of God has been sent to the Gentiles; they will listen" (Acts 28:28). Luke has in view, of course, the growth of the largely Gentile church. But a few lines earlier Paul spoke with the Jewish leaders in Rome and he described his Christian faith as "the hope of Israel" (Acts 28:20): "It is because of the hope of Israel that I am bound with this chain." Again we can see how well this fits with the understanding of Christianity as fulfilled Judaism.

If Christianity is rightly regarded as the fulfillment of Judaism, then the gospel is also *for* the Jews.[19] It is a Jewish gospel for the Jewish people.

---

19. See D. A. Hagner, "Jesus: Bringer of Salvation to Jew and Gentile Alike," in *Who Was Jesus? A Jewish-Christian Dialogue*, eds. C. A. Evans and P. Copan (Louisville: Westminster John Knox, 2001) 45–58.

The fact that the gospel is for the Jews and yet so many Jews have failed to believe the gospel is, of course, the problem that Paul addresses in Rom 9–11. The urgency of Paul's own conviction that the gospel is for the Jews can be seen in passages such as Rom 1:17, where Paul says that the gospel "is the power of God for salvation to every one who has faith, to the Jew first and also to the Greek" and 1 Cor 9:20: "To the Jews I became as a Jew, in order to win Jews; to those under the law I became as one under the law–though not being myself under the law–that I might win those under the law."

We have seen that Paul looks forward to the salvation of Israel at the end of the present era. That fact, however, does not cool his fervor to preach the gospel to the Jews. And if we are to be faithful to the NT, then the church's mission to Israel cannot cease. There are some who think that evangelizing the Jews is somehow anti-Semitic. In fact, the opposite is true. Failure to evangelize the Jews is what is really anti-Semitic, since it withholds from the Jews what is rightfully theirs–the great treasure of God's salvific faithfulness in Christ. Paul writes in moving words: "For I tell you that Christ became a servant to the circumcised to show God's truthfulness, in order to confirm the promises given to the patriarchs, and in order that the Gentiles might glorify God" (Rom 15:8–9). This is the reason that the gospel must continue to be proclaimed to the Jews. The Jews have served the universal church, becoming a light to the nations through Christ, and now the church must in turn serve the Jews in the proclamation of the gospel. Again, note Paul's words: "they have now been disobedient in order that by the mercy shown to you they also may receive mercy" (Rom 11:31).

It is one thing to say, as Paul does, that a time is coming when all Israel will be saved. But inevitably the question arises, what about Jews of the past and present who were and are unable to accept the truth of the gospel? This is a question one does not ask in polite society, but it is an important one that should not be swept under the carpet. Faithful Jews, as contrasted with secular Jews, are, it seems to me, in a very special category. To the extent that they live in accord with the light they have, they, like all others, are in the hands of God. Yet they remain a special people in God's eyes, unlike all others. From a Christian perspective, they resemble to an extent those strange people we meet in Acts 19:1–7, who are called "disciples,"–disciples, however, not of Jesus, but of John the Baptist. They were not yet Christians since they had not yet been baptized in the name of Jesus and had not yet received the Holy Spirit. If we analyze their situation, we may say that they had believed in the beginnings, so to speak, but had not yet come to believe in the fulfillment. They stand in the NT as a strange anomaly. In a similar way, faithful Jews, past and present, may be said to have believed in the beginnings (from a Christian perspective), but not in the fulfillment. Totally different from pagans, such Jews stand already in a special relationship with God. Many of these Jews were and are unable to hear the gospel with an open mind—especially, of course, after the tragedy of the holocaust. If we grant the premise that there is no salvation apart from the cross–a viewpoint I think the NT affirms–then they too will ultimately be saved only by Christ's death on the cross. In this way they will become recipients of God's mercy, though presently unaware of cross and its significance, even as faithful Jews of the generations before Jesus of Nazareth were also unknowingly saved by the death of Jesus, something that for them lay in the distant future.

2. The Jews Are a People Special to the Church

In the commonness of our theology and in the commonness of our relationship with God, we stand together with faithful Jews as brothers and sisters. In the contemporary world, which is increasingly secular, on the one hand, and where other religions are growing rapidly, it is extremely important for us to stand together. We must together defend theism and our common ethics and values in a torn and troubled world that desperately needs them.

We also, of course, await together the coming transformation of the present world order into the full reality promised by the prophets. For the work of the Messiah is not finished. The Apostle Peter acknowledged this from the very beginning of Christianity, speaking to a Jewish audience in the temple: "Repent, therefore, and turn again, that your sins may be blotted out, that times of refreshing may come from the presence of the Lord, and that he may send the Christ appointed for you, Jesus, whom heaven must receive until the time for establishing all that God spoke by the mouth of his holy prophets from of old" (Acts 3:19–21). The Messiah has more to do.

It is not surprising that Paul concludes his discussion in Rom 9–11 with a doxology that refers not only to the depths of God's riches, wisdom and knowledge, but also to his unsearchable judgments and inscrutable ways. For God's ways are mysterious and wonderful. God's work with

Israel, then the church, and then Israel again, represents a plan that is quite beyond our understanding. Israel and the church together embody the mysterious plan of God in view from the beginning. According to that plan, the Jewish Messiah is also the church's Lord. Israel first, but the Gentiles too, are meant as the recipients of God's great gift. The devout Simeon, "looking for the consolation [*paraklēsin*] of Israel," expressed this point wonderfully when he took into his arms the baby Messiah and said these words: "Lord, now let thy servant depart in peace, according to thy word; for my eyes have seen thy salvation which thou hast prepared in the presence of all peoples, a light for revelation to the Gentiles, and for glory to thy people Israel" (Luke 2:29). The Christian gospel is meant to bring glory to the Lord's people. Yet so often it has often brought hatred and suffering to Israel, and therefore become a stumbling block.

It is appropriate to end this essay with an emphasis on the shame of anti-Semitism. Anyone who has read the Bible should know how absolutely intolerable is any thought of Christian persecution of the Jews. When Saul the Pharisee persecuted the Christians, the risen Christ appeared to him on the Damascus Road and identified himself with the words: "I am Jesus, whom you are persecuting" (Acts 9:5; 22:8; cf. 26:14). In a similar way, Christians who would persecute Jews are in effect persecuting Jesus, persecuting the very one they name as Lord. Though we may necessarily differ with the Jews on many important points, we Gentile Christians are of the same family of faith with the Jews, adopted like orphans into the relationship between God and the Jews that already existed millennia before Christianity began.

If we Christians would follow Jesus Christ, our Jewish Master and Lord, we will love his people, the Jews, stand with them in solidarity in this present age, even as together–as Jews and Christians–we eagerly await that day of the eschatological transformation of this world and our amalgamation into one great family, when we will finally be united in the worship of our one Messianic King.

16

Jesus: Bringer of Salvation to Jew and Gentile Alike

Explanatory Note: This essay was written as a response to a Jewish-Christian dialog concerning Jesus that took place in 1993 between Jewish NT scholar Peter Zaas, Professor of Religious Studies at Siena College in Londonville, NY, and William Lane Craig, Christian theologian and apologete.

It is refreshing, as Peter Zaas points out, to encounter Jewish-Christian dialogue that does not sidestep the difficult questions of disagreement between Jews and Christians, but rather attempts to address them with frankness.[1] And there is no point at which the difference of opinion is greater than on the question of the significance of Jesus of Nazareth. As in the Gospels, so too today, it is the question of Jesus, in particular the estimate of his person, that constitutes the deep chasm that divides Jews from his followers.

The obvious truth of this observation should caution us from the start about the correctness of Zaas's statement that there is no Jewish position on Jesus.[2] Strictly speaking, of course, it is true that there is no official Jewish estimate concerning the person of Jesus. That is, there is

---

1. Paul Copan, "Introduction," in *Who Was Jesus? A Jewish-Christian Dialogue*, ed. Paul Copan and Craig A. Evans (Louisville: Westminster John Knox, 2001) 5, cf. 42.
2. Peter Zaas, *Who Was Jesus?*, 15–16.

no statement about who Jesus was, no description of his significance, that can be said to reflect universal Jewish opinion on the subject. The same was true in the time described by the Gospels: "Some say [you are] John the Baptist, but others Elijah, and still others Jeremiah or one of the prophets" (Matt 16:14). But if there is no agreement today among Jews concerning who Jesus was, there clearly is agreement on *who he was not*. And the reason is clear. If Jews accept the significance of Jesus attributed to him in the New Testament, they are no longer Jews (so far as faith is concerned) but Christians. Jesus, in short, is defined by the Jewish community not positively, but negatively. There is universal agreement among Jews about what he cannot have been. He cannot have been what the church believes him to be. Again, this is no different than it was from the beginning. The Jews in the Gospels who did not follow Jesus at least agreed that however he was to be categorized, he was not what he claimed to be.

It will be seen from the preceding paragraph that I am defining Jews religiously and not ethnically, as Zaas does.[3] I realize, of course, that there is an ethnic dimension to Jewishness and that when Jews believe in Jesus as Messiah and Kyrios, they do not stop being Jews, but can well be regarded as "completed" or "fulfilled" Jews. This was indeed the case with all the first Christians of the Jerusalem church, and there is no reason why the same may not be true today. Indeed, one could even say that for Jews to become believers in Jesus is one of the most Jewish things they could do. And there is no reason to my mind why such individuals cannot retain many if not all their Jewish distinctives after believing in Jesus. But from the New Testament's point of view, ethnicity has become essentially unimportant. *All* of humanity, Jew and Gentile alike, are trapped in sin and are in the same dire need of salvation, a salvation that can be provided only through the death and resurrection of Jesus Christ. The very idea of Jewishness is redefined by Paul, indeed in dependence on the Scriptures of Israel, as a matter of spiritual, not literal, circumcision (Rom 2:28–29), and Gentiles of faith who thereby fulfill the Abrahamic covenant are now designated the descendants of Abraham (Gal 3:6–9). In Christ, Paul concludes, "there is no longer Jew or Greek" (Gal 3:28). Ethnic Jewishness remains a relatively unimportant factor in the whole picture.

At one point, Zaas comes close to using the word "Christian" in an ethnic sense, (i.e., when he assigns responsibility for the Holocaust to

---

3. Zaas, *Who Was Jesus?*, 16, 34.

people who claimed to be "Christians").[4] Here "Christians" must mean "Gentiles" since most Nazis were Christians in name only. The perpetrators of the Holocaust were *not* Christians. At least the adjective "nominal" is required before the word is used in this way. Christians, who have been taught to love even their enemies (not that the Jews are to be regarded as such!), can have nothing to do with anti-Semitism, except to be the first to stand with the Jews against every manifestation of it.

The problems addressed in Jewish-Christian dialogue concern Jewishness not as a matter of mere ethnicity, but as a matter of religious faith. It is the differences between *Judaism* and Christianity that we must address, not differences between Jewish ethnicity and Christianity. It does not seem to me that one can justifiably reduce Judaism to Jewish ethnicity, as does Zaas, merely because there is no official Jewish theological orthodoxy. This matter is brought up by William Lane Craig, who insists, rightly in my opinion, that there are beliefs that matter very much to Judaism. For all of its emphasis on orthopraxy, Judaism does have beliefs that are of critical importance.[5]

Zaas correctly warns us about the dangers of an anachronistic approach wherein one makes statements about the time of Jesus based on information drawn from the present: "I would really caution you to try to be sensitive to these kind of things as they would sound in antiquity, not through the lens of millennia of Christian theologizing."[6] In my opinion, however, Zaas does something similar when he implies that the religious leadership of Israel in the time of Jesus would have exhibited the same broad-minded tolerance of viewpoints that we find in modern forms of Judaism. Without minimizing the great diversity we find in first-century Judaism, it is not hard to imagine that the Gospel reports of the reaction of the leadership to Jesus represent the truth and that the leaders regarded the self-claims of Jesus as blasphemous in character and his teaching as a threat both to the people as well as to their own privileged status.

It is true that the blasphemy spoken of in the trial narratives is not blasphemy in the technical sense. Jesus does not pronounce the divine Name. Nor would it have been blasphemy to claim to be the Messiah—Zaas is of course right on this. But if Jesus insulted God by arrogating to himself prerogatives that belong to God alone, this could well have been

---

4. Zaas, *Who Was Jesus?*, 18.
5. William Lane Craig, *Who Was Jesus?*, 33–34.
6. Zaas, *Who Was Jesus?*, 32.

regarded as blasphemous. Jesus did not claim (i.e., accept the claim) that he was an ordinary messiah (i.e., a special person anointed for leadership) as did other messianic claimants. On the contrary, he redefined messiahship by his claim to be uniquely the Son of God ("David's Lord"; Matt 22 :41–46), "the Son of the Blessed One" (Mark 14:61–64), who was to be seated at the right hand of Power [a circumlocution for "God," deliberately showing that he did not technically blaspheme]" and who would come "on the clouds of heaven" at the end of the age (Matt 26:64–65), and this was an outrage to the Jewish leadership. It was, in effect, to make himself equal to God (cf. John 5:18). I find it difficult to believe that orthodox Jews today would not regard a man making such claims as guilty of blasphemy. I cannot imagine, furthermore, that these leaders in the first century would have endorsed a reduction of Judaism to merely a matter of Jewish ethnicity.

Having made these random remarks, I now want to address more directly some of the central issues before us in the discussion of the significance of Jesus. I will do this under three headings: the Gospels as historical sources, the aims of Jesus, and the birth of the church.

THE GOSPELS AS HISTORICAL SOURCES

I find it intriguing that in the discussion between Zaas and Craig that the question of the reliability of the Gospels as historical sources finds such little place. It is Craig alone who raises the question explicitly. Zaas, as a New Testament scholar, might well have picked up on this and pushed it in his favor. Most Jewish scholars, indeed, make a frontal attack on the reliability of the statements in the Gospels that cannot be reconciled with the conclusion that Jesus was merely another Jewish teacher, calling people back to the righteousness of Torah, a prophet-like reformer of Judaism. In this rejection of the historical reliability of material that is consonant with the high Christology of the post-resurrection church, Jewish scholars are happy to follow the negative conclusions of radical Christian scholars. They are bound to find comfort these days in the views of the Jesus Seminar, which concludes that a meager 18 percent of the sayings of Jesus in the Gospels are authentic.[7] The Jesus profiled by the Jesus Seminar is, not surprisingly, basically similar to the Jesus of

---

7. See Robert W. Funk, Roy W. Hoover, et al., *The Five Gospels: The Search for the Authentic Words of Jesus* (New York: Macmillan, 1993).

twentieth-century Jewish scholarship, namely a teacher/prophet/healer who stands in considerable discontinuity with the Christ proclaimed by the church.

This is not the place to address this issue in the fullness it deserves, but at least a few observations may be made. It cannot be denied that the faith of the post-resurrection Christians has had an impact on the Gospel tradition and that the Gospels were written not as neutral historical documents but as theological documents designed to defend and promote the Christian faith. It is clear that they present *interpreted* history, and it must be admitted that sometimes the degree of interpretation is considerable, especially when we turn to the Fourth Gospel—which is thus seldom used in the discussion of the historical Jesus. Yet the truth of this observation should not be absolutized, for when all the above is conceded, it simply does not follow that the Gospels are therefore not basically historical documents or that they convey to us no reliable history.

There is something terribly wrong in an approach to this problem that concludes that 82 percent of the sayings of Jesus in the Gospels cannot be safely regarded as historical. There is also an extraordinary flaw in a methodology that assumes without discussion a historicist orientation to the Gospels that consistently rules out a priori that which is not acceptable to a naturalistic perspective on reality. Presuppositions are everything here, and if one's presuppositions go against the common statements of the Gospels, so much the worse for the Gospels! If our presuppositions will not allow otherwise, of course Jesus can have been only a teacher, an interpreter of the law, and a reformer of Judaism and nothing more. We may add charismatic healer, too, but only if the healing miracles are capable of psychosomatic (i.e., naturalistic) explanations. But how can we know with any confidence that such presuppositions are justified?

With a different starting point and different presuppositions, a more positive view of the Gospels emerges. Once it is admitted that the sayings of Jesus were exceptionally important to the disciples (is this not self-evident?) and indeed that they regarded it as their responsibility to preserve and guard those sayings by means of a carefully sustained oral tradition, the reliability of the sayings of Jesus in the Gospels takes on a high degree of probability. The situation has been set out illuminatingly by Birger Gerhardsson[8] and Rainer Riesner,[9] who have shown among other things that the context is one that favors the careful transmission of oral materials, that the oral tradition was held in the highest esteem, and that the tradition as it is actually found in the Gospels bears this out and is highly reliable. The fact that the Gospel accounts are accounts reflecting the faith of the evangelists does not mean they cannot also be historical.

Contrary to popular opinion, then, the transmission of the sayings of Jesus by oral tradition—in this case, what amounts to a holy or sacred tradition—is not a threat to the stability or reliability of the materials, but serves rather as a kind of guarantee of the integrity of the content of that tradition. To be sure, there were slight modifications of the sayings as they were transmitted in different contexts, and as the evangelists collected the materials and integrated them into their narratives, they received some interpretation and elaboration. But the degree to which this took place has been greatly exaggerated by scholars in the twentieth century. The idea of wholesale creation of sayings of Jesus or even of the radical alteration of them in the brief forty-year period of oral tradition before the writing of the Gospels is highly unlikely. The tradition maintained a relatively stable core.[10] Because of this, any attempt to understand Jesus while dismissing from consideration great amounts of the sayings tradition is doomed to failure. Indeed, the more material in the Synoptic Gospels one regards as inauthentic, the greater the distortion of the resultant picture of Jesus will likely be, and the greater confusion there will be concerning what to make of Jesus.

THE AIMS OF JESUS

No portrayal of Jesus as merely a teacher or healer can do justice to the New Testament record. He did teach and he did heal, but these activities were subordinate to his main calling and accomplishment.

---

8. Birger Gerhardsson, *Memory and Manuscript: Oral Tradition and Written Transmission in Rabbinic Judaism and Early Christianity* (Grand Rapids: Eerdmans, 1998); and *The Reliability of the Gospel Tradition* (Peabody, MA: Hendrickson, 2001).

9. Rainer Riesner, *Jesus als Lehrer: Eine Untersuchung zum Ursprung der Evangelien-Überlieferung*, 3rd ed., WUNT 2/7 (Tübingen: Mohr Siebeck, 1988).

10. See David Wenham, *From Good News to Gospels: What Did the First Christians Say About Jesus?* (Grand Rapids: Eerdmans, 2018).

But what was the purpose of Jesus' teaching? And how did it relate to Judaism and the law of Moses? This subject is given attention by both Zaas and Craig. Zaas records his impression that the teaching of Jesus is Jewish, and he concludes that "the Jesus of the Gospels is a Jewish teacher of righteousness, no matter how unrecognizable to Jews the church has made him,"[11] and that "Jesus offered a new way of looking at Judaism."[12] For Zaas, then, Jesus was simply a reformer of Judaism. With almost all other Jewish scholars—Neusner being a recent notable exception—Zaas concludes that Jesus was an upholder of the Torah, and he alludes to the "jot or tittle" of Matt 5:18.[13] Craig, on the other hand, rightly points to the antitheses of the Sermon on the Mount (Matt 5:21–48) and to the editorial comment in Mark 7:19 ("thus he declared all foods clean") as indications of the fact that Jesus relates to the law as no other teacher did.[14] In this regard, one might also point to Jesus' teaching concerning the Sabbath and divorce.

Both Zaas and Craig have valid points to make here. In my opinion, the question of Jesus and the law can be understood only as involving a paradox. This paradox is already apparent in Matthew 5, where Jesus' affirmation of the law is juxtaposed with the antitheses. The latter involve more than mere interpretation, Zaas notwithstanding. They involve a transcending of the law (see especially the third, fourth, and fifth antitheses) that immediately brings into focus the unique authority of Jesus. But for Matthew this transcending of the law by the Messiah is by no means to be understood as the overthrowing of the law. It is its authoritative interpretation. And the obedience to the teaching of Jesus is for Matthew (as for Paul!) the fulfillment of the Torah, and the very embodiment of the righteousness of the Torah. Thus it is true that Jesus is both the upholder of the righteousness of the Torah, as well as a sovereign interpreter of the Torah who can transcend it in favor of its ultimate meaning.

Craig is surely right that the key issue here is the authority of Jesus. This is a common and important motif in the Gospels, and it is hard to see how Zaas can minimize it in the way he does. We see that authority, of course, in the definitive way that Jesus interprets the Torah. He does not say "the law says" or "Moses says," but "*I* say to you." As the Messiah, he is the *only* teacher, the *one* tutor of his people (Matt 23:8–10).

11. Zaas. *Who Was Jesus?*, 19.
12. Zaas, *Who Was Jesus?*, 17.
13. Zaas, *Who Was Jesus?*, 33.
14. Craig, *Who Was Jesus?*, 32–33.

But more than that, Jesus puts himself at the center of everything. He calls his disciples not so much to Torah as to himself: "Come to *me*," he says to the weary and burdened. "Take *my* yoke upon you," he says, rather than referring to the yoke of the Torah (Matt 11:28-30). It is he who is crucial in the relation between God and humanity. He talks about losing one's life for *his* sake (Mark 8:35; Matt 10:39), not that of Torah or the kingdom, or being persecuted for *his* sake (Matt 5:11). He says with all boldness: "Everyone therefore who acknowledges *me* before others, I also will acknowledge before my Father in heaven; but whoever denies *me* before others, I also will deny before my Father in heaven" (Matt 10:32-33 = Luke 12:8-9). The love of Jesus is more important than all other human relationships, and "whoever does not take up the cross and follow *me* is not worthy of *me*" (Matt 10:37-38). His relation with God is utterly unique: "All things have been handed over to me by my Father; and no one knows the Son except the Father, and no one knows the Father except the Son and anyone to whom the Son chooses to reveal him" (Matt 11:27 = Luke 10:22).

Jesus is, in brief, the unique Agent of God, who takes upon himself nothing other than the prerogatives of God. He forgives sins, as Craig emphasizes, and not as an intermediary, but directly and on his own authority (thus the reaction of astonishment among the crowd in Mark 2:7). More than that, he identifies himself as the eschatological Judge. He will come on the clouds with power and great glory, he will send out his angels and gather his elect (Matt 24:30-31). *He* "will sit on the throne of his glory" and "all the nations will be gathered before him, and he will separate people one from another as a shepherd separates the sheep from the goats" (Matt 25:31-32). Furthermore, the final judgment is pronounced on the grounds of relationship to Jesus: "you did it to me"; "you did not do it to me" (Matt 25:35-46). When reinforced by the disciples' encounter with the glorified, resurrected Jesus, this material leads readily to the high Christology of the early church, as articulated, for example, already by Paul a mere two decades later. This is the Jesus who could be identified as the "Emmanuel" ("God with us") of Isaiah 7:14 (Matt 1:23), who could promise his presence where two or three gather in his name (Matt 18:20; cf. the presence of the Shekinah glory among two who study Torah), and who indeed promised his presence with his disciples "always, to the end of the age" (Matt 28:20).

In the twentieth century, Jewish scholars have been engaged in what can be called the Jewish reclamation of Jesus. That is, they have been at work showing the full Jewishness of Jesus. The important corollary to their conclusion that Jesus was but a reformer of Judaism is that it was Paul, and not Jesus, who was the creator of Christianity. It is obvious that for such conclusions to be drawn, the material we have been considering in the last few paragraphs must simply be rejected outright. Jewish scholars have thus relied heavily on the negative results of radical scholarship applied to the Gospels. Their focus has accordingly been on the ethical teaching of Jesus, for it is here that they see the greatest possibility of bringing Jesus again into their ranks.

In a book that I have written on this subject, I attempted to show, however, that even the ethical teaching of Jesus cannot be successfully reclaimed for Judaism, for at a number of key points it does not fit into the normal framework of Jewish teaching, at least as we know it from the Jewish sources available to us.[15] The reason for this is that the teaching of Jesus is inseparable from his announcement of the dawning of the kingdom of God in his own person (see, e.g., Matt 12:28; Luke 17:21). Repeatedly the ethical teaching of Jesus has a strange ring to it when compared to typical Jewish ethical teaching. We have seen it in reference to Jesus' authoritative stance in his interpretation of the law. We see it also in such things as the command to love one's enemies, the teaching not to resist an evildoer but to turn the other cheek, the "otherworldliness" of Jesus with its self-renunciation and its negative view of wealth, the prohibition of divorce, the advocacy of voluntary celibacy, and finally the general tone of Jesus' ethical teaching (i.e., its absolute and idealistic character). Again and again one encounters in Jesus' teaching material that is not comfortable in a straightforward Jewish context. There is one clear reason for this: *the teaching of Jesus is ultimately inseparable from his personal claims.* More exactly, the ethical teaching assumes the new presence of the eschatological kingdom, which is in turn based on the person and work of Jesus—namely, the presence and the death of God's Messiah, the unique Son of God.

Although Jesus was a preacher of righteousness, he did not come to reform Judaism. The full import of his work can be known only after the cross and the resurrection, but it is clear already from the Gospel narratives that in his announcement of the kingdom Jesus sees his mission as a turning point in the aeons. Quoting the prophecy of Isaiah 61:1–2a in the sermon at Nazareth, Jesus announces that "Today this scripture has been

---

15. Donald A. Hagner, *The Jewish Reclamation of Jesus: An Analysis and Critique of the Modern Jewish Study of Jesus* (Grand: Rapids: Zondervan, 1984), especially 133–70.

fulfilled in your hearing" (Luke 4:21). Elsewhere Jesus says: "The law and the prophets were in effect until John came; since then the good news of the kingdom of God is proclaimed" (Luke 16:16; Matt 11:12–13). It is the day of the bridegroom, of new cloth and new wine (Matt 9:14–17; Luke 5:34–38). It is the day of messianic fulfillment (Matt 11:2–6). Jesus calls his disciples blessed, adding that "many prophets and righteous people longed to see what you see, but did not see it, and to hear what you hear, but did not hear it" (Matt 13:16–17 = Luke 10:23–24).

We have thus moved into a new era of the history of salvation. Any assessment of the significance of Jesus that ignores or denies this must necessarily be fundamentally .inadequate. The Jewish attempt to explain Jesus quite apart from any forward movement in salvific time-frames is therefore bound to fall short. Jesus cannot be understood as "one messiah among many," as Zaas puts it.[16]

And this brings us to the cross. As has long been stressed, the heart of the Gospels is the passion narratives. Indeed, in the absence of a passion narrative, a document such as the so-called *Gospel of Thomas*—which consists almost exclusively of sayings of Jesus—hardly qualifies to be designated a Gospel at all. It is very interesting to me that in almost all Jewish discussion of the death of Jesus, the *meaning* of that death is neglected, with the present dialogue being no exception. It comes up only briefly in the first question of the question-and-answer session.[17] There Zaas tips his hat to the importance of sacrifice in the Hebrew Bible, but then indicates that since the destruction of the Second Temple, atonement is accomplished by mere repentance. The logic underlying such a leap is not explained, and the only apparent reason remains the mere nonexistence of the literal Temple.

Jewish discussion of the death of Jesus focuses understandably on the exceptionally sensitive matter of the determination of responsibility (more on that below). My point here, however, is that the death itself is apparently regarded as the tragic end of one who should really have been honored as a loyal teacher of Israel. Jesus, however, seems to have interpreted his imminent death in terms of the servant of Isaiah 53 (especially vv. 10–12). That is, his death was to be understood as a sacrifice that atoned for the sins of the world: "For the Son of Man came not to be served but to serve, and to give his life a ransom for many" (Mark 10:45

---

16. Zaas, *Who Was Jesus?*, 19.
17. *Who Was Jesus?*, 36.

= Matt 20:28). "Ransom" is used here metaphorically in reference to the payment of the penalty of sin at the cost of the sacrificial death of Jesus. Similarly, at the institution of the Lord's Supper, Jesus referred to the cup as "my blood of the covenant, which is poured out for many for the forgiveness of sins" (Matt 26:28; cf. Mark 14:24). This is the heart of the new covenant that Jesus came to effect, and thus "this cup that is poured out for you is the new covenant in my blood" (Luke 22:20). The death of Jesus brings about a turn in the aeons and is itself the pivot of that turning.

The death of Jesus was therefore not merely a vital mission of Jesus; it was his *central* mission. He came to die. The fulfillment he brings and the kingdom he inaugurates depend squarely on his death. And therefore the death of Jesus is not a tragic event wherein a great teacher and healer was unfortunately put to death at a young age. It was, on the contrary, nothing less than the accomplishment of the will of God for the salvation of humanity. The demeanor of Jesus all through the passion accounts of the Gospels bears out this conclusion. Rather than being the helpless victim of all that happens, he is strangely and quietly sovereign throughout, even to the final moment.

By no means, however, did Jesus deserve to die. And by no means are those who put him to death made into heroes for doing in ignorance what ultimately was the will of God! To my mind, it is impossible to deny the centrally important role of the Jewish leadership in the death of Jesus. As I indicated in my opening remarks, I accept the Gospels' record that Jesus was put to death for blasphemy, but a blasphemy involving a totally unacceptable self-aggrandizement. The old question, posed again by Craig, has never received an adequate answer: Why would the Jewish leaders—much less the Romans—desire the death of a charismatic teacher and healer who was fully loyal to Judaism? What was it about him, what threat did he pose, that the Jewish authorities were moved to such extreme measures against him?

The answer, as we have tried to say above, is that Jesus put himself at the center of God's purposes and made himself determinative and irreplaceable in the relationship of humanity and God. He calls humanity to himself, to follow him as their sole Master, to offer their lives in a pattern of discipleship modeled after him, to represent the good news of the gospel of God's free grace and forgiveness based on his cross. The Gospels from beginning to end thus call their readers to a decision concerning Jesus. The question posed in all three Synoptic Gospels—"Who do *you* say I am?"—is not meant as an academic exercise, but as an existential question of the greatest importance to all of humanity, Jews and Gentiles. If we are to judge by the Gospels, therefore, Zaas is completely off the mark when he argues that this question "remains as it has always been, entirely irrelevant to the Jewish enterprise."[18]

From the point of view of the Gospels (and more clearly from the epistles), the death of Jesus was for sin. That is, Jesus died bearing the sin of the world—more precisely the sin of the myriads of individual sinners who make up humanity. Theologically, it is here that we should look for the cause of Jesus' death. The responsibility of the Jewish leaders and mob is ultimately one of a quite limited scope, namely one that could be designated as merely a responsibility of historical instrumentality. It should be regarded as of little consequence, and certainly as nothing that would warrant hatred or persecution of the Jews—or indeed as a sanction for any form of anti-Semitism. The substantive responsibility must be placed on each sinner's shoulders. If blame is to be placed, it is I who am guilty of crucifying Jesus. My sin put him on the cross.

THE BIRTH OF THE CHURCH

In my opinion, Craig is absolutely right, in discussing the significance of Jesus, to focus on the resurrection of Jesus. The reason the resurrection is so important is that, apart from its validation of the claims and identity of Jesus, we are left only with so many words and deeds, however unusual they may be. The resurrection serves as the vindication of Jesus' self-claims—indeed, of his whole mission. It is the determinative point in the Gospel tradition that brings meaning to the entirety.

The resurrection is both the key to the faith of the early church and the cornerstone of its proclamation. As the key to the faith of the early church, it is the single, indisputable fact that authenticated, made possible to assimilate, and brought understanding to all that the disciples had experienced through the words and works of Jesus. After the death of Jesus and prior to the resurrection, the disciples were confused, disillusioned, and disheartened. It is understandable that they were in this pitiable condition, for in light of what he said, a dead Jesus could only leave them with question upon question. The eschatological signs of the resurrection of Jesus and the outpouring of the Holy Spirit served as a demonstration of the truth of the dawning of a new era of salvation that

---

18. Zaas, *Who Was Jesus?*, 18.

was the fulfillment of the expectations of the prophets, albeit in a proleptic way, short of the consummation of the age. The resurrection and the outpouring of the Spirit were not only thereby the foreshadowing of the last day, but also its guarantee.

As the cornerstone of the church's proclamation, the reality of the resurrection is preeminently that to which the disciples were witnesses. In addition to the twelve disciples, the risen Jesus appeared to more than 500 people, as Paul testifies, adding the important point that most of these were still alive in the mid-50s when Paul wrote 1 Corinthians (1 Cor 15:6). The church preaches the cross and the resurrection, not merely the former, not merely the latter. Either without the other is incomplete, for the new age owes its existence to the death of Jesus. But the resurrection is the powerful demonstration of the truth of the words, of the truth of the good news of a new era of fulfillment. It thus simultaneously underlines the high and mysterious significance of the death of one who is now seen as the glorified Son of God.

Craig sets forth the strength of the evidence for the resurrection of Jesus concisely and effectively: the witnesses, the empty tomb, the birth of the church. These are persuasive in themselves, but even more so when combined with one other fact. *Every other attempted explanation of the phenomena is plainly inadequate.* If historical sense is to be made of the facts of the witnesses, the tomb, and the rise of the church, then an adequate cause must be found. No naturalistic explanation has been offered that accounts for the facts. Indeed, the feeble attempts that *have* been made to explain away the resurrection are laughable and strain credibility far more than the the resurrection itself.

It must be stressed, as Craig rightly does, that the resurrection of Jesus was not the resuscitation of a corpse followed by a return to life in this world. When Zaas says that he does not dispute the fact of the resurrection of Jesus, he means the resuscitation of Jesus.[19] The same is clearly true of the claim of Jewish writer Pinchas Lapide when he says that he accepts the truth of the resurrection of Jesus. As Craig points out in his response to a question, there is a world of difference between revivification and resurrection. In the former instance, one comes back to life only to die again later.[20] In the case of resurrection, however, one enters into a new order of existence altogether. As Paul puts it in 1

---

19. Zaas, *Who Was Jesus?*, 38.
20. Craig, *Who Was Jesus?*, 39

Corinthians 15:35-55, the body that is "sown" is physical, perishable, and weak whereas the body that is raised is spiritual, imperishable, and glorious. Flesh and blood are transformed into a new "spiritual body," one that is appropriate to eschatological existence. Such was the resurrection of Jesus, which Paul describes as "the first fruits of those who have died" (1 Cor 15:20). In short, in resurrection we are talking about a new order—nothing less than dramatic reversal of the effects of sin on the world, the restoration of the perfection of the creation at the beginning. This transformation of the world is what the prophets spoke of when they foresaw a time when there would be no more evil, no more suffering or sorrow, no more death, when life would be filled with an extravagant abundance, and above all when men and women would be in unbroken fellowship with their Creator. It is all of this that the resurrection of Jesus symbolizes and points to. His resurrection is the beginning of that new creation and tangible evidence of its reality. It is furthermore a guarantee of the eventual realization of this hope in fullness at the final consummation. And the Holy Spirit in the life of the Christian provides a foretaste of the glory that shall be.

A resurrection of this kind—a true resurrection—has universal consequences that necessarily touch on the existence of every human who has ever lived. Paul traces this out too when he writes in the same context: "For since death came through a human being, the resurrection of the dead has also come through a human being; for as all die in Adam, so all will be made alive in Christ" (1 Cor 15:21-22). Therefore it is impossible to reduce the resurrection to a "Christian" question that is of no particular relevance to the Jews, as Zaas would do. This might be the case if we were dealing with a resuscitation, but not if we are dealing with a true resurrection. By its very nature the resurrection of Jesus impinges on every person, Jew or Gentile. And this is why the Christian wants to evangelize others—all others, including the Jews. This gospel became the driving force in the life of Paul, the Jew who had previously been a zealous Pharisee. He wrote of the gospel that "it is the power of God for salvation to everyone who has faith, to the Jew first and also to the Greek" (Rom 1:16). The resurrection of Jesus is of the utmost importance to the Jew as well as the Gentile. In no way does the New Testament condone the idea that Christianity is a religion for the Gentiles only.

CONCLUDING REMARKS

There is a remarkable difference in the way Zaas and Craig approach the basic question before us. This, I suppose, is not particularly remarkable in itself, since after all, Craig believes in Jesus as proclaimed in the New Testament, while Zaas does not. But the difference does account for much of the discussion between them, as it does for the tone of my own response to the discussion.

As I see it, the difference is due to the way in which the central question is addressed. For Zaas, the question "Who is Jesus?" is merely an academic question. It is a question of some mild interest, but basically one for the intellect alone. Thus Zaas can be playful, open, provocative, stimulating. In the end nothing really significant is at stake, and Zaas is tolerant of a wide range of opinions (which is perhaps all they can be, in his view). To each his own. It matters not.

Craig, on the other hand, understands the question "Who is Jesus?" not merely as an intellectual challenge, but as involving a call to personal response. On this Craig follows the Gospels. When Jesus posed the question himself, the real issue was not correct information alone, but a response of the will that brought one into personal relationship with him. Thus for Craig there is a gravity to the question that is simply not there for Zaas. The answer one gives to the question matters vitally to Craig. There is only one correct answer to the question, and Craig wants to show as well as he can the strength of the evidence for that answer.

These comments should not be taken to mean that Craig is not or cannot be a good scholar. Nor do they imply that Zaas is a priori more objective than Craig. The fact is that no Christian can answer the question "Who is Jesus?" without becoming an evangelist! The question brings one close to the heart of a Christian as perhaps no other question can. But a faith commitment is not necessarily a hindrance to good scholarship. On the contrary, it may be an asset to be able to approach these matters from within.

It is right and good for these issues to be discussed openly, between persons of different opinions, in a friendly manner and with mutual respect. We can continue to learn from one another, and we are in need of having our misunderstandings corrected. Differences will nevertheless remain. I am convinced, however, that it is possible to love others—i.e., to wish them well and to work for their well-being in every regard—even when one disagrees with them on matters of the deepest significance.

It may well be our deepest wish and prayer that they might share the conclusion to which we have come. But that is not in our hands to accomplish. As Christians, however, we must continue to share the truth as we have been led to sec it. Like Craig, I am convinced of its cogency and that it is the authors of the New Testament who have the right answer to the question of the significance of Jesus.

APPENDIX 1

Passages Pointing to Discontinuity/Supersession/Displacement

(Note: The lists in this and the following appendix are presented as a sampling of passages, chosen subjectively, and are presented as neither exhaustive nor definitive.)

1. ISRAEL HAS NO ADVANTAGE OVER THE GENTILES

Election

- Acts 10:34–35, "Truly I perceive that God shows no partiality, but in every nation any one who fears him and does what is right is acceptable to him."
- Acts 28:28, "Let it be known then that this salvation of God has been sent to the Gentiles; they will listen."
- Rom 2:11, "God shows no partiality"
- Rom 2:25, "if you break the law, your circumcision becomes uncircumcision"
- Rom 3:9, "What then? Are we Jews any better off? No, not at all; for I have already charged that all people, both Jews and Greeks, are under the power of sin."

APPENDIX 1

- Rom 4:14, 16, "If it is the adherents of the law who are to be the heirs, faith is null and the promise void . . . That is why it depends on faith, in order that the promise may rest on grace and be guaranteed to all his descendants not only to the adherents of the law, but also to those who share the faith of Abraham, for he is the father of us all."

- Rom 5:18, "Then as one man's trespass led to condemnation for all men, one man's act of righteousness leads to acquittal and life for all people."

- Rom 10:12, "For there is no distinction between Jew and Greek; the same Lord is Lord of all and bestows his riches upon all who call upon him."

- Rom 9:6–7, "For not all who are descended from Israel belong to Israel, and not all are children of Abraham because they are his descendants."

- Gal 3:7, "So you see that it is people of faith who are the children of Abraham."

- Gal 3:29, "And if you are Christ's, then you are Abraham's offspring, heirs according to promise."

- Gal 6:15, "For neither circumcision counts for anything, nor uncircumcision, but a new creation."

- Gal 6:16, "Peace and mercy be upon all who walk by this rule, even upon the Israel of God."

- Eph 2:19, "So then you are no longer strangers and sojourners, but you are fellow citizens with the saints and members of the household of God."

- Eph 3:6, "that is, how the Gentiles are fellow heirs, members of the same body, and partakers of the promise in Christ Jesus through the gospel."

- Phil 3:3, "For we are the true circumcision, who worship God in spirit, and glory in Christ Jesus, and put no confidence in the flesh."

- Col 2:11, "In him also you were circumcised with a circumcision made without hands, by putting off the body of flesh in the circumcision of Christ."

- Col 3:11, "Here there cannot be Greek and Jew, circumcised and uncircumcised . . . but Christ is all, and in all."

- 1 Tim 3:15, "you may know how one ought to behave in the household of God, which is the church of the living God, the pillar and bulwark of the truth."
- 1 Pet 2:9–10, "But you are a chosen race, a royal priesthood, a holy nation, God's own people, that you may declare the wonderful deeds of him who called you out of darkness into his marvelous light. Once you were no people but now you are God's people; once you had not received mercy but now you have received mercy."

Covenant

- 2 Cor 3:6, "who has made us competent to be ministers of a new covenant, not in a written code but in the Spirit; for the written code kills, but the Spirit gives life."
- 2 Cor 3:11, "For if what faded away came with such splendor, what is permanent must have much more splendor."
- Gal 4:24–26, "Now this is an allegory: these two women are two covenants. One is from Mount Sinai, bearing children for slavery; she is Hagar. Now Hagar is Mount Sinai in Arabia; she corresponds to the present Jerusalem, for she is in slavery with her children. But the Jerusalem above is free, and she is our mother."
- Heb 8:6–7, "But as it is, Christ has obtained a ministry which is as much more excellent than the old as the covenant he mediates is better, since it is enacted on better promises. For if that first covenant had been faultless, there would have been no occasion for a second."
- Heb 8:13, "'In speaking of a new covenant he treats the first as obsolete. And what is becoming obsolete and growing old is ready to vanish away."

2. THE ROLE OF THE LAW HAS COME TO AN END

- Rom 7:4, "you have died to the law through the body of Christ"

APPENDIX 1

- Rom 7:6, "But now we are discharged from the law, dead to that which held us captive, so that we serve not under the old written code but in the new life of the Spirit."
- Rom 7:10, "the very commandment which promised life proved to be death to me"
- Rom 10:4, "For Christ is the end of the law, that everyone who has faith may be justified."
- Rom 13:10, "love is the fulfilling of the law"
- Rom 14:5, "One person esteems one day as better than another, while another person esteems all days alike. Let every person be fully convinced in his or her own mind."
- Rom 14:14, "I know and am persuaded in the Lord Jesus that nothing is unclean in itself"
- 1 Cor 9:20–21, "To the Jews I became as a Jew, in order to win Jews; to those under the law I became as one under the law though not being myself under the law that I might win those under the law. To those outside the law I became as one outside the law not being without law toward God but in the law of Christ that I might win those outside the law."
- Gal 3:13, "Christ redeemed us from the curse of the law, having become a curse for us."
- Gal 3:24–25, "So that the law was our custodian until Christ came, that we might be justified by faith. But now that faith has come, we are no longer under a custodian."
- Eph 3:9, "and be found in him, not having a righteousness of my own, based on law, but that which is through faith in Christ, the righteousness from God that depends on faith."
- Col 2:14, "having cancelled the bond which stood against us with its legal demands; this he set aside, nailing it to the cross."
- Col 2:16–17, "Therefore let no one pass judgment on you in questions of food and drink or with regard to a festival or a new moon or a sabbath. These are only a shadow of what is to come; but the substance belongs to Christ."
- Heb 7:18–19, "On the one hand, a former commandment [concerning the Levitical priesthood] is set aside because of its weakness and

uselessness (for the law made nothing perfect); on the other hand, a better hope is introduced, through which we draw near to God."

3. THE TEMPLE IS PASSÉ

- Rom 3:25, "whom God put forward as a *hilastērion* by his blood, to be received by faith."
- Rom 5:9, "Since, therefore, we are now justified by his blood, much more shall we be saved by him from the wrath of God."
- 1 Cor 5:7, "For Christ, our passover lamb, has been sacrificed."
- 1 Cor 3:16–17, "Do you not know that you are God's temple and that God's Spirit dwells in you? . . For God's temple is holy, and that temple you are."
- 2 Cor 6:16, "For we are the temple of the living God; as God said, 'I will live in them and move among them, and I will be their God, and they shall be my people.'"
- Eph 1:7, "In him we have redemption through his blood, the forgiveness of our trespasses, according to the riches of his grace."
- Eph 2:21–22, "in whom the whole structure is joined together and grows into a holy temple in the Lord; in whom you also are built into it for a dwelling place of God in the Spirit."
- Eph 5:2, "And walk in love, as Christ loved us and gave himself up for us, a fragrant offering and sacrifice to God."
- 1 Tim 2:5–6, "and there is one mediator between God and humanity, the man Christ Jesus, who gave himself as a ransom for all."
- Tit 2:14, "who gave himself for us to redeem us from all iniquity and to purify for himself a people of his own who are zealous for good deeds."
- Heb 6:19–20, "We have this as a sure and steadfast anchor of the soul, a hope that enters into the inner shrine behind the curtain, where Jesus has gone as a forerunner on our behalf, having become a high priest for ever after the order of Melchizedek."
- Heb 9:11–12, "But when Christ appeared as a high priest of the good things that have come, then through the greater and more perfect

tent (not made with hands, that is, not of this creation) he entered once for all into the Holy Place, taking not the blood of goats and calves but his own blood, thus securing an eternal redemption."

- Heb 9:26, "But as it is, he has appeared once for all at the end of the age to put away sin by the sacrifice of himself."
- 1 Pet 1:18–19, "You know that you were ransomed . . . .with the precious blood of Christ, like that of a lamb without blemish or spot."
- 1 Pet 2:5, "and like living stones be yourselves built into a spiritual house, to be a holy priesthood, to offer spiritual sacrifices acceptable to God through Jesus Christ."
- 1 Pet 3:18, "For Christ also died for sins once for all, the righteous for the unrighteous, that he might bring us to God, being put to death in the flesh but made alive in the spirit."
- 1 John 2:2, "and he is the expiation for our sins, and not for ours only but also for the sins of the whole world."
- 1 John 4:10, "In this is love, not that we loved God but that he loved us and sent his Son to be the expiation for our sins."
- Rev 1:5–6, "To him who loves us and has freed us from our sins by his blood and made us a kingdom, priests to his God and Father, to him be glory and dominion for ever and ever."
- Rev 3:12, "He who conquers, I will make him a pillar in the temple of my God; never shall he go out of it, and I will write on him the name of my God, and the of the city of my God, the new Jerusalem which comes down from my God out of heaven."
- Rev 11:19, "Then God's temple in heaven was opened, and the ark of his covenant was seen within his temple."
- Rev 21:22, "And I saw no temple in the city, for its temple is the Lord God the Almighty and the Lamb."

4. THE LAND IS CONSPICUOUS BY ITS ABSENCE FROM THE NEW TESTAMENT

- Rom 4:13, "The promise to Abraham and his descendants, that they should inherit the world [*kosmos*] did not come through the law but through the righteousness of faith."
- Heb 11:9–10, "By faith he [Abraham] sojourned in the land of promise, as in a foreign land, living in tents with Isaac and Jacob, heirs with him of the same promise. For he looked forward to the city which has foundations, whose builder and maker is God."
- Heb 11:16, "But as it is, they desire a better country, that is, a heavenly one. Therefore God is not ashamed to be called their God, for he has prepared for them a city."
- Heb 12:22, "But you have come to Mount Zion and to the city of the living God, the heavenly Jerusalem, and to innumerable angels in festal gathering."
- Heb 13:14, "For here we have no lasting city, but we seek the city which is to come."
- Rev 21:1–3, "And I saw a new heaven and a new earth; for the first heaven and the first earth had passed away, and the sea was no more. And I saw the holy city, a new Jerusalem, coming down out of heaven from God, prepared as a bride adorned for her husband; and I heard a loud voice from the throne, saying, 'Behold, the dwelling of God is with men. He will dwell with them, and they shall be his people, and God himself will be with them.'"

Passages for Special Consideration:

- Matt 21:40–43, "'When therefore the owner of the vineyard comes, what will he do to those tenants?' They said to him, 'He will put those wretches to a miserable death, and let out the vineyard to other tenants who will give him the fruits in their seasons.' ... 'Therefore I tell you, the kingdom of God will be taken away from you and given to a nation [*ethnē*] producing the fruits of it.'"

APPENDIX 1

- Matt 27:25, "And all the people [*pas ho laos*] answered, 'His blood be on us and on our children.'"
- John 8:44, "You are of your father the devil."
- 1 Thess 2:14–16, "For you, brothers and sisters, became imitators of the churches of God in Christ Jesus which are in Judea; for you suffered the same things from your own countrymen as they did from the Jews, who killed both the Lord Jesus and the prophets, and drove us out, and displease God and oppose all people, by hindering us from speaking to the Gentiles that they may be saved—so as always to fill up the measure of their sins. But God's wrath has come upon them at last [*eis telos*]."
- Rev 2:9 and 3:9, "those who say that they are Jews and are not, but are a synagogue of Satan"

APPENDIX 2

Passages Pointing to Continuity/ Ongoing Significance/Salvation

1. THE SPECIALNESS OF ISRAEL CONTINUES

Election

- Matt 10:5–6, "Go nowhere among the Gentiles, and enter no town of the Samaritans, but go rather to the lost sheep of the house of Israel."
- Matt 15:24, "I was sent only to the lost sheep of the house of Israel."
- Matt 19:28, "Truly, I say to you, in the new world, when the Son of man shall sit on his glorious throne, you who have followed me will also sit on twelve thrones, judging the twelve tribes of Israel."
- Matt 23:38–39, "Behold your house is forsaken and desolate. For I tell you, you will not see me again, until you say 'Blessed is the one who comes in the name of the Lord.'"
- [for Luke, see under "land"]
- Acts 28:20, "it is because of the hope of Israel that I am bound with this chain"

APPENDIX 2

- Rom 1:16, "the gospel is the power of God for salvation to every one who has faith, to the Jew first and also to the Greek"
- Rom 2:25, "Circumcision indeed is of value if you obey the law"
- Rom 3:1–2, "Then what advantage has the Jew? Or what is the value of circumcision? Much in every way. To begin with, the Jews are entrusted with the oracles of God."
- Rom 3:3, "What if some were unfaithful? Does their faithlessness nullify the faithfulness of God? By no means."
- Rom 3:29, "Or is God the God of Jews only? Is he not the God of Gentiles also? Yes, of Gentiles also, since God is one; and he will justify the circumcised on the ground of their faith and the uncircumcised through their faith."
- Rom 4:9, "Is this blessing [Ps. 32:1–2] pronounced only upon the circumcised, or also upon the uncircumcised?"
- Rom 4:11, "The purpose was to make him [Abraham] the father of all who believe without being circumcised and who thus have righteousness reckoned to them, and likewise the father of the circumcised who are not merely circumcised but also follow the example of the faith which our father Abraham had before he was circumcised."
- Rom 9:4, "They are Israelites, and to them belong the sonship, the glory, the covenants, the giving of the law, the worship, and the promises; to them belong the patriarchs, and of their race, according to the flesh, is the Christ, who is God over all, blessed for ever."
- Rom 9:24, "even us whom he has called, not from the Jews only but also from the Gentiles"
- Rom 10:2, "I bear them witness that they have a zeal for God, but it is not enlightened."
- Rom 11:12, "I ask, then, has God rejected his people? By no means! ... God has not rejected his people whom he foreknew. "
- Rom 11:11, "So I ask, have they stumbled so as to fall? By no means!"
- Rom 11:1–2, "Now if their trespass means riches for the Gentiles, how much more will their full inclusion mean!"
- Rom 11:15, "For if their rejection means the reconciliation of the world, what will their acceptance mean but life from the dead?"

- Rom 11:23-24, "And even the others, if they do not persist in their unbelief, will be grafted in, for God has the power to graft them in again. For if you have been cut from what is by nature a wild olive tree, and grafted, contrary to nature, into a cultivated olive tree, how much more will these natural branches be grafted back into their own olive tree."
- Rom 11:25-26, "I want you to understand this mystery, brothers and sisters: a hardening has come upon part of Israel, until the full number of the Gentiles come in, and so all Israel will be saved."
- Rom 11:28, "As regards the gospel they are enemies of God, for your sake; but as regards election they are beloved for the sake of their forefathers."
- Rom 11:29, "For the gifts and the call of God are irrevocable."
- Rom 11:30-31, "Just as you were once disobedient to God but now have received mercy because of their disobedience, so they have now been disobedient in order that by the mercy shown to you they also may receive mercy."
- Rom 15:8, "For I tell you that Christ became a servant to the circumcised to show God's truthfulness, in order to confirm the promises given to the patriarchs, and in order that the Gentiles might glorify God for his mercy."
- 1 Cor 10:32, "Give no offense to Jews or to Greeks or to the church of God."
- 2 Cor 11:21-22, "But whatever any one dares to boast of—I am speaking as a fool—I also dare to boast of that. Are they Hebrews? So am I. Are they Israelites? So am I. Are they descendants of Abraham? So am I."
- Gal 6:16, "Peace and mercy be upon all who walk by this rule and upon the Israel of God."
- Eph 2:19, "So then you are no longer strangers and sojourners, but you are fellow citizens with the saints and members of the household of God"
- Rev 21:12, "It [the heavenly Jerusalem] had a great, high wall, with twelve gates, and at the gates twelve angels, and on the gates the names of the twelve tribes of the sons of Israel were inscribed."

APPENDIX 2

2. THE LAW

- Matt 5:17–19, "Think not that I have come to abolish the law and the prophets; I have not come to abolish them but to fulfill them. For truly, I say to you, till heaven and earth pass away, not an iota, not a dot, will pass from the law until all is accomplished. Whoever then relaxes one of the least of these commandments and teaches others so, shall be called least in the kingdom of heaven; but the one who does them and teaches them shall be called great in the kingdom of heaven."
- Rom 3:31, "Do we then overthrow the law by this faith? By no means! On the contrary, we uphold the law."
- Rom 7:12, "So the law is holy, and the commandment is holy and just and good."
- Rom 7:22, "For I delight in the law of God, in my inmost self"
- Rom 8:4, "in order that the just requirement of the law might be fulfilled in us, who walk not according to the flesh, but according to the Spirit."

3. THE TEMPLE

- 2 Thess 2:4, the man of lawlessness "opposes and exalts himself against every so-called god or object of worship, so that he takes his seat in the temple of God, proclaiming himself to be God."

4. THE LAND

- Matt 5:5, "Blessed are the meek, for they shall inherit the earth [*gē*]."
- Matt 19:28, "Truly I say to you, in the new world, when the Son of man shall sit on his glorious throne, you who have followed me will also sit on twelve thrones. judging the twelve tribes of Israel."
- Luke 1:68, "Blessed be the Lord God of Israel, for he has visited and redeemed [*epoiēsen lutrōsin*] his people."

APPENDIX 2

- Luke 2:25, Simeon, "was righteous and devout, looking for the consolation [*paraklēsis*] of Israel"
- Luke 2:38, "And coming up at that very hour she gave thanks to God, and spoke of him to all who were looking for the redemption [*lutrōsis*] of Israel."
- Luke 21:24, "and Jerusalem will be trodden down by the Gentiles, until the times of the Gentiles are fulfilled."
- Luke 24:21, "But we had hoped that he was the one to redeem [*lutrousthai*] Israel."
- Acts 1:6–7, "they asked him 'Lord, will you at this time restore [*apokathistēmi*] the kingdom to Israel?' He said to them, 'It is not for you to know the times or seasons which the Father has fixed by his own authority.'"

Special Passage for Consideration

- Luke 2:29–32: "Lord, now lettest thou thy servant depart in peace, according to thy word, for mine eyes have seen thy salvation [*sōtērion*] which thou hast prepared in the presence of all peoples, a light for revelation to the Gentiles, and for glory to thy people Israel."

www.ingramcontent.com/pod-product-compliance
Lightning Source LLC
Chambersburg PA
CBHW071147300426
44113CB00009B/1119